PN
1271
.J32

Jarrell, Randall

Kipling, Auden &
Co.

DATE DUE

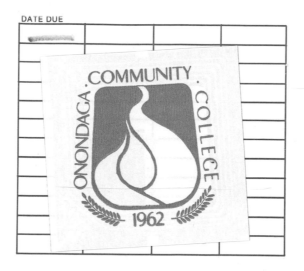

Onondaga Community College
Rte. 173, Onondaga Hill
Syracuse, New York 13215

Books by Randall Jarrell

· ❊ ·

POETRY

ESSAYS

FICTION

CHILDREN'S BOOKS

TRANSLATIONS

ANTHOLOGIES

Kipling, Auden & Co.

Randall Jarrell, *1914-1965*

KIPLING,

AUDEN & CO.

Essays and Reviews

1935–1964

FARRAR, STRAUS AND GIROUX

NEW YORK

All rights reserved
Library of Congress catalog card number: 80-80161
Published simultaneously in Canada by
McGraw-Hill Ryerson Ltd., Toronto
Printed in the United States of America
DESIGNED BY HERB JOHNSON

FIRST EDITION, 1980

Note

· ❀ ·

THIS fourth and final collection of Randall Jarrell's essays and reviews follows *Poetry and the Age* (1953), *A Sad Heart at the Supermarket* (1962), and *The Third Book of Criticism* (1969), and makes available virtually all of Jarrell's previously uncollected criticism.

"Malraux and the Statues at Bamberg," "The Taste of the Age," "Poets, Critics, and Readers," "The Woman at the Washington Zoo," and "On Preparing to Read Kipling" were first collected in *A Sad Heart at the Supermarket*, which is now out of print. "The English in England," included in *The Third Book of Criticism*, is reprinted here so as to gather all of Jarrell's criticism of Kipling between the covers of one book.

The contents of *Kipling, Auden & Co.* are arranged chronologically, and the place and date of first publication are cited at the beginning of each essay or review. All are reprinted exactly as they originally appeared, except for the five essays from *A Sad Heart at the Supermarket*, which Jarrell revised for that book, and "The End of the Line," which he revised for Morton Dauwen Zabel's anthology *Literary Opinion in America* (second edition, 1951).

Two complete reviews that appeared in *The Nation* as Verse Chronicles are included under that title. Five additional selections are headed "From Verse Chronicle"; in these instances, portions of the original reviews appear in *Poetry and the Age*, and only the remaining material is reprinted here.

It was initially intended that Jarrell's lectures on Auden, delivered at the Princeton Seminars in Literary Criticism, 1951–52, would be included in this book, but these lectures were not left in a form that justifies their appearance alongside Jarrell's published work. However, they are likely to be of interest to students of both Jarrell and Auden, and will be made available in a scholarly journal.

Contents

· ❋ ·

[1947]

[1948]

[1949]

[1950]

[1951]

[1953]

[1954]

[1955]

Kipling, Auden & Co.

Ten Books

THE SOUTHERN REVIEW, AUTUMN 1935

Vein of Iron by Ellen Glasgow   *Kneel to the Rising Sun* by Erskine Caldwell   *Feliciana* by Stark Young   *The Furys* by James Hanley   *Lucy Gayheart* by Willa Cather   *A Preface to Maturity* by Jule Brousseau   *We Too Are Drifting* by Gale Wilhelm   *Time: The Present* by Tess Slesinger   *Time Out of Mind* by Rachel Field   *Chance Has a Whip* by Raymond Holden

A GROUP of Scotch emigrants settled in Pennsylvania, then went south to Virginia; their minister was John Fincastle, called by his Presbyterian congregation the "Scholar Pioneer." He was something of a philosopher; his great-great-grandson, John Fincastle, was so much more of one that he was turned out of the ministry for heresy. When Miss Glasgow's book begins, in 1901, he is living in the Fincastles' old house, in a small Virginia town, Ironside. With him live Grandmother Fincastle, his wife, Mary Evelyn, his sister, Meggie, and his ten-year-old daughter, Ada. *Vein of Iron* is the story of this family.

If Miss Glasgow had been writing fifty or a hundred years ago, she would have given directly the history of Ironside and the Fincastles; today, she chooses to inform the reader obliquely. "Toward Life," the first part of the book, tells the story of one day in the child Ada's life. Different chapters are narrated from the points of view of Ada, Grandmother Fincastle, John Fincastle, Mary Evelyn, and Meggie Fincastle. The characters occupy themselves little with action or perception; their concern is recollection. They repeat with unvarying delight the histories of their families, the names of their mothers, the events of their childhood—things familiar to them, no doubt, but things which the reader has to learn. If one were to begin a novel by making the hero almost drown, so that all his life might "flash before his eyes," the readers would feel that he had chosen a somewhat arbitrary mechanism of information; the reminiscences of Miss Glasgow's characters are almost as extensive, and they have not the excuse of being about to drown. Miss Glasgow selects for their reveries that form of presentation halfway between the modern novelist's version of James's stream of consciousness and an earlier convention of the reporting of thought: that is, some of the character's thoughts are given in direct quotation, and some are told about indirectly, and, further to vary the texture of the mass, momentary sensory details are constantly thrown in. To handle this method satisfactorily, the writer must have sensibility of almost exaggerated delicacy so far as stylistic effects are concerned. Generally, the method handles the writer.

Telling a story from several points of view has its disadvantages and difficulties. For one thing, the characters' turns of thought, their styles of rumination, must be differentiated; in this, it seems, Miss Glasgow usually fails. What differences of content or elevation there are, are obscured by a certain regularity and heaviness of style. In the novel the little girl differs from the adults mainly in that she thinks in shorter sentences; one reviewer cites this as a notable example of Miss Glasgow's artistry.

Vein of Iron is, in short, what Ada did and what her father thought. It is unnecessary to do more than briefly summarize the course of the Fincastle family.

The story brings them down to the present time; in the last part, "The Dying Age," they move to the city, and Ada (who stands for a sort of pioneer courage and obstinacy) and her father (who adds to these qualities the detachment and skepticism of the philosopher) serve as norms against which Miss Glasgow can set up an industrialized urban life.

Miss Glasgow's attitude toward our time is uncompromising. Burke once said you can't indict a whole people; such a thought would never enter Miss Glasgow's head. It would be difficult to exaggerate her dislike for the superficial qualities of our age. The next paragraph, of excerpts from Miss Glasgow's book, will give a good idea of both the matter and form of her indictment.

"Whatever could not feed the machine was discarded as rubbish . . . They were all alike, especially the women . . . like rows of shallow saucers slopping with idealism . . . A world that had mistaken sensation for happiness . . . Through sheets of rain a drunken man lurched against her as he tossed a pint flask into an alley . . . Drunken boys . . . sprawling . . . The rosy knees and red mockery of their lips . . . The wide insatiable mouth, painted red as a wound, and the flaunting bare knees above rolled stockings . . . Unreal and fantastic as a nightmare . . . Distraught, chaotic, grotesque, it was an age, she told herself, of cruelty without moral indignation, of catastrophe without courage . . . Could the human race, glutted with horrors of its own making, survive upon a material basis alone? . . . A strange country, with its watered psychology, its vermin-infested fiction, and its sloppy minds that spill over . . . There were still teas without tea, and motion-picture faces without a film, and endless gin-drinking, and hastily bitten-back hiccoughs, and stories just a little funnier that went just a little farther than last year, and much talk of prize fighting, which was Puritanically forbidden, and of fox-hunting, which was Cavalierly allowed, and ardent prophecies that the next legislature would permit horse racing and gambling and pari-mutuel betting . . ."

This hardly requires much comment. There is a troubling flavor of the tabloids about most of Miss Glasgow's judgments. Short skirts and rouge have for her the fascination of obscenity. What she says is very familiar, and very obviously said; she has given us her dislike pure, not bothering to make it over into art. A greater writer has said it better:

> *Turning and turning in the widening gyre*
> *The falcon cannot hear the falconer;*
> *Things fall apart; the centre cannot hold;*
> *Mere anarchy is loosed upon the world.*

Possibly the last great German idealist, according to Miss Glasgow, said that the American people might some day realize that John Fincastle was their greatest thinker; writing about a great philosopher has its difficulties and its rewards. The smallest feather of so rare a bird should engage the reader. We are charmed to know that Kant liked "any music, just so it's loud and military," not because of the opinion but because it was the great Immanuel Kant who held it. But for this interest to attach to John Fincastle, we must feel that he *is* a great philosopher. To convince us, Miss Glasgow would have to be either a great philosopher or a great writer: that is, either give the philosophy itself, or else make a character whose acts and sayings are so entirely consistent and point so certainly in one direction that they force us to believe in him unreservedly, and to feel that it is merely because it would take too long, and because we might not be able to understand it, that we are not given the philosophy as well as the philosopher.

Miss Glasgow is of course not interested in the first of these alternatives; the most definite thing she says about Fincastle's great book is that it was a "reconciliation between the will and the intellect." This has a familiar ring; a Kantian might say that the reconciliation has already been effected, a psychologist repeat, with some irony, the word *will.* Fincastle believes that "God is essence, not energy." It is hard to interpret the statement, and it reminds us too much of Santayana.

Miss Glasgow has not the professional's attitude toward philosophy, and so fails to give it to John Fincastle. (Quoting Miss Glasgow: "Philosophy is not a reform but a consolation . . . it is still what it has always been, the only infallible antidote to life." The function of philosophy is to—console! One assures Miss Glasgow that this is *not* what philosophy "has always been.") Philosophy for her is essentially ethics; she is decidedly what James called "tenderminded." If Miss Glasgow were aroused in the middle of the night by a burglar, who clapped a pistol to her head and demanded, "Name me a philosopher!" you can be certain it would not be Hume. John Fincastle occasionally says things worthy of himself; but his thoughts in general, his judgments about the "Dying Age," are not so much those dramatically proper to the character of a great philosopher as those that Miss Glasgow happens to have herself. His sayings too often make up in sententiousness for what they lack in logical acuteness. The reader believes in him as a religious thinker, a noble and sympathetic character—not, however, as a great philosopher.

Miss Glasgow's style may be called commonplace; she is fond of the most obvious and familiar rhetorical devices, and these are most evident in important scenes, scenes in which she depicts some irresistible emotion, some mystical rapture. In general, her style is a good, average, useful style, but when one compares it with a first-rate one, both its inadequacies and ornaments become obvious. This style is at its best in occasional very slight, very sensitive, discriminations, especially in similes designed to convey the effect of sense perceptions. Some of these are unusually successful: "The syllables were as empty as old wasps' nests . . . The row of sandstone slabs, as yellow as old teeth . . ."

Miss Glasgow is generally better in handling unpleasant scenes than in handling pleasant ones. In fact, it is surprising to see how much she depends upon shock as an aesthetic device; Miss Glasgow, in a review, once spoke with energetic despair of the methods and effects we associate with such Southern writers as Faulkner and Caldwell. Miss Glasgow is at times not so far removed from them as she might think.

One feels about *Vein of Iron* that it was intended to be a great book; the plan of the whole novel is very impressive; and yet the texture and details are too often commonplace, the words of the characters too often have the value of something overheard in the street or over the telephone—no more. Miss Glasgow has seen to the spirit, and let the letter take care of itself. Then, too, Miss Glasgow comes to her work hardened, full of prejudice and presupposition.

Still, Miss Glasgow's book has considerable power. We readily believe in the characters as real people, in the story as something that really happened; some of the book, about the pioneers, about Grandmother Fincastle, about John Fincastle, will affect the reader unreservedly. Particularly affecting is such a scene as that in which Grandmother Fincastle comes to Ada, at the birth of her child.

Mr. Caldwell's effects range from particularly brutal to quite unusually sensitive ones; who else would have named three poor girls on a Georgia farm Rosamunda, Griselda, and Darling Jill? He is certainly a born humorist—if one ever doesn't laugh when Mr. Caldwell wants one to, it is only because one is too horrified. He is equally at home with the typical and the odd, a deputy sheriff and an albino. He generally depends on understatement and repetition, rather than exaggeration, for comic effect. The best thing one can do with Mr. Caldwell's peculiar variety of humor is to accept it with gratitude.

However, there is another element in his serious work—a preoccupation with brutal, violent, and obscene subject matter—that is not in the least peculiar to Mr. Caldwell. It is more evident than it has ever been in his latest book of short stories. There is no mixture of elements in them; they class themselves automatically as serious or humorous. Not a single story in *Kneel to the Rising Sun* is without a murder, a rape, or some scene of the utmost violence and brutality. Most of them, if merely related baldly as anecdotes, would have a considerable physiological effect on the reader; told by Mr. Caldwell, who lavishes all of his very considerable powers on them, and whose attitude and methods are those of the humorist, they are horrible to an extraordinary extent: the reader can actually feel his stomach contracting. If Mr. Caldwell is subjecting one to this nausea gratuitously, it is difficult not to feel for him a violent dislike; one is forced to look for circumstances which will explain or justify his methods.

About most of these stories one can say, as Goya did, "I have seen it," or, as Ambrose Bierce said in a different connection, "Can Such Things Be?" That is, they are social documents, instruments of protest against society; we accept the discomfort that attends reading such a story because we feel that it is true, that we ought to know it. After reading the *Agamemnon* or *Lear* we feel no desire to *do* anything at all; but after reading a successful story of this other kind, we are full of a horrified protest, we wish very violently that we could do something about such things.

Some of the stories, however, are not of this sort. In them the obscene or gruesome subject matter is used deliberately, merely to increase the effect of the story. This is, in the last analysis, an insult to the reader, an implicit assumption of his aesthetic stupidity; the writer believes that the reader will not be able to differentiate the effect of the shocking subject matter from the effect of the story as a work of art proper, and, since the total effect is so large, will assume that the story must have been extraordinarily fine. I do not mean this condemnation to be so sweeping as it sounds (nor do I mean to say that this assumption about the reader is necessarily conscious on the part of the writer), but certainly the indiscriminate or evident use of the principle can only result in failure. After all, the entire point of a trick is that you don't see how it is done. In such scenes as the death of Emma Bovary, Kirilov's suicide, the blinding of Oedipus, the subject matter has its effect; but, in the first place, the scenes are so carefully done that we notice the form more than the matter; and, in the second place, the blinding of Oedipus means something, it has an obvious relevance. Mr. Caldwell would have told you of the act for its own sake, and besides have told you so vividly, and in so much detail, that you would virtually feel your own fingernail against your own eyes. The writer had better remember that even the most gruesome and tragic art must give the reader pleasure. If the aesthetic pleasure we get from these stories outweighs the unpleasant effect of the subjects, then they are successful; but if this is not the case, there is no reason why we would show the slightest mercy to Mr. Caldwell.

It is much easier to understand than to pardon such conduct on the writer's part. In the first place, if you habitually write about murders and rapes, under peculiarly trying circumstances, in a peculiarly brutal manner, who will have the courage to call you sentimental?—and we live in an age that eschews sentimentality as if it were a good deal more than the devil. (Actually, of course, a writer may be just as sentimental in laying undue emphasis on sexual crimes as on dying mothers: *sentimental,* like *scientific,* is an adjective that relates to method, and not to matter.)

There is another more important cause. Valéry says about the poet that he is like a man who carries ten-pound weights up to the roof, and finally drops them all at once on the head of a passer-by. That is, the writer does not get from his work as he writes and reads it the same aesthetic shock that the reader does; and since the writer is accustomed to reading other stories, and having them produce a decided effect on him, he is disquieted at not being equally affected by his own.

But the bare facts of murder and rape have as much effect on the writer as on the reader: and the writer, confusing this shock with aesthetic shock, may take always to writing stories of the kind that have so much effect on him as he writes them. (Just so, an author frequently chooses solemn or overwhelming subjects to write about; he is so impressed at writing about Life and Death that he does not notice that he is saying nothing of the slightest importance about either. Miss Millay's "Renascence" is one of the best examples of this fault.) The writer's subject matter will of course become more violent and more shocking all the time; the appetite grows with feeding, and the writer after a time will be unmoved by things that would have once made him shake like an aspen.

Mr. Caldwell's technical ability is quite unusual. He writes his stories almost as if he were writing music. He has set themes or motifs, which he repeats time and time again—there are few writers who use repetition to the same extent. He brings you with extraordinary delicacy and care up to a climax or anticlimax; he loves that sort of suspense you get in the movies when someone is about to be killed by gangsters. He has a peculiar style, bare, precise, about halfway between the conversational-commonplace and the naïve-literary—the latter element is almost chemically pure in such first-person stories as "The Cold Winter."

About half the stories in his present volume are sketches rather than stories; but certainly no one could think of saying that about such a story as "Kneel to the Rising Sun." Mr. Caldwell's people are frequently not people at all, but merely very much simplified response systems. The easiest way of seeing what he lacks is to read Chekhov's stories about peasants. Nevertheless, such stories as "Kneel to the Rising Sun," "The Growing Season," and "A Day's Wooing" are stories well worth reading. "The Growing Season" is, in fact, one of the most extraordinarily ingenious stories I have ever seen. It is about the extremely bloody murder of something called "Fiddler." Fiddler is chained to a tree in Jesse English's yard; whether Fiddler is an imbecile, a dog, God himself couldn't say for certain, since never once is he called anything but Fiddler. Fiddler, "with his undeveloped legs," "rattling his chain," "crawling around the tree," getting up "as if to stand," Fiddler "making more noise than he had ever made before," is something the reader will hardly forget.

Most of the sketches in *Feliciana*—fourteen or fifteen out of nineteen—belong to the category of stories about the baby. Mr. Young tells you, with rather obtrusive precision and casualness, about cooks, servants, and cowboys he has known, Southern ladies of whom he approves, megalopolitan ones of whom he does not. It is hard to define exactly Mr. Young's attitude; as people tell you about the Grand Canyon, it must be seen to be believed. You can use, in characterizing it, the adjectives *patronizing, ironic, knowing;* it has in it something of the feeling of the more learned toward the less learned, of the cultured representative of a great tradition toward the representative of an inferior one. (The Greeks spoke of all other peoples as barbarians. It was an objective enough term; still, its use at about the beginning of the Christian era, as contrasted with its use at the time of the battle of Plataea, must have lacked good temper. Mr. Young's attitude has its affinities in the latter period.) An attitude of this sort is like omniscience: one mistake and the whole thing falls through. If the reader at any time finds himself considering Mr. Young's sensibility or moral values as, for the moment, inferior to his own, he will have difficulty in keeping the same awe for Mr. Young. This, perhaps, does happen; sometimes Mr. Young is snobbish, sometimes sentimental—sometimes he shows a disquieting admiration for moral perceptions or stylistic effects which do not seem to the reader admirable at all. Mr. Young is too often, as one of his characters says about himself, "myself strutting in my own procession."

Still, there are some stories in *Feliciana* to which most of this criticism does not apply. Mr. Young at his best is decidedly worth reading. He is really not a novelist, not a writer of short stories, but an essayist; the essay in this book called "Echoes at Livorno" is the best thing in it. Some of this essay will give the reader the most exquisite pleasure; and yet there are parts of it so disappointing one hardly knows what to say. The best moments of his style are graceful and beautiful; for instance: ". . . And sometimes in that silence, while he hung listening, a gentle shock of mild surprise carried far into his heart the voice of mountain torrents; or the visible scene entered unawares into his mind, with all its solemn imagery, its rocks, its woods, and its uncertain heaven received into the bosom of the steady lake." This sentence has some flaws, and fails badly at the end; still, it is a fine one. Queerly enough, the best part of it reads almost like a paraphrase of Wordsworth; yet Mr. Young shows in another essay some contempt for the English "nature poets," contrasting their "botany, profundity, pantheism, and rapture" with the "passionate humanity," the "classicism" of the Italians. If Mr. Young thinks so, it is a pity he does not copy them instead of Wordsworth.

As a matter of fact, all this merely shows how almost completely Latin Mr. Young is. There are innumerable references in the book to Spain, Mexico, France, Italy, even Turkey; in the whole book there is one reference to any northern European country: a sentence about "Teutonic foreigners." To another country of northern Europe, England, there is no reference at all.

The Furys, by Mr. Hanley, is a book about working-class people in a west-of-England port; it is done on a big scale and, except for one unfortunate exception, to be discussed below, it is a well proportioned and sensible book. The texture of *The Furys* is terse, minute, witty; the author occasionally shows a sort of violence or extravagance that overflows into something resembling surrealism (Grandfather reliving his boyhood, Professor Titmouse and his apparition). There is really a great deal in the book; instead of getting, by temperament or industry, a few favorite effects, and repeating them indefinitely, Mr. Hanley absolutely deluges you with the most varied ones, all quite justified by the plan of his book. The scenes range from funny to almost Apocalyptic ones. There are fifteen or sixteen characters who can be remembered with the utmost vividness; Mr. Fury, in particular, is an extraordinary success.

There is one big fault about *The Furys,* and anyone who has read *Boy,* Mr. Hanley's first novel, can see just what the fault is, and just what caused it. *Boy* is a powerful, but extremely limited, book—a tour de force, a book whose effects are all of one kind. It is a book about a boy who runs away to sea: the boy gets to Alexandria and dies, in a flood of meaningless and violent circumstances, especially horrible, the reader feels, because of the boy's failure to understand anything that is happening to him. Near the end there is a sort of nightmare of pure lust. *The Furys* is written on an entirely different scale, it is a more sensible, a better-balanced book; but Mr. Hanley has given it an ending that would fit *Boy,* an ending that stops, but does not finish, *The Furys.*

Lucy Gayheart is very unpretentious, a quiet book on a small scale. The book depends on two accidental deaths—the death of Sebastian, the singer with whom Lucy Gayheart is in love, and Lucy's own death. This is a structural flaw; as Maupassant said, people are killed every day by bricks falling from scaffoldings, but you mustn't write novels about them. Everyone knows the statement (with which, of course, one may disagree violently) that the best style is one which the reader does not notice at all. Miss Cather's style and general treatment almost satisfy this demand; or at least, one notices the faults of her style more than its virtues. This is not intended to be ironic; I mean that it is only by careful rereading that one sees all the virtues of Miss Cather's style; her faults, on the other hand, are of a sort that our age particularly notices. Her style has very distinct limits, but inside these limits she writes with ease and grace. (The last sentence in Book II is the worst sentence in the book; it was probably just bad luck, one of those unaccountable lapses during which we forget our names, that kept Miss Cather satisfied with it.) Miss Cather's style and sensibility are not those of a first-rate writer; but she does not strain them, and there is nothing false about *Lucy Gayheart.*

You know Lucy Gayheart only in the way you might know yourself, if you were badly forgetful, and not very introspective. Sometimes things people say about you surprise you a good deal, and one or two of the things other people say about Lucy surprise you almost as much. Very few people know their own characteristic locutions, or turns of thought; you do not know Lucy's. She is made a rather general and lyrical figure throughout, and this prepares you for the way in which she is regarded near the book's end. In telling you, very beautifully and sensitively, about her footprints, Miss Cather compares them to those of "the herald Mercury"; and Miss Cather has written so gently and restrainedly, what she has said seems so just, that they have that much significance for you, too.

Miss Cather's treatment of Lucy's grief seems unsuccessful; she tells only the general things everybody knows, just the things she could have taken for granted. She writes of emotion better than of sensation; yet she frequently describes an emotion so that you remember having felt the one she means, but decide that her description of it is not good enough. I do not say that Miss Cather is rather romantic and sentimental, and that she pays no attention to economics and sociology. Mr. Hanley is very much interested in the economic implications of *his* story, and it is a good story; but there is no reason to hold him up to Miss Cather and say, "Go thou and do likewise."

Miss Cather is especially good in the cultural levels she gives to her characters in the speeches she has them say; there is no mistake to hurt your confidence in her. Her attitude toward music, her great singer, are very convincing and satisfying. Besides, Miss Cather knows so much about writing; you do not need to look at the list of "other books by this author" to realize that she has written a great many books, and learned a great deal while she was writing them. Miss Cather is somehow so sympathetic, and so interesting, that *Lucy Gay-*

heart demands both liking and respect. *Lucy Gayheart* is not an "important" book at all; but surely, if it affects one so, it has enough of virtue.

A Preface to Maturity is what is commonly known as an "autobiographical first novel." Miss Brousseau is more interesting when she writes about other people than when she tells about her own adjustments to, and conclusions about, life; she is more often deceived by herself than by her fellows. Perhaps it had better be said that D. H. Lawrence is not included among her fellows—she seems to have swallowed Lawrence hook, line, and sinker. Her love scenes, as a result, have a sort of cheerful absurdity that recommends them to the reader; the characters analyze their emotions at inordinate length, and you feel that it is only a lack of proper facilities (and a certain antipathy to science) that keeps them from recording their blood pressure at the same time. The book is overwritten at times. On the other hand, Miss Brousseau's observation is sometimes unusually acute; one feels, then, that she has had no interest in either substantiating or discrediting her presuppositions, and has said what she really saw, what the world and her integrity forced her to say. What the book mainly needs is more experience in writing and a different attitude toward writing. If Miss Brousseau were forced to write about animals or automata, and could not depend so much upon ideas, ideals, sentimentality, whole sheets of emotion, if she would once stop and ask herself, "What good are all these purple patches, these carefully written rhapsodies?" she might write a great deal better second book.

Sometimes book advertisements are designed to interest a limited public; for instance, the announcement of a reprint of *Black Beauty* will be accompanied by the information that "This is a book no horse lover can afford to miss." The advertisements of *We Too Are Drifting* have been rather of this sort. After all, it is only a pleasant, if unimportant, book. Miss Wilhelm has definite notions of economy and structure, and her book makes very easy reading. This story of three women in love has the extrinsic charm lent by a novel situation; perhaps it seems both more original and more interesting than it actually is. It is certainly a very innocent and idealistic book. A great many things are beautiful and noble and strange, and Miss Wilhelm tells you so bluntly. If it were only as easy as that! Her characters, like Hemingway's, are *noble.* I can recall some characters in literature who I thought were virtuous in the highest sense—Prince Myshkin, for instance—but none of them was ever *noble.*

Miss Wilhelm's artists qua artists are not very convincing; bad ones probably talk like that, but good ones at least ought not to. (Miss Wilhelm might look at the conversations in Vollard's life of Degas.) The accidental death of the sculptor seems unnecessary. As far as her style is concerned, it is only necessary to quote a sentence, and let the reader decide for himself by whom Miss Wilhelm is influenced: "The sun was bright and hot but there was wind off the sea and there was smooth bright green grass and dark clotted trees and the white sheep clotted and the blue sky with white wreaths and the smooth road curving."

Miss Slesinger's *Time: The Present* is a collection of magazine short stories, most of which are hardly worth reprinting. The stories are generally choppy, jumbled, and derivative; Miss Slesinger is easily influenced by contemporary writers, and both her mechanisms and effects are familiar. "On Learning That Her Second Husband Has Taken His First Love," for instance, reads like a schoolgirl's parody of Dorothy Parker; to Miss Parker's peculiar qualities it adds a sentimentality and self-absorption all its own. Miss Slesinger's irony is essentially aimless, since her own attitude and sensibility impress the reader as very little superior to those of the characters she satirizes. A humorist has always to be funny; the satirist, faced with the like necessity of always attacking something, is often either barbarous or dull. Miss Slesinger is sometimes tedious, and sometimes manifests a peculiar feminine brutality.

The work is very uneven, in regard to both sentiment and merit. You can find in it sentimental bits, disgusting bits, witty bits—almost anything you please. The publishers have put brightly colored coarse-paper inserts between the stories, and have printed the titles of the stories on these; it makes quite an ugly book.

Time Out of Mind is an ingenuous story about a proud Maine family, the Fortunes, whose son becomes, in spite of his father's opposition, a great composer. He is truly loved, not by his selfish wife and sister, but by the poor girl who writes the story to soothe her age. He comes to a tragic end, and she is accused of his death; Miss Field solves the problem of the presentation of her heroine's trial by quoting from the local newspaper—the quotation, incidentally, occupies eleven pages of small type. On a certain level, *Time Out of Mind* is quite a good story; but this level is surprisingly low. The book is full of rather pretty and idealistic sayings about life and art and love. The author has the habit of quoting from the Old Testament, and her prose suffers from the comparison.

Anthropologists periodically go off to Africa or the South Seas, to return a year or two later with a substantial monograph on the sexual life of the natives. Mr. Holden has had the happy inspiration of not bothering with Africa at all; his book, *Chance Has a Whip,* might very well be called *The Sexual Life of the American Business Man.* Insofar as serious writing is concerned, Mr. Holden is a thorough amateur. His hero has a very happy love affair; on the other hand, he almost dies of a burst appendix, his daughter commits suicide, he accidentally kills one of his wife's former lovers, and is accidentally killed by gangsters escaping from prison. An occasional scene or simile is vivid enough—the story as a whole is irrelevant.

The Morality of Mr. Winters

KENYON REVIEW, SPRING 1939

Maule's Curse by Yvor Winters

"God," said the dying man, pointing his finger, with a ghastly look, at the undismayed countenance of his enemy, "God will give him blood to drink!"—The House of the Seven Gables

SO FAR as these essays—on Hawthorne, Cooper, Melville, Poe, Very and Emerson, Dickinson, and Henry James—are related, it is by this thesis: Maule's curse was a real one, Punic in its completeness; every major American writer of the nineteenth century, except Dickinson, Melville, and Cooper (who escaped in their shirts), had his life left "in moral confusion" by his "New England heritage." Dickinson saved herself by attaining the insights of "a more nearly Catholic Christianity," Melville "escaped the curse by comprehending it," Cooper got off, rather more prosaically, by being "an unmitigated New Yorker," and so not coming under its influence at all.

The Puritans were doubly heretical: as Calvinists, they had abandoned Catholic dogmas for deterministic ones; they next substituted for the Calvinist doctrine of the Inner Light one that made conduct alone indicative of election. They held to determinism in theory and denied it in practice; they substituted an inadequate morality for religion, and made its interpretation and enforcement blankly Manichaean. As time mitigated its rigor, as the non-moral and supernatural elements associated with it grew vestigial ("The doctrine of predestination would naturally lead to religious apathy, for it offered no explicit motive to action"), it became Unitarianism, a "mildly moralistic creed"; the Unitarians, by "depriving the ethical life of the more impressive aspects of its supernatural sanction," had before long "all but extinguished intensity of moral conviction." These wretched creatures soon succumbed "to Romantic ethical theory, especially as expounded by the Transcendentalists"; here we end our journey, groping laboriously along the huge limbs of Emerson, who, this Vergil tells us, "eliminated the need of moral conviction and moral understanding alike," whose universe is one "of amiable but perfectly unconscious imbeciles."

All this had disastrous consequences. Emerson, cut off from his "heritage, his source of significance," confused "Romantic amoralism" and New England mysticism "so inextricably that we have not yet worked ourselves free of them." Hawthorne, corrupted by "provincial sentimentalism," closer to Emerson than to Edwards, produced a merely negative criticism of the Puritans. New England gave James a moral sense "unsupported by any clear set of ideas"; it left Melville spotty, Dickinson impoverished, and Henry Adams entirely bewildered. This whole account, all these writers, illustrate the characteristic American dilemma: "the choice between abstractions inadequate or irrelevant to experience on the one hand, and experience on the other as far as practicable unilluminated by understanding."

This part of *Maule's Curse,* which is supposed to relate "the history of ideas [a history of ideas that, neglecting both science and philosophy, is almost wholly theology] to the history of literary forms," is interesting and plausible; but some of the parts of the argument are unproved, one or two unprovable—for instance, the vital point that the doctrine of predestination necessarily leads to religious apathy—and a disproportionate importance is given to causes that were certainly partial. Many or most of the good writers of the nineteenth century were similarly cut off from the religion of their predecessors. Mr. Winters might just as well have named his book *Copernicus' Curse* (or Galileo's, or Darwin's, or a hundred others'): for it is the development of the sciences (along with a good many minor causes) that has produced the changes in the world that seem to Mr. Winters so unqualifiedly evil. His indictment of the Puritans boils down to this: their mistaken dogmas led to religious apathy, thence to moral confusion; their continued emphasis on a harshly inadequate morality permanently soured their dispositions, and left them with an exaggerated moral sense after the morality which had produced and directed it had disappeared. The first point hardly seems of paramount importance, since the correct dogmas, throughout Europe and America, led to an equal apathy and confusion; the second point anybody who has known a New Englander admits already.

Still, Mr. Winters's approach has helped produce the extraordinary criticism that makes up most of *Maule's Curse;* it is, all in all, illuminating; but I am afraid it lights Mr. Winters even more piercingly than it does American literature. The abstractions Mr. Winters has chosen— which are, roughly, the traditional Catholic ones—will seem to many of the inhabitants of this planet "inadequate or irrelevant to experience"; he too is a victim of his characteristic American dilemma. His readers will find in Mr. Winters an absolute moral dogmatism, an aesthetic that reduces art to morals, and a metaphysic conscious of hardly any problems except those of determinism. If Emerson's universe is one of amiable but unconscious imbeciles, Mr. Winters's is that of a crèche (I must admit there are a good many devils hiding among the sheep).

Whitehead is supposed to have said of Russell: "Bertie thinks me muddleheaded and I think Bertie simple-minded." Now Mr. Winters is simple-minded, in this sense, to an astonishing degree; to him there are few questions unanswered, and none unanswerable. If ours is not the most rational of all possible worlds (for even Mr. Winters sometimes entertains the doubt), that does not excuse any confusion about it on our part; we *have* absolutely valid standards, both adequate and relevant, by which the universe can be understood and evaluated; if we are unfortunate or foolish enough to disregard these, we must take the consequences—which are disastrous. He writes as if the last three hundred years had occurred, but not to him: I know no one of comparable merit so wholly uncorrupted by "science," in any sense of the word. To him, fine art is correct moral judgment, highly formed and entirely unambiguous; here are two characteristic assertions from *Primitivism and Decadence:*

> In traditional verse, each variation [in meter], no matter how slight, is exactly perceptible and as a result can be given exact meaning as an act of moral perception . . . The moral intelligence is merely the knowledge and evaluation of evil, and the moral intelligence is the measure of the man and the poet alike.

It is the rigorous application of inadequate and inflexible standards which produces occasional judgments that a tactful admirer might characterize as trembling on the brink of absurdity. Mr. Winters calls Jones Very "one of the finest of poets"; thinks Elizabeth Daryush great, the "finest British poet since T. Sturge Moore"; ranks Bridges (whom he considers a thoroughly major poet) above Hopkins, Moore above Yeats—Yeats is not mentioned by Mr. Winters except to illustrate vices; thinks Lady Winchilsea's "The Tree" and "The Change" "flawlessly beautiful poems" which typify almost uniquely the traditional norm of English poetry; puts Gray and Collins below Churchill, a great poet who "all but equals Pope's brilliance and range"; states that any American who wants an education richly instead of superficially literary must read the complete works of James Fenimore Cooper (a stylist superior to Hawthorne); and is so intolerant of any great deviation from his own standards of order and significance that he finds "madness" (a term carefully qualified, however) in James, Eliot, Henry Adams, Hawthorne, Melville, Collins (the melancholy of the "Ode to Evening" in the lines *The weak-eyed bat / With short shrill shriek flits by on leathern wing* "verges on disorder"), and—of all people—Cooper.

But these are the lapses of a critic whose thoroughness, clarity, and real penetration are almost unequaled today; *Maule's Curse* is the best book on American literature I ever read, and I make so great a point of its author's vices only because his virtues are apparent and indeed overwhelming. He puts into exact and lucid shape judgments informed by an unusual sensitivity, a rigorous intelligence, and a dismayingly thorough knowledge. He reads each writer as if he had never been read before; he is a critical instrument completely uninfluenced by any fear of ridicule or consideration of expediency. We know precisely what he thinks and his reasons for thinking so. Most of his essays are intended to be definitive—a surprising number are. He is valuable both in widening taste (his own likings are unusual, and no one is better at championing neglected merit) and in correcting it (his attacks on the real excesses of modern literature are devastating). If I said just how good the essays on Melville and James are, I should seem extravagant; that on Poe (which leaves him looking like a china shop after a visit of the Marx brothers) is not far behind; Dickinson and Hawthorne are handled with intelligence and love, Cooper with a large and tremendously detailed surplus of the latter. Mr. Winters demolishes his old butt, Emerson, with automatic ease, and a gaze averted to Very. Jones Very, Mr. Winters's latest find, is a sort of New England Traherne, who writes as a rule bad Herbert with an eighteenth-century stutter and as an exception rather good mystical verse. He is a better poet than some of his contemporaries—Lowell and Longfellow, for instance—and deserves being hauled from oblivion; but he all too usually writes stuff like this:

> And in thy rambles, e'en the creeping vine
> Shall keep with thee a jocund holiday . . .
> I plunge me in the river's cooling wave,
> Or on the embroidered bank admiring lean,
> Now some endangered insect life to save . . .

—lines which Mr. Winters uses as proof of Very's greatness and calls "lovely."

Texts from Housman

KENYON REVIEW, SUMMER 1939

THE LOGIC poetry has or pretends to have generally resembles induction more than deduction. Of four possible procedures (dealing entirely with particulars, dealing entirely with generalizations, inferring the relatively general from the relatively particular, and deducing the particular from the more general), the third is very much the most common, and the first and second are limits which "pure" and didactic poetry timidly approach. The fourth is seldom seen. In this essay I am interested in that variety of the third procedure in which the generalizations are implicit. When such generalizations are simple ones, very plainly implied by the particulars of the poem, there will be little tendency to confuse this variety of the third procedure with the first procedure; when they are neither simple nor very plainly implied, the poem will be thought of as "pure" (frequently, "nature") poetry. This is all the more likely to occur since most "pure" poetry is merely that in which the impurity, like the illegitimate child of the story, is "such a little one" that we feel it ought to be disregarded. Of these poems of implicit generalization there is a wide range, extending from the simplest, in which the generalizations are made obvious enough to vex the average reader (some of the "Satires of Circumstance," for instance), to the most complicated, in which they entirely escape his observation ("To the Moon"). The two poems of Housman's which I am about to analyze are more nearly of the type of "To the Moon."

II

Crossing alone the nighted ferry
With the one coin for fee,
Whom, on the wharf of Lethe waiting,
Count you to find? Not me.

The brisk fond lackey to fetch and carry,
The true, sick-hearted slave,
Expect him not in the just city
And free land of the grave.

The first stanza is oddly constructed; it manages to carry over several more or less unexpressed statements, while the statement it makes on the surface, grammatically, is arranged so as to make the reader disregard it completely. Literally, the stanza says: *Whom do you expect to find waiting for you? Not me.* But the denying and elliptical *not me* is not an answer to the surface question; that question is almost rhetorical, and obviously gets a *me;* the *not me* denies *And I'll satisfy your expectations and be there?*—the implied corollary of the surface question; and the flippant and brutal finality of the *not me* implies that the expectations are foolish. (A belief that can be contradicted so carelessly and completely—by a person in a position to know—is a foolish one.) The stanza says: *You do expect to find me and ought not to* and *You're actually such a fool as to count on my being there?* and *So I'll be there, eh? Not me.*

Some paraphrases of the two stanzas will show how extraordinarily much they do mean; they illustrate the quality of poetry that is almost its most characteristic, compression. These paraphrases are not very imaginative—the reader can find justification for any statement in the actual words of the poem. (Though not in any part considered in isolation. The part as part has a misleading look of independence and reality, just as does the word as word; but it has only that relationship to the larger contexts of the poem that the words which compose it have to it, and its significance is similarly controlled and extended by those larger units of which it is a part. A poem is a sort of onion of contexts, and you can no more locate any of the important meanings exclusively in a part than you can locate a relation in one of its terms. The significance of a part may be greatly modified or even in extreme cases completely reversed by later and larger parts and by the whole. This will be illustrated in the following discussion: most of the important meanings attached to the first stanza do not exist when the stanza is considered in isolation.) And the paraphrases are not hypertrophied, they do not even begin to be exhaustive.

Stanza 1:   Do you expect me to wait patiently for you there, just as I have done on earth? expect that, in hell, after death, things will go on for you just as they do here on earth? that there, after crossing and drinking Lethe and oblivion, I'll still be thinking of human you, still be waiting faithfully there on the wharf for you to arrive, with you still my only interest, with me still your absolutely devoted slave—just as we are here? Do you really? Do you actually suppose that you yourself, then, will be able to expect it? Even when dead, all alone, on that grim ferry, in the middle of the dark forgetful river, all that's left of your human life one coin, you'll be stupid or inflexible or faithful enough to *count* on (you're sure, are you, so sure that not even a doubt enters your mind?) finding me waiting there? How are we to understand an inflexibility that seems almost incredible? Is it because you're pathetically deluded about love's constancy, my great lasting love for you? (This version makes the *you* sympathetic; but it is unlikely, an unstressed possibility, and the others do not.) Or is it that you're so sure of my complete enslavement that you know death itself can't change it? Or are you so peculiarly stupid that you can't even conceive of any essential change away from your past life and knowledge, even after the death that has destroyed them both? Or is it the general inescapable stupidity of mankind, who can conceive of death only in human and vital terms? (Housman's not giving the reasons, when the reasons must be thought about if the poem is to be understood, forces the reader to make them for himself, and to see that there is a wide range that must be considered. This is one of the most important principles of compression in poetry; these implied foundations or justifications for a statement might be called *bases*.) Are you actually such a fool as to believe that? So I'll be there? Not me. You're wrong. There things are really different.

One of the most important elements in the poem is the tone of the *not me*. Its casualness, finality, and matter-of-fact bluntness give it almost the effect of slang. It is the crudest of denials. There is in it a laconic brutality, an imperturbable and almost complacent vigor; it has certainly a sort of contempt. Contempt for what? Contempt at himself for his faithlessness? contempt at himself for his obsessing weakness—for not being faithless now instead of then? Or contempt at her, for being bad enough to keep things as they are, for being stupid enough to imagine that they will be so always? The tone is both threatening and disgusted. It shivers between all these qualities like a just-thrown knife. And to what particular denial does this tone attach? how specific, how general a one? These are changes a reader can easily ring for himself; but I hope he will realize their importance. Variations of this formula of alternative possibilities make up one of the most valuable resources of the poet.

The second stanza is most thoroughly ambiguous; there are two entirely different levels of meaning for the whole, and most of the parts exhibit a comparable stratification. I give a word-for-word analysis:

Do not expect me to be after death what I was alive and human: the *fond* (1. *foolish;* 2. *loving*—you get the same two meanings in the synonym *doting*) *brisk* (the normal meanings are favorable: *full of life, keenly alive or alert, energetic;* but here the context forces it over into *officious, undignified, solicitous, leaping at your every word*—there is a pathetic ignoble sense to it here) *lackey* (the most contemptuous and degrading form of the word *servant:* a servile follower, a toady) *to fetch and carry* (you thought so poorly of me that you let me perform nothing but silly menial physical tasks; thus, our love was nothing but the degrading relationship of obsequious servant and contemptuous master), *the true* (1. *constant, loyal, devoted, faithful;* 2. *properly so-called, ideally or typically such*—the perfectly slavish slave) *sick-hearted* (1. cowardly, disheartened in a weak discouraged ignoble way, as a Spartan would have said of helots, "These sick-hearted slaves"; 2. sick at heart at the whole mess, his own helpless subjection. There was a man in one of the sagas who had a bad boil on his foot; when he was asked why he didn't limp and favor it, he replied: "One walks straight while the leg is whole." If the reader imagines this man as a slave he will see sharply the more elevated sense of the phrase *sick-hearted slave*) *slave* (1. the conventional hardly meant sense in which we use it of lovers, as an almost completely dead metaphor; this sense has very little force here; or 2. the literal *slave:* the relation of slave to master is not pleasant, not honorable, is between lovers indecent and horrible, but immensely comprehensive—their love is made even more compulsive and even less favorable). But here I leave the word-by-word analysis for more general comment. I think I hardly need remark on the shock in this treatment, which forces over the conventional unfelt terms into their literal degrading senses; and this shock is amplified by the paradoxical fall through *just city* and *free land* into *the grave.* (Also, the effect of the *lackey / carry* and versification of the first line of the stanza should be noted.)

Let me give first the favorable literal surface sense of *the just city and free land of the grave,* its sense on the level at which you take Housman's Greek underworld convention seriously. The house of Hades is the *just city* for a number of reasons: in it are the three just judges; in it are all the exemplary convicts, from Ixion to the Danaïdes, simply dripping with justice; here justice is meted equally to the anonymous and rankless dead; there is no corruption here. It is the *free land* because here the king and the slave are equal (though even on the level of death as the Greek underworld, the horrid irony has begun to intrude—Achilles knew, and Housman knows, that it is better to be the slave of a poor farmer than king among the hosts of the dead); because here we are free at last from life; and so on and so on.

But at the deeper level, the *just* fastened to *city,* the *city* fastened to *grave,* have an irony that is thorough. How are we to apply *just* to a place where corruption and nothingness are forced on good and bad, innocent and guilty alike? (From Housman's point of view it might be called mercy, but never justice.) And the *city* is as bad; the cemetery looks like a city of the graves, of the stone rectangular houses—but a city without occupations, citizens, without life: a shell, a blank check that can never be filled out. And can we call a land *free* whose inhabitants cannot move a finger, are compelled as completely as stones? And can we call the little cave, the patch of darkness and pressing earth, the *land* of the grave?

And why are we told to expect him not, the slave, the lackey, in the just city and free land of the grave? Because he is changed now, a citizen of the Greek underworld, engrossed in its games and occupations, the new interests that he has acquired? Oh no, the change is complete, not from the old interests to new ones, but from any interests to none; do not expect him because he has ceased to exist, he is really, finally different now. It is foolish to expect *anything* of the world after death. But we can expect nothingness; and that is better than this world, the poem is supposed to make us feel; there, even though we are overwhelmed impartially and completely, we shall be free of the evil of this world—a world whose best thing, love, is nothing but injustice and stupidity and slavery. This is why the poet resorts to the ambiguity that permits him to employ the adjectives *just* and *free*: they seem to apply truly on the surface level, and ironically at the other; but in a way they, and certainly the air of reward and luck and approbation that goes with them, apply truly at the second level as well. This is the accusation and condemnation of life that we read so often in Housman: that the grave seems better, we are glad to be in it.

We ought not to forget that this poem is a love poem by the living "me" of the poem to its equally living "you": *when we are dead, things will be different—and I'm glad of it.* It is, considerably sublimated, the formula familiar to such connections: *I wish I were dead;* and it has more than a suspicion of the child's *when I'm dead, then they'll be sorry.* It is an accusation that embodies a very strong statement of the underlying antagonism, the real ambivalence of most such relationships. The condemnation applied to the world for being bad is extended to the *you* for not being better. And these plaints are always pleas; so the poem has an additional force. Certainly this particular-seeming little poem turns out to be general enough: it carries implicit in it attitudes (aggregates of related generalizations) toward love, life, and death.

III

It nods and curtseys and recovers
When the wind blows above,
The nettle on the graves of lovers
That hanged themselves for love.

The nettle nods, the wind blows over,
The man, he does not move,
The lover of the grave, the lover
That hanged himself for love.

This innocent-looking little nature poem is actually, I think, a general quasi-philosophical piece meant to infect the reader with Housman's own belief about the cause of any action. (I am afraid it is a judgment the reader is likely neither to resist nor recognize.) The nettle and the wind are Housman's specific and usual symbols. Housman's poetry itself is a sort of homemade nettle wine ("Out of a stem that scored the hand / I wrung it in a weary land"); the nettle has one poem entirely to itself, XXXII in *More Poems*. No matter what you sow, only the nettle grows; no matter what happens, it flourishes and remains—"the numberless, the lonely, the thronger of the land." It peoples cities, it waves above the courts of kings; "and touch it and it stings." Stating what symbols "mean" is a job the poet has properly avoided; but, roughly, the nettle stands for the hurting and inescapable conditions of life, the prosperous (but sympathetically presented and almost admiringly accepted) evil of the universe—"great Necessity," if you are not altogether charmed by it. What the wind is Housman states himself (in "On Wenlock Edge the wood's in trouble"; but it is given the same value in several other poems, notably "The weeping Pleiads wester"): the "tree of man" is never quiet because the wind, "the gale of life," blows through it always.

What I said just before the analysis of the first stanza of "Crossing alone the nighted ferry" is true here too; many of one's remarks about the first stanza of this poem will be plausible or intelligible only in the light of one's consideration of the whole poem. In the first line, *It nods and curtseys and recovers,* there is a shock which grows out of the contrast between this demure performance and its performer, the Housman nettle. The nettle is merely repeating above the grave, compelled by the wind, what the man in the grave did once, when the wind blew through him. So living is (we must take it as being) just a repetition of little meaningless nodding actions, actions that haven't even the virtue of being our own—since the wind forces them out of us; life as the wind makes man as the tree or nettle helpless and determined. This illustrates the general principle that in poetry you make judgments by your own preliminary choice of symbols, and force the reader who accepts the symbols to accept the judgments implicit in them. A symbol, like Bowne's "concept," is a nest of judgments; the reader may accept the symbols, and then be cautious about accepting judgments or generalizations, but the damage is done.

The images in the poem are quite general: "the nettle on the graves of lovers that hanged themselves for love" is not any one nettle, not really any particular at all, but a moderately extensive class. (If Housman were writing a pure poem, a nature poem, he would go about it differently; here the generality is insisted on—any lover, any nettle will do well enough: if you prove something for *any* you prove it for *all,* and Housman is arranging all this as a plausible *any.*) There is of course irony, at several levels, in a nettle's dancing obliviously (*nod* and *curtsey* and *recover* add up to *dance*) on the grave of the dead lover. All flesh is grass; but worse here, because the grass which is the symbol for transitoriness outlasts us. (The reader may say, remembering *The stinging nettle only will still be found to stand*: "But the nettle is a symbol of lasting things to Housman, not of transitory ones." Actually it manages for both here, for the first when considered as a common symbol, for the second when considered as Housman's particular one. But this ambiguity in symbols is frequent; without it they would be much less useful. Take a similar case, *grass*: this year's grass springs up and withers, and is shorter than man; but *grass,* all grass, lasts forever. With people we have different words for the two aspects, *men* and *man*. The whole business of thinking of the transitory grass as just the same more lasting than man—in one form or another, one of the stock poetic subjects—is a beautiful fallacy that goes like this: *Grass*—the year-after-year process—is more lasting than *men;* substituting *man* for *men* and this year's blade for the endless grass, you end by getting a proposition that everybody from Job on down or up has felt, at one time or another, thoroughly satisfactory.) Why a nettle to dance on the grave? Because in English poetry flowers grow on the graves of these lovers who have died for love, to show remembrance; Housman puts the nettle there, for forgetfulness. In the other poems the flower "meant" their love—here the nettle means it. All the nettle's actions emphasize its indifference and removedness. The roses in the ballads were intimately related to the lovers, and entwined themselves above the graves—the nature that surrounded the lovers was thoroughly interested in their game, almost as human as they; the nettle above this grave is alone, inhuman and casual, the representative of a nature indifferent to man.

The fifth and sixth lines of the poem are there mainly to establish this shocking paradox: here is a sessile thing, a plant, that curtseys and nods, while the man, the most thoroughly animate of all beings, cannot even move. Looked at in the usual way this is gloomy and mortifying, and that is the surface force it has here; but looked at in another way, Housman's way, there is a sort of triumph in it: the most absolute that man can know. That is what it is for Housman. Once man was tossed about helplessly and incessantly by the wind that blew through him—now the toughest of all plants is more sensitive, more easily moved than he. In other words, death is better than life, nothing is better than anything. Nor is this a silly adolescent pessimism peculiar to Housman, as so many critics assure you. It is better to be dead than alive, best of all never to have been born—said a poet approvingly advertised as seeing life steadily and seeing it whole; and if I began an anthology of such quotations there it would take me a long time to finish. The attitude is obviously inadequate and just as obviously important.

The triumph here leads beautifully into the poem's final statement: the triumph at being in the grave, one with the grave, prepares us for the fact that it was the grave, not any living thing, that the lover loved, and hanged himself for love of. The statement has some plausibility: hanging yourself for love of someone is entirely silly, so far as any possession or any furthering of your love is concerned, but if you are in love with death, killing yourself is the logical and obvious and only way to consummate your love. For the lover to have killed himself for love of a living thing would have been senseless; but his love for her was only ostensible, concealing—from himself too—the "common wish for death," his real passion for the grave.

. But if this holds for this one case; if in committing this most sincere and passionate, most living of all acts (that is, killing yourself for love; nothing else shows so complete a contempt for death and consequences, so absolute a value placed on another living creature), the lover was deceiving himself about his motives, and did it, not for love of anything living, but because of his real love for death; then everybody must do everything for the same reason. (This is a judgment too exaggerated for anyone to expect to get away with, the reader may think; but judgments of life tend to this form—"Vanity, vanity, all is vanity.") For the lover is the perfectly simplified, extreme case. This is what is called a crucial experiment. (It is one of Mill's regular types of induction.) The logic runs: If you can prove that in committing this act—an act about the motives of which the actor is so little likely to be deceived, an act so little likely to have the love of death as its motive—the actor was deceived, and had the love of death as his motive, then you can prove it for any other act the motive of which is more likely to be the love of death, and about the motives of which it is more likely that the actor might be deceived.

But for the conclusion to be true the initial premise must be true, the lover's one motive must have been the wish for death; and Housman has of course not put in even a word of argument for the truth of that premise, he has merely stated it, with the most engaging audacity and dogmatism—has stated it innocently, as a fact obvious as any other of these little natural facts about the wind and the nettle and the cemetery. He has produced it not as a judgment but as a datum, and the sympathetic reader has accepted it as such. He is really treating it as a percept, and percepts have no need for proof, they are neither true nor false, they are just there. If he had tried to prove the truth of the premise he would have convinced only those who already believed in the truth of the conclusion, and those people (i.e., himself) didn't need to be convinced. With the poem as it is, the reader is convinced; or if he objects, the poet can object disingenuously in return, "But you've made the absurd error of taking hypothetical reasoning as categorical. My form is: *If* A, *then* B; I'm not interested in *proving* A. Though, of course, if you decide to remove the *if,* and assert A, then B is asserted also; and A is awfully plausible, isn't it?—just part of the data of the poem; you could hardly reject it, could you?"

Two of the generalizations carried over by this poem—that our actions are motivated by the wish for death, that our ostensible reasons for acts are merely rationalizations, veneers of apparent motive overlying the real levels of motivation—are, in a less sweeping form, psychological or psychoanalytical commonplaces today. But I am not going to hold up Housman's poem as a masterly anticipation of our own discoveries; so far as I can see, Housman was not only uninterested but incapable in such things, and pulled these truths out of his pie, not because of wit, but because of the perverse and ingenious obstinacy that pulled just such gloomy judgments out of any pie at all. Here the shock and unlikeliness of what he said were what recommended it to him; and the discovery that these have been mitigated would merely have added to his gloom.

From That Island

KENYON REVIEW, AUTUMN 1939

Modern Poetry: A Personal Essay by Louis MacNeice

M R. MACNEICE'S matter is more personal than his manner, which is
highly unindividual; the straightforward, general, elevating tone,
varied judiciously with jokes or pieces of slang, the reassuringly commonplace analogies, the frequent little guidebook summaries, the general air of more or less talking down, of good-humoredly and sensibly
overlooking any unprofitable or embarrassing complications, make his
book remind you of one of those endowed series of lectures by some
prominent physicist, who also gets you to accept what he knows by putting it simply, what he believes by putting it inspiringly. (Sometimes
Mr. MacNeice does worse, and his sentences have a haunting ring of
the *Scout's Handbook:* for instance, when he decides that rhyme is
desirable because it presents a "healthy technical problem," or that
writing light lyrics for music is a "healthy" occupation.) He writes an
efficient undifferentiated prose, without much strength or possibility of
emotion, but with a disquieting tropism for obvious wordings: in his
prose the ballads have "a savour of the earth," and there are lounge
lizards and highbrows and physiques and "tortured but vital person-
alities" and verse "memorable for its music" and "forces which make
for progress" and "honest surveys" and "unflinching recognitions"—
things one hardly expected from the author of "Bagpipe Music." His
book is full of truisms you consent to without much pleasure, and half-
truths you dissent from without much heat; so that you end by observing everything with sleepy enjoyment, like H. G. Wells reflecting that
somehow Reason always does muddle through.

This book falls halfway between those ingenuous anomalies "explaining" modern poetry, full of easily assimilable misinformation, and
the less ingratiating performances of the real critics: *Some Versions of
Pastoral* or *Reactionary Essays* or *Primitivism and Decadence* or *The
Double Agent.* It is useless and cruel to compare *Modern Poetry* with

these last (my sympathies are all with them, I admit, and they make MacNeice's book seem very dashed-off and amateurish and negligible), since he seems to be deliberately writing down, in an attempt to reach the intelligent but uninformed reader. For this his method of handling is admirable; but the impressive limitations of his sympathy and knowledge, their rigid localization in both time and space (the time is Auden and the place London), the largely apologetic character of his criticism, make his book misleading as well as useful, and most misleading to the sort of reader it will interest most. It is hard not to be upset at how much MacNeice takes for granted, at how much (looking at the poetry and criticism of the recent past) he has forgotten or simply never learned; one again realizes uncomfortably that "progress," in poetry at least, comes not so much from digesting the last age as from rejecting it altogether (or, rather, from eating a little and leaving a lot), and that the world's dialectic is a sort of neo-Hegelian one in which one progresses not by resolving contradictions but by ignoring them. I certainly don't mean that MacNeice's criticism is not both intelligent and well informed; but his own hypotheses and the hypotheses of his friends, with constant verification, have long ago come to seem to him natural principles; the unquestioning acceptance which he extends to his and their particular abstractions and tastes and prejudices comes at times uncomfortably near provincialism.

There are two things which very noticeably warp his book. In the first place, it is a sort of apologia, a justification of his own and his friends' poetry; his evolutionary account of how the poetry of the last hundred years, developing through all sorts of degenerate and over-specialized types, finally culminated in the poetry of Auden and (Mac-Neice is what I should like to say, and MacNeice, naturally, is what MacNeice has in mind; but he is modest, and settles on Spender as his second hero, and devotes to him a good deal of rather awkward and pale attention—in handling Day Lewis his shyness has increased to such a point as almost to have become embarrassment) Spender, may seem to the unsympathetic not so much history as propaganda. I too think Auden the most engaging of poets; but MacNeice's version of him (one far-off divine event, / To which the whole creation moves) is hardly one I can share.

The second reason for the distortion of MacNeice's account is that occupational disease of Englishmen, a real ignorance of anything American. A reader given to exaggeration might in an excess of enthusiasm call his knowledge of American poetry sketchy. This is a *Modern Poetry* which has never heard of, or disregards, Marianne Moore, Allen

Tate, Wallace Stevens, Robert Frost—but there is no point in going on with the omissions; MacNeice handles Eliot and Pound at length, mentions, just, Ransom and Prokosch and Cummings ("the 'tough-guy' American poet"), and that is all. *Modern British Poetry,* I think we agree, is the name? An explanation that he is not attempting a complete survey of contemporary poetry does not help; the accident that most good modern poetry has been American poetry makes his ignorance of it a disaster, and makes his account of the development of modern poetry one likely to seem plausible only to a not exactly exhaustive class: Englishmen born after about 1905.

But I am afraid that my disappointment with *Modern Poetry* will give the impression that it is a bad book, which it is not; it is full of interesting and sensible, if rarely very brilliant or seductively put, judgments. His fireside chats on fundamentals (he has something of the politician's tendency to the agreeably general) and his appealing case history of his own development are things anyone will like. But I finished his chapters on obscurity and imagery with the uneasy consciousness that he had never left the surface; and his discussion of meter reduces to "anything goes if you think it goes," *you* being the reader. What Hopkins says about sprung rhythm is for MacNeice no more than a justification of licenses that needed none; this because he has a real understanding neither of accentual nor of accentual-syllabic verse. (He comments naïvely that the first line of *Paradise Lost* "appears to have only four stresses instead of five," because one of the metrical stresses falls on an *and*.) I liked least of all his opinion of the function of the poet: "The poet is a blend of the entertainer and the critic or informer . . . His criticism will cut no ice unless it entertains . . ." The sugar-coated pill theory once again, and all unsugared; that unlucky criticism which "cuts no ice" because it fails to "entertain" is enough to make a crocodile weep. "As informer, he is not a photographic or scientific informer, but more like the 'informer,' in the derogatory sense—he is grinding an ax or showing off, telling tales about his enemies, flattering his friends." As a convenient test, I started applying this to all those poets whose names begin with H; when I had got through Hardy, and Hopkins, and Herbert, I gave up angrily, vexed at my having mistaken for description so regrettable a piece of advice.

In the terms of one of the best sections of the book, MacNeice's criticism is all Jekyll and no Hyde. It is thin after his poetry; the violence and wit and emotion have gone away, and what is left is a tepid journalistic reasonableness; one straggles gracelessly through a wilderness of common sense. It is an experience for which the reader of modern criticism is unprepared: in that jungle through which one wanders, with its misshapen and extravagant and cannibalistic growths, bent double with fruit and tentacles, disquieting with their rank eccentric life, one comes surprisingly on something so palely healthy: a decorous plant, without thorns or flowers, rootless in the thin sand of the drawing room.

Poetry in a Dry Season

· ·

PARTISAN REVIEW, MARCH–APRIL 1940

*Chorus of Bird Voices, Sonnets, Battle-Dore, Unconventional Verse,
etc.* by William Bacon Evans   *Farewell to Walden* by Florence
Becker   *Panorama* by Walter Roberts   *The Connecticut River
and Other Poems* by Reuel Denny   *America Was Promises* by
Archibald MacLeish   *First Will and Testament* by Kenneth
Patchen   *Collected Poems* by Robert Graves   *A Turning
Wind* by Muriel Rukeyser   *The World I Breathe* by Dylan
Thomas   *Another Time* by W. H. Auden

M R. EVANS's title is almost enough of a review for his book. While
ailing in Syria, he wrote a song for every species of North American bird (I am no ornithologist, but there *can't* be any more of the
damn things); it has seldom been better done. This is poetry which
instructs its writer and entertains its reader (the functions of poetry,
I have read); a missionary could hardly be more harmlessly employed.
Mr. Evans is an amiable, unpretentious, and tolerant person—he apparently dislikes nothing but cigarettes—and won my heart immediately: more than I can say for most of the poets I am reviewing. But
then, Mr. Evans is no poet.

If I were a dust jacket, I should call *Farewell to Walden* "sonnets
of love and social protest"; being what I am, I can say only that they
are all Italian, all regular, and all bad. Miss Becker in her "streamlined
hydroplane tractor," going "wherever the campaign / Has need of us
... aware / Of enemies and directions," is a version of May Day I shall
be sorry to forget. *Panorama* has the faults and favorites of Auden,
MacNeice, Lewis, Prokosch, Spender, Allott, and all the others: class
reunion on the Ark, a charity bazaar at the Tower of Babel. One often
sees an animal one likes, a phrase worth picking up cheap; but the
whole is formless, meaningless, and useless.

Mr. Denny's family crest consists of a man with his mouth open;
underneath is the inscription, "Who will deliver us from these Greeks

and Romans?" For Mr. Denny is wonderfully academic—here at last is what everyone has been dreading, a poet to take Robert Hillyer's place (going on the safe assumption that Mr. Hillyer is dead): carefully "American" and "contemporary," a real "left-wing opportunist." (His own term for himself.) He uses a piece of slang as though he had just looked it up in the dictionary, and puts it in the middle of phrases that look as if he had found them illustrating a definition of poetic diction. He goes with "a pouch of pemmican, skis maybe, and a rifle" to search for "Liberty," a "sleeping woman" with "marble knees" and "wild, magnanimous eyes." Here is a typical description of a "steel hawk" (i.e., an airplane): "His polished power fled / Through the vast court of midnight like a prayer's wan word / Whose syllable, in the shrine, flies whispering down the floor / Toward the carved ear, unseen, of an unawakened god."

America Was Promises is a brilliant and malicious parody of MacLeish's public-speaking period. Here on the platform, huge against the leaves, the sea, the night (courtesy of Maxfield Parrish); flanked by Freedom, Truth, Justice, stiff in their collapsible chairs, a nominating committee to be periodically apostrophized; stands the declaiming "I": he speaks for Man. How ready with accusation, exhortation, condemnation! And yet accused and condemned smile and applaud with the exhorted, like them do nothing: who could bear to soil that strained and sentimental solemnity, that innocuous generality, the last refuge of the patriot, with anything so petty as understanding or objection or action? The parodist makes the Public Speaker just another armchair fist-waver. The argument of *America Was Promises* might have been devised by a YMCA secretary at a home for the mentally deficient—the reader ends by sympathizing with Mr. MacLeish, the parody is too exaggerated to be convincing. Whoever wrote it has been foolish enough to make an elaborate hoax of it (*Archibald MacLeish* is actually printed on the title page); but no one is likely to believe that any poet would end any serious poem: "Believe / America is promises to / Take! / America is promises to / Us / To take them / Brutally / With love but / Take them. / [Big gap] O believe this!"

First Will and Testament is enormously like Cummings: surprise and sex and slang and sentimentality; Life, shiny with blood, dew, and printer's ink; jokes, puns, parodies, good, bad, and unbelievable; prostitutes, gangsters, and burlesque: America; and all the rest. But Mr. Patchen is less delicate, very much less original, and very much more disorganized, strained, and sentimental. (His poetry has a big violet streak of Original Swinburne-with-a-dead-baby; and his detailed version of "Sex is *wonderful*" gets much worse than Swinburne's "It's *wicked*.") He relies on violence, on bigness, on social protest for its own sake, on allusions to everything and everybody; he always works with a shotgun, his motto is *Too Much!* He is influenced a great deal by Cummings and Joyce, most of all by general contemporary practice; even when he is at his best, you feel that you are so *used* to this sort of thing. Critics, who write about "sawdust . . . out of the heads of tenth-rate poets"—and on occasions, certainly, they do—he despises; his own criticism (pp. 167–168) is nonsense, gush, or Homely Wisdom à la Frost ("The way to build a house is to build it"). He has a real, but disorganized, self-indulgent, and rather commonplace talent.

This is not Mr. Patchen's opinion of himself. (Nor is it that of William Carlos Williams, who almost invents a new language, a kind of system of emotional nonsense syllables, in his effort to praise Mr. Patchen properly. For instance, Mr. Patchen is "a hawk on the grave of John Donne." I should have called him a parrot on the stones of half a cemetery.) He hints at his full stature—when Mr. Patchen hints, the pigs run in from miles around—in his prose introduction to the first section of a seven-part introduction to a seven-volume poem which he is to write. It is to be called *The Hunted City*; it is "conceived as a life-work"; it "will be an attempt to write the history, spiritual, and real, of these times and this country"; it consists of these books "in preparation": *Horrible Ghost, Holy Ghost*; *The Shadow of the Gunman*; *Chamber Music for a Madman*; *The Counterfeit Is Crucified*; *The History of the Headless Statue*; *The Housecarpenter and the Hangman's Angel*; and *Lie There Loving, Lie There in My Own Honor*.

Robert Graves's poems are pleasant, rather interesting, nicely constructed, noticeably his own; he is agreeably sensible and able; so it is really unpleasant to decide that he is not a good poet, that even his best poems just miss. There is too much comment, fancy, anecdote; one thinks, "Sensible! rather witty! nicely put!" but never how moving or extraordinary or *right*. I did not enjoy Miss Rukeyser's poems as much, and disapproved of them more: *A Turning Wind* is full of gratuitous disorganization and obscurity, lapses in taste, hit-or-miss symbolism, muddy intensity; yet she might become a better poet than Graves. Her poems are too self-indulgent—they think themselves profound and difficult versions of a confused and obscure world, and do not notice, or take as inevitable, their own helpless confusion and obscurity. (They also don't notice about a hundred early-Auden echoes or imitations.)

With luck, hard work, and some unkind self-regard, Miss Rukeyser would become a good poet; as it is, she is no more than a promising one.

Dylan Thomas is very Welsh (he reminds me a little of Owen Glendower) and very good. People compare his poems with Crane's; but (I think) Thomas's are more original, show a more extraordinary feeling for language and rhythm, and are better organized. They often mean much less than Crane's—but when you consider Crane's meanings, this is not altogether a disadvantage. If poetry were nothing but texture, Thomas would be as good as any poet alive. The *what* of his poems is hardly essential to their success, and the best and most brilliantly written pieces usually say less than the worst. (This is a condemnation one cannot extend to the three or four best stories in *The World I Breathe,* which "mean" quite as much as anyone could wish.) Even at his worst he is a sort of *idiot savant* of language, a poet anyone interested in poetry will read. At his best he is the outside of a first-rate poet.

Now I have much to say about *Another Time,* and no space. Auden at the beginning was oracular (obscure, original), bad at organization, neglectful of logic, full of astonishing or magical language, intent on his own world and his own forms; he has changed continuously toward organization, plainness, accessibility, objectivity, social responsibility. He has gone in the right direction, and a great deal too far. *Another Time* is Auden's eighteenth century; rational, didactic, social, full of abstractions, comment, light verse—the forms are automatic, the language is plain or formally rhetorical. Now, in too many of the poems, we see not the will, but the understanding, trying to do the work of the imagination (I use these charming fictions for convenience's sake); they are moral, rational, manufactured, written by the top of the head for the top of the head. The mechanical operation of the fancy produces too many of the light poems. Auden has lost the quick animal certainty of his daemon, his "gift": the good poems are magnificently and carefully right, the bad ones full of effects that have almost the wrongness of a fallacy.

The poems say often now, "Be good." They ascend through moral abstractions, gnomic chestnuts, to a vaguish humanitarian mysticism. (Between the liberals who attacked Auden as a Communist and the Communists who attacked him as a liberal, the Communists were right: he is a Mann by more than marriage.) He wants to show "an affirming flame," and says that "life must live." Once few of Auden's poems had titles; now most of them are descriptions of, comments on, titles: famous writers (dozens), events, cities, "The Composer," "The Novelist," etc. They are really occasional. The comments are often interesting or clever or amusing; poetry is not comments. And there is so much that is simply *bad*: facetiousness, sentimentality, vagueness, commonplaceness. The "Epithalamion" sounds as if it were celebrating a marriage between the Encyclopedia of the Social Sciences and J. Middleton Murry. And who would believe that *Auden* could end a somnambulistic sonnet on "The Composer": "And pour out your forgiveness like a wine"?

But the handful of good poems makes up for it all. Clear, delicate, organized, intelligent; the statements of a poet with very much to say, and with both the genius and technique for its saying; the best poems in *Another Time* are worth all the rest of these books put together. The characteristic poetic strategy of our time—*refine your singularities*—is something Auden has not learned; so his best poems are very peculiarly good, nearly the most interesting poems of our time. When he writes badly, we can afford to be angry at him, and he can afford to laugh at us.

A Job Lot of Poetry

· ·

THE NEW REPUBLIC, NOVEMBER 11, 1940

Joyce Kilmer: Poems, Essays, Letters   *New Journey* by Sidney Salt   *Narration with a Red Piano* by J. Calder Joseph   *The Cock of Heaven* by Elder Olson

"THERE COULD BE no more fitting time for the appearance of this book," begins the dust jacket, truthfully enough. I suppose it would take some external stimulus to get most of us to read the collected works of the "great soldier-poet," Joyce Kilmer; and a Second World War is of the right order of magnitude. Kilmer is a simple compound:

$$\frac{\text{war} + \text{Catholicism}}{\text{Literature}}$$

Franco's soldiers—Moors and Germans excepted—might have gone to battle with his songs upon their lips. His regiment, "the bravest and best in the army," is celebrated with a song that ends, "With the Potsdam Palace on a truck and the Kaiser in a sack / New York will be seen one Irish green when the Sixty-ninth comes back." Kilmer writes home from the front lines: "It is wrong for a poet—especially a Gael—to be listening to elevated trains when there are screaming shells to hear . . . the bright face of danger to dream about." (Yeats, "On Being Asked for a War Poem," answered that he had better keep his mouth shut.)

Some of Kilmer's poems are better than "Trees," but not enough better for it to matter. He calls the Milky Way "Main Street, Heaventown," and ends a Thanksgiving poem, "And Oh, thank God for God!" But I do not want to give the impression that his poems are unusually absurd—unusually anything; if they had not existed, it would have been necessary only to copy them. His criticism—this volume includes poems, essays, letters, photographs, and one incredible memoir—is either moral or theological. The silly and sickly evil that is modern (non-Catholic) literature, the "obscene absurdity" of the "materialist theory"—loved subjects—yield only to the finally important: "But is this *truly Catholic?"* He remarks of one poet that his Catholicism is "not so convincing" as that of two other poets; and, speaking of "infidel poets," he confesses, "I have never been able to enjoy the recital, however skillful, of a sacred story by a poet who did not believe in it." The letters are better.

Mr. Sydney Salt's *New Journey* is uneven enough to be puzzling. The book is a sort of pease-porridge-cold of (invented) excerpts from Columbus's log, disconnected lyrics, letters from Columbus to a monk, from the monk to Columbus, from the monk to the author, from the author to the reader. They are full of childish mysticism, a naïveté that delights in such dream statements as "Man is Destiny, Will his Fate; and Fear is Death." Columbus stands for Man struggling into the Unknown to gain Progress. And—I forgot—Love. Mr. Salt clothes these Sunday-school sentiments in Sunday-school prose, and in verse derived from—*Conquistador* and late Eliot! And, often, the words are fresh, the images come over. So should I spare Mr. Salt for his skin, or damn him for his bones? Let me put it too kindly for the sake of the joke: *New Journey* is intensively good and extensively silly.

The *I* of *Narration with a Red Piano,* by Mr. J. Calder Joseph, is one's old friend of the twenties, Behaviorist Man—the Noble Savage very much *manqué,* the child stammering his truths from the slums: sentimental, brutal, naïve, gasping out his grief and exultation—sexual or humanitarian—in conscientiously formless and prosy lyrics. "I got a crazy terrible love for you . . . Got Prayer. Got Coin. Got Fight! . . . the rain glistens / baby tears on the window pain"—why go on? These are the familiar subjects, the familiar method: the man in the street talking to the woman of the streets, in plain American. "It's d' system, see?" So it is, a system that has ruined better writers than Mr. Joseph. There is an introduction by Saroyan: same old Saroyan.

The Cock of Heaven, by Mr. Elder Olson, presents the contradiction of *New Journey* at a higher level. It is a much more artful and elaborate version of an even less promising conception; in the words of the dust jacket (few books are as rewarding as their dust jackets): "This is no sentimental piece of religiosity, but a work of significance and variety—serious and satiric, straightforward and ironic, mystical and realistic . . . It tells of the Magi who forever seek a Messiah, of the seven Messiahs who are sent to combat the sins (and who invariably fail), and finally, of the modern world, the advent of the ultimate Messiah, and universal catastrophe." And it tells this tale—one a gruff old scientist might think a shade literary—in dozens of the most extravagantly literary styles.

Mr. Olson's sources are many and apparent. Poem Number IV on page 40, V on page 58, XI on page 82, XIII on page 85 (the second line is Donne), are almost pure late Yeats, full of his characteristic properties, words, and rhythms; so are parts of a number of others, for instance, XXIV on page 96 and V on page 28. Here is some early Yeats: "Visited but by the hooded wave, / Aye, and all dream-wandering souls." Here is one of the samples of MacLeish: "Invisible / Turner of Seasons! Artificer of Storms! Thou!" All Eliot's periods are surprisingly fully represented—a list would take half a page. I love Hopkins (as Mr. Roosevelt would say, *I hate war*): I simply cannot trust myself to say what Mr. Olson's imitation of Hopkins is like. His Hamlet soliloquy reads more like a Browning parody: "And love— Hewgh, love! Foh, love! What, love, quotha?" And there are echoes of Aiken, Baudelaire, Browning—but I must stop. One can even identify structures: "Animula," "Gerontion," "The End of the World," the choruses of *Murder in the Cathedral.*

The reader may say, "What of it?" And I agree: these are symptoms, not causes—but symptoms of the inveterate literariness that vitiates everything it touches. Mr. Olson is the Will to Believe, the Renascence of Wonder: he gives precisely the same credence to everything—everything! "Cold sea-girls," vampires, "ice-pure unicorns," the "rose-blood" (elsewhere, "rose-rain-light") from Christ's wounds, "the horned voluminous worm amid Asian snows"; a ship bears "writ on her wreathèd counter, *Dream.*" And he throws together cave men and Magi, Eliot's rats and Andromeda's dragon, Stalin and the "Enchanted Pilgrims." It is simply impossible to take *The Cock of Heaven* as anything more than a fairy tale, the literary equivalent of (say) *Scheherazade* or a good Silly Symphony. But it's a swell fairy story; I read it several times with delight. Mr. Olson has a great faculty for getting things over, for really doing something; and he actually organizes (rather obviously, certainly) both single poems and larger units. You feel, as you do with *L'il Abner* in the comic strips, that you are reading someone with a positive delight in invention, a facility and fertility adequate to any demand. And Mr. Olson is at times charmingly witty; his little Middle English rondo, III on page 65, is absolutely perfect of its kind. He is a chameleon almost anyone would like to have for a pet. But he could say with Hamlet (I'd better look through *The Cock of Heaven* to make sure he doesn't): *The time is out of joint;* he belongs to a simpler age; whenever I think of him, it is with a sword cane, a green beard, and an opera cloak, applauding passionately the first performance of *Hernani.*

Poets: Old, New, and Aging

THE NEW REPUBLIC, DECEMBER 9, 1940

Sunderland Capture and Other Poems by Leonard Bacon
Against the Cold by Witter Bynner   *Cantos LII–LXXI* by Ezra
Pound   *Death at Sea* by Frederic Prokosch

MR. BACON and Mr. Bynner are what are called "traditional"
poets—i.e., neo-romantics who, working inside the usual forms,
do nothing to shock us from our dogmatic (or in this case academic)
slumbers. Their poems are the poems of very late Victorian epigoni;
Swinburne's ghost, picking its way through an unfriendly world, would
cry out to recognize, under the disguising letter, the familiar and
delighting spirit—shrunken, ineffectual, but still indomitably Victorian.

Mr. Bacon and Mr. Bynner are traditional in the sense that an
appendix is traditional; they are the remains of something necessary
under no longer existing conditions. In their poems the romantic, the
sentimental, and the "beautiful" are, still, the rhetorical flesh of some
edifying or diverting reflection. Their quarrel with modernism is the
romantic quarrel, they are dissatisfied with it only because they are not
yet up to it; they are, so to speak, modernists *manqués,* the souls of
modernists yet unborn. The breakup of modernism, the attempt at
something to take its place, is for them something in a remote Wellsian
future. But both are somewhat affected by the practice of their—
evolutionarily speaking—immediate descendants; Mr. Bacon has even
the rudiments of a sort of anti-romantic censor. But it is one gullible
enough to be wholly mollified by the wit, learning, and occasional
shocking or prosaic detail that Mr. Bacon throws it, and it hardly attempts resistance to the romantic or sentimental excesses naturally congenial to him. (Mr. Bynner's censor gets no sop at all; the poet has
adopted a policy of starving it into submission.) Being in the age but
not of it, both poets write with impressive ease; their forms are strict, if
awkward, their speech fluent, if unreflecting; how easily they triumph
over the difficulties of which they are unaware! *They* are not deterred
by the doubts that have harassed poets like Tate and Eliot. And yet

even their triumphs have a hollow and dreary ring; the spectators cry, "I have seen it!" but add reluctantly, "before"; their poems are debates with, victories over, the ghosts of straw men.

Has the reader seen those soldiers' or tourists' postcards which themselves supply the skeleton of the message, and which need only the insertion of a few words to be complete? In the same way Mr. Bacon and Mr. Bynner (and the class they represent) work by *filling* in a form; it is as if they had taken the examples in a textbook of prosody and substituted their own words. Into the shining little jelly molds that constitute the poet's repertory of forms, they pour a quaking and formless gelatin—and when the molding is finished, they are satisfied to be deceived by the illusion of form; but the jelly is as soft as ever. Poets like these are Pharisees who have not learned that the forms were made for man, and not man for the forms—that a form is yours or nothing; consequently form is something they neither possess nor understand. A sonnet Hopkins writes is primarily a *Hopkins* sonnet, a sonnet by Milton is a *Milton* sonnet: Mr. Bacon's sonnets and Mr. Bynner's sonnets are, first and foremost, *sonnets*—just good old sonnets.

Mr. Bacon carries over into *Sunderland Capture* something of the attitude of his humorous poems. He is (cf. De Voto, Hogben, Hooton, Zinsser) the *blunt* man, who comes right out and tells you what he thinks, who damns all sorts of things, conservative as well as radical— the knowing, irascible, crusty professor who is permitted the excesses he inveighs against in others and whose eccentric outspokenness, used as it is in their interest, is no more held against him by the authorities than his jokes or ties. He is the licensed jester of the conservatives, a sort of muscle man of *The Saturday Review of Literature*. (The political analogue would be General Johnson.) But he is no mere humorist or scholar, we are made to feel; look, here is this lovely or sentimental or romantic line to disprove it. Mr. Bacon says that his poetry burns "with that instructive and sardonic burning / Which teaches beauty to the undiscerning"; the reader—the undiscerning reader, I mean—may find such a view enthusiastic. I have unkindly spent all my space talking about the limitations of Mr. Bacon's poetry; but inside these there are a good many rewards: vigor, arresting phrases, nice turns of wit, the reflections of an acute, if conventional, mind. I should call his poems fairly good examples of a fairly bad sort of poetry.

After Mr. Bacon, Mr. Bynner is all lamb. His mild and discreet wit hardly ruffles the ecstatic hush that broods around his lyrics—he too broods, dissolved in contemplation or quiet tears. I remember a psychological experiment in which the subject does nothing but differentiate shades of gray. In the account of his experiences there is a certain monotony—a monotony I am not going to risk by any description of all the lovely and touching and rhetorical things that trail through the pages of *Against the Cold;* what need to describe things so familiar? Mr. Bynner is thoroughly in a convention—his emotions, images, and rhetoric can be predicted almost as if they were eclipses. What one feels angry at is the automatic rhetorical romanticism of this convention, not Mr. Bynner himself—who makes a very pleasant impression; but his battles are lost before they're started . . .

I had thought of Ezra Pound as the one thing constant in this fleeting world. Continents sank under the sea, empires fell: Vienna fell, Canton fell, Warsaw fell: the unmoved sage sat on at Rapallo, like Idiosyncrasy on a monument—the warm Italian breeze bore out over a universe of cretins his condemnations and invective, his economic panaceas, his *wd*'s and *cd*'s and *shd*'s, his American slang unparalleled outside the pages of an English novel. But as Hitler says, *there are no more islands:* Mr. Pound has deteriorated with the world. *Cantos LII–LXXI* contains the dullest and prosiest poetry that he has ever written. These cantos are so bad that they would not seem his at all, if they were not so exactly like the very worst portions of the old ones. Mr. Pound has become himself to the ∞ th degree, his daydream is at last absolute. One sees implicit in every page: *"Le droit, c'est moi."* Prejudice, whim, idiosyncrasy, have been hypostatized into a universal imperative. Mr. Pound is obviously one of the most talented poets of our time; yet these cantos are almost unreadable. What has happened?

That would take a book to tell. Mr. Pound has always had likings or prejudices rather than standards—his strength has lain mainly in disconnected insights. Organization and logic have been his weak point; the Browning monologue (which was designed to be effectively dramatic precisely because of its formlessness) has been his favorite form almost from the beginning, and his and Eliot's use of it has made it and its variants standard for the age. His talents are primarily lyric—not narrative, certainly not expository or didactic. He is not really a "thinker" at all: any sort of thinking, outside of the German system-making Heine makes fun of, requires a certain submissiveness to facts, and Mr. Pound has never submitted to a fact (or anything else, for that matter) in his life. He has taken all culture for his province, and is naturally a little provincial about it: one of the touching things about him is his entire Americanism, an Americanism that could survive unimpaired fifty years in a lunar crater. He has an enormous amount of talent, wit, and courage, but he has the literary man's characteristic vanity and omniscience, a magpie's eclecticism, a mania for absolutes and a conviction that they are accessible: to him everything is fairly simple Black or White. He repeats, *Hold to the middle*—meanwhile, the middle hardly exists for him; his feeling for Confucius is less appreciation than identification. He is not the Fool-Killer—life is a short blanket—but the Fool-Damner; he has shouted so long into the intense inane that his yells, by a natural protective metamorphosis, have taken on something of the character of their surroundings.

Early in his life Mr. Pound met with strong, continued, and unintelligent opposition. If people keep opposing you when you are right, you think them fools; and after a time, right or wrong, you think them fools simply because they oppose you. Similarly, you write true things or good things, and end by thinking things true or good simply because you write them. For Mr. Pound, both circumstance and predisposition made the process inescapable. His friends and disciples were eager to encourage him in his worst excesses; and modernist poets or critics hated, by caviling at the work of their talented fellow, to expose him to the jeers of the academic masses, who already condemned indiscriminately all that he had done. (Eliot, for instance, has written appreciations, not criticisms, of Pound.) Mr. Pound's universe became more and more a solipsistic one; the form, logic, and amenities of his criticism some time ago assumed the proportions of a public calamity. And his special poetic gifts—and performance—succumbed in their turn. Writing good poetry is only occasionally difficult: usually it is impossible. But writing what seems to you good poetry is always easy, if only, somehow, your standards of what constitutes a good poem can be lowered (and specialized) to what you write; this unconscious and progressive lowering of taste, a sort of fatty degeneration of the critical faculties, is the most common of ends. Mr. Pound seems no longer able to discriminate between good and bad in his poetry: to him it is all good because it is all his.

Half of *Cantos LII–LXXI* is a personal, allusive, and wildly eccentric retelling of Chinese history, full of names, dates, quotations, ideograms, abbreviations, underlinings, and slang. Everything is seen as through a glass darkly, the glass being Mr. Pound: 1766 B.C. talks exactly like A.D. 1735, and both exactly like Ezra Pound. To the old complaint, "All Chinamen look alike," Mr. Pound makes one add, "And talk alike, and act alike—and always did." Little of the intrinsic interest of the events manages to survive the monotonous didacticism of the account. The rest of the book is more interesting, since it consists mostly of quotations—intelligent, informative, or just odd—from John Adams, its subject. (On the dust jacket New Directions twice insists that Pound's subject is John Quincy Adams—a queer mistake to make; whoever made it must have found Pound's style too entrancing ever to determine what he was writing about.) Mr. Pound has a fine feel for anecdotes that carry the quality of a person or an age; but I should prefer to see a collection of his favorites in some more appropriate form.

The versification of these cantos is interesting: there is none. The prose is an extremely eccentric, slangy, illogical, sentence-fragment, note-taking sort of prose—but prose; the constant quotations from letters or documents or diaries are no different from the verse that frames them. The technical skill that went into some of the earlier cantos has almost disappeared.

An unsympathetic reader will find Mr. Prokosch a sort of decerebrate Auden, an Auden popularized for mass consumption; and since Auden himself has been, lately, so successful in the attempt to provide one, it is hard to see in Mr. Prokosch much more than a work of supererogation. But this is a shallow view; Mr. Prokosch's success in the romantic and superficial exploitation of Auden's materials and methods is really incomparable—a triumph unmitigated by the odd intelligence and sensibility that adulterate obstinately even the laxest and most mechanical of Auden's pages. (A person who knows Auden's poetry well will notice his influence in *Death at Sea* many hundreds of times, in tone, form, images, rhetoric, and content. Mr. Prokosch's earlier poetry is less singularly derivative.) Mr. Prokosch has sublimated Auden's worst vices and Auden's easiest virtues into a method; it is the mechanical operation of this method that produces the mass of *Death at Sea*—the poems pour out like sausages, automatic, voluptuous, and essentially indistinguishable. The "Love" that is the *deus ex machina* of Auden's worst lapses is the tutelary deity of Mr. Prokosch's poetry: his world view is too sentimental and palely irresponsible—too *fashionable*—to be valued as much more than an effective romantic pose. He replaces Auden's Freudianism with a psychology that amounts to— *To know anything is to forgive anything;* and for Auden's demi-Marxism he substitutes the *Weltanschauung* of *Manfred* or a Sunday-supplement Spengler. (He has a Shelleyan fondness for the atlas as a bedside book; the argument of many of his poems is virtually, Death and darkness fall over Samarkand, Bokhara, Timbuktu—fall, in fact, over the great big world.) The list or panorama, a tangle of picturesque details resolved by the blankest of generalizations, is his favorite structural device: *the consumptive cries on the dear Danubian banks, the Senegalese sheds his scalding tears beside the Niger, the Eskimo weeps icicles into Hudson Bay*—why, they're all *crying:* and you have your poem. (You're wrong if you think the *dear Danubian banks* is mine.)

But do not let me give the impression that Mr. Prokosch's poems are failures; the effects are second-hand and second-rate—but oh, so effective! The surface of the poetry has the immediate appeal the able and sensational popularization of a new technique always has; and under that surface bubbles the same old romanticism that infected us all in our cradles. How many ladies' clubs yet unorganized will prickle to the raptures of this verse! Naturally, not everyone will be pleased with such easy and florid romanticism; I read the poems with annoyance and mild pleasure, and thought Mr. Prokosch's obvious gifts childishly misused. But so much glitter and flow and scope have turned better heads than mine. On the dust jacket of *Death at Sea* are testimonials by Stephen Spender, Robinson Jeffers, Michael Roberts, Edwin Muir, and the *Manchester Guardian*—and others by Yeats and Eliot are referred to; I mention these to bear out my last statement, and to show that my own opinion is a dissenting one which the reader should be properly cautious about accepting.

A Note on Poetry

I MAY AS WELL say what the reader will soon enough see, that I don't want to write a preface. I am not even sure what sort I am expected to write: one telling what I meant these poems to be or do, I suppose, along with sections about the function of poetry and its state at present. Now the reader may be interested in what the poems are; but why should he care what I meant them to be? And the thought of saying anything about the function of poetry or its present condition, in a couple of pages, makes me uncomfortable. Worse, suppose I say "modern" poetry is A; then the reader will probably think I meant my poems to be A, if I consider myself a "modern" poet, not-A if I don't. I could give plenty of other reasons; but the best reason is simply that I don't want the poems mixed up with my life or opinions or picture or any other regrettable concomitants. I look like a bear and live in a cave; but you should worry.

If, after all this, I go on and write my preface, surely the reader will pay no attention to it?

If you consider "modern" poetry—Pound, Eliot, Crane, Tate, Stevens, Cummings, Marianne Moore, and so on—in isolation, it will seem both more original (this is the favorable side of the mistake) and more disquieting (or *crazy* or *inexplicable* or any other disapproving adjective) than it really is; if you consider it as an end product, a limit, in most cases a *reductio ad absurdum,* of a long historical process, what will puzzle you is why it didn't happen sooner. (That is, as early as it did in France: Rimbaud wrote "modern" poetry. The causes are mostly economic, I think: France didn't have the Victorian prosperity which slowed up the whole series of changes in England; also, the rate of change could be greater because romanticism was more of a surface phenomenon there.) When I say *historical process* I use it in the full sense of the word, I don't mean literary-historical; without the economic and scientific and political changes that accompany—and, mostly, cause—the changes in the poetry itself, the history of English poetry is nothing but a magician's catalogue. I don't mean that I believe in the sort of psycho-physical parallelism between literature and economics in which literary phenomena are merely shadows of economic ones, with no causal efficacy of their own; once a literary process is really started, it works itself out on its own momentum. But the great changes in literature are non-literary in origin; and the same causes that produce the new work produce, in time, its audience. Wordsworth's poems did not produce the Wordsworthians—the things that made Wordsworth write a certain type of poetry at the beginning of the nineteenth century, by the middle of the century had prepared its readers. If poetry were produced by large groups and consumed by a few responsive individuals, the order would be reversed, and the consumers would have to hunger vaguely for something not even ready to exist for thirty or forty years.

"Modern" poetry is, essentially, an extension of romanticism; it is what romantic poetry wishes or finds it necessary to become. It is the end product of romanticism, all past and no future; it is impossible to go further by any extrapolation of the process by which we have arrived, and certainly it is impossible to remain where we are—who could endure a century of *transition?* Modernism, like Spinoza's *substance,* is the den from which no tracks return: at least, none whose makers have not come to an understanding with the lion. One is reminded of some species which carried evolutionary tendencies so far past the point of maximum utility that they actually became destructive to them: Titanotherium, whose size and horns increased until the species became extinct; or certain shellfish whose coils became so complicated they could at last barely be opened. Romanticism is necessarily a process of extension, a vector; this is striking even when the observer looks at it as a purely literary process, and leaves out of account the changes in society that are forcing it to its extremes. (Neoclassicism, *in theory,* is a static system.) Most of the tendencies which differentiate romantic from neoclassical poetry exist in an hypertrophied state in modernist poetry, but there are a great many factors that help conceal this: a big quantitative change looks like a qualitative one; the best modern criticism of poetry is extremely anti-romantic, and the change in theory covers up the lack of any essential change in practice—because of Eliot's critical opinions, many people think his poetry a sort of classicism; modern poetry often so noticeably lacks some romantic qualities that the reader disregards all the others it possesses, especially since many of them are too common to be noticed as specifically romantic; the reader tends to be confused by the continual surface novelty romanticism demands; and, finally, there are some genuinely non-romantic tendencies—premonitions, perhaps—in modern poetry. I have no space for the enormous amount of evidence all these generalizations require; but consider some of the qualities of typical modernistic poetry: very interesting language, a great emphasis on connotation, "texture"; extreme intensity, forced emotion—violence; a good deal of obscurity; emphasis on sensation, perceptual nuances; emphasis on details, on the part rather than on the whole; experimental or novel qualities of some sort; a tendency toward external formlessness and internal disorganization—these are justified, generally, as the disorganization required to express a disorganized age, or, alternatively, as newly discovered and more complex types of organization; an extremely personal style—*refine your singularities;* lack of restraint—all tendencies are forced to their limits; there is a good deal of emphasis on the unconscious, dream structure, the thoroughly subjective; the poet's attitudes are usually anti-scientific, anti-common-sense, anti-public—he is, essentially, removed; poetry is primarily lyric, intensive—the few long poems are aggregations of lyric details; poems usually have, not a logical, but the more or less associational structure of dramatic monologue; and so on and so on. This complex of qualities is essentially romantic; and the poetry that exhibits it represents the culminating point of romanticism.

I obviously do not mean that the poets and their public have arrived at this point en masse; the poetry of the age is extremely heterogeneous, and the indifferent mass of poets and readers are distributed haphazardly through the various earlier stages of romanticism, unwilling or unable to go any further—cultural liberals, so to speak; or, to put it more prettily, vestiges, anachronisms, reptiles surviving into an age of mammals. For modernistic poetry has certainly been the most successful and influential body of poetry of this century; most good poets outside it have been influenced by it, the most successful poet of the time, Yeats, had his poetry so changed by it that his later work is neglected or disliked as "modern" by most of the admirers of his earlier poems. What has begun to weaken so much the enormous attraction (in the physical sense) that modernist poetry exerted? What has become of the animal certainty with which the young poet of the twenties began to write experimental poetry? Why have not the successful modernist poets continued confidently their original lines of development?

Modernist poetry exerted its attraction because it was carrying the tendencies of romanticism to their necessary conclusions; now most of those conclusions have been arrived at; and how can the poet go

any further? How can poems be written that are more violent? more
disorganized? more obscure? more—the adjectives throng to me—than
those that have already been written? And the poets, at the ends of their
processes of specialization, are more or less conscious of what has
happened. Some of them have tried to make their poetry conform to
their critical principles, spoiling their poetry in the process: Winters is
my *locus classicus,* but I can spare Eliot a glance. (Here I am certainly
not recommending any divergence of practice and theory, I am simply
noticing that it is difficult for a poet in an advanced state of romanticism to write good non-romantic poetry because he thinks he ought to.)
Imagism was a *reductio ad absurdum* of one or two tendencies of romanticism, such a beautifully and finally absurd one that it is hard
to believe it existed as anything but a logical construction; and what
imagist found it possible to go on writing imagist poetry? A number
of poets have stopped writing entirely; others, like recurring decimals,
repeat the novelties they commenced with, each time less valuably than
before. And there are surrealist poetry, and political poetry, and all the
other refuges of the indigent. Auden is the only poet who has been
influential very recently; and this is because, very partially and uncertainly, and often very mechanically, he represents new tendencies, a
departure from modernist romanticism.

We have reached one of those points in the historical process at
which the poet has the uncomfortable illusion of choice; when he too
says, "But what was it? What am I?" The *it* he asks about is the dying
tradition (which dies because the world it represented is dying)—the
determinants which once were axiomatic, permitting neither disagreement nor understanding; today, for him, they are no longer determining: the marionette looks reluctantly for another hand. So the poets
repeat the old heartlessly, or make their guesses at the new; meanwhile,
quantity is being transformed into quality, the water goes over into
steam—today, for most of Europe, even the illusion of choice is impossible, and we see or shall see literature being determined, in the
strictest and most immediate sense, by economics.

I have not been saying that modernist poetry is romantic, hence
bad; *romantic,* as I used it, is a neutral descriptive term. I wished to
stress the fundamental kinship of modern and romantic poetry because
it is their differences that are insisted on by the two common critical
positions: the essentially Victorian view that regards metaphysical,
eighteenth-century, and modern poetry as regrettable divergences from
the real tradition of English poetry, which skips from the Elizabethans
(i.e., Spenser and Shakespeare) and Milton on to the romantics and

Victorians; and the other view, which approves of the Elizabethans, metaphysicals, and moderns, tolerates the eighteenth century, and condemns the Victorians and romantics.

I have had no space for evidence, qualification, or detail—and there needs to be a great deal of each; I hope the reader will be indulgent toward a tentative sketch. During the course of the article, the reader may have thought curiously, "Does he really suppose he writes the sort of poetry that replaces modernism?" Let me answer, like the man in the story, "I must decline the soft impeachment." But I am sorry I need to.

The Rhetoricians

THE NEW REPUBLIC, FEBRUARY 17, 1941

And in the Human Heart by Conrad Aiken   *The Arrow at the Heel* by Raymond Holden

AND IN THE HUMAN HEART is a sequence of forty-three Shakespearean sonnets. They are written with impressive fluency and command; their materials and mechanisms are ones Mr. Aiken has used so many times before, under so much more difficult circumstances, that he seems as much at ease as Merlin pulling a quarter from a schoolboy's nose. Merlin is the right comparison, I think; Mr. Aiken has always traded in rhetorical magic, and his incantations have grown more traditional as he has aged. A few months ago, returning from England to *The Atlantic Monthly,* he began a crusade against contemporary poetry. It was hard not to be impressed with it: anyone would be impressed with a crusader who says that Auden, Tate, Ransom, Warren, MacNeice, and Muriel Rukeyser all write just alike; and he ended by demanding a romantic revival. A hundred and fifty years of romanticism have culminated in a situation that even the romanticist decides is impossible: so he proposes, as a cure, a return to romanticism. And he lives up to his advice; on the strength of these poems Mr. Aiken can be called, as he would wish to be called, a straight romantic.

What are these sonnets about? Their ostensible subject is a very generalized love affair; but their real subject is a particular rhetoric Mr. Aiken has been developing for a long time. He is in love with a few dozen words, and their permutations and combinations have assumed for him a weight and urgency that would be quite incomprehensible to his readers, if it were not for the fact that most of these terms are the traditional magic-making words of English romantic poetry. "The Good, the True, the Beautiful / Those are the things that pay!" wrote Lewis Carroll; add to these Love and Nature—and the more common particulars that represent such abstractions in poetry—and you have, in its rudest beginnings, the machinery of Mr. Aiken's rhetoric. In forty-three sonnets the sun, moon, and stars are mentioned more than fifty times: *love,* 50; *flower* and flower names, 58; *time,* 33—*space* comes close behind; *golden,* 16; *world,* 23; the blackness or darkness of things is spoken of twenty-five times, their brightness or fiery lightness more than a hundred times. Chaos, infinity, eternity, the sea, the snow, fire, ice, leaves, birds, dreams, angels, heaven and hell, the heart, the soul—such favorites as these are more emotional and meaningful for Mr. Aiken, more essential to the poems, than the "subject" that serves as their pretext. He could write fairly pleasing and interesting poetry about any subject whatsoever; deprive him of the use of his favorite words and he would be simply unable to write poetry at all.

The content of Mr. Aiken's best poems has almost disappeared; these are only their emptied and enormously inflated rhetorical shells. To him, now, the world exists as a thesaurus from which to derive the glittering and immaculate counters that arrange themselves, almost automatically, into a poem. Any similarity between the poems and reality is purely coincidental: they are produced by the extravagantly emotional, rhetorical, and sentimental manipulation of the beautiful objects of an imaginary universe. But if they are empty, they are still beautifully able. Are there any finger exercises by Liszt? They would be like these poems. If you have been waiting for a magician's encore in the land of Faëry, here is your chance. Personally, I think that Merlin is stuck in the oak tree for good; what goes on now goes on only in that best of all possible worlds, one's own head.

In *And in the Human Heart* the rhetoric is the poem; in *The Arrow at the Heel* the rhetoric is, instead, what ruins the poem. Mr. Holden's way of saying anything is so painstakingly, conventionally, and determinedly rhetorical that even his most emotional or farfetched statement sounds positively legal: it is as if one of Millay's or Wylie's poems had been rewritten to serve as the majority opinion of the Supreme Court. Mr. Holden's forms are traditional in the deadest sense of the word; often one can hardly pay attention to the poem for staring at the terrible I AM A SONNET writ large on every feature. The poems are competent, sincere, thoroughly respectable productions; many of the phrases are effective, some of the ideas are interesting; but phrases and ideas survive only as random notes, barely heard over the terrible din of the machinery. The subject is picked and the mills begin to grind; Mr. Holden's mills grind slowly and oh! so small. The reader emerges from them a little wiser and a whole lot sadder: he has had what the advertisements call An Experience. Reading *The Arrow at the Heel* is like attending Dali's lecture from a diving suit; but Mr. Holden never comes out of the diving suit. If he only could get free of it somehow—but I suppose he never will. The poem's ruin, here, is the poet's delight; for it is the very machinery that crushes the poem that assures Mr. Holden he has turned out a really competent, finished, professional job.

New Year Letter

THE NATION, APRIL 12, 1941

The Double Man by W. H. Auden

IN 1931 Pope's ghost said to me, "Ten years from now the leading young poet of the time will publish, in *The Atlantic Monthly,* a didactic epistle of about nine hundred tetrameter couplets." I answered absently, "You are a fool"; and who on this earth would have thought him anything else? But he was right: the decline and fall of modernist poetry—if so big a swallow, and a good deal of warm weather, make a summer—were nearer than anyone could have believed. The poetry which came to seem during the twenties the norm of all poetic performance—experimental, lyric, obscure, violent, irregular, determinedly antagonistic to didacticism, general statement, science, the public— has lost for the young its once obsessive attraction; has evolved, in Auden's latest poem, into something that is almost its opposite. "New Year Letter" (which, with many notes and a few lyrics, forms *The Double Man*) is a happy compound of the *Essay on Man* and the *Epistle to Dr. Arbuthnot,* done in a version of Swift's most colloquial couplets. Pope might be bewildered at the ideas, and make fun of, or patronizingly commend, the couplets; but he would relish the Wit, Learning, and Sentiment—the last becoming, as it so often does, plural and Improving; and the Comprehending Generality, Love of Science, and Social Benevolence might warm him into the murmur, "Well enough for such an age." How fast the world changes! and poetry with it! What he would have said of the more characteristic glories of "Gerontion," the *Cantos,* or *The Bridge,* I leave to the reader's ingenuity.

"New Year Letter" contains Auden's ideas about everything (Life and the Good Life, Art and Society, Politics, Morals, Love, the Devil, Economic Man), organized inside a successfully concrete framework of what he has read and seen and met with. Auden's ideas once had an arbitrary *effective* quality, a personality value, almost like ideas in Lawrence or Ezra Pound. They seem today less colorful but far more correct—and they are derived from, or are conscious of, elements over most of the range of contemporary thought. Sometimes the reader exclaims delightedly, "What a queer thing for a *poet* to know!" (This replaces the resentful remark of the twenties: "What a queer thing for anybody to know!") The poets of the last generation were extremely erudite, but their erudition was of the rather specialized type that passed as currency of the realm in a somewhat literary realm. About Darwin, Marx, Freud and Co., about all characteristically "scientific" or "modern" thinkers most of them concluded regretfully: "If they had not existed, it would not have been necessary to ignore them." (Or deplore them.) In their comparison of the past and the present, the present came off, not even a poor, but a disgraceful second; "and this was not surprising," as Carroll says, since the values by which they judged—the whole climate of their judgment—were desperately and exclusively those of the past. They constituted a forlorn hope we must admire but understand. Auden's culture and doctrines are more accessible and plausible than theirs to the ordinary cultivated person, whose thought is not now essentially religious, literary, reactionary, or anti-scientific. And the manner of Auden's knowledge surprises as much as the matter; there is none of the atmosphere of stupefying scope and profundity of information that has accompanied Pound's and Eliot's application of the methods of the industrial revolution to literature: so far as Auden's tone is concerned, London and Rome are still untouched by American hands, the great Völkerwanderung of the barbarian scholars has never occurred.

"New Year Letter" seems to me, within certain limits, a great success. It is thoroughly readable: Auden handles with easy virtuosity humorous and serious material—sometimes his method of joining them verges on simple Byronic alternation, but they tend to be swept together by the tone and verse movement, rapid, informal, and completely adaptable. The poetry, strained through so many abstractions, is occasionally a little pale; but it *is* poetry. Auden has accomplished the entirely unexpected feat of making a successful long poem out of a reasonable, objective, and comprehensive discussion. It is kept concrete or arresting by many devices: wit, rhetoric, all sorts of images (drawn from the sciences, often); surprising quotations, allusions, technical terms, points of view, shifts of tone; he treats ideas in terms of their famous advocates, expresses situations in little analogous conceits; and he specializes in unexpected coordinates, the exquisitely ridiculous term—he is remarkably sensitive to the levels and interactions of words. The poem is not quite first-rate. It lacks the necessary finality of presentation; it is at a remove; the urgency and reality have been diluted. Evil is talked about but not brought home; there is a faint sugary smell of *tout comprendre est tout pardonner*: everything is going to be all right in the end. When one remembers his earlier poetry at its best, one feels unreasonably homesick for the fleshpots of Egypt. But these are almost too many qualifications: it is a valuable, surprising poem.

In the notes there are quotations, aphorisms, exposition, verse, a few poems: if not God's plenty, at least, plenty. Some notes are valuable in themselves, some amplify or locate the poem's ideas; but these water a positive desert of Good Sense: machine-made parables, forced definitions, humorless half-truths, with which we wearily dissent or impatiently agree. (The notes specialize in neither the High nor the Low, but the Mean Sublime.) To the question, "What is the only thing that always remains work, that can never give us aesthetic satisfaction?" Auden replies, *the ethical;* the victims of his insistent raids on the Moral can ruefully agree. The lyrics called "The Quest" (conscientiously flat, abstract, and characteristic parables) seem to me rather uninterestingly unsuccessful.

I've made my review general because I wanted to emphasize, like the advertisements: "This poem's *different*"; some people who don't ordinarily read modern poetry might enjoy "New Year Letter." Since I've no space for what I should like—a careful discussion of its ideas and technique—let me finish simply by saying that it is worth buying.

Contemporary Poetry Criticism

THE NEW REPUBLIC, JULY 21, 1941

A POEM, today, is both an aesthetic object and a commodity. It is an unimportant commodity for which there is a weak and limited demand; it is produced, distributed, and consumed like any other commodity. Poems are produced by a peculiar submarginal class, only a dozen or so of whom live by the sale of their products. They are distributed, as a relatively negligible sideline, by publishers. The consumers are a heterogeneous group; their demand is, for the most part, characterized by a somewhat apathetic and pious conventionality. A cynical observer might say that many of them have inherited from another age both their respect for and their taste in poetry, and are afraid that if one is questioned the other will disappear. What this public likes (and buys) the publisher publishes. Some people—regular publishers, occasionally—are shocked at what the public does like, and publish unprofitably what it won't buy.

A commercial magazine or newspaper is a rather elaborate device for inducing people to read advertisements. Most present-day poetry criticism consists of reviews in such magazines and newspapers; if we disregard its function and the conditions of its production—both commercial—we must misunderstand it. Reviews are demanded by both publishers and public; publishers buy advertisements, the public buys magazines (and advertising rates vary with circulation): so an editor necessarily demands reviews that will satisfy publishers and public. (Here, let me emphasize, I am disregarding subsidized non-commercial magazines and magazines only secondarily supported by advertising; however, the criticism of these to some extent influences and is influenced by that of the commercial magazines and newspapers.)

From the publisher's point of view criticism is a quite important subspecies of advertising; reviews are free publicity, free testimonials. Good criticism is criticism that sells books. A good critic is a man who likes as much as possible as persuasively as possible. (Woollcott's pallbearers will all be publishers; and those tears will be real.) The publisher naturally advertises in magazines that print *good* criticism—

naturally; so, naturally, an editor farms out his reviews to reliable pro-
ducers of just such criticism; there is a process of natural selection
going on all the time among reviewers. In heaven all reviews will be
favorable; here on earth, the publisher realizes, plausibility demands
an occasional bad one, some convincing lump in all that leaven, and
he accepts it somewhat as a theologian accepts Evil. Newspapers sometimes print free news stories about their advertisers; reporters call such
a story a Business Office Must. To the publisher reviews are a kind of
Business Office Must.

The public—let me put it bluntly—the public wants a review
to tell it what it is going to think of a book. The critic usually avoids
the ambiguity of "You'll like this, you won't like that," and tactfully
or ingenuously phrases his prediction: "This is a good book; that is
a bad." The public likes the good, dislikes the bad, and is pleased with
both its taste and the reviewer's. The reviewer preferably is someone
who can be considered an expert: there is more prestige in agreeing
with him, and he can speak with a knowledge and finality that will
reassure the reader (that what he likes *is* art)—and since modern
poetry is to the average reader, if not terra incognita, at least No Man's
Land, he welcomes reassurance. But often the reviewer is not expert on
any subject except Reviews: he derives his authority from his position,
rather than the reverse. The reviewer, from the public's point of view,
should be the Collective Me, a sort of hypostatized, apotheosized common denominator of public taste. (Many people—booksellers and li-
brarians, for instance—have an actual commercial interest in the coin-
cidence of the reviewer's taste and the public's.) The reviewer is like
the juror, drawn by lot, who nevertheless takes on the authority and
prestige of the People he represents. But all the reviewer's powers are
delegated powers; if he tries to elevate the public taste, writes real criticism and consistently disagrees with the public, these powers are withdrawn, and he will be revealingly condemned for arbitrary dogmatism,
the assumption of powers that are not his.

Reviews are codified in critical articles and anthologies; it is the
nature of both to be approving, or to manifest their disapproval only
negatively. Editors seldom print unfavorable articles on poets, so critics
rarely write them. The anthologist has a vital financial interest in there
being a large body of current poetry that can be called—that he can
call—good. Poetry is always reviving today from yesterday's revival.

This is the system; but there is a good deal of play in it, precisely
because the publishing of poetry is commercially such a negligible
affair. Publishers are hardly vitally concerned; no one, so far as I know,

makes a living by reviewing poetry. Another thing that makes the system more disapproving than it otherwise would be is that so much of the poetry of the last twenty years has been modernist poetry (often printed by non-commercial publishers) which the public dislikes, misunderstands, and enjoys seeing condemned.

I have given a rather abstract analysis of the situation. Now I could go in for details, and tell you about the prominent reviewer Mr. B., who said, when Auden was first published here, that his six-year-old boy could write better poetry than Auden; or about the most prominent Mr. U., who says that Marianne Moore's poetry isn't poetry at all, but criticism; or about that inveterate reviewer Miss W., who has just published a textbook full of explanations of modern poetry—explanations that show she is quite incapable of understanding any modern poem of even the slightest difficulty. But it is like trying to define a haystack by drawing straws from it. And I am not interested in the individual depravity of reviewers; they are standardized, eminently replaceable parts of the machine: I suppose even for Louis Untermeyer a substitute could be found. I am afraid I have not exaggerated the situation; if for a few months the reader will look at the poetry reviews in the *Times* and the *Herald Tribune, The Saturday Review,* and other such places, he can see for himself. Such reviews are extraordinarily similar—that is because they are a technique not for pointing out but for obscuring differences; from the hands of most reviewers best and worse emerge with the same winning and vacant smile. In the dark all cats are gray.

Most of the criticism of any age is bad—for instance, who were the popular reviewers and critics of the year 1841? But today the only commercially practicable body of criticism is a bad one. Good criticism, which points out badness or mediocrity, and actually scares away buyers from most books, is something the publishers necessarily cannot tolerate. Good criticism, which is often involved or difficult, and which always tells the public not what it wants but what is good for it, is something the commercial public doesn't care for either. I am not condemning the body of criticism for being as bad as it is, I am giving it a certificate of necessity: for it to be anything else is a commercial impossibility.

The poetry of the present is mostly written about by reviewers; that of the past is mostly written about by scholars: i.e., English professors. Scholars produce scholarly articles, for which there is a great demand; the steady publication of quantities of scholarly articles will obtain for a person with the proper academic qualifications steadily increasing salaries. Consequently, scholarly criticism is being produced in immense amounts. Unfortunately, most scholarly criticism is negligible as scholarship and worthless as criticism. Much of the performance is bad, of course, because the performers are incompetent or mediocre; but the real trouble is the nature of the performance.

During the last part of the nineteenth century the prestige that had formerly attended the methods and practitioners of literary, philosophical, and theological wisdom was largely transferred to those of scientific knowledge. Professors of English tried to "cash in on" (Burke's phrase) this prestige by the naïve application of scientific quantitative methods to literature. They tried to make "English" a science, and they succeeded in making it a pseudo-science of the most forbidding variety, in amassing a gigantic rubbish heap of facts about literature. (Of scholars, as of bees, the criterion is industry.) Criticism is necessarily based on very fine qualitative distinctions, the critic's responses to and judgments about works of art; the discipline that neglects and condemns these as subjective, unreliable, impressionistic, that is satisfied only with the "objective reliability" of "facts"—such a discipline is absurd in theory and disastrous in practice, and can produce criticism of any value only in spite of itself. Some scholars have attained their ideal of perfect objectivity, and seem unwilling or even unable to make the slightest distinction between good, bad, and mediocre—all are data for scholarship. Robert Graves was examined by such a professor, who gave him the considered reproof: "Mr. Graves, I believe you *prefer* some authors to others." Carl Becker has defined a professor as a man who thinks otherwise; a scholar is a man who otherwise thinks.

But, do what he will, feeling, taste, the subjectivity of judgment constantly do creep into the scholar's articles and teachings; not the trained and scrupulous taste, the reasoned critical judgment of the expert, but the unexamined conventions, prejudices, and idiosyncrasies that the scholar has acquired at random in the course of his career of facts. His taste in poetry is, very slightly modified, the academic late-Victorian taste of his high-school and college teachers. The last twenty-five years have seen part of a great change in taste, a revaluation of most English poetry—I do not believe there is a good critic living who shares the taste of the scholars. So the scholar, who already looks down on the critic in theory, is able in practice to condemn him, even more severely and sincerely, for the immense disparity in all their judgments. Today there is not merely a division between scholars and critics, but open war; and since scholars are a thousand to one, and occupy every important position in the colleges, there is not much hope for the critic.

I hope the summary quality of this account has not antagonized the reader; I do not question the value of scholarship. But most scholarship is a means, and when it is exalted into an end—as it is today—the real end of scholarship is defeated. Our universities should produce good criticism; they do not—or, at best, they do so only as federal prisons produce counterfeit money: a few hardened prisoners are more or less surreptitiously continuing their real vocations.

I might have taken as a motto for this essay, "If a way there be to the Better, it exacts a full look at the Worse." Now I have come to the Better—the Best, even: I do not believe there has been another age in which so much extraordinarily good criticism of poetry has been written. (Incidentally, it is usually printed in non-commercial magazines and often published by non-commercial publishers.) Too much of the criticism of the past seems to us morals or biography or information—anything but criticism. Modern criticism of poetry, at its best, is relatively pure; it is really concerned, as it should be, with understanding (in the most active and comprehensive sense) and evaluating poetry. This criticism has been extremely catholic and extremely acute; there has been no analysis too complicated, delicate, or surprising for these critics to undertake. Modern criticism has accomplished a change in taste, a critical revolution, even greater than the change in poetic performance which modernist poets have effected. I myself believe that modernist poetry is essentially an extension of romanticism (with a few neoclassic elements à la Stravinsky), and that along with great virtues it exhibits many of the vices of romanticism in their most exaggerated form. This certainly could not be said of modern criticism, which has repudiated romanticism so wholeheartedly that many critics condemn in their criticism the vices that they exploit in their poetry. This criticism has helped us understand and value modernist poetry—which academic criticism simply rejected—but its work with the poetry of the past has been even more important: it has resurrected or defended dozens of poets whom academic criticism had discarded or disgracefully undervalued. One immediately thinks of Donne, Webster, Raleigh, Jonson, Wyatt, Fulke Greville, Herbert, Marvell, Hopkins, and those poets who Matthew Arnold said were not poets at all: Dryden and Pope. And modern criticism has reexamined, carefully and often damningly, many of the Victorians and romantics whom academic criticism so uncritically received and exalted. It is only by connecting the past with the present, by examining the past in the light of the present, that we can really either understand or value the past; academic and scholarly criticism have failed because they have not done this. After knowing the best modern criticism, one reads more poetry and reads it better: English poetry is, one sees, more varied, complicated, and astonishing than anybody had thought.

I have been speaking of such critics as William Empson, T. S. Eliot, R. P. Blackmur, Allen Tate, Yvor Winters, John Crowe Ransom, I. A. Richards, Morton Dauwen Zabel, Cleanth Brooks, Robert Penn Warren, Delmore Schwartz, and five or six others. They have written a good many books, almost any of which is worth reading; their criticism is often printed in such magazines as *The Southern Review,* the *Kenyon Review,* and *Partisan Review.* I do not mean to be saying, "Here they are—all perfect!" They are highly imperfect; the reader and I will probably agree that we would not be caught dead saying some of the things they say; but, all in all, they are about as good as we can find—and better than we deserve.

This criticism is not better known for several reasons. Much of it has been published recently and rather obscurely. It is *hard* criticism, of unusual depth and complication, written—one might almost say—by critics for critics. It makes great demands of its readers in more than one way: its characteristic complication of surface, its self-conscious employment of so much knowledge, sensitivity, and superiority may dishearten or antagonize the reader. Another deterrent is the political and social position of the majority of these writers. It is an odd fact that most good criticism of poetry today is being written by critics who can only be called—who call themselves—reactionary. (The best leftist critics of poetry, men like Edmund Wilson and Kenneth Burke, have gone over almost entirely into general criticism.) But neglecting criticism because we are annoyed at the critic's politics (or tone or style or anything else) is a fool's game; if we can learn nothing at all from his political views—that is unlikely, but possible—we can simply disregard them, and have that much more time for the criticism. As readers of criticism, we must allow ourselves to be disheartened or antagonized by nothing but bad criticism.

Personally, I believe that it would be profitable for critics to show less concern with poets, periods, society (big-scale extensive criticism), and more concern with the poems themselves (intensive criticism). In extensive criticism the data on which the critic bases his judgments are necessarily not given. The critic says that A.'s poetry is such-and-such because of the influence of So-and-So on the age; you summon your memories, clear or vague, of a few dozen of A.'s poems—the right ones, you hope—and after comparing these with your memories of So-and-So and the age, you make up your mind about the critic's remark. Your need and understanding of the remark vary inversely. In intensive criticism, the analysis of specific poems, what the critic says and exactly what he is saying it about are both there: the criticism is ideally accessible. Nothing would have more value for criticism than the existence of a few hundred or thousand detailed critical analyses, done by first-rate critics, of important English poems—*important* includes both good and bad. Good criticism is based on very good reading: unless we can do the same sort of reading the critic does we cannot even understand his judgments, much less accept or reject them. These intensive critical analyses at once convict and improve our own reading—there is no way in which we can learn so much about poetry so quickly and surely. I know plenty of critics who agree with me about such analyses; why aren't they being written? Because there are one or two magazines in the world that occasionally print such analyses; because no publisher has ever published a book of them. The critic not only can't make his living by them; he can't even get them printed.

We have a good many critics who are perfectly capable, under favorable conditions, of producing a large amount of extremely valuable criticism of poetry; they are, instead, producing a small amount under quite unfavorable conditions. All through this article, with shy persistence, I have kept recurring to the topic of money. This is an incongruous subject for a critic—what does he know about money? Only what everybody else knows: that he must get some somehow; by writing criticism if that is possible, by doing something else if that is not. People who are interested in criticism can do something for it in two ways: by being good critics or by encouraging good critics. *Encouraging* means buying or publishing their books, running magazines for them, giving them fellowships, hiring them in universities: it is a mercenary word.

Tate versus History

THE NATION, JULY 26, 1941

Reason in Madness by Allen Tate

THESE are critical essays: some are literary criticism in a narrow sense, some in a broad, and some are not literary criticism at all. The essays are disconnected and occasional, the preface says, but that is not one's impression; Mr. Tate's style, method, and point of view give the book a surprising unity. The style will please anyone: few people write English with so much strength, ease, and wit. The method is what Mr. Tate confesses it is—the attack. The point of view—well, most of this review will be about that; roughly, it is an American variant of Eliot's, more downright and logical, not so religious, evasive, or "humble."

Mr. Tate's criticism of critics—Arnold, Coleridge, Richards, Daiches—is sound, brilliant, and crushing; he altogether avoids the filial relaxation of standards that is our customary tribute to the distinguished dead. His criticism of poetry, less intensive, is generally quite as good. His critical standards resemble Blackmur's, Winters's (minus Winters's incomparable neoclassical excesses), or Eliot's (minus Eliot's unconscious residual passion for the experimental). As a critic of poetry he has the initial advantage of being one of the four or five greatest living poets; his judgments are occasionally perverse, always acute, and usually simply right. He rarely amplifies or justifies these judgments; consequently he misses the advantage critics like Blackmur and Empson get from showing the reader exactly what they are saying, and why. He has an odd habit of conclusively demonstrating the quality of a poet by means of a little metrical analysis: it is an idiosyncrasy that almost assumes the proportions of a vice. Most of the literary criticism in this book is obviously first-rate; and there is, besides, the most brilliant attack on scholarship—*PMLA* variety—that I have ever seen.

Mr. Tate, fighting desperately to preserve traditional European culture, is part of an old and growing campaign against science, progress, humanitarianism, Economic and Perfectible Man. The movement has had two wings, both right: the irrational, which has attacked in the name of intuition, blood, the folk; and the rationalistic, which has attacked, with remorseless scholastic logic, in the name of the religion, art, philosophy it has seen being destroyed. Men like Mr. Tate have denounced the evils of what they call finance-capitalism; they have denounced the scientists and industrialists who, discarding art, religion, and philosophy as meaningless luxuries, have tried to throw away half our culture. But they are themselves eager to sacrifice the scientific, mathematical, and technical half of European culture, in order to return to the good society (traditional, theological, based on property, the "primary medium through which man expressed his moral nature") that is the womb from which the rest of us have struggled to get free. They approximate to that familiar limit, the thirteenth century, by means of an odd neo-Cartesian program of Systematic Belief. They are more hardhearted than hardheaded; about their attitude there is something conscientiously partial, pre-scientific, provincial in both space and time—they can believe so much more and ignore so much more than other people. It is not so much the truth as the necessity of religion that impresses Mr. Tate; his theology is a blank and hypothetical quasi-Catholicism—the Christianity of *as if.* The education he wants is Latin, Greek, and philosophy. (He is a dualist—the Carnation or contented kind.) He writes: "I may look at English history with Hilaire Belloc—as I happen to do with reservations—as the decline of moral standards and human liberty from the twelfth century to our day." Well—such men are a distinguished and very forlorn hope; what they are fighting is history. Their attitude seems to me mistaken as truth and badly mistaken as tactics: they are all campaigning for the philosopher-King Stork. It has been later than they think for four hundred years.

But today, when everybody realizes that what we have been needing wasn't a change of system but a change of heart, that it wasn't economics we should have been studying but ethics (or should I say military tactics?); when all the fellow travelers lie home with their heads under their pillows, dreaming of democracy and liberalism and religion—today one gets a perverse pleasure from a confirmed old reactionary like Mr. Tate, who sticks to his opinions for all the worst reasons, instead of deserting them for all the best. He calls his book *Reason in Madness,* a light surviving in the "mad abstract dark"; we can get nowhere by retorting that we are reason, and Mr. Tate and his fellows the mad concrete dark. We must manage, somehow, a climate of opinion in which both are varieties of reason—and of madness too. A good many things are going to be taken from us; really to be reasonable, to be *willing,* to get where we can what good we can, is something we must lose for ourselves.

Town Mouse, Country Mouse

THE NATION, SEPTEMBER 20, 1941

The Listening Landscape by Marya Zaturenska   *Poems 1930–1940* by Horace Gregory

MISS ZATURENSKA is the country mouse, in the sense that Marie Antoinette was a shepherdess. How did the pastoral first enchant Miss Zaturenska? One sees her, perplexed with this sick disease of modern life, standing in the subway reading *Finnegans Wake;* she frowns; across sits Einstein reading the *Anti-Dühring;* he frowns; it is like a nightmare. A schoolgirl begins to recite her homework, "Corinna's Going a-Maying." Word by word, stanza by stanza, the repose and order of the pastoral settle over Miss Zaturenska's troubled mind, over Miss Zaturenska's feverish spirit, like a wet blanket. Joyce, Einstein, Engels fade away, are quite forgot; the subway is a mass of ivy. Miss Zaturenska goes home, sits down among her geraniums, and writes a pastoral; another; she sits there to this day, like the salt mill at the bottom of the ocean, grinding out pastorals.

Miss Zaturenska is as efficient as a sheet of carbon paper. She includes reasonably exact facsimiles of all the physical properties of pastoral, excludes any embarrassing interference from actuality, and hopefully supposes that she has attained the classical order that has fascinated her. But the classicism of exclusion is academicism; the real strength and use of pastoral are what Miss Zaturenska, obsessed with the trimmings, never guesses. All these clouds, marbles, legends, ferns, and nymphs ("by Fragonard") are only bystanders, innocent, unemployed, unemployable; their *esse* is purely *percipi,* they are powerless as a mirage. (I made up a motto for Miss Zaturenska: Every Man His Own Poussin.) Her curious literalness—combined with an unreflecting facility for language, the immediate, approximate, and smothering word—make her read, generally, like a rather good translation; she reminds one of the man who played the violin "by main force." Miss Zaturenska reads Auden and Yeats (once or twice they shake her branches like a breeze), yet she is satisfied with the stalest romantic diction—"Elysium-echoes of far worlds unborn," and so forth. She is handicapped, for poetry, just as Santayana was: by not having spoken English as a child. And she is regrettably literary—one picks one's way through a landscape full of painters and authors and goddesses; her *tableaux* are less *vivant* than Tussaud.

But Miss Zaturenska has obvious virtues: force, emotion, sweep, some amount of form; her poems often have a real subject, are recognizably hers, really get somewhere. Her pieces are like stage scenery, imposing and successful to the glance, coarse to a closer look: approximations. Poems like "The White Dress" or "Forest of Arden" show her at her rather disquieting best; they are rough and evitable successes—the work of a poet who has a real talent, but not for words.

Everyone is familiar with the romanticism of the far away and long ago; but what is today a more popular kind goes almost unrecognized—the exoticism of the ticker tape, let me call it. Crane said that poetry must assimilate the machine, metropolitan existence; this sort of romanticism *exploits* the machine, and considers intrinsically valuable the showily topical and megalopolitan terms it translates everything into. Mr. Gregory (a mouse from Twenty-third Street) tells you that Macbeth embezzled, the market fell, his life insurance went to the banks; this is the strategy, intensive and extensive, of his most typical poems. "Ticker tape / on private yachts: ring them up on the cash register / cable them" will show how concentrated and willful such imagery often becomes. Unfortunately, the modernity of its terms does not guarantee the truth or even the modernity of an insight. Imagine a writer of the nineties who conscientiously put everything in the latest metropolitan terms—bicycles, incandescent lamps, streetcars—and you will see how much power, in themselves, such things keep after a generation. This whole fashion of writing (and it has been enormously fashionable) rests on a variant of the old fallacy that there are classes of words or objects which are themselves poetic. The romantics had failed before, had to escape from, the modern world: they had employed, as much as possible, "poetic" words and objects; what they rejected as anti-poetic—the mechanical, the sordid, the prosaic—was perhaps a sure means to success? A fortuitous collocation of the anti-poetic (plus, for emotion or profundity, the same old romantic and sentimental excesses) was too many poets' solution of the problem of how to express the modern world. It was a mistake, of course; to the Muse of Poetry—a neutral monist from way back—Crane's burnt match skating in a urinal is just another primrose by the river's brim.

For poems like these Mr. Gregory employs a suitable rhetoric composed largely of parodied quotations, tags, literary clichés, mixed with slang or advertising or tabloid banalities, non-literary clichés. He gets both from his main source, Eliot; the second also derives from Joyce, Cummings, and Crane. His use of this rhetoric is heavily ironic; the automatic undifferentiating irony of many of the poems is full of the easy "disillusionment" of the twenties, the favorite defense mechanism of the sentimentalist. It is the debunker's attitude: we're all rotten, what's the good of anything? Well, what's the good of this sort of irony? Marx said that he had stood Hegel on his head; often Mr. Gregory has simply stood Pollyanna on her head. Right side up she accepts all, upside down she rejects all. And her inversion is disconcertingly inconsistent; the irony and disillusionment are never extended to the poet's own sentimentality, or to the past with which the present is unfavorably compared. The Cummings-like sentimentality of the earlier poems (a consumptive lover "coughs the moon and a gallon of stars") persists throughout the book; the embarrassingly romantic and sentimental are Mr. Gregory's Mount Sinai, a haven that is the source of all ultimates. This is natural; sentimentality and cynicism (or brutality) are complementary excesses. Mr. Gregory is Whitman on a spot—the spot being contemporary New York. The old confused and rhapsodic acceptance no longer is possible, is broken up or overlaid by an equally confused rejection; we still get all the lists' details, but ironically presented as decadence, and it is only by a sort of temperamental sleight of hand that the poet manages to rise into emotional acceptance. (Mr. Gregory's favorite model for passage-work is the conclusion of "Gerontion." Eliot uses an illogical series of terms so well selected that they generate their own emotion, a whole attitude; most imitators make a list and paste on an emotional conclusion.) Mr. Gregory even seems to admire this confused acceptance in other people: he speaks of "wide-breasted Whitman" (surely so ironic a poet might have said "soft"), and Emerson, at least in these poems, seems his favorite writer—subject too.

Some of Mr. Gregory's poems have merely appeared in *The New Yorker;* others are *New Yorker* poems: the inclusive topicality, the informed and casual smartness, the flat fashionable irony, meaningless because it proceeds from a frame of reference whose amorphous superiority is the most definite thing about it—they are the trademark not simply of a magazine but of a class.

Mr. Gregory's radicalism—I am talking not about his personal beliefs but about their manifestation in his poetry—seems to me more a sentiment than a body of ideas, something the age furnished him just as it did his irony or his prosody. There is more social sympathy (Mr. Gregory knows and cares about poor and ordinary people) and social satire (a radical point of view is a great additional source of irony) than social insight in the poems. His radicalism is contradicted by his Whitmanish acceptance, his Eliotish insistence on the inferiority of the present; but these are so much stronger one hardly notices or cares about the contradiction.

Most of Mr. Gregory's poems do not have regular meters, line lengths, or stanzas; any poet knows how hard it is really to organize a poem without these. But his feeling for speech and tone, his real selectivity, plus his absolutely magnificent rhymes, do manage to hold his poems together surprisingly often. The rhythmical flow of the poems, which in his middle period is broken up into a fashionable sort of stream-of-consciousness collage, is restored in the fantastic reveries of the later poems, monologues of a queer improbable verisimilitude, full of the "feel of the times."

I have talked so much about Mr. Gregory's weaknesses because they are fascinating to me, so beautifully representative; but he has most of the representative virtues of the time as well. He belongs more to the conversational-colloquial half of modern poetry than to the rhetorical-obscure half; his textures often have the particularity and precision and bareness of successful prose. He is an accomplished, sensitive, and complicated poet; honest, too: he never fools his readers without fooling himself. I found his poems much better than I had remembered, and felt for them much respect and a little enthusiasm. But one must not make out too imposing a case for his poetry: there is something curiously passive and automatic about even his individuality, as if he were the age's Trilby. His poetry is the sort the next age will take only at a tremendous discount. Probably he has been overrated; but he is a rather creditable sort of poet to overrate; anyone who can write poems as good as his best ones—"Interior: the Suburbs," for instance—deserves one's affection or awe.

Kafka's Tragi-Comedy

· ·

KENYON REVIEW, WINTER 1941

Amerika by Franz Kafka, translated by Edwin Muir

IN *Amerika* one sees the beginnings of the method that is developed in *The Trial* and perfected in *The Castle*. The unity, concision, and apparent *necessity* of *The Castle,* the completeness of its realization, make it seem incongruous to talk of development in connection with its method; but even Pallas Athena began as no more than a bad headache, and in *Amerika* one is awed and amused to recognize, in their humble, methodical, or inconsequential beginnings, the bewildering successes of *The Castle*. One can imagine—perhaps with badly concealed pleasure—cutting *Remembrance of Things Past, Ulysses, The Magic Mountain*: fifty or a hundred pages of place names, of Dublin details, of debates between Naphta and Settembrini, never would be missed. And we can say of these great or extremely good novels, "This part is successful, that less so, that scarcely at all so." But who would have the courage to declare part of *The Castle* unnecessary or unsuccessful? Its most grudging reader could hardly refuse it the epithet, "perfect of its kind"; K. and the assistants will last as long as Alice or Gulliver or that traveler who called himself Noman.

Karl Rossman, the hero of *Amerika,* is a quite primitive ancestor of K.—they have in common, principally, their initials and methods of presentation. (Karl, like K. or Joseph K., is given in the third person; but everything is presented through him, he is never judged overtly, and the third person consequently acquires some of the characteristics of the first.) I am not implying that *Amerika* is in any way negligible; even if one's primary interest in it—genetic, I regret to say—were lacking, it would remain thoroughly worth reading. It is a charming and often extremely funny story, a sort of *Candide* à la Hans Christian Andersen, with extraordinary overtones. Kafka's familiar themes receive a slighter treatment, but one full of a grace and mastery reminiscent of some of his last stories. In other words, *Amerika* is a minor work by a great writer. When I read it first, in the English edition, I was bitterly disappointed—as some of my readers may be—to find that it was not another *Castle;* but when I reread it for this review, I was delighted with so much of it that I could hardly understand my first disappointment.

The worlds of Kafka's three novels are quite different. The world of *Amerika* is the real world seen through a pair of oddly distorting glasses: if it is unlike Europe, its unlikeness has the partial, ostensible excuse that it is far-off and hardly known. There is a casual, accurately accidental, faintly comic pastoral quality about it; it is full of the humor or pathos of the irrelevant or absurd. This world is hardly *judged* at all; its cruelties and barbarities elicit only the blankly anthropological interest we extend to the vagaries of savages or children. The conscientious naïveté, the more-than-scientific suspension or tentativeness of judgment of the later books, are already surprisingly well developed in *Amerika.* In its capacity for generating ambiguity and irony (reinforced in the later books by the similar possibilities of allegory), the attitude resembles that of Socrates, that of the scientist making minimal assumptions, or that of the "humble observer": child, fairytale simpleton or third son, fool. And it allows Kafka to employ at will his favorite comic method, the use of irrelevant or absurd amplifications or qualifications. (Kafka is the incomparable master of the detail that convinces not by its plausibility but by its absurdity; the detail that is improbable or impossible and—in its context—profoundly *right.*) But this method is more than comic. The blank innocence with which relevant, irrelevant, sensible, absurd, are set down beside each other, the absence even of any implication or suspicion of separation (accompanied by the characters' interminable analysis of motive and logic), suggest more disquietingly than anything else could: In *this* world how can we possibly believe that we know what is important and what is unimportant?—here where the most fantastically difficult and well-nigh interminable research, the whole world-high heap of piled-on qualification, amplification, contradiction, leaves us no nearer the truth than when we started—for we must stop somewhere, one place is as good or as bad as the next, and our result is utterly different according to the accident of our stopping place.

In *The Trial,* treated quite naturalistically, there is the real world, the world of banks, boardinghouses, and tenements. But alongside it, inside it, exists a not so much super- as extra-natural world: the legal-bureaucratic nightmare, complete with officers, judges, clerks, janitors, executioners, paupers, that reaches out into the real world, accuses, condemns, and executes Joseph K. The two worlds are, so to speak, the

Body and Soul whose debate forms *The Trial*. These worlds are in explicit contradiction; the constant strain between them, the lack of the unity and humor of *The Castle,* make *The Trial* a much more wearing book—few things are more frightening than these courts where justice is reached only by means of an infinite regress of the most incredibly complicated and stupid varieties of injustice, where the very injustice that destroys you goes under the name of justice.

In *The Castle* the "real" world has ceased to exist: Kafka's wonderful substitute is an almost unrecognizably improved version of the world of the law courts in *The Trial*. But I am not reviewing *The Castle,* and I need not attempt a description. It is allegory of a sort that former literature has simply not prepared us for, an extension of the method that almost revolutionizes our conceptions of the method. The subject of *The Castle* is, I suppose, *How shall a man be saved?*—and Kafka's answer is, if anything, more difficult than the question.

It is customary to make Freudian remarks about Kafka: but let me make a couple of more or less Marxist ones. His world is the world of late capitalism, in which individualism has changed from the mixed but sought blessing of the romantics, to everybody's initial plight: the hero's problem is not to escape from society but to find it, to get any satisfactory place in it or relation to it. How shall a unit of labor power be saved? The hero—anomalous term—struggles against mechanisms too gigantic, too endlessly and irrationally complex even to be understood, much less conquered. Kafka understands that there is no separation between ideas and things, that contradictions are the shocking ends of a continuum, that everything is a *process*: justice and salvation both are represented as a sort of infinite regress. The law courts of *The Trial*, the governing system of *The Castle* (which have a unicellular ancestor in the hotel of *Amerika*) are the conditions of the universe presented in terms of those of monopoly capitalism; the fusion gives a singular richness and plausibility to Kafka's allegory of man's relation to the world. God is the trust, the state, all over again at the next higher level. God's justice and the world's contradict each other; and yet what is God's justice but the world's, raised to the next power, but retaining all the qualities of its original? Dante tells you why you are damned (or saved, if we want to consider the jackpot), and supplies the details of the whole mechanism; Kafka says that you are damned and can never know why—that the system of your damnation, like those of your society and your universe, is simply beyond your understanding; and he too gives the details of the system, and your confusion grows richer with each detail. Consider where and when the two lived, and it is plain

why each says what he does. If religions are affected by the econo-
mies of the societies that produce them—something not too unlikely—
Kafka's is a wonderful illustration of the process; its terms and insights are those of—or are impossible without—a highly developed
scientific and industrial technique.

Indeed, Kafka's whole method is rooted in the immense complication of our whole society. The perfect calm, the dispassionate rigor, that
might be called either scientific or classical, clothe an insight too profound ever to be blinded by indignation. In Kafka there is an unex-
ampled extension of the methods of comedy to the material of tragedy.
K. is seeking for salvation, for truth, Joseph K. for justice, for his very
life; their search is presented with the utmost possible concern and
intensity; and yet Kafka's method of treatment, his whole attitude,
make us see at the same time that the details are somehow comic, that
the whole, looked at in one way, is itself comic. It is absurd not to call
the world evil, and it is impossible to take the condemnation seriously:
either laughter or tears are impossibly inadequate, we have for it only
the stare we give Medusa's head.

The End of the Line

THE NATION, FEBRUARY 21, 1942

WHAT HAS IMPRESSED everyone about modernist poetry is its *differentness*. The familiar and rather touching "I like poetry—but not modern poetry" is only another way of noticing what almost all criticism has emphasized: that modernist poetry is a revolutionary departure from the romantic poetry of the preceding century. Less far-reaching changes would have seemed a revolutionary disaster to "conventional" poets, critics, and readers, who were satisfied with romantic poetry; a revolutionary improvement to more "advanced" poets and critics, who disliked romanticism with the fervor of converts. *Romantic* once again, after almost two centuries, became a term of simple derogation; correspondingly, there grew up a rather blank cult of the "classical," and poets like Eliot hinted that poets like Pound might be the new classicism for which all had been waiting.

All this seems to me partially true, essentially false. The change from romantic poetry was evolutionary, not revolutionary: the modernists were a universe away from the great-grandfathers they admired; they *were* their fathers, only more so. I want to sketch this evolution. But if the reader understands me to be using *romantic* as an unfavorably weighted term, most of what I say will be distorted. Some of the tendencies of romanticism are bad; some of the better tendencies, exaggerated enough, are bad; but a great deal of the best poetry I know is romantic. Of course, one can say almost that about any of the larger movements into which critics divide English poetry; and one might say even better things about the "classical tradition" in English poetry, if there were one. (It is not strange that any real movement, compared to this wax monster, comes off nowhere; but it is strange that anyone should take the comparison for a real one.) If I pay more attention to unfortunate or exaggerated romantic tendencies, it is because these are the most characteristic: the "good" tendencies of movements are far more alike than the "bad" ones, and a proof that two movements are essentially similar needs to show that they share each other's vices.

Modernist poetry—the poetry of Pound, Eliot, Crane, Tate, Stevens, Cummings, MacLeish, et cetera—appears to be and is generally considered to be a violent break with romanticism; it is actually, I believe, an extension of romanticism, an end product in which most of the tendencies of romanticism have been carried to their limits. Romanticism—whether considered as the product of a whole culture or, in isolation, as a purely literary phenomenon—is necessarily a process of extension, a vector; it presupposes a constant experimentalism, the indefinite attainment of "originality," generation after generation, primarily by the novel extrapolation of previously exploited processes. (Neoclassicism, in theory at least, is a static system.) All these romantic tendencies are exploited to their limits; and the movement which carries out this final exploitation, apparently so different from earlier stages of the same process, is what we call modernism. Then, at last, romanticism is confronted with an impasse, a critical point, a genuinely novel situation that it can meet successfully only by contriving genuinely novel means—that is, means which are not romantic; the romantic means have already been exhausted. Until these new means are found, romanticism operates by repeating its last modernist successes or by reverting to its earlier stages; but its normal development has ended, and—the momentum that gave it most of its attraction gone— it becomes a relatively eclectic system, much closer to neoclassicism than it has hitherto been. (A few of these last romanticists resort to odd varieties of neoclassicism.) If this account seems unlikely to the reader, let me remind him that a similar course of development is extremely plain in modern music.

A good many factors combine to conceal the essentially romantic character of modernist poetry. (1) A great quantitative change looks like a qualitative one: for instance, the attenuation or breaking up of form characteristic of romanticism will not be recognized or tolerated by the average romantic when it reaches its limit in modernist poetry. (2) The violent contrast between the modernist limits of romantic tendencies and the earlier stages of these tendencies, practiced belatedly and eclectically by "conventional" poets, is an important source of confusion. (3) Most of the best modern criticism of poetry is extremely anti-romantic—a poet's criticism is frequently not a reflection of but a compensation for his own poetry; and this change in theory has helped to hide the lack of any essential change in practice. (4) Modernist poems, while possessing some romantic tendencies in hypertrophied forms, often lack others so spectacularly that the reader disregards those they still possess; and these remaining tendencies may be too common for him to be conscious of them as specifically romantic. (Most of the romantic qualities that poetry has specialized in since 1800 seem to the average reader "normal" or "poetic," what poetry inescapably is.) (5) Romanticism holds in solution contradictory tendencies which, isolated and exaggerated in modernism, look startlingly opposed both to each other and to the earlier stages of romanticism. (6) Both modernist and conventional critics have been unable to see the fundamental similarities between modernist and romantic poetry because they were unwilling to see anything but differences: these were to the former a final recommendation, and to the latter a final condemnation.

We can understand modernist poetry better by noticing where and how it began. The English poetry that we call *fin de siècle*—the most important tendency of its time—was a limit of one easily recognizable extension of romanticism. These "decadent" poets were strongly influenced by Baudelaire, Verlaine, and similar French poets. Rimbaud, Laforgue, and Corbière—who had already written "modern" poetry—had no influence on them. Why? Because a section of French poetry was developing a third of a century ahead of English poetry: Rimbaud wrote typically modernist poetry in the 1870's; in the nineties a surrealist play, Jarry's *Ubu Roi,* scared the young Yeats into crying: "After us the Savage God!" France, without England's industrial advantages and enormous colonial profits, had had little of the Victorian prosperity which slowed up the economic and political rate of change in England—had still less of that complacent mercantile Christianity the French dismissed as "English hypocrisy." And—if we stick to a part of the culture, literature—the rate of change could be greater in France because romanticism was more of a surface phenomenon there. English poetry was not *ready* to be influenced by French modernism for many years. Meanwhile, there were two movements particularly suited to criticism. Accompanying the triumph of prose naturalism there was a prosy, realistic, rather limited reaction against "decadent" poetry (it included Robinson, Frost, Masters, Masefield, some of the Georgians, etc.). The other movement, imagism, carried three or four romantic tendencies to their limits with the perfection of a mathematical demonstration.

French modernist poetry first influenced poetry in English through Americans who, lacking a determining or confining tradition of their own, were particularly accessible and susceptible: Pound and Eliot (like Picasso, Stravinsky, and Joyce) were in some sense expatriates in both space and time. They imported modernism into English rather more deliberately and openly than Wordsworth and Coleridge had imported romanticism; but all Pound's early advice to poets could be summed up in a sentence half of which is pure Wordsworth: Write like prose, like speech—and *read French poetry!* The work of this most influential of modern poets, Ezra Pound, is a recapitulation of the development of our poetry from late romanticism to modernism. His early work is a sort of anthology of romantic sources: Browning, early Yeats, the *fin de siècle* poets, Villon and the troubadours (in translations or imitations that remind one of Swinburne's and Rossetti's), Heine. *His* variety of imagism is partly a return to the fresh beginnings of romantic practices, from their diluted and perfunctory ends; partly an extension to their limits of some of the most characteristic obsessions of romanticism—for instance, its passion for "pure" poetry, for putting everything in terms of sensation and emotion, with logic and generalizations excluded; and partly an adaptation of the exotic procedures of Chinese poetry, those silks that swathe a homely heart. When Pound first wrote poems that are modernist in every sense of the word, their general "feel" is reminiscent of what one might call a lowest common denominator of Corbière, Laforgue, and Rimbaud; but Heine had by no means disappeared; and the original Cantos I and II, gone now, were still full of Browning. But if Eliot was willing to base his form on Browning's (the dramatic monologue is primarily a departure from the norm of ordinary poetry; but in modernist poetry this departure *itself becomes the norm*), he had no interest in Browning's content and manner; in even his earliest poems one is seeing romanticism through Laforgue, and one can reconstruct this romanticism, in the pure form in which it had once existed, only from Eliot's remarks about his early feelings for Rossetti and Swinburne . . . All during this time the Irish expatriate Joyce was making his way from late-romantic lyrics (in verse, though there is much that is similar in his early prose) to the modernist poetry (in prose) that crops up here and there in *Ulysses,* and that is everywhere in *Finnegans Wake.*

But it would take fifty or a hundred pages to write about this development in terms of specific poets. One can indicate the resemblances of romanticism and modernism more briefly, by making a list of some of the general characteristics of modernist poetry:

(1) A pronounced experimentalism: "originality" is everyone's aim, and novel techniques are as much prized as new scientific discoveries. Eliot states it with surprising naïveté: "It is exactly as wasteful

for a poet to do what has been done already as for a biologist to re-discover Mendel's discoveries." (2) External formlessness, internal disorganization: these are justified either as the disorganization neces-sary to express a disorganized age or as new and more complex forms of organization. Language is deliberately disorganized, meter becomes irregular or disappears; the rhythmical flow of verse is broken up into a jerky half-prose *collage* or *montage*. (3) Heightened emotional in-tensity; violence of every sort. (4) Obscurity, inaccessibility: logic, both for structure and for texture, is neglected; without this for a ground the masses of the illogical or alogical lose much of their effectiveness. The poet's peculiar erudition and allusiveness (compare the Alexandrian poet Lycophron) consciously restrict his audience to a small, highly specialized group; the poet is a specialist like everyone else. He intimi-dates or overawes the public by an attitude one may paraphrase as: "The poet's cultivation and sensibility are of a different order from those of his readers; even if he tried to talk down to them—and why should he try?—he would talk about things they have never heard of, in ways they will never understand." But he did not despair of their understanding a slap in the face. (5) A lack of restraint or proportion: all tendencies are forced to their limits, even contradictory tendencies—and not merely in the same movement but, frequently, in the same poet or the same poem. Some modernist poetry puts an unparalleled emphasis on texture, connotation, violently "interesting" language (attained partly by an extension of romantic principles, partly by a more violent rhetoric based on sixteenth- and seventeenth-century prac-tices); but there has never before been such prosaic poetry—conversa-tional-colloquial verse without even a pretense at meter. (6) A great emphasis on details—on parts, not wholes. Poetry is essentially lyric: the rare narrative or expository poem is a half-fortuitous collocation of lyric details. Poetry exploits particulars and avoids and condemns generalizations. (7) A typically romantic preoccupation with sensation, perceptual nuances. (8) A preoccupation with the unconscious, dreams, the stream of consciousness, the irrational: this *surréaliste* emphasis might better have been called *sousréaliste*. (9) Irony of every type: Byronic, Laforguian, dryly metaphysical, or helplessly sentimental. Poetry rejects a great deal, accepts a little, and is embarrassed by that little. (10) *Fauve* or neo-primitive elements. (11) Modernist poets, though they may write about the ordinary life of the time, are removed from it, have highly specialized relations with it. The poet's naturalism is employed as indictment, as justification for his own isolation; pro-saic and sordid details become important as what writers like Wallace

Stevens and William Carlos Williams somewhat primitively think of as the *anti-poetic*. Contemporary life is condemned, patronized, or treated as a disgraceful aberration or special case, compared to the past; the poet hangs out the window of the Ivory Tower making severe but obscure remarks about what is happening below—he accepts the universe with several (thin) volumes of reservations. What was happening below was bad enough; the poet could characterize it, truthfully enough, with comparative forms of all those adjectives that Goethe and Arnold had applied to their ages. But its disasters, at least, were of unprecedented grandeur; it was, after all, "the very world, which is the world / Of all of us,—the place where, in the end, / We find our happiness or not at all"; and the poet's rejection or patronizing acceptance of it on his own terms—and, sometimes, what terms they were!—hurt his poetry more than he would have believed. (12) Individualism, isolation, alienation. The poet is not only different from society, he is as different as possible from other poets; all this differentness is exploited to the limit—is used as subject matter, even. Each poet develops an elaborate, "personalized," bureaucratized machinery of effect; *refine your singularities* is everybody's maxim. (13) These poets, typically, dislike and condemn science, industrialism, humanitarianism, "progress," the main tendencies of Western development; they want to trade the present for a somewhat idealized past, to turn from a scientific, commercial, and political world view to one that is literary, theological, and personal.

This complex of qualities is essentially romantic, and the poetry that exhibits it is the culminating point of romanticism.

It is the end of the line. Poets can go back and repeat the ride; they can settle in attractive, atavistic colonies along the railroad; they can repudiate the whole system, à la Yvor Winters, for some neoclassical donkey caravan of their own. But Modernism As We Knew It—the most successful and influential body of poetry of this century—is dead. Compare a 1940 issue of *Poetry* with a 1930 issue. Who could have believed that modernism would collapse so fast? Only someone who realized that modernism is a limit which it is impossible to exceed. How can poems be written that are more violent, more disorganized, more obscure, more—supply your own adjective—than those that have already been written? But if modernism could go no further, it was equally difficult for it to stay where it was: how could a movement completely dynamic in character, as "progressive" as the science and industrialism it accompanied, manage to become static or retrogressive without going to pieces? Among modernist poets, from 1910 to 1925, there was the same feeling of confident excitement, of an individual but irregularly cooperative experimentalism, of revolutionary discoveries just around the corner, that one regularly sees at certain stages in the development of a science; they had ahead of them the same Manifest Destiny that poets have behind them today. Today, for the poet, there is an embarrassment of choices: young poets can choose—do choose—to write anything from surrealism to imitations of Robert Bridges; the only thing they have no choice about is making their own choice. The Muse, forsaking her sterner laws, says to everyone: "Do what you will." Originality can no longer be recognized by, and condemned or applauded for, its obvious experimentalism; the age offers to the poet a fairly heartless eclecticism or a fairly solitary individuality. He can avoid being swept along by the current—there is no current; he can congratulate himself on this, and see behind him, glittering in the distance of time, all those bright streams sweeping people on to the wildest of excesses, the unlikeliest of triumphs.

For a long time society and poetry have been developing in the same direction, have been carrying certain tendencies to their limits: how could anyone fail to realize that the excesses of modernist poetry are the necessary concomitants of the excesses of late-capitalist society? (An example too pure and too absurd even for allegory is Robinson Jeffers, who must prefer a hawk to a man, a stone to a hawk, because of an individualism so exaggerated that it contemptuously rejects affections, obligations, relations of any kind whatsoever, and sets up as a nostalgically awaited goal the war of all against all. Old Rocky Face, perched on his sea crag, is the last of *laissez faire;* Free Economic Man at the end of his rope.) How much the modernist poets disliked their society, and how much they resembled it! How often they contradicted its letter and duplicated its spirit! They rushed, side by side with their society, to the limits of all tendencies. When, at the beginning of the thirties, these limits were reached, what became of these individualists? They turned toward anything collective: toward Catholicism, communism, distributism, social credit, agrarianism; they wrote neoclassical criticism or verse; they wrote political (Marxist or fellow traveler) criticism or verse; they stopped writing; and when they read the verse of someone like E. E. Cummings, as it pushed on into the heart of that last undiscovered continent, *e. e. cummings,* they thought of this moral impossibility, this living fossil, with a sort of awed and incredulous revulsion.

I have no space to write of later developments. Auden was so influential because his poetry was the only novel and successful reaction away from modernism; and a few years later Dylan Thomas was so influential—in England—because his poetry was the only novel and successful reaction away from Auden. But his semi-surrealist experimentalism could be as good as it was, and as influential as it was, only in a country whose poets had never carried modernism to the limits of its possibilities. No one can understand these English developments if he forgets that, while we were having the modernism of Pound, Stevens, Williams, Moore, Eliot, Tate, Crane, Cummings, and all the rest, England was having the modernism of the Sitwells.

I am afraid that my hypothesis about romanticism and modernism, without the mass of evidence that can make a theory plausible, or the tangle of extensions and incidental insights that can make it charming, may seem improbable or unpleasant to some of my readers. It is intended to be partial: I have not written about the hard or dry or "classical" tendencies of some modern verse—what Empson and Marianne Moore have in common, for instance; and I have not listed the differences between modernism and romanticism that everybody has seen and stated. But I hope that nobody will dislike my article because he thinks it an attack on romanticism or modernism. This has been description, not indictment. Burke said that you can't indict a whole people, and I hope I am not such a fool as to indict a century and a half of a world. Besides, so far as its poetry is concerned, it was wonderful. Wordsworth and Blake and Heine, Baudelaire and Corbière, Hardy and Yeats and Rilke—the names crowd in; and there are dozens more. That some of these poets were, sometimes, as strange as they were wonderful; that some of their successors were, alas, rather stranger: all this is as true as it is obvious. But the "classical" prejudice which hints that these poets were somehow deceived and misguided as (say) Dryden and Valéry were not seems every year more grotesque. One repeats to oneself, *Whom God deceives is well deceived,* and concludes that if these poets were not classical, so much the worse for classicism.

In All Directions

PARTISAN REVIEW, JULY–AUGUST 1942

New Directions: 1941, edited by James Laughlin

WHEN I FINISHED *New Directions* I felt angry and amused and helpless. It is a sort of encyclopedic contradiction in red sackcloth: *The Boyg Rides Again,* they might have called it. It commences with seven pages of Notes on Contributors, written by an anonymous Goody Two-shoes who rattles like Mr. Laughlin—nobody else errs with the same aura of optimistic benevolence. The Notes announce, among other things, that Kafka's famous parable from *The Trial* has never before been translated into English, and then *print* it (Knopf's suit for infringement of copyright should be instructive); kill off Roger Roughton in the Spanish revolution; and explain that the Italian government, by putting pressure on "close dependents," is forcing the unwilling Ezra Pound to broadcast Fascist propaganda. (I suppose Major Douglas got him to advocate Social Credit by kidnapping Homer Shakespeare Pound). But these are nothing; as Kipling says, "It was the tone, man! the tone!"

Brecht's long play is an episodic thieves' pastoral which presents the Thirty Years' War in terms of a wandering sutler: "Tilly's victory at Leipsic costs Mother Courage four officers' shirts." Mother Courage (the part is obviously intended for Hattie McDaniel) has a son named Swisscheese: the whole play's soul is contracted into that name. The play is a kind of anti-historical romance, a *Mother Horse-Sense's Progress;* the methodical collision of history and horse sense resulted, so far as I was concerned, in the complete triumph of history. *Mother Courage* tastes like a raw potato: good, but crude and simple and special case; and I feel like Feuerbach, when it comes to living on potatoes. But even potatoes show to a little advantage by Delmore Schwartz's *Paris and Helen*—self-conscious, self-indulgent, a literary and embarrassing failure. No character does anything without lengthily explaining what he is doing, preferably in some famous writer's words; the Dramatist then explains why the character has done it, and what it all means, and why the famous writer's language is better than *his* could ever be; then the Producer does a little commenting of his own; and the Audience does I don't know what—the author has unaccountably forgotten to say. This is not complex, just diffuse—the literary equivalent of washing your hands fifty times a day; it is a commentary on a commentary on a commentary. It is a real grief to see so good a writer (the most promising extensive poet of the time) wasted on this; his essay on modern poetry, later in the book, is sensible and interesting. *Paris and Helen* is dedicated to Metro-Goldwyn-Mayer; Universal would have done.

Georg Karl Friedrich Mann's *Azeff Wischmeier, the Bolshevik Bureaucrat* reads like a James Joyce–S. J. Perelman parody of the *Encyclopaedia Britannica;* its 108 pages are a Russian Joke to end all Russian Jokes. Mr. Mann, a great deal of the time, is a wonderfully funny writer; but there is something wonderfully humorless about his methodical and remorseless extravagance—the reader, blind and bleeding in these graceless toils, finds it hard to remember that the machine which is destroying him is, after all, funny.

Half the stories are heavily influenced by Kafka, who by now has become a non-naturalistic convention at everyone's disposal; used badly enough, it is as dreary and unimaginative as naturalism. Roger Roughton's plausible and disquieting death journey is the best of these stories; Miss Eustis and Mr. Gedanken come next, probably. Wright Morris's prose is plain honest neo-primitive stuff, mildly successful; Ben Field's story is as naturalistic as a can of angleworms; Paul Goodman's stories are witty, indulgent, trivial essays; Julien Gracq's "Chateau d'Argol" is "Ulalume" + Hegel (all uninverted) + *The Castle of Otranto*, done rather nicely—but why? The Swiss de Rougemont's fables are pleasanter than his armchair metaphor-mongering about society, which finds a *summum bonum* in—surprise, surprise—Switzerland, that "combination of a resort hotel and a safety-deposit vault." Eve Merriam's parables are pleasant; her scenario for a socially conscious animated cartoon is almost the crudest piece of writing I've ever seen.

"Augment of the Novel" is third-rate Pound—prejudice, idiosyncrasy, and reminiscence have almost wrestled free from the protean intelligence that has always burdened them. "Symbols in Portugal" is a surrealist's amusingly fantastic psychoanalysis. Mr. Calas writes that "what we call solutions of genius are in their essence paranoiac"; so here. André Breton's "Fata Morgana" is Art's answer to nonsense syllables. Clarence John Laughlin's "Poems of Desolation" are photographs of window dummies and black lace shawls in graveyards: these represent "the impasse reached in sexual relationships by western civilization," etc. Harry Thornton Moore, "our leading authority on poetry recordings," especially admires Welles's recording of *Macbeth* because "the cauldron hisses when the baboon's blood is poured in, and the toads and snakes that are dropped in can be heard to plop."

Hugh McDiarmid does better in Scots: "The Divided Bird," a confusion of genres such as you rarely see, reads like the *Critique of Practical Reason* put into excruciating verse by some Erasmus Darwin of the day. But it is, if not refreshingly different, at least different from *A Little Anthology of Contemporary Poetry,* half the poets of which are for any reasonable purposes indistinguishable (even their friends have nicknamed them Comme Ci, Comme Ça). Hugh Chisholm reads like the complete files of *New Verse;* Mr. Brinnin is a competent, faintly American version of this fashion; and Mr. Kees, in spite of some good touches, is lost there too. Miss Young has a couple of interesting, awkwardly written poems; Miss Miles is manner—a clever one— carried to the point where the returns almost stop coming in at all. Mr. Ford is nice words and words and words. Nicholas Moore is Thomas-and-water. John Berryman's "Five Political Poems" have lots of Yeats, lots of general politics, a *1939* reissue of *1938,* and a parody of "Lord Randall" that—but nothing can make me believe that Mr. Berryman wrote this himself, and is not just shielding someone. There is an unpublished section of *The Ghost in the Underblows;* it is exactly like the published sections. For all I can remember of either (I've read both), it *is* one of the published sections. Mr. Fisher is like the gold in sea water: valuable, but in impracticable concentrations. Poetry seems hardly congenial to Mr. Hivnor and Mr. Hays; with Mr. Kaufman congeniality reaches absolute zero. Mr. Laughlin's "What the Pencil Writes" is a modest, appealing appraisal. Paul Wren seems unformed, inexperienced, but rather promising. F. T. Prince is represented by five monologues of a Zulu chief; their style is consistent, delicate, fairly original, distinguished by some charmingly innocent alliteration and some surprisingly awkward rhythms; and how can one resist a writer who makes a chief say that he has "called my regiments Decoys, / Slashes, Gluttons, or else Bees / Ambushes, Mountains, the Blue Haze"? Rider Haggard was never like this.

I don't know what to say about all the Russian poems. The translations seem reasonably bad; most of the poems are crude but alive, the productions of a culture that still takes poetry for granted, as a necessity. The critical essays are fairly interesting as information. I was charmed by a quotation about a hero who "stepped out of his little tent, / He washed his fair face / With spring water cold, / His face he wiped with a little towel. / As he played on his birch-bark horn, / The whole people heard him." Guess who? Lenin.

New Directions is a reviewer's nightmare; it's enough punishment to read it all, without writing about it too. It is a queer mediocre hodge-podge in which a few nice and a good many awful things are smothered. Le Petit Chose, in my high school, was always insisting that everything have a *raison d'être; New Directions* doesn't—or rather, it has one that was dead and unburied ten years ago, like Hoover. Now-adays, seeing people being conscientiously experimental together has the brown period smell of the Masonic ceremonies in *War and Peace;* even Mr. Laughlin and the few Constant Experimenters know that something has happened to experiment—so *New Directions,* especially the experimental sections, gets more conventional every year. (In such matters, it is the first step that counts.) What use is it now, anyway? Maybe Mr. Laughlin could make a magazine out of it; seeing 200 pages four times a year, instead of 800 once, might be bearable quantitatively. Qualitatively I don't know. I sit here with it; it weighs down my lap, it makes my head ache. Think who writes it, who prints it, what it is: what a symbol! Yes, nature is witty.

The Development of Yeats's
Sense of Reality

THE SOUTHERN REVIEW, WINTER 1942

I HAVE MET many people whose idea of Yeats is this: Yeats, when young, was a bad romantic poet with all sorts of queer supernatural ideas; when he grew older his ideas became even queerer, but his poetry—God knows how—was miraculously transformed. (Many others think him a good romantic poet who somehow—God knows why—degenerated into a writer of queer, violent, obscure, almost-modernist verse.) Certainly the change was great enough to seem miraculous; but why did the miracle happen to Yeats, and not to the rest of the bad romantic poets? And how did it happen? To guess that, one has to remember how Yeats lived and what he thought; and one has to know the first before one can even begin to understand the second—because Yeats was not an objective thinker at all, but had to a mouth-opening degree the philosopher's or mystic's ability to distort some facts and leave out the rest, to make the universe conform to a private system at any cost. With Yeats it was not so much a question of what was there as it was a question of what, to satisfy his whole being, it was necessary for him to find there. His life was one long struggle with reality. At first he won a temporary equivocal victory by neglecting or ignoring it; then reality had its revenge, and forced itself into his life and poetry in spite of everything he could do; but finally he managed, in the strangest way possible, a complete triumph over reality. (In his life and poetry, I mean; where his thought is concerned, there is no doubt which had the victory.) But in making this division between Yeats and reality, I have of course been cheating: if his victory was a triumph over one reality, it was at the same time the triumph of another reality, his own nature; and it was accomplished not by rejection but by acceptance. The whole play is a comedy because it has a happy ending; but the triumph was real. Yeats saved his poetry and himself, was—if any poet in our time was—a success. It will seem disrespectful, but I cannot resist giving him Blake's proverb: "If a fool would persist in his folly, he would become wise." And Yeats became, if not wise, at least a great poet: so that his last poems and letters and sayings, no matter how biased or silly or incredible, are full of an overwhelming sense of life, of vigor, of justification—and he can remind one, at the last, of that other foolish fond old man who clenched his fist at the lightning, who on his deathbed learned to multiply.

In this essay I am going to neglect Yeats's poetry—which seems to me far and away the best of our time—in order to give a sketch of what he did and thought during the first half of his life; because if we understand that, the change in Yeats's poetry will lose its blank miraculous look, and will seem instead a fulfillment, the expression of his own experience, his own desires, his own essential being.

It is hard to make oneself remember how old Yeats was—he was born in 1865; how old-fashioned, pre-industrial, almost anachronistic his first surroundings were—he spent most of his early childhood in Sligo, a small port on the west coast of Ireland. Compared with London, Sligo was another world, an island precariously surviving, still relatively intact, in the midst of the new world that commerce, industry, and science had built up around it. (For example, Yeats's family, like a medieval one, still ate only two meals a day.) Compared with England, Ireland was another such island, an exploited colony, deliberately condemned to an agricultural non-industrial economy, its people sellers of food and raw materials, buyers of consumers' goods, payers of rent. Anyone who has read Yeats's wonderful *Autobiography* will remember his Sligo—shabby, shadowed, half country and half sea, full of confused romance, superstition, poverty, eccentricity, unrecognized anachronism, passion and ignorance and the little boy's misery. Yeats was treated well and was bitterly unhappy; he prayed that he would die, and used often to say to himself: "When you are grown up, never talk as grown-up people do of the happiness of childhood." Part of this unhappiness came from his fear of his grandfather, an old sea captain, a man of legendary passion and silence and violence, of ignorant and helpless strength, so feared and so admired that bonfires would be lighted along the railway line to celebrate his return. The little boy confused him with God; "I often wonder," Yeats wrote when old, "if the delight in passionate men in my plays and in my poetry is more than his memory." Another part of Yeats's unhappiness came from his loneliness; but most of it, so far as Yeats could remember, was without any cause at all. "I have grown happier with every year of life as though gradually conquering something within myself, for certainly

my miseries were not made by others but were a part of my own mind."
Remembering the completeness of that conquest, the old Yeats's deliberate actual joy, one can say that his final happiness was also his own
doing, a part of his own mind.

Yeats's early world was different from ours in other ways. He saw
supernatural birds in the rooms; once he screamed in his sleep, and
described the wreck of a steamer with his grandfather on board. There
were the ghosts of smugglers, the death coach, a relative with second
sight, a buried treasure guarded by "a spirit that looked like a flatiron."
Worrying about the voice of conscience, the little boy heard a voice in
his head which always, after that, spoke to him in moments of crisis;
the voice commenced by saying, "What a tease you are!" (I can't
think of any comment good enough for this remark.) "All the well-
known families had their grotesque or tragic or romantic legends";
even the servants' stories were full of tradition, superstition, violence,
arbitrary eccentricity, romance. It was an aristocratic traditional society,
contemptuous of commerce, oblivious of industry or science; Yeats
was surrounded with family anecdotes, portraits, and relics.

When Yeats was eight or nine an aunt said to him: "You are
going to London. Here you are somebody. There you will be no one at
all." It was true. There in England he and his sister told each other,
almost in tears, how they longed for Sligo and hated London; he wanted
even a piece of Sligo earth to hold in his hand; his mother talked always
of Sligo, and "it was assumed between her and us that Sligo was more
beautiful than other places." He went to a cheap school, was jeered at
for being Irish, a painter's son, was beaten in constant fights with the
English boys; as he walked home from school he would tell himself
that whatever he cared for most had been taken away from him. He
was a foreigner among foreigners. Everyone at home had always despised the slow ignorant English; now, afraid of the boys who fought
with him and beat him, he doubted himself for the first time, and tried
to find reassurance in daydreams of his own courage, in the one poor
athletic ability he had, in his pride in his own cleverness—although,
idle, slowly learning disliked things, he was always near the bottom of
his classes. "When I was ten or twelve years old and in London, I would
remember Sligo with tears, and when I began to write, it was there I
hoped to find my audience."

So from the time Yeats was eight his world was split in two; into
the real and detestable world of London, where he was imprisoned and
miserable; and into the ideal world of Sligo, that he longed for all

year, revisited every summer. One was the world of trade and industry and science, of smoke and streets and school, of the coarse dull English; the other world was all that he loved and remembered, the world of myth and superstition and romance, his own country. Many of the romantic poets have been full of nostalgia for the wonderful country of childhood, the remembered fantastic antithesis of the grown-up world they are miserable in; few of them have had Yeats's justification, this situation that made any other response almost impossible. Yeats had no illusion about the condition of childhood: "I remember little of childhood but its pain," he wrote; he was homesick for a real country that love and remembrance exaggerated into romance.

I have made so much of this division because it persists through Yeats's whole life. When Yeats grew a little older, it was there to serve as a foundation for his poetry and philosophy and politics, his whole thought; and, almost unrecognizably expanded and distorted, this antithesis of two worlds, the world of the past and the world of the present, persists through the last page he ever wrote. One might almost say that his whole life represents an attempt to reconcile these worlds; to learn, not so much to understand as to bear, the historical necessity that was replacing the one he loved with the one he despised. And since that necessity was really unbearable to him, he began, as so many others have, by refusing to believe it: by altogether accepting one world, altogether rejecting the other.

Yeats's family moved to Dublin when he was fifteen. He was bewildered and bored with school, and learned so little he had always to read the classics in translation. What he cared for was, astonishingly, natural history; he collected specimens, read Darwin and Huxley, and vexed a pious geologist with his arguments. He would spend most of his nights outdoors or in caves; and losing interest in the natural history he had learned so little of, he began instead to pretend to be a sage, magician, or poet—Manfred, Athanase, Alastor. He thought constantly about poetry, enormously influenced by what his father read and admired; his father hated any abstraction, generalization, rhetoric, and cared only for passion or revery, the dramatic idealization of real speech. Yeats wrote fantastic incoherent plays, imitating Shelley or Spenser in unscannable verse. He kept on with his queer abstract unobservant love of nature; planned to live alone on a little island, Innisfree; sailed out to find what sea birds stirred before dawn—he had a conscious passion for the dawn, the cold windy light and tumbling clouds that, as a child, he had always associated with God.

Yeats was living, as always, in the midst of more supernatural occurrences, anecdotes, and legends than I can begin to tell. This supernatural world was already as real and obvious to him as the city world of business and science—though he was still embarrassed and willing to make a joke of it if pressed. To the native Irish superstitions, the country miracles, he soon joined "psychical research and mystical philosophy"; he became a member of the Theosophical Society, studied Odic Force and esoteric Buddhism, made experiments that ended in the showers of supernatural occurrences that always rewarded or afflicted him. It is impossible to overrate the influence of all this on Yeats; it kept up his entire life, in one form or another. His world view, like it or not, was entirely supernatural, magical, anti-scientific; when in his last period he became "philosophical," he was philosophical about in the sense that Paracelsus was scientific—his whole philosophical system was dictated to him by spirits who used his wife as a medium. Our ordinary views grew to seem to him a kind of weird conspiracy of silence, the compulsive ignorance of a hypnotized subject: "How trust historian and scholar that have for three hundred years ignored . . . so momentous a part of human experience? Was modern civilization a conspiracy of the subconscious . . . had some seminal illusion been imposed upon us by beings greater than ourselves for an unknown purpose?" The young Yeats hoped to make an authoritative religion out of—what the great poets have said; and for many years his main dream was to set up a monastic society on a fake Gothic castle in the middle of a lake. (He tells of a literary society that ceased to meet because the girls got the giggles whenever anyone made a speech. I must confess that some of the time I too get the giggles.) He defined truth as "the dramatically appropriate utterance of the highest man"; this was too much for his father, an admirer of John Stuart Mill. They quarreled bitterly about science, which Yeats had grown to hate "with a monkish hate." He went to art school and drew casts absent-mindedly, longing for "pattern, for pre-Raphaelitism, for an art allied to poetry." His father's London friends were pre-Raphaelite painters who had "lost their confidence"; Yeats wanted them all to return to their old ways. Yeats tells about his own vanity, pretension, and childishness, his sense of exclusion from the bourgeois families of the Dublin suburb—who laughed at him, whose children called when he passed, thin and thoughtful, "Oh, here is King Death again." He was "as prudish as a girl"; he fell in love with a girl already engaged, wrote her poems and was miserable, and established the pattern of unrequited love that he was to follow for so long. A timid gregarious man who loved "proud lonely things," he began his long struggle to set up a mask or pose, to become his own opposite; and he would make political speeches in public, hoping in vain to become self-possessed.

Yeats became a disciple of John O'Leary, the Fenian, a man of so much "moral genius" that he seemed to Yeats somebody out of Plutarch; he and, a little later, Maude Gonne, informed Yeats with their own political zeal. "From these debates, from O'Leary's conversation, from the Irish books he lent or gave me, has come all I have set my hand to since," Yeats later wrote. He believed that it would be possible to join Catholic and Protestant Ireland by means of a great national literature. And, moved by bad patriotic Irish poetry, he decided that all poetry needs is personal utterance, passionate sincerity—by avoiding rhetoric and abstraction, à la Verlaine, he could make his poetry "not a matter of literature at all"; it would be "pure," the direct representation of his life. He did not realize that life is nothing but impurities. The formula did not work; in his writing there was, as he understood later, "little but romantic convention."

When Yeats was twenty-two his family moved back to London; so he kept on, not with politics, but with pre-Raphaelitism and mysticism. He loved everything that was the opposite of the world he lived in—the world he summed up in that often-repeated group of hated names: "Huxley, Tyndall, Carolus Duran, Bastien-Lepage." The names stand for science, naturalism, mechanization, specialization, and a thousand other things. He tried to make for himself, out of scraps of poetry and mysticism and emotion, out of anything that felt old to the hand, a religion, a church, dogma; and he was willing to go anywhere for his materials—to cabalistic societies, to groups of alchemists, to Madame Blavatsky.

Henley and Wilde, Yeats's friends, did not influence him; but Morris did. Morris's medievalism, Morris himself enchanted Yeats, and he became for a while—imagine!—a socialist. But a Marxist workman's continual arguments got on his nerves; not one of the socialists was religious enough to suit him; and he finally burst out that "there must be a change of heart and only religion could make it." So he quarreled with them and left for good; but kept hoping, nevertheless, for some "near sudden change."

A little later Yeats and a friend started the Rhymers' Club, where Johnson, Dowson, and most of the *fin de siècle* poets met and talked. Yeats did all the generalizing; his passion for philosophy and abstraction (so carefully excluded from his verse) was alien and disquieting to the rest, late romantics united in an instinctive opposition to all generalizations. Yeats writes: "I was full of thought, often very abstract thought, longing all the while to be full of images, because I had gone to an art school instead of a university"; and he reflects, ruefully or proudly, "Le Gallienne and Davidson, and even Symons, were provincial in their setting out, but their provincialism was curable, mine incurable." (Certainly this provincialism did as much as anything else to save him.) Yeats, reacting against Tennyson and Browning and Swinburne, believed that they had filled their work with "impurities," that he and his friends "must create once more the pure work." So poor Yeats tried to give up whatever made him generalize; and, full of remorse and shame, used "to pray that my imagination might somehow be delivered from abstraction." Naturally his poetry, so rigorously partial, willed to exclude an essential powerful part of his being, was weak and shallow—had, as Yeats later understood, "an element of sentimentality." He created "pure" work, what those art-for-art's-sake times desired; but it was precisely the impurities that his poetry needed. He was using a point of view and technique appropriate enough for Dowson or Symons or Verlaine, those late-romantic late-capitalist individualists; but it was all wrong for Yeats. It was impossible to write anything resembling folk poetry or political poetry in such a style; and Yeats was collecting Irish folk stories, thinking constantly about Ireland—he believed that he could create a national half-anonymous folk art, a "sensuous musical vocabulary" that future generations could use. But Yeats had borrowed his whole machinery and technique from the adulterated and decadent romanticism of an industrialized society; and, no matter how hard he tried to produce his folkish art, he "did something entirely different." What could have been more specialized than this "pure" poetry he was writing? Yet Yeats detested specialization, felt that the modern world was only a bundle of fragments, and longed for its return to the "Unity of Beings" of the Middle Ages. Europe had once "shared one mind and heart"; and now, like Miss Beauchamp or the traveler Lawrence tells of, it had split to pieces, to specialized abstractions. Even character seemed abstraction to Yeats, and he avoided it in his own plays, disliked it in Shakespeare—whom he preferred to Chaucer unwillingly and resentfully. Yeats thought that he could reverse the whole process of history, take the world which had split to pieces and unify it again; or do that at least to Irish life—or at least to Irish poetry—or at least to one man's life and poetry, his own.

But Yeats was working hard at all his queerly assorted projects. As it had been, as it continued to be, his life was packed with mysticism, spiritualism, magic—with all sorts of esoteric supernatural studies and experiments; the more-than-surrealist flavor of his world may be suggested by a casual sentence: "I am sitting in a Café with two French Americans, the German poet Douchenday, and a silent man whom I discover to be Strindberg, and who is looking for the Philosopher's Stone." Meanwhile he was engaged in the unending, always difficult political work with O'Leary and Maude Gonne; he had founded the National Literary Society, at a time when "no educated man bought an Irish book," and had begun to argue, to make speeches, to write for newspapers, to hold meetings and collect money, to do all the things that made him enemies, that divorced him from his natural surroundings and friends, that used up his time and strength, and that seemed to end only in his complete defeat. (How important that work was for Irish literature no one needs to say now; it may have been, in the end, just as important for Yeats's poetry.)

If you look at the poems Yeats was writing in the first year or two of this century, you are surprised at how much they resemble the poems he was writing fifteen years before, at how little he had managed to improve; even the improvement had been, largely, technical improvement, growth inside the narrow limits his poetry had originally confined itself to. The lyrics are thin, pale tapestries of a sentimental and romantic past—at first Indian, later Irish, but always completely unreal. The poetry is intolerably pure; the qualities that make Yeats's later poems notable are exactly what these lack. The most common subject of the poems is a passive, Platonic, and hopelessly unrequited love. They are an odd combination of pre-Raphaelite and *fin de siècle* poetry—the pre-Raphaelite corpse possessed by the decadent spirit: they represent a culminating point of one kind of romanticism, so much so that the worst of them are their own most effective parodies. A list of the words Yeats used most frequently will show exactly what kind of poetry he was writing. His early poetry is full of the following words (and of words derived from them or related to them): *dream, rose, heart, lonely, wandering, gentle, sorrow, sweet, mournful, holy, tender, quiet, faery, Druid, beauty, peace, lofty, high, pitiful, wan, murmur, worn, grief, tears, weary, sigh, old, desolate, piteous, faint, dreaming, foam, flame, fade, woven, tremble, shadowy, grey, dim, white, pale* (*curd-pale, cloud-pale, honey-pale, pearl-pale, death-pale*). The meter and construction match the words; the limp wan rhythms, the enormous quantities of adjectives and intransitive verbs, are exactly what one would expect. (I always think with affection of the poem in which a woman expresses her hatred of a rival by saying: "And may some dreadful ill befall her quick!")

The reader may want to compare with these the words that occur most frequently in Yeats's late poetry: *foul, passionate, ignorant, ignorance, malicious, abstract, crazy, lunatic, mad, bitter, famous, frenzy, frenzied, violent, violence, fantasy, rage, daemonic, horrible, furious, bloody, triumphant, insolent, arrogant, arrogance, mock, mockery, murderous, bone, blood, stone, malice, sensual, fanatic, intellect, shriek, rascal, knave, rogue, fool, gyres, miraculous, cold, indifferent, raddled, blind, wild, naked, dumb, rag, ragged, tumult, joy, death, hate, night, wine, ditch, mummy, barren, murderous, torn, terrible, great, brilliant, fabulous, drunken, mire.* The words are full of violence, of toughness and strength; some have a rhetorical magnificence, others a sensual colloquial sharpness. This list is the antithesis of the other; one needs only to read the two to realize how completely Yeats's poetry changed.

Just then there were several reasons for a change. He had carried these particular romantic tendencies to a limit and exhausted them; he began constantly writing for the theater, and soon saw the necessity for a language that would be balder and more dramatic, more like speech; and, most important of all, the dreams that made up his life were going to pieces, and his poetry changed with their ruin. He had loved and worked for several things, and only one of them (mysticism, supernaturalism) remained whole. Another one was Irish independence, which he had worked hardest at during the last years of the century, traveling all over England and Scotland, taking pride in evenings spent with "some small organizer into whose spittoon I secretly poured my third glass of whiskey," enduring "some of the worst months of my life," always hoping to become what he was not and could never be. All this was mixed with, partly caused by, the "miserable love affair" that was for a great many years the most important thing in his life; he was in love with a revolutionary agitator who cared for nothing but Irish independence—he once said ruefully that his devotion "might as well have been offered to an image in a milliner's window, or a statue in a museum." Both his private life and his political life, from year to year, grew more and more hopeless; and Yeats began slowly to realize that his other great desire—bringing himself, his country, and its literature back to the "Unity of Culture" of the Middle Ages—was hopeless too. For years the chief subject of his lyrics was his despair at seeing what was happening to himself and his love, his disillusionment with the politics he had wasted himself on. He became full of bitter resentment at the revolutionary politics that made it impossible for his love to be anything but miserable and hopeless; that seemed to him to be transforming the woman he loved into a fanatic; that separated him both from his natural work and his natural surroundings. Years later he could write angrily that he had always forsaken poetry for anything: "One time it was a woman's face, or worse— / The seeming needs of my fool-driven land." Still later he wrote that he had seen "the loveliest woman born" ruin herself "for an old bellows full of angry wind"; the woman ruined by fanaticism became one of his obsessions.

It was all this, and what happened because of it, that began to put reality into Yeats's poetry. Yeats had identified Irish politics with his own interests and desires: his own love affair, his own hope for the restoration of an aristocratic, legendary, theological, folkish state like those he calls the "pure" Asiatic cultures. All his life his one overwhelming desire was for the defeat of science and industrialism, the return of the world to the old order of things—and everything he ever cared about, from politics to spiritualism, he managed to join to this desire. Until the time we have come to—when Yeats was almost forty—he believed that he and people like him could *make* the world change, "reverse the cinematograph" of history. (But he made his poetry represent, not the struggle to get the world he wanted, but a vague, wistful, and sentimental propaganda picture of an unreal universe; he made a romantic Utopia out of a legendary past.) Now Yeats began to realize that it was impossible to make all this happen—that it was impossible, really, to make any of it happen: he saw the Ireland he wanted, the world he wanted, the woman he wanted, moving farther and farther away—and he saw, too, that his work and misery had been useless, that all these things had from the beginning been beyond his reach. Reality had crushed Yeats's picture of it, his plans for it; the real world—and the real Yeats who lived in that world—began to force their way into the poetry that had for so long been innocent of either.

I have treated the first half of Yeats's life in some detail; now I have no more space for events, and will end with a summary account of the last great changes in his poetry. During his middle period Lady Gregory particularly influenced his poetry, getting him to write for the theater, making him collect folk stories and poetry, helping give him a real world—the remains of the aristocratic folkish Ireland of the past—to substitute for the romanticized Morris-world of the early poetry, lending him money so that he could write, seeing that he actually did write. A good deal of this poetry is doubtful, searching, gloomy; Yeats hopes, now the "lying blossoms" are falling, to "wither into truth"; and the poetry, compared with the old, is full of "impurities," logic, wit, the troubling present. One can say, phrasing it to be a joke, that this was Yeats's "liberal" period: under the perplexed doubtful strength he had gained, the difficulties and contradictions of his own life and thought were always waiting; and he often fell into a queer passive negative despair, wishing to be "colder and deafer and dumber than a fish," to be—"for no knowledge is worth a straw— / Ignorant and wanton as the dawn." This cold ignorance, a catatonia like death, seemed to him his only escape from the Chinese puzzle box of dilemmas that his life had become. Many of his poems were bitter or nostalgic reminiscences of his dying love; more things than that were dying in him, and he wrote, in a gloomy projection: "Romantic Ireland's dead and gone." In 1916, grieved and perplexed, he could give only a reluctant aesthetic assent to the deaths at the Post Office: "Was it needless death after all? / For England may keep faith . . . What if excess of love / Bewildered them till they died?" This from the man who had worked beside Maude Gonne, from the man who, older, wrote out of his cult of violence: "When all words are said / And a man is fighting mad, / Something drops from eyes long blind, / He completes his partial mind . . ." When asked to write a war poem, he replied that a poet should be silent in times like these, having no gift for such matters; that "he has had enough of meddling who can please / A young girl in the indolence of her youth / Or an old man upon a winter's night." This was the man who a few years later wrote "Meditations in Time of Civil War" and "1919." During these years Yeats was more realistic, prosaic, and sensible than he had ever been before or managed to be after. He had become a good poet; after a little, by an extraordinary reversal, he was to become a great one.

The source of the change was that one thing that had never failed him, that had grown more important during his whole life—mysticism, supernaturalism; and the change came about, appropriately, through a woman, his wife. Certain spirits, by means of the automatic writing and, later, the mediumistic trances of Yeats's wife, gave Yeats an elaborate system of mystical philosophy, that seemed to offer a schematized, highly comprehensive understanding of world history, of character, of almost every phase of human (or superhuman) experience. This system for the first time made it possible for Yeats to accept the modern world—as one phase of an inexorable historical cycle; the present he hated became only a necessary step toward the return of the past he loved, the scientific materialistic thought of our time became only a childish superficial understanding of one limited aspect of a great supernatural reality. Yeats had first tried to *make* the world change, to persuade it to go back to the society he wanted; then for some gloomy years he realized that it was impossible to change it, that the world he wanted was gone for good; but finally he found the one way out—he discovered a philosophical and historical system by which history itself, the universe itself, *made* the present change into the past. Now, instead of rejecting or escaping from the modern world, the process of history; instead of accepting it under compulsion, full of doubt and hatred; he could fully accept it, urge it violently on. History, politics, the modern world became enormously meaningful for Yeats, became material that he could accept and use as finally important. And it was in this way that Yeats escaped from the greatest weakness of modernist poetry, the modernist poet's highly specialized relationship to contemporary life: his rejection of the present, his inability to write about the life of his own times (which is, in the end, his only material) as anything but a special case, an aberration, a degeneration. Yeats's version of Aristotle is: *History is more philosophical than drama, more dramatic too;* he had what can literally be called a tragic view of life, since all history became for him a drama on a tremendous scale, a meaningful tragedy worked out by great supernatural powers, where spectators and actors live each other's death, die each other's life, and laugh out in tragic joy. When people who admire Yeats's poetry ridicule or deplore his "crazy system," they do not realize that it was the system which enabled him to produce the poetry. Consider what would have happened to Yeats if he had had to accept the ordinary scientific, liberal, "sensible" views of our times: views that contradicted his own experience (all the supernatural experience that he valued most), his own desires, his own essential being.

We are always complaining that the men of our time cannot unify, take any view of the whole of things: Yeats (by what seem to us fantastic distortions and omissions) managed to get a system that *was* his view of the whole of things, that enabled him to say all that he had to say about himself and his world. And he said it with an organized violent intensity (*formal violence* is the best short description of his late poetry) that reminds us that in our times the best, the most sensible, minds *have* lacked conviction—and organization too—the worst *have* been full of passionate intensity. And Yeats's extraordinary system got for him, sometimes, extraordinary insights valid for everyone else as well. However wrong that system is for you and me, it was magnificently right for Yeats: it made his last poetry the fulfillment of his whole life, it made him write about our times as no other poet has.

At first Yeats was overwhelmed with the system that came to

him through his wife's trances, and he offered to give up poetry and spend his whole life working out that system; the spirits answered (to appreciate the superb wit of their reply you must remember that Yeats believed them to an extent dramatic projections of his own desire and thought): "No, we have come to bring you metaphors for poetry." They brought more than metaphors—they brought him the whole possibility of the poetry that he was to write. We can understand his whole system best if we remember what he answered when he was asked if he believed in the actual existence of the fixed historical cycles of his system. He replied: "They have helped me to hold in a single thought reality and justice."

The Fall of the City

THE SEWANEE REVIEW, SPRING 1943

*This article was written some time ago, about a play that was written
six years ago; it is a criticism of the 1937 MacLeish who wrote* The Fall
of the City, *not of the 1942 MacLeish who writes government reports.*

ANY successful play in verse—in a time when the phrase sounds like
an Irish bull—is worth an analysis; and *The Fall of the City* has
been extraordinarily successful. Almost anyone with a radio has heard
it, almost anyone with an anthology has read it; even the college text-
books print it, with prefaces calling it a really topical play, one that has
both comprehended and predicted the actual history of our times.
"Pioneering in a new medium, the verse play for radio, MacLeish fore-
told the fate of Vienna by eleven months," one editor writes; "Prague,
Warsaw, Oslo, Amsterdam, Paris—the play was repeated with tragic
variations." But if this is so, *The Fall of the City* is exactly what everyone has been wanting—a good poetic drama about contemporary reality;
Poetry and Drama and Society, miserably separated for so many ages,
have at last been reunited. How has it been done?

The play begins with the "orotund and professional" voice of the
Studio Director. After the conventional "Ladies and gentlemen: / This
broadcast comes to you from the city," he rises for a moment into
orotund and professional verse, in a passage full of the abstract, glossy,
and geographical lyricism that is a MacLeish trademark. He gets back
to business with, "For three days the world has watched this city";
through the newspapers and through broadcasts like this one, the audience assumes. Each day, at twelve o'clock, a dead woman has risen from
the grave! MacLeish's exclamation point notes how unusual such an
event is; that such an event is being broadcast is still more unusual, most
hearers will think. It is very easy to believe in broadcasting, fairly easy
to believe in dead women rising daily from the grave; but to believe in
both at the same time takes the Red Queen. The hearers cannot help
distrusting the Studio Director when he tells them, in a conventional
Shakespearean passage about omens, that "in a time like ours seemings

and portents signify"; that this old-fashioned miracle is a finally important expression of our time, and not merely an expression of the author's liking for a sensational dramatic device.

The announcer takes us away to the city, at "precisely four minutes to twelve," in order to broadcast the fourth resurrection of the dead woman. (Where was he the second and third times? By the fourth time any real broadcasting company would have made it a regular program with a sponsor.) It is a city more suited to miracles than to microphones: a kind of generalized Aztec town, far away in space, farther away in time; there are temples, pyramids, hawks, kites, water sellers, peasants, horse raisers, cattle herders, priests with knives (stone, I regret to say). The announcer, a country boy from way back, is much impressed with the "enormous crowd" of ten thousand people; in their midst, surrounded with plumed fans, sit the "cabinet ministers"! One can see already that the play is a queer and sometimes unfortunate mixture, a kind of allegory: it exists on two levels, one a literal Aztec level, the other an allegorical topical level. These levels, by their conflict, produce all sorts of surface incongruities and anachronisms; and perhaps, under the surface, they never fuse, but remain contradictory—the reader can judge.

The announcer's description of the exotic city rises into suspense; it is almost noon. The dead woman punctually, miraculously rises; she recites a mannered, consciously archaic, conscientiously vague lyric about death. Then after mechanically repeating a prophecy she does not understand, she trails away in a few elegiac measures. Her prophecy is: "The city of masterless men / Will take a master. / There will be shouting then / Blood after."

To see all the laws of nature broken, four times running, because a small Aztec city is about to be conquered, may very well seem disproportionate to a modern audience. Shakespeare has these miraculous omens because he and his hearers were sure that the world is made that way, that such things always happen; since we are just as sure of the opposite, a contemporary playwright needs an overwhelmingly good reason for using such miracles, especially if his play is an allegorical representation of modern history. MacLeish has none; he simply wants a sensational exotic device to make his play more impressive, and he feels that the play's sensational and exotic setting, along with the announcer's continual reassurances, will soothe us into belief.

The announcer, still afraid that we may still be doubting, makes another Shakespearean speech on the validity of omens; meanwhile the people, after reiterating fragments of the prophecy, suddenly go to pieces, and run yelling around the square, "milling around us like cattle that smell death." Before this MacLeish has made the crowd seem very tough and stolid, full of peasants, farmers' wives, armed horse raisers and cattle herders who "look at the girls with their eyes hard / And a hard grin and their teeth showing." Why do they suddenly act like a Girl Scout troop with hysterics? like frightened animals? Because Mac-Leish makes them act that way throughout the play, no matter what the situation; they are without sense, courage, or any other creditable quality; they respond to everything like complete fools and cowards, are several times compared to animals, and remind you of nothing so much as Hamilton's "great beast."

Suddenly the First Messenger staggers in; helped over to the cabinet ministers, he gives a couple of perfunctory ritual pants, and speaks—not a few gasping sentences, but an energetic and rhetorical two pages. He has run day and night, all the way from the ocean (presumably he was on bad terms with the broadcasting company). The bouncy two-stress lines, like unrhymed Skeltonics; the Anglo-Saxon alliteration ("He was violent in his vessel: / He was steering in her stern: / He was watching in her waist: / He was peering in her prow . . ."); the mannered archaic parallelism; the primitive syntax ("East over sea-cross has / All taken / Every country . . ."); make one think of Hengist and Horsa carrying a message to Garcia, and lend the messenger a charming but slightly Mother Goose-ish air; his method is one of simple exaggeration. He warns that a mighty conqueror has landed, after overcoming all the lands east of the sea. Those he conquers lead lives of unbelievable shame and degradation; nevertheless, says the messenger, many or all of you will welcome him. Why? The messenger doesn't say. We know all about Fascism, so we are prepared to believe that some of the people will welcome him; but dramatically, in terms of the play, not of its topical application, the welcome is quite unmotivated—we have to assume, as MacLeish does, that the people of the city have some sort of tropism toward slavery and degradation.

How do the people take this additional bad news? with additional hysterics? Their response is exactly the opposite: not one speaks, not one moves; they stand there like docile animals, patiently waiting for the ministers to tell them what to do and what to think. A minister comes from the "huddle" (notice the weight of this word) on the plat-form; and this First Orator makes a long, highly rhetorical speech. (There is no dialogue in the whole play—nothing but long speeches, songs, the announcer's descriptions, and choppy phrases from the crowd.) His oration is full of vulgar and specious effectiveness, inflated generalities, plays on words, childish logic-chopping, mechanical and repetitive antitheses and analogies. MacLeish wants the speech to sound entirely false and unsympathetic to his own audience; it does; but he makes most of it so obviously pompous and empty that the crowd in the square could not have been fooled by it either. MacLeish, out to discredit the Orator and his position, the crowd and its response, has none of the objectivity or breath of sympathy of the true dramatist, and consequently gives the Orator none of the genuinely effective things he might have said. The people are, of course, entirely won over by the speech; forgetting the Dead Woman and the Conqueror, they shout with joy, sit down and eat their lunches (wrapped in corn shucks), play on flutes—the children and old men begin to dance. What could the Orator have said to reassure them so completely? to make them act like complacent fools?

He has made them a speech about pacifism, about passive resistance. These Aztecs, with their spears and bows, their human sacrifices, their generals in feather mantles, absolutely eat up a speech that would embarrass the most confirmed pacifist. This is false on the literal Aztec level of the play, quite as false on its allegorical topical level: when countries have been threatened by Fascist conquerors, their governments have *not* made empty pacifist appeals—it would not have worked either with their own people or with the Fascists. This minister is made a wordy demagogue, Hitler's idea of a parliamentary orator. The first half of his speech consists of inflated variations on *They that take the sword shall perish by the sword.* Then he asserts that doing nothing will conquer the conqueror; that the *snickers* of *road-menders*, the *titters* of *laundresses,* the *coarse guffaws* of *chambermaids* will make the conqueror "sweat in his uniform foolishly. / He will disappear: no one hear of him!" He says that "scorn conquers," mentions reason and truth, and concludes with a thoroughly disgraceful and thoroughly unlikely peroration: "Words . . . win!"

MacLeish shows contempt for the Orator even more drastically by having the announcer, at the climax of the speech, break in with a FitzPatrick Traveltalk description of the scene. This immense discourtesy (it would be as plausible for an announcer to interrupt one of Roosevelt's speeches with a description of Washington) shows the audience, as forcibly as a blow, that the minister is not even worth listening to; that his empty talk is less important than a travelogue's local color. And the empty romantic exoticism of the description shows the critic, just as forcibly, how completely MacLeish has managed to dodge the whole problem of representing contemporary reality; how much he values these gaudy properties for their own sake.

The people's little fair is broken up by the arrival of the Second Messenger, as panting, exhausted, and long-winded as the first. "Stand by: we're edging in," says the announcer, reminding his hearers as sharply as possible, with the cliché, of the incongruity between the radio and this horseless (and, presumably, signal-drum-less and signal-fire-less) culture of the Messenger. The conqueror is coming fast, warns the Messenger; "No man opposing him / Still grows his glory." It seems that the Conqueror has a straw man, a bloody and hateful figure of horror, whom he sets up and fights with "at every road-corner"; and the alien people everywhere, overwhelmed by his prowess, bring him flowers and gold, sing songs to him, hold his hands and feel his thighs, worship him and are conquered. (This odd method of conquest is quite incomprehensible on the literal Aztec level of the play—the reader can make sense of it only if he knows that it represents the Fascist use of anti-Semitism.) This great conqueror is already crossing the mountains.

There is another complete shift in the people's behavior; "frantic with anger and plain fear," they behave like vindictive lunatics. "The mob . . . crazy with terror" is "boiling around us like mullet that smell shark." (Before, they "milled like cattle.") "Down with the government!" they shout. *"Down with liberal learned minds!"* (For pure bathos, for inexcusable incongruity and anachronism, this italicized phrase is hard to beat.) Unless the people are completely inconsistent fools, sure to respond in the worst way to anything, this response to the Second Messenger—fifteen minutes after an exactly opposite response to the First Messenger—is impossible.

The priests interrupt with the second panacea, religion. They are made to seem emotional obscurantists, pure escapists; their arguments are specious and hackneyed; nevertheless, the people immediately fall for them, for the second time forgetting all about the Dead Woman and the Conqueror. The announcer, whom MacLeish makes gullible as a stage Watson, has helped discredit the minister's speech by his vacuous acceptance of it; he receives the priests' speeches with the same enthusiasm, describing the people's response in approving clichés that would, as Wilde puts it, compromise a locomotive. The priests, with drums and songs, promptly move the people to frenzy; the crowd dances to the pyramid, tears the clothes from a girl's "bare breast," drags her to the altar, and "shrieks" (notice how the orgiastic *shrieks* influences us against the crowd) in ecstasy. All this is unlikely enough on the literal level of the play—the Aztec priests who cut the hearts from tens of thousands of prisoners are not likely to advise submission to an alien conqueror, a withdrawal from the world of action. On the topical allegorical level of the play this is senseless: no country has met a Fascist attack with hysterical religiosity—it is the last thing that would occur to anybody except a tent-show revivalist or a playwright. MacLeish makes his democracy fall because its people stupidly follow their political leaders when they counsel passive resistance; because its people stupidly follow their religious leaders when they counsel a religious withdrawal; because they stupidly and cravenly forsake their military leaders when they tell them to fight. It is hard to see how anyone could make so bad an analysis accidentally.

But now MacLeish pulls from his Sodom one lonely Lot, a brave, honest, and intelligent man of action. He is—a general! Yes, a tough old general in a feather coat. He rescues the girl, drives the people down from the pyramid, and bawls them out in the most hard-boiled and violent rhetoric the admiring MacLeish can find for him. In a deep voice that drowns the "chatter" of the crowd, he shouts: "You ought to be flogged for your foolishness! / Your grandfathers died to be free / And you—you juggle with freedom! . . . You thought you could always quibble!" And so on. Those grandfathers have a familiar ring.

The general then makes a speech about freedom (libretto by Dorothy Thompson). All he thinks about is freedom; "there's nothing in this world worse," he warns them, "than doing the Strong Man's Will." Generals are famous for feeling that way about democracy and authority, I am told; and for trying to save the rights of the democracies from Fascism, when the people of the democracies want to throw those rights away. Certainly in MacLeish's New Found Land they're famous for it; though I'll bet that, before long, some repressed general breaks up a performance of *The Fall of the City* by establishing a military dictatorship and successfully defending the city from its conqueror.

The General makes a last appeal to the people to fight and die for their liberties: in other words, to do what the Spanish loyalists, what the Chinese, what half the nations of Europe have done and are doing. But of the people of this democracy—who allegorically stand for The People, who topically stand for the people of our own time—not one even listens to the General, not one fights for his liberty or his life. As always in this play, they scream and run around and around the square in their terror. The square is choked with *deserters*. We have been told of no troops, of no resistance; their own government has ordered them not to resist; yet MacLeish twice calls the people who flee into the square *deserters*. The citizens (who behave, from beginning to end, exactly like a mob in *Little Orphan Annie*) now give up completely, shouting the most frantic, craven, vindictive, or ridiculous sentences. "Opinions and talk! Deliberative walks beneath the ivy and the creepers!" cries one, as men mad with terror will. "He's one man: we are but thousands!" reasons another pessimistic citizen—an emigrant from *Through the Looking-Glass,* no doubt. The people tear off their plumes, make bonfires of their bows, throw away their spears (Aztecs would hardly do this, modern populations would hardly have the arms to throw away); they shout wilder and wilder things: "Freedom's for fools! . . . Freedom has eaten our strength and corrupted our virtues! . . . Fools must be mastered! . . ." They end with the extraordinary, "Chains will be liberty!" The mere prospect of a Conqueror makes the people become the Conquered, servile wretches who deny all their liberties, welcome their degradation in impossible speeches.

The announcer finishes the play with a long and extremely effective narrative. The people wait in breathless terror, minute after minute, until the Conqueror enters, helmed, mailed, "broad as a brass door: a hard hero." The people "cover their faces with their fingers. They cower before him. / They fall; they sprawl on the stone." The Conqueror mounts the pyramid, opens his visor; and the announcer whispers, cries out, "There's no one! . . . The helmet is hollow! . . . The armor is empty . . . The push of a stiff pole at the nipple would topple it."

And the people?

They don't see or they won't see. They are silent . . .
The people invent their oppressors: they wish to believe in
    them.
They wish to be free of their freedom: released from their
    liberty—
The long labor of liberty ended!
                    They lie there!

Suddenly the Conqueror's arm rises, and the people "shout with happiness"; so great is their joy at being slaves, the conquered, that the announcer cries, "You'd say it was they were the conquerors." The people, "like troops in a victory," shout out exultantly: "The city of masterless men has found a master. The city has fallen." The announcer repeats, flatly: "The city has fallen." And the play ends.

The whole play has systematically discredited the people of the democracy, who are represented as stupid and treacherous cowards, without a single redeeming trait. It has discredited their leaders, who are represented as fatuous word spinners. The people are conquered not by force, but by their own yearning to be mastered, to throw away their irksome liberties for the satisfying rule of the Strong Man. I have encountered such people before: in Hitler's and Mussolini's speeches. The only brave or intelligent man in the whole democracy is a professional soldier, a Strong Man; because of his rather implausible passion against authority and for "freedom," he does not take command of the city, but only implores the people to fight—as a result the people are conquered. (If I were a general about to set up a military dictatorship—in order to save people from themselves, of course—I should be able to think of no other play that would so suitably influence the public and my troops.) The author's tone is: "I don't care what you want—you'll be free if I have to make you." This is the message of the play: the people are cowardly fools who *want* to be degraded, to be subjugated, to throw away their freedom—we must force them, in some way, to fight for it. The play must surely have reminded many people of Huey Long's remark that Fascism in this country will have an anti-Fascist platform. "The people invent their oppressors"! A man who has spent time interviewing those oppressors for *Fortune* should know better than that. The oppressors are real; that suit of armor was never empty: it is MacLeish who has invented, not the people. In these last years many millions of these people, over the entire world, have died fighting their oppressors. Say to them that they invented their oppressors, wished to believe in them, wished to be free of their freedom; that they lie there.

If MacLeish put his philosophy in a book, he should call it *The World as Will and Nothing but Will*. He is an extraordinary case of arrested development, a survival from an almost extinct past; there is something consciously neo-primitive about his eager adoption of the optimistic voluntarism of frontier days, when—with plenty of land, plenty of jobs, and plenty of room on top—plenty of people thought that you can if you think you can; that the world is what we make it; that there's no limit. This is as far as possible from any tragic view of life, from the point of view of any great dramatist—who is, necessarily, a specialist on limits; who knows that the world is, at a given moment, what we find it; who understands well enough to accept, with composure even, the inescapable conditions of existence. MacLeish passionately dislikes any determinism, even an optimistic one; his one response to an inescapable condition is to look strong and deny that it exists. So, in his play, it's the people's *fault;* they *choose* to be slaves; they are weak and *bad*. Burke said that you can't condemn a whole people; I'm sure MacLeish would reply, "Why not?" Why not write a play condemning them? exhorting them to reform, to act just like their grandfathers, to stop quibbling about freedom and *fight?* MacLeish does not have any sort of religious or philosophical determinism, as most of the great dramatists had; the determinism of character or motivation he neglects—there is not a character in the entire play; and all the economic and social factors that may, in modern plays, furnish a kind of substitute for Fate or Necessity, he has made it his profession to avoid. So there is something curiously partial and shallow and oratorical about the play: it represents a positively political view of life.

As everybody since Aristotle has said, a play must have struggle, conflict, action—and this means more than waving weapons and making violent speeches. There is no real conflict in *The Fall of the City*. It is a play-by-play account of how an ignorant and cowardly people slide into their ruin, continually hoodwinked by everybody, until the crowning swindle is put over by an empty suit of armor. The city is not taken, it falls. (And we are convinced from the beginning that it is going to fall; surely God—MacLeish either—doesn't raise women from the grave to tell us lies.) People talk, talk, talk, may even run around and around the square; but no one really does anything—not even the Conqueror. The General, late in the play, attempts to put some conflict into it; and is promptly disregarded. The structure of the play is extraordinarily simple, like a series of arias or recitations; it is extraordinarily unlike the complicated system of stresses and strains that is the structure of a real play.

Let me give a simplified structural analysis. The Dead Woman prophesies the fall of the city; the people become frightened. The First Messenger warns them that the Conqueror is coming; the people wait dumbly for advice. The Minister (First Orator) tells them to do nothing; they forget their fears, and dance or eat lunch. The Second Messenger warns them that the Conqueror is nearer; the people become *very* frightened. The Priests (Second Orators) tell them to be religious; they forget their fears, and dance religiously. The General (who, structurally speaking, combines the functions of Third Messenger and Third Orator) warns them that the Conqueror is upon them, that they must fight; the people go mad with fear. The Conqueror, an empty suit of armor, marches in and raises its arm; the people don't or won't see, and shout with happiness at being conquered. I am not sure what this is the structure of; but it is certainly not the structure of a play.

The Fall of the City exists on two levels: the literal or Aztec level; the allegorical or topical level. Its action is impossible on either of these levels alone: taken as a play about a primitive people, it is absurd; taken as a play about contemporary reality, it is equally absurd. It never really joins these levels at all, but gets along by uneasily and surreptitiously shifting back and forth between the two, in an attempt to evade the difficulties that would be insurmountable if it stuck to either. MacLeish makes his easy equation between a generalized Spanish conquest of an Aztec city, a generalized Fascist conquest of a democracy, only because, as a dramatist, he has no conception of the real forces that operate in either culture: he does not bother to observe or understand how people act, why they act as they do—and so makes them do impossible things or do possible things for impossible reasons. The one thing a dramatist *must* understand is motivation; if he does not—and MacLeish does not— his play can have only an external and arbitrary unity, the specious organization of a fallacy. The people of MacLeish's city are fantastically unlike the real Aztecs, the real population of any traditional, agricultural, non-industrialized culture. If a culture is archaic and exotic enough, he seems to think, economic and technological factors stop operating. Who are the people *with power* in this city? The elected demagogues? Apparently; but the question never occurs to him. There everything happens because of emotions, of will; it is a city of free choice. This horseless and metal-less city, with its spears and pyramids and cloaks of feathers; the corpse rising from the grave with its prophecy; the priests with their human sacrifice; the empty and all-conquering suit of armor —are these necessary to a play about contemporary political reality, about Fascism? Obviously not. They are gratuitous decorations, employed because they satisfy the author's taste for the romantic, the exotic, the sensational; because he believes that "verse is easily accepted on the stage only where the scene is made remote in time and so artificial to begin with"; because, after *Conquistador,* they were a familiar machinery that he had already learned to employ effectively; because they made it possible for him to distort or disregard facts, contemporary reality, and to present as real actions that would be plainly false in a contemporary scene; because his point of view is, essentially, as romanticized as his machinery of effect. His play, by accident or design, completely disregards what anyone knows: that Fascism is a highly specialized economic and political manifestation of a late stage of our own particular economic system, capitalism; that it springs from all kinds of real causes, not simply from people's cowardice and stupidity, their shameful longing to be slaves. Since he disregards all the characteristic and essential aspects of our own culture, his explanation of how Fascism operates seems not merely mistaken but childish.

The Fall of the City is false as an interpretation of reality. It is a schematized, arbitrarily one-sided, and melodramatic oversimplification, full of useless sensationalism and exoticism; a black-and-white political cartoon, plainly at variance with most of the facts. It is also false as an imaginative creation; the world the author creates is internally inconsistent, full of incongruities, anachronisms, arbitrary or impossible behavior; there are no characters, only the blankest of types; the motivation and organization of the play are wholly inadequate. A good deal of it, as a dramatic creation, is impossible, since it can be understood only if it is referred to some contemporary political event, accepted only if we are willing to concede, "All right, since it really happened that way." We need to suspend not only our disbelief but our capacity for disbelieving: to open our mouths and shut our eyes and take what the mother bird gives us.

This essay is not intended to be a sympathetic or comprehensive analysis of *The Fall of the City;* I came to bury it if I could manage to. Let me admit that it is not stillborn, as most verse plays are, but has a hump and teeth. I believe that, on a fairly low level, it is an effective play; I have not tried to show why it is effective. I believe that it is a bad play; and I have tried to show why it is bad. But the point of view from which the play is written, the "message" of the play, seems to me far worse than the play itself. A critic, as critic, can say that the poet's analysis seems mistaken, his point of view unfortunate; but, speaking as a private citizen, the critic may want to be a good deal blunter. A philosopher I know once lent a copy of *Alice in Wonderland* to an old lady; when she returned it he asked, "Well, what did you think of it?" She murmured: "What a lie!"

Ernie Pyle

THE NATION, MAY 19, 1945

H E WROTE like none of the rest. The official, press-agent, advertis-
ing-agency writing that fills the newspapers, magazines, and
radio with its hearty reassuring lies, its mechanical and heartless super-
latives; the rhetorical, sensational, and professional pieces of ordinary
Time–Life journalism—the same no matter what the subject, who
the writer; the condescending, preoccupied work of "real writers"
officially pretending to be correspondents for the duration: all this writing
about the war that by its quality denies the nature and even the existence
of the war, he neither competed with nor was affected by. He was
affected by, obsessed with, one thing—the real war: that is, the people
in it, all those private wars the imaginary sum of which is the public
war; and he knew that his private war, his compulsive obligation, was
to write what he had seen and heard and felt so that neither those who
had felt it nor those who had not could ever again believe that it was
necessary for anyone to be ignorant of it. He was their witness; and he
looked not to find evidence for his own theories or desires, to condemn,
to explain away, to justify, but only to *see,* and to tell what he saw.
What he cared about was the facts. But facts are only facts as we see
them, as we feel them; and he knew to what a degree experience—
especially in war—is "seeing only faintly and not wanting to see at all."
The exactly incongruous, the crazily prosaic, the finally convincing fact
—that must be true because no one could have made it up, that must
be Pyle because no one else would have noticed it—was his technical
obsession, because he knew it was only by means of it that he could
make us understand his moral obsession: what happens to men in our
war. (A few reporters cared almost as much and tried almost as hard;
but their work is hurt by emotional forcing, self-consciousness, the hopeless strain between their material and their technique. To the reporter's
trained consciousness there is something incidental, merely personal, almost meretricious, about his exact emotions or perceptions or moral
judgments; these things are not part of "the facts," and he professionally
supplies only as much of their generalized, familiar equivalents as his

readers immediately demand and immediately accept. These things, for many years, had been the only facts for Pyle.) Pyle did not care how he told it if he could make us feel it; there is neither self-protectiveness nor self-exploitation in his style. What he saw and what he felt he said. He used for ordinary narration a plain, transparent, but oddly personal style—a style that could convince anybody of anything; but when his perceptions or emotions were complex, far-reaching, and profound, he did his utmost to express their quality fully—at his best with the most exact intensity, at his worst with a rather appealingly old-fashioned spaciousness of rhetoric. It is easy to be critical of some of these last passages, and of the flat homeliness of others: he possessed few of the unessential qualities of the accomplished writer but—at his rare best— many of the essential qualities of the great writer. It was puzzling and disheartening to read some of the reviews of his books: the insistence that this was not "great" reporting, the work of a "real" writer, but only a good reporter, a good man—nobody missed *that*—reproducing what the "G.I. Joes" felt and said. (Some writers seemed compelled to use about him, as they do about all soldiers who are at the same time enlisted men, the words *simple, plain,* or *little*—so disquieting in their revelation of the writers' knowledge and values.) And yet all of us knew better. We felt most the moral qualities of his work and life; but we could not help realizing that his work was, in our time, an unprecedented aesthetic triumph: because of it most of the people of a country *felt,* in the fullest moral and emotional sense, something that had never happened to them, that they could never have imagined without it—a war.

In war the contradictions of our world, latent or overt, are fantastically exaggerated; and what in peace struggles below consciousness in the mind of an economist, in war wipes out a division on atolls on the other side of a planet. So in Pyle war is the nest of all contradictions; the incongruous is the commonplace homogeneous texture of all life. All of them know it: a cannoneer, playing poker by two candles in a silent battery, says to him "as though talking in his sleep," *"War is the craziest thing I ever heard of."* A man builds a raft to float on the water of his foxhole; another goes to sleep, falls over in the water, and wakes up, until he finally ties himself by a rope to a tree; four officers of a tank company fix themselves a dugout with electric lights, a pink stove, an overstuffed chair, and "a big white dog, slightly shell-shocked, to lie on the hearth." Men in shallow foxholes, under severe strafing, try to dig deeper with their fingernails, are commonly "hit in the behind by flying fragments from shells. The medics there on the battlefield would either cut the seats out of their trousers or else slide their pants down, to treat the wounds, and they were put on the stretchers that way, lying face down. It was almost funny to see so many men coming down the hill with the white skin of their backsides gleaming against the dark background of brown uniforms and green grass." Pyle "couldn't help feeling funny about" fighter pilots who had just strafed a truck convoy, and who, "so full of laughter . . . talked about their flights and killing and being killed exactly as they would discuss girls or their school lessons." Soldiers pile out of their jeeps for an approaching bird, thinking it a Stuka ("I knew one American outfit that was attacked by Stukas twenty-three times in one day. A little of that stuff goes a long way"); and a digger testifies, with utter magnificence: "Five years ago you couldn't have got me to dig a ditch for five dollars an hour. Now look at me. You can't stop me digging ditches. I don't even want pay for it; I just dig for love. And I sure do hope this digging today is all wasted effort, I never wanted to do useless work so bad in all my life. Any time I get fifty feet from my home ditch you'll find me digging a new ditch and, brother, I ain't joking. I love to dig ditches." And yet it is a war where "few ever saw the enemy, ever shot at him, or were shot at by him"; where "physical discomfort becomes a more dominant thing in life than danger itself"; where everything is so scarce that passing soldiers stop Pyle six times in a day to borrow a pair of scissors to cut their nails—"if somebody had offered me a bottle of castor oil I would have accepted it and hidden it away."

Pyle is always conscious of the shocking disparity of actor and circumstance, of the little men and their big war, their big world: riding in a truck in the middle of the night, so cold he has to take off his shoes and hold his toes in his hands before he can go to sleep, he feels shiveringly "the immensity of the catastrophe that had put men all over the world, millions of us, to moving in machine-like precision through long nights—men who should have been comfortably asleep in their warm beds at home. War makes strange giant creatures out of us little routine men that inhabit the earth." And, flying from the Anzio beachhead to D-Day in the Channel, passing at sunset over the peaks of the Atlas, he thinks longingly of the worlds inside the world: "Down below lived sheep men—obscure mountain men who had never heard of a *Nebelwerfer* or a bazooka, men at home at the end of the day in the poor, narrow, beautiful security of their own walls." His column describing the apotheosis of another world, the debris of the Normandy beachhead, is so extraordinary in its sensitivity, observation, and imagination that I wish I could quote all of it; but, taken at random from "this long thin line of personal anguish": from the sleeping, dead, and floating men; from the water "full of squishy little jellyfish . . . in the center of each of them a green design exactly like a four-leaf clover"; from the ruined tanks, trucks, bulldozers, half-tracks, typewriters, office files, steel matting, and oranges—a banjo and a tennis racket; from the dogs, Bibles, mirrors, cigarette cartons (each soldier was given a carton of cigarettes before embarking), and writing paper of that universe where "anything and everything is expendable," here are two objects:

> I stooped over the form of one youngster whom I thought dead. But when I looked down I saw that he was only sleeping. He was very young, and very tired. He lay on one elbow, his hand suspended in the air about six inches from the ground. And in the palm of his hand he held a large, smooth rock.
>
> I stood and looked at him for a long time. He seemed in his sleep to hold that rock lovingly, as though it were his last link with a vanishing world . . .
>
> As I plowed out over the wet sand, I walked around what seemed to be a couple of pieces of driftwood sticking out of the sand. But they weren't driftwood. They were a soldier's two feet. He was completely covered except for his feet; the toes of his G.I. shoes pointed toward the land he had come so far to see, and which he saw so briefly.

Yet their war's grotesque unnaturalness finally becomes for them a grotesque naturalness, all that they have known or done—except for that endlessly dwelt-on fantasy that was before and may be after the war, their civilian lives and families and home. Pyle one night— back in one world after weeks in the other—"never wide awake, never deeply asleep," thinks fitfully: "One world was a beautiful dream and the other a horrible nightmare, and I was a little bit in each of them. As I lay on the straw in the darkness they became mixed up, and I was not quite sure which was which." From his long experience of front-line troops, divisions used steadily for months or years, he creates calmly and objectively and prosaically—under their jokes and addresses and grammatical errors, the speech of the farms and garages of America —their extraordinary suffering: the "endlessness of everything," their "state of exhaustion that is incomprehensible . . . past the point of known human weariness . . . one dull, dead pattern—yesterday is tomorrow and Troino is Randazzo and when will we ever stop and, God, I'm so tired." He and an officer look at some muddy, exhausted troops and decide "they haven't been up in the line at all." They don't have "that stare" of front-line troops. Pyle continues: "It's a look of dullness, eyes that look without seeing, eyes that see without conveying any image to the mind. It's a look that is the display room for what lies behind it—exhaustion, lack of sleep, tension for too long, weariness that is too great, fear beyond fear, misery to the point of numbness, a look of surpassing indifference to anything anybody can do." Nobody else makes you feel so their *long* dreary suffering, everything going on past not only their own lives but the lives of their replacements, until a whole division is "only a numbered mechanism through which men pass"; you remember Mauldin's bearded and filthy soldier, so exhausted he looks middle-aged, staring at his rifle and saying to it slowly: "I've given you the best years of my life."

And these are not professional soldiers but only ordinary people: we feel behind every word the ironic pathos of what they are doing and what they are, of the threadbare shiny scraps that are all that remain to them of the old life they hope their way back to, from this dream where they lie "shooting at the darkness from out of the dark." These scraps— jobs, families, and states—repeated with the same perpetual heartbreaking plainness to the listening Pyle, are a bridge pushed back shakily to their real lives; and he understands and puts down what they tell him, always; and the foolish think it a silly habit of his. Even his generals seem human, as he tells how one is waked: the sentry kneeling beside the general, asleep on the ground in his long underwear, repeating softly, "General, sir, general, sir." The desperate antinomies of war are held together by their common ground, the people who endure them: in the foreground, overshadowing the great convulsions, the appalling strengths, are always "the individual cells of that strength"—their stubbornly and precariously stable commonplaceness, their wonderful pathetic persistence in all they can keep of their old understanding and lives and world. If there are few of the regular heroes, there are many of Pyle's: men chosen by chance, sent out "across the ageless and indifferent sea," doing determinedly and unwillingly what they have to do, heroic if they have to be, and not for a public cause but for their own private moral obligations—fighting "for . . . for . . . well, at least for each other." So Pyle stays with them year after year and finally dies with them, because of them—the lives that, with their pets, their dreams of after and before, their pictures of their children and wives and girls, their intermittent unending exhaustion and suffering and despair, inch out their marginal existence under the 88's.

Nobody else in the world but Pyle makes you feel so intensely *sorry* for them, makes you feel how entirely against their will and aside from their understanding it all happens. The terrible particulars of their misery, of this catastrophe beyond anything they could have deserved or even imagined, drive home to anybody who can understand anything the final moral contradiction of such a war: that though from it come, along with suffering and brutality and death, courage and stubborn endurance and sacrifice, people's real love for one another—*all these things have their price;* and this price is so much too great that it is absolutely incommensurable. Though our victory in this war is better than our defeat, though there is a difference between the two sides that is essential, still what has to be done, the actual substance of the war, is almost entirely evil. The sergeant says to Pyle about the replacements: "I know it ain't my fault they get killed, and I do the best I can for them. But I've got so I feel like it's me killing 'em instead of a German. I've got so I feel like a murderer." For Pyle, to the end, killing was murder: but he saw the murderers die themselves.

His condemnation of war seems to the reader more nearly final than any other, because in him there is no exaggeration, no hysteria, no selection to make out a case, no merely personal emotion unrecognized as such; he has nothing to prove. He has written down all that is favorable or indifferent—his readers have noticed this most, the commonplace courage and endurance and affection of his soldiers; but after all this his condemnation is so complete, detailed, brought home to us so absolutely, that it is unforgettable and unarguable. This proper evaluation of things, his calm, detachment, and objectivity (some of his most humorous and equable columns were written while he himself was in the depths of frustration and revulsion) help to give his work its serious truth.

Here are the soldiers of this war:

I was sitting among clumps of sword grass on a steep and rocky hillside that we had just taken, looking out over a vast rolling country to the rear. A narrow path wound like a ribbon over a hill miles away, down a long slope, across a creek, up a slope, and over another hill. All along the length of that ribbon there was a thin line of men. For four days and nights they had fought hard, eaten little, washed none, and slept hardly at all. Their nights had been violent with attack, fright, butchery, their days sleepless and miserable with the crash of artillery.

The men were walking. They were fifty feet apart for dispersal. Their walk was slow, for they were dead weary, as a person could tell even when looking at them from behind. Every line and sag of their bodies spoke their inhuman exhaustion. On their shoulders and backs they carried heavy steel tripods, machine-gun barrels, leaden boxes of ammunition. Their feet seemed to sink into the ground from the overload they were bearing.

They didn't slouch. It was the terrible deliberation of each step that spelled out their appalling tiredness. Their faces were black and unshaved. They were young men, but the grime and whiskers and exhaustion made them look middle-aged. In their eyes as they passed was no hatred, no excitement, no despair, no tonic of their victory—there was just a simple expression of being there as if they had been there doing that forever, and nothing else.

This is how they die:

When a man was almost gone, the surgeons would put a piece of gauze over his face. He could breathe through it but we couldn't see his face well.

Twice within five minutes chaplains came running. One of those occasions haunted me for hours. The wounded man was still semi-conscious. The chaplain knelt down beside him and two ward boys squatted nearby. The chaplain said, "John, I'm going to say a prayer for you."

Somehow this stark announcement hit me like a hammer. He didn't say, "I'm going to pray for you to get well"; he just said he was going to say a prayer, and it was obvious to me that he meant the final prayer. It was as though he had said, "Brother, you may not know it, but your goose is cooked." Anyhow, he voiced the prayer, and the weak, gasping man tried vainly to repeat the words after him. When he had finished, the chaplain added, "John, you're doing fine, you're doing fine." Then he rose and dashed off on some other call, and the ward boys went about their duties.

The dying man was left utterly alone, just lying there on his litter on the ground, lying in an aisle, because the tent was full.

There are many passages in Pyle that, in their extraordinary intensity and exactness of observation and presentation, seem to the reader to have reached a pure truth of statement. (When we read his famous column about the dead Captain Waskow we are no longer separated from the actual event by anything at all.) In the hospital tent he sees that all the wounded and dying look alike, their faces reduced to a "common denominator" by dirt and suffering and exhaustion—except for any extremely fair soldier, who looks like "a flower in a row of weeds." As the bombs from hundreds of our heavy bombers were falling toward Pyle (by that mistake that killed General McNair and hundreds of other Americans), he heard how "the universe became filled with a gigantic rattling as of huge ripe seeds in a mammoth dry gourd"; he and a stranger wriggled desperately under a farm wagon, and waiting for the bombs already exploding around them, he saw that "we lay with our heads slightly up—like two snakes—staring at each other." Is there any imaginable way in which the next quotation could be altered?

> Our fighters moved on after the enemy, and those who did not fight, but moved in the wake of the battles, would not catch up for hours. There was nothing left behind but the remains—the lifeless debris, the sunshine and the flowers, and utter silence. An amateur who wandered in this vacuum at the rear of a battle had a terrible sense of loneliness. Everything was dead—the men, the machines, the animals—and he alone was left alive.

I do not need to write about Pyle's humor and honesty and understanding, all the precious and "human" qualities—this use of *human* seems an inexorable rationalization, a part of the permanent false consciousness of humanity—that no reader has missed. Along with them there is the charm of those frailties which he insisted on so much. He told beautifully, and often, how scared he was *(Lord, but I felt lonely out there);* but his extraordinary courage—no, his ordinary courage, the courage which, as he showed endlessly, had to be ordinary for millions of men—his readers could only guess, from the long voluntary succession of those situations he was so scared in. His steady humility and self-forgetfulness—without any of the usual veneration of the self for what it is forgetting—were reinforced by his peculiarly objective amusement at his own relation to the world. (When he landed on Okinawa he borrowed a combat jacket with "U.S. Navy" on the back. Later a marine told him: "You know, when you first showed up, we saw that big Navy stenciled on your back, and after you passed I said to the others: 'That guy's an admiral. Look at the old gray-haired bastard. He's been in the navy all his life. He'll get a medal out of this sure as hell.'") His affectionate amused understanding and acceptance of all sorts and levels of people come from his imaginative and undeviating interest in, observation of, these people; he is as unwilling to look away from them because they do not fit his understanding of them as he is to reject them because they do not satisfy the exacting standards he keeps for himself.

He was very much more complex than most people suppose; and his tragedy—a plain fatality hung over the last of his life, and one is harrowed by his unresigned *I've used up my chances*—was not at all that of the simple homogeneous nature destroyed by circumstances it is superior to. People notice how well he got along with people and the world, and talk as if he were the extrovert who naturally does so; actually he was precisely, detailedly, and unremittingly introspective, and the calm objectivity of his columns is a classical device—his own confused and powerful spiritual life always underlies it, and gives it much of its effect. This contradictory struggle between his public and private selves, between the controlled, objective selectivity of the pieces and his own intense inner life, one must guess from fragments or the remarks of those who knew him best; it is partly because this one side of him is incompletely represented in his work that one regrets his death so much.

His writing, like his life, is a victory of the deepest moral feeling, of sympathy and understanding and affection, over circumstances as terrible as any men have created and endured. By the veneration and real love many millions of people felt for him, their unexplained certainty that he was *different* from all the rest, and theirs, they showed their need and gratitude for the qualities of his nature, and seemed almost to share in them. He was a bitter personal loss for these people. Most of his readers could not escape the illusion that he was a personal friend of theirs; actually he was—we meet only a few people in our lives whom we ever know as well or love as much. There are many men whose profession it is to speak for us—political and military and literary representatives of that unwithering estate which has told us all our lives what we feel and what we think, how to live and when to die; he wrote what he had seen and heard and felt himself, and truly represented us. Before his last landing in the Ryukyus, he felt not only fear and revulsion but an overwhelming premonition that he would die there: "repeatedly he said he knew he would be killed if he hit another beachhead. Before he finally settled the question of whether or not to go ashore in his own mind, he spent three sleepless days and nights. Then on the fourth day he made up his mind." He told a good friend, "Now I feel all right again"; to other people he said merely that he didn't want to go there, but he guessed the others didn't either. He had to an extraordinary degree the sense of responsibility to *the others,* the knowledge of his own real duty, that special inescapable demand that is made —if it is made—to each of us alone. In one sense he died freely, for others; in another he died of necessity and for himself. He had said after visiting the lepers in the Hawaiian Islands: "I felt a kind of unrighteousness at being whole and 'clean.' I experienced an acute feeling of spiritual need to be no better off than the leper."

After he died I saw, as most people did, a newsreel of him taken in the Pacific. He is surrounded by marines trying to get his autograph, and steadies on the cropped head of one of them the paper he is signing. He seems unconscious of himself and the camera; his face is humorous, natural, and kindly, but molded by the underlying seriousness, almost severity, of private understanding and judgment. I remembered what the girl in *The Woodlanders* says over another grave: "You were a *good* man, and did good things." But it is hard to say what he was or what we felt about him. He filled a place in our lives that we hardly knew existed, until he was there; and now that he is gone it is empty.

These Are Not Psalms

COMMENTARY, NOVEMBER 1945

Poems by A. M. Klein   *Story of a Secret State* by Jan Karski

MR. KLEIN'S poems are academic, semi-religious verse about (1) representative experiences of the moderately religious life and (2) the persecution of the Jews during the present quantitatively unique intensification of the Diaspora. Let me consider them first as poetry; second, as religious poetry; third, as responses to, expressions of, the Third Reich's systematic liquidation of the Jews of Europe.

In the first place, pieces like these are not poetry but verse; even a glance at their language is enough to bring this home to the reader. The language has none of the exact immediacy, the particular reality of the language of a successful poem; it has instead the voluntary repetition of the typical mannerisms of poetry in general—mannerisms that become a generalized, lifeless, and magical ritual without the spirit of which they were once the peculiar expression. Mr. Klein uses forms and meters, epithets and rhetoric, with the innocent freedom of the born writer of verse—who is always, willing or unwilling, at ease in Zion. If he were to make himself into a poet he would be appalled to see everything suddenly difficult beyond hope, to find himself without even the illusion of freedom.

Mr. Klein uses a form, writes about a subject, simply because he wants to; but this, for a poet, is as impossible as it is for you to love your enemies, to dream virtuous dreams, or to have "lots of will power" simply because you want to. The general lack of freedom of the poet is grotesquely intensified in the specific lack of freedom of the poem—in which each part is determined not only by the demands of the incomplete tentative mass of the already existing parts, but by the overriding demands of the obscurely divined, problematic, and unique whole. These demands are grounded in the demands of the subject itself. Mr. Klein, in writing about the mass slaughters of Jewish populations, has retained so much freedom that he can regularly use little jokes or satirical remarks, in the style of the light verse that is perhaps most congenial to him, in order to make the slaughterers ludicrous in our eyes; the poet who could treat this subject would be so possessed and dominated by it that such thoughts would not even occur for him to reject.

Thus one can say of Mr. Klein's verse that some of the jokes are possible, some of the rhetoric is effective, some of the emotion is felt— but all these works are useless without Grace. This is a typical enough quotation, about an adulterous generation that not only seeks but provides itself with signs:

> *Sir Aries Virgo, astrology-professor,*
> *Regards the stars, and prophesies five truces.*
> *Herr Otto Shprinzen, of the same guild, a guesser,*
> *From the same stars the contrary deduces.*
>
> *. . . Ides is foretold, and doomsday, and God's thunders.*
> *January greets the unseen with a seer.*
> *Augurs prognosticate, from signs and wonders,*
> *Many a cradle, yea, and many a bier.*

Here are rhymes and meter and images and allusions and jokes and rhetoric, as thick as suet in plum pudding. The rhymes are mechanical, those of a reasonably perfunctory writer of light verse; the meter is, paradoxically, at once sloppy and banging; most of the metaphors are dead, most of the jokes are embarrassingly obvious; and the most hopeful effect, the parody of Browning's "greet the unseen with a cheer" is ineffective because Browning's phrase has so much more rhetorical shock than Mr. Klein's. (Greeting the unseen with a cheer—a pathological response—is incomparably odder than greeting it with a seer, a normal procedure among the majority of mankind; Browning's phrase reads like a parody of Mr. Klein's.) In the approximate, stagy air of such verse everything seems manufactured, nothing born; and Mr. Klein's serious poems, though full of feeling, blunder to us from the same industrial, confused, perpetually smoky realm of being. Contrast with Mr. Klein's verse this passage without rhymes, meter, allusions, or "poetic" effects—a real poetry on which it would be difficult to base any verse:

> *How he follow'd with them and tack'd with them three days*
> *　　and would not give it up,*
> *How he saved the drifting company at last,*
> *How the lank loose-gown'd women looked when boated from*
> *　　the side of their prepared graves,*

*How the silent old-faced infants and the lifted sick, and the
    sharp-lipp'd unshaved men;*
*All this I swallow, it tastes good, I like it well, it becomes
    mine,*
I am the man, I suffered, I was there.

The exactness of epithet is only a little less notable than the wonderful
evocative rightness of movement, the change from the slow, night-
marishly fixed rocking of the swells into the rush of the poet's envelop-
ing, intent acceptance of, merging with, this edged fragment of his
universe. And notice how seriously he produces its exact reality, how
seen and felt each atom of it is. We learn from Mr. Klein's passage
much about the devices of verse, from Whitman's much about the
nature of poetry.

    It was a mistake to call most of these poems psalms, and to num-
ber them as psalms, since this device keeps too sharply before us those
real Psalms which Mr. Klein's resemble only externally. He has borrowed a little of their letter; but their whole spirit—the terrible immediacy, reality, seriousness, and *personalness* that make them read like
some extraordinarily sublimated case history of the religious life—is
alien to Mr. Klein, a pleasant, "well-adjusted," civilized man, as unconsciously secular as he is consciously religious. He often seems less to
represent a religious culture than to reproduce it, with something of the
outsider's conscious, objective, relishing appreciation of the picturesque:
the events of life are given form by religion, but are not themselves
religious in content. (Compare the saint who, asked what he would do
if he had only an hour to live, replied that he would go on with his
game of chess, since it was as much worship as anything else he had
ever done.) In Mr. Klein's conscious mind there are no "doubts"—the
religious triumphs over the secular with almost unseeing ease; he asks,
in one of his best passages:

> *O Lord, in this my thirtieth year*
> *What clever answer shall I bear*
> *To those slick persons amongst whom*
> *I sat, but was not in their room?*

He answers, turning Milton upside down, that the Lord will justify his
ways to them. Yet in another poem he proposes to break into heaven,
"seek out the abominable scales on which the heavenly justice is mis-
weighed," and "leave those scales gloriously broken, that ever thereafter
justice shall be done." That a religious poet should say it and not even

notice that he has said it, not even attempt to mediate between it and the absolutely contradictory sayings that form the substance of his work, is more than extraordinary. When the world judges those leagued against it, the soul and its God, and the soul obliviously consents to that judgment as its own, who can fail to see the significance of so Freudian an error? In a real psalm this judgment against His justice would be recognized as suffering, only to be condemned, canceled out, and sublimated into an acceptance incapable of any judgment; the structure of such religious poems has its ground in the structure of such religious experiences—in their irrational, almost physiological dialectic of suffering, with its opposites struggling into a final reconciled, accepting ecstasy.

But this guaranteeing particularity, personalness, is what Mr. Klein's work always lacks; everything he writes about seems bookish, unimmediate, not at all out of his own personal experience. He writes about tortures, mass executions, concentration camps, the cattle cars in which men die standing in quicklime, so that the first thing one thinks is, "He was never there, either in the flesh or in the spirit." One picture or one quoted speech tells more about them than everything in his poems; his knowledge is a knowledge he possesses like any other, but is not possessed by. Mr. Klein—speaking, rather extraordinarily, through the mouth of the Emperor Solomon, surrounded by SS men—predicts that his oppressors will perish:

> *Tomorrow no bright sun may rise to throw*
> *Rays of inductive reason on Judaeophobic foe.*

How reasonable and inductive a conclusion! A Pangloss come to judgment! Contrast with this the Psalm beginning "By the rivers of Babylon, there we sat down, yea, we wept, when we remembered Zion"—and ending, as people so often forget: "O daughter of Babylon, who art to be destroyed; happy shall he be, that rewardeth thee as thou hast served us. Happy shall he be, that taketh and dasheth thy little ones against the stones." This appalling ferocity is the other side of the passive longing sadness that people remember; both are *so*, the poet has hidden neither. Can anyone imagine the writer of this Psalm making fun of his oppressors as ludicrous lunatics and scoundrels? We permit the peasant of the Middle Ages to present Herod as a comic bogeyman; but such an attitude, besides being historically jejune, is fantastically inappropriate to those whose crimes make Herod's real or imagined ones seem mere personal failings. Maidanek, Birkenau, Dachau—all those names that are more terrible for the living than any others will ever be—stand for the most forbidding, inexorable, and compulsive subject of our century. Mr. Klein, understandably and even laudably, has been drawn to a type of writing and a subject that are not only uncongenial to but completely beyond the scope of his gentler talents. But which of us, swallowed up in the sackcloth of the prophet, can by his own doing give more than a few brave and wooden squeaks?

If the reader wishes to see and to feel what happened at Maidanek or in the Warsaw ghetto, he should read the twenty-ninth and thirtieth chapters of Jan Karski's *Story of a Secret State.* Mr. Karski (if I may judge from the rest of his book) is a man without any literary talents worth mentioning; but in these chapters what he saw and heard and felt has made for itself an expression independent of either Mr. Karski or his readers—an expression that will force from the dullest or most heartless reader a helpless *I was the man, I suffered, I was there.* When one reads the terrible words of the Zionist leader and the head of the Jewish Socialist Alliance—spoken in the darkness of a ruined house at the edge of the Warsaw ghetto—one realizes that there have been men living in our time who were not the epigoni but the true heirs of the men who wrote the Psalms.

Poetry in War and Peace

PARTISAN REVIEW, WINTER 1945

Nevertheless by Marianne Moore   *The Wedge* by William Carlos Williams   *The Walls Do Not Fall by* H.D.   *Five Young American Poets: 1944* (Eve Merriam, John Frederick Nims, Jean Garrigue, Alejandro Carrión, Tennessee Williams)   *Land of Unlikeness* by Robert Lowell

POETS are in the beginning hypotheses, in the middle facts, and in the end values. One looks from the new window and murmurs, like the lady who read *Alice*: "What a lie!" But in a quarter of a century even the chairs see through that window not a landscape but the Beautiful. So Miss Moore is reviewed not as a poet but as an institution—though not yet, like Auden, as an eleemosynary institution; one reviewer calls Miss Moore the greatest living poet and *Nevertheless* her best book, ending with the demand that she be placed in Fort Knox for the duration. Certainly she writes better poetry than any other woman alive; but I have used up my small share of the superlative in previous reviews of her—this time let me look through Miss Moore and see neither lies nor Beauty, but some trees. (Whoever you are, I like her as much as you; so don't complain.)

Miss Moore's method is analytic, an illogical atomism: the static particulars with which she operates are at the farthest level of abstraction from the automatically dynamic generalizations of the child or animal. The usual English accentual-syllabic meter produces in the reader the feel of the emotion or generalization *passing through* the particulars, a wave as real as the elements that compose it; Miss Moore's syllabics merely fix her specimens on their slides. She has said that the deepest feeling manifests itself in restraint, and certainly in her lines the crude natural rhythm of the primitive emotion has been restrained away to nothing. So her rhymes, rejecting the firm kinesthetic confidence of the common English rhyme, force us to slow or stumble in our efforts to feel or even to find them. Everything combines to make the poem's structure visual and instantaneous rather than auditory and temporal, a state rather than a process. With some poets we are confused about where we began and where we ended, but are sure that we have been moved; with Miss Moore we know just where we are, but we stay there. Poetry has its own principle of Indeterminacy: if the position of something is fixed with the highest degree of accuracy, its movement cannot be. (Thus in Virginia Woolf, as in Hume, there is no "action": the sense data are a pack of cards which organize themselves into a game of poker—so we are told; and there is as much brute credulity needed to work up her states into drama as there is, in Hume, to put impressions together into the precarious collocations we pretend are things.) In Miss Moore's poems even the animals' processes are habits, norms, and thus get the stability and finality of things. All her zoos are Egyptian.

How often Miss Moore writes about things (hers are aesthetic-moral, not commercial-utilitarian—they persist and reassure); or plants (how can anything bad happen to a plant?); or animals with holes, a heavy defensive armament, or a massive and herbivorous passivity superior to either the dangers or temptations of aggression (masks, in Yeats's sense, of Miss Moore). The way of the little jerboa on the sands —at once True, Beautiful, and Good—she understands; but the little shrew or weasel, that kills, if it can, two or three dozen animals in a night? the little larvae feeding on the still-living caterpillar their mother has paralyzed for them? We are surprised to find Nature, in Miss Moore's poll of it, so strongly in favor of Morality; but all the results are implicit in the sampling—like the *Literary Digest,* she sent post-cards to only the nicer animals. In her poems the lion never eats Androcles—or anything else except a paste made of rotten apples. The virtuous individual is precariously, but necessarily and finally, safe; Miss Moore's poetry is one long set of variations on Socrates' *Nothing can happen to the good man.* Why do her animals never die? Because of the pre-established harmony in Adam Smith. Both her economic practice and moral theory repeat wistfully, *Laissez faire, laissez aller.* Poor private-spirited citizen, wandering timidly but obliviously among the monoliths of a deadlier age, will they never let you alone? To us, as we look skyward to the bombers, this urban Frost, the frequenter of zoos, calls *Culture and morals and Nature still have truth, seek shelter there*; and this is true; but we forget it beside the cultured, moral, and natural corpse . . . At Maidanek the mice had holes, but a million and a half people had none.

Miss Moore's war poem, "In Distrust of Merits," has been called the best war poem so often that it should be treated in detail.

The title is humility, not understanding—she distrusts her own merits, but trusts, accepts almost as if she were afraid to question, those of the heroic soldiers of her poem. She does not understand that they are heroes in the sense that the chimney sweeps, the factory children in the blue books, were heroes: routine loss in the routine business of the world. She sees them (the recurring triplet is the major theme of the poem) *fighting fighting fighting;* she does not remember that most of the people in a war never fight for even a minute—though they bear for years and die forever. They do not fight, but only starve, only suffer, only die: the sum of all this passive misery is that great activity, War.

Miss Moore thinks of the war in blindingly moral terms. We are fighting "that where there was death there may be life." This is true, in a sense; but the opposite is true in a more direct sense. She writes at the climax of her poem, "If these great patient / dyings—all these agonies / and woundbearings and bloodshed / can teach us how to live, these dyings were not wasted"; and she is certain that they were not wasted, and ends the poem with "Beauty is eternal / and dust is for a time." (The armies and the peoples died, and it meant that Beauty is eternal.) Since Pharaoh's bits were pushed into the jaws of the kings, these dyings —patient or impatient, but dyings—have happened, by the hundreds of millions; they were all wasted. They taught us to kill others and to die ourselves, but never how to live. Who is "taught to live" by cruelty, suffering, stupidity, and that occupational disease of soldiers, death? The moral equivalent of war! Peace, our peace, is the moral equivalent of war. If Miss Moore had read a history of the European "colonization" of our planet (instead of natural histories full of the quaint animals of those colonies) she would be astonished at nothing in the last world war, or in this one, or in the next. She should distrust us and herself, but not at the eleventh hour, not because of the war (something incommensurable, beside which all of us are good): she should have distrusted the peace of which our war is only the extrapolation. It is the peace of which we were guilty. Miss Moore's seeing what she sees, and only now, betrays an extraordinary but common lack of facts, or imagination, or *something.* But how honest and lovable—how genuinely careless about herself and caring about the rest of the world—Miss Moore seems in this poem, compared to most of our poets, who are blinder to the war than they ever were to the peace, who call the war "this great slapstick," and who write (while everyone applauds) that *they* are not going to be foolish enough to be "war poets." How could they be? The real war poets are always war poets, peace or any time.

For this poem Miss Moore has given up her usual method, because of the emotion and generality that have overwhelmed her. I wish that she had—as the world has—taken her little animals, her bric-a-brac with all their moral and aesthetic qualities, her individuals with their scrupulous virtues, and shown them smashed willy-nilly, tortured, prostituted, driven crazy—and not for a while but forever: that is, till the day they died. As it is she has handled not these real particulars but abstractions she is unfamiliar with and finds it hard not to be heroic about; and her poem is neither good nor bad, but a mistake we sympathize with thoroughly.

I don't want to finish my review of Miss Moore without saying what a good poet she is, and how lucky we are to have her.

William Carlos Williams is almost too much of a fact to be criticized. In the best of his poems the Nature of the edge of the American city—the weeds, clouds, and children of vacant lots—and its reflection in the minds of its inhabitants exist for good. His ironic (but certainly correct) *Am I not / the happy genius of my household?* suggests the charm, honesty, and rather astonishing limitations of his work. These limitations are neither technical nor moral but intellectual. (Even his good critical remarks sound as if they had been made by Henry Ford; his critical sense seems kinesthetic, only intermittently conscious, so that he is unable, generally, to exploit his regular style for dramatic monologue, as he most effectively might.) His poems are, in a way, the diaries of another Sally Beauchamp; but the tough responsible doctor-half that says and does, the violent and delicate free-Freudian half that feels and senses, have their precarious connection in one of the great mythological attitudes of our country: Brooklyn, the truck driver looking shyly at the flower. *In the suburbs, there one feels free*: his optimism comes not from closing his eyes to the serpents but from strangling them. He is young forever; so this optimism of ability and courage—touchingly wrong in the old Hercules, dying in his shirt of fire—is still precariously right for the young one. He is the America of poets.

The bombers came over H.D. as she was making (1) an apology for poetry in wartime, (2) a theory of the primacy of theory over practice, (3) a believing study of Egyptian religious machinery. The poem that combines the three is felt, queer, sincere, more than a little silly: the smashed unenclosing walls jut raggedly from the level debris of her thought (which accepts all that comes from heaven as unquestioningly as the houses of London). H.D. is History, and misunderstands a later stage of herself so spectacularly that her poem exists primarily as an anachronism: Churchill in his shelter suit reading *The Battle of Britain,* the new poem of a Mr. Addison.

Miss Garrigue is much the best of New Directions' Five Young American Poets. Her poems often have the guaranteeing and personal queerness of a diary; her most successful (urgent dream-landscapes) are not the most promising. The poems seem to say: I don't exactly *believe* in modernism, but what else is there? Except myself? The *myself* is what we value. But she should ask herself: How much is sensibility worth?

Miss Merriam's poems are fluent, effective, full of emotion and reality—if one could suspend even the capacity for disbelief, and pretend that they are poems at all. Their aesthetic distance is negative; they are really pre-poetry, verse for Pavlov's dogs. *Lax, undone, like trembling legs of bride / spread wide and sweet / for him to enter in*: these are real toads in real gardens . . . Mr. Nims gets his methods from Shapiro, Auden and the rest, his matter from newsreels, and his principles of understanding from Maritain's textbook of philosophy (this is not a very nasty remark for people who have not read the textbook); his poetry has the efficiency and charm of one of Joyce's Jesuits. He and Miss Merriam are sisters under the skin, and both of them are flayed.

Tennessee Williams must be one of those hoaxes people make up to embarrass *Poetry* or *Angry Penguins*: no real person—no fictional one except Humpty Dumpty—would say about poets, "For others, I know, the Army has offered a haven." (That haven, Dachau.) If Tennessee Williams wrote more like W. C. Williams I should think him another of Laughlin's pseudonyms; this would render a little more plausible the carefully fantastic localization of the poems: Darien, Gloucester, Santa Monica, Jacksonville, Washington, New Mexico, Vero Beach, Memphis, New Orleans, Boston, Manhattan, Acapulco, St. Louis, St. Augustine, and Summer. The romany chal! Mr. Williams writes two prefaces, a Serious Version and a Frivolous Version; I have printed only a Frivolous Version of my criticism, but I assure his friends that they would not willingly exchange it for the other.

When it comes to poems in Spanish I am in the position of the orangoutang Furness taught to say *Papa* and *cup;* Alejandro Carrión's real productions can evoke from me only *Ah, sí* or *¡Que lindo es Michoacán!*—the two phrases Mexico taught me to love or to pronounce. The translations are collocations of images and sentiments unexceptionable enough to remind one of the identity of indiscernibles, or of the Egyptian letters Gardiner mentions, where the reader understands every word and every sentence, but neither why they were written nor what they were intended to convey. One can be too neighborly.

Some of Mr. Lowell's poems are so good ("The Drunken Fisherman" is the best poem in any of these books) and all are so unusual that it makes reviewing his book a pleasure. A "traditional" poet is one who uses the usual properties and images to say the usual things; Mr. Lowell, a really traditional poet, is sometimes able to exploit the resources of language and the world for the organization of a poem almost exactly as some of the poets of the seventeenth century were able to. His language is nouns and verbs and the necessary connectives—a few adjectives, next to no adverbs; its exceptional strength is not merely the strength of intensity, emotional and rhetorical, but the basic intrinsic strength of language itself. Often he knows (as almost no contemporary poets know except in theory) that language at its strongest is *not* language that remains at the highest emotional and textural intensity as long as one can force it to; that sensibility is like money—good only for what it can buy; that the whole is what the parts are for. He has never been fooled into the vulgar belief in the separation (opposition, even) of the "connotative" and "denotative" functions of language—a belief that reaches its most primitive level of absurdity in Winters's positively pre-Socratic view. Mr. Lowell's essential source is early Milton; obvious but unimportant sources for a few details are Hopkins (*You are their belle / And belly too . . . Celestial Hoyden*) and Tate. *What* Mr. Lowell says could not have been said, guessed at, or tolerated before. His world is our world—political, economic, and murderous—cruelly insisted upon, with all our green and pale hopes gone, their places taken by a blind and bloody Heaven. (He has succeeded in making salvation seem as real, and almost as frightening, as damnation.) In these poems the blood of the martyrs is the creed of the Church; his Christ (named as one names Madonnas) is the Christ of the Tabloids. When over this coiling darkness there is a grave, indistinct, and serene lightening of pity, one is more than usually moved. His world, his rhetoric, and his beliefs are joined in an iron unity of temperament; in a day when poets aspire to be irresistible forces, he is an immovable object.

Of New England he has the grim affectionate knowledge one has of one's damned kin. Here are the *fearful Witnesses* who *fenced their gardens with the Redman's bones*; the clippers and the slavers, the seaman knitting at the asylum; the Public Gardens *where / The bread-stuffed ducks are brooding, where with tub / And strainer the mid-*

Sunday Irish scare / The sun-struck shallows for the dusky chub; and here is *the faith / That made the Pilgrim Makers take a lathe / To point their wooden steeples lest the Word be dumb.* (These parodies of quotations, or slurred references to them, are sometimes a wonderful source of wit and depth, sometimes a senseless habit: *all manmarks from this world man never made.*) Here his harshest propositions flower out of facts. But his satires of present-day politics and its continuation often have a severe crudity that suggests Michael Wigglesworth rewriting the "Horatian Ode"; airplanes he treats as Tate does, only more so—he gives the impression of having encountered them in Mother Shipton. Several of his poems are harsh and arbitrary (though surprisingly realized and surprisingly felt) exercises "in the manner of" the seventeenth century. But most of these excesses seem temporary; what is permanently excessive is an obstinacy of temperament extreme enough to seem a form of violence.

Mr. Lowell's Christianity has nothing to do with the familiar literary—not to say economic—Christianity of *as if,* the belief in the necessity of belief: all that links *Time,* Auden, Werfel, and the Caudillo in one believing band. He *is* a Christian, and consequently knows that Christianity is true, just as physicists used to know that physics is true. Among the usual rout of Catholic converts he looks like another John the Baptist, all zeal and hair; one would have said, a priori, that he is the ideal follower of Karl Barth. A few years ago he would have supported neither Franco nor the Loyalists; one sees him sending a couple of clippers full of converted minutemen to wipe out the whole bunch— human, and hence deserving. (I wish Mr. Lowell could cast a colder eye on minutemen. His treatment of the American Revolution is in the great tradition of Marx, Engels, and Parson Weems.) When the Roman Empire (in his "Dea Roma") evolves into the Roman Catholic Church, there is a change in degree, but not in kind; in his poems the Church is, among other things, an overwhelming social-historical *fact,* a State as frightening as any secular one. (His imagery for it is always Bismarckian.) His religious poems are not the familiar bad new sort, but the familiar good old sort, in terms of us and now; "The Drunken Fisherman" is as interesting and strange a piece of "religious" writing as any since *The Castle.* A good religious poem, today, is ambergris, and it is hard to enjoy it for thinking of all those suffering whales; but martyrs are born, not made.

Mr. Lowell is in a certain sense a poet's poet: properly to admire his command of those three horses you need to have tried to ride three horses yourself. Many of his phrases are memorable in that wonderful and unfashionable way in which some of Empson's are.

> *When the ruined farmer beat out Abel's brains,*
> *Our Father laid great cities on his soul.*

A man who can begin a poem like that can do anything. (In this case, alas, he can turn the poem into "Onward, Christian Soldiers.") At his best Mr. Lowell is a serious, objective, and extraordinarily accomplished poet. He is a promising poet in this specific sense: some of the best poems of the next years ought to be written by him.

FROM *Verse Chronicle*

THE NATION, DECEMBER 29, 1945

Tribute to the Angels by H.D.

FOR H.D. the Education of Hellas was more than a place and less than an education: it was a religion. But she has worn out the place names and the olives; wandering among barbarians, patching what religious scraps she can pick up into a quilt to warm her bombed old bones, she evokes a wondering and amused affection. Yet imagism was a *reductio ad absurdum* upon which it is hard to base a later style: H.D.'s new poem is one for those who enjoy any poem by H.D., or for those collectors who enjoy any poem that includes the Virgin, Raphael, Azrael, Uriel, John on Patmos, Hermes Trismegistus, and the Bona Dea.

FROM *Verse Chronicle*

THE NATION, FEBRUARY 23, 1946

Selected Poems by Marsden Hartley

M ARSDEN HARTLEY'S collection of verse shows observation, sentiment, humor, and indignation but no knowledge of how to organize and concentrate these into poems; the sympathetic magic that
takes the place of knowledge he seems to have borrowed, with un-
grudging and rather unreflecting admiration, from whatever passed as
lingua franca among modernist poets in the twenties. If there were
only some mechanism—like Seurat's proposed system of painting, or
that projected Universal Algebra Gödel innocently believes Leibnitz to
have perfected and mislaid—for reasonably and systematically converting into poetry what we see and feel and are! When one reads the
verse of people who cannot write poems—people who often have
more intelligence, sensibility, and moral discrimination than most of
the poets—it is hard not to regard the Muse as a sort of fairy god-
mother who says to the poet, after her colleagues have showered on
him the most disconcerting of gifts: "Well, never mind. You're still
the only one that can write poetry."

FROM *Verse Chronicle*

THE NATION, MAY 25, 1946

That's All That Matters by Oscar Williams   *Perilous Balance* by
Arnold Stein   *The Music Makers* by Stanton A. Coblentz
The Bridge by Ruth Pitter

OSCAR WILLIAMS'S new book is pleasanter and a little quieter than
his old, which gave the impression of having been written on a
typewriter by a typewriter. In his random search for some new machinery to be the victim of, he samples an extraordinary lot of images,
rhythms, and rhetorics, all of them wild and poetic in a rather tame and
prosaic way; and one breathes in the poems, instead of air, the vacant
and flowing spirit of George Barker. The logical picture behind the
sometimes successful detail of the poems—the premise lurking under
anything in them, like the observer in a book on relativity—is always
the poet working away at his work: the poems themselves are the true
subjects of these poems, and the "subjects" seem no more than ignorant, accidental victims of the breaking up of a reservoir of poetic emotion that pours itself arbitrarily out on anything.

Arnold Stein is an innocent, academic, giftless poet. Since his love
poems use words exactly as the songs on the Hit Parade do—but have
no tunes—they are extremely embarrassing to read. He writes to a
girl that he is "a part of you and of the beauty of the world and man";
he writes, "And my throat swelled with the beauty of it"; he writes,
"The stir of things made music in your soul." He is perfectly capable of
writing in this way about the war. He says about a heavy-bomber raid
preparing a tank breakthrough:

> *And you were tender and warm inside and you thought:*
> *Men—giving themselves (though blindly) to a goal*
> *(Not understood), and to each other (unknown);*
> *Moving, working, dying, and together,*
> *And aware of each other, and feeling the beauty of it.*

(Just so, in *The Waste Land,* a woman cooks a roast and calls in her neighbors "to get the beauty of it hot.") One thinks helplessly, "There is nothing in the whole world that this man wouldn't call beautiful"; but the uneasy confusion of a few poems written in occupied Germany seems to show that Mr. Stein is not actually one of Leibnitz's monads after all, since he has at last seen something in the world besides the reflection of his own tender and warm insides, something in the war besides the beauty of it.

Any poem must be (1) singing, (2) magical, (3) easy to understand: this is a (very) synthetic a priori judgment of Stanton A. Coblentz's, and by a sufficiently unreflecting use of it he is able to condemn the Benéts as modernist poets, and to compile an anthology of "traditional" contemporary poems that is the most nearly conclusive—and the most awingly dreary—justification of modernist poetry that has ever been devised. These poems are the imitation not of nature but of Poems; and at their worst they make Frederick the Great's adaptations of Voltaire seem *res gestae.*

Ruth Pitter's poems are, in approximate silhouette, Robert Bridges versions of Walter de la Mare; she is "traditional" in the bad sense of the word, but her own sensibility and formal intelligence interrupt and occasionally transfigure her delicate, orthodox, and reasonably interesting exercises in what one might call Attic modes. What Miss Pitter is herself is sympathetic and valuable; but this no more than colors the aggregations of attitudes and techniques of which she is the unquestioning inheritor. She does not fully comprehend that these, like the linens in a tomb, vanish to the digger's "Ah!"—that the lives and possessions of the dead are inaccessible to us until we ourselves have lived and repossessed them—that, as the painter Elstir has said:

> There is no man, however wise, who has not at some period of his youth said things, or lived in a way, the consciousness of which is so unpleasant to him in later life that he would gladly, if he could, expunge it from his memory. And yet he ought not entirely to regret it, because he cannot be certain that he has indeed become a wise man—in so far as it is possible for any of us to be wise—unless he has passed through all the fatuous and unwholesome incarnations by which that ultimate stage must be preceded. I know that there are young fellows, the sons and grandsons of famous men, whose masters have instilled into them nobility of mind and moral refinement in their school days. They have, perhaps, when they look back upon their past lives, nothing to

retract; they can, if they choose, publish a signed account of everything they have ever said or done; but they are poor creatures, feeble descendants of doctrinaires, and their wisdom is negative and sterile.

Miss Pitter's poems, so far as their continual animals are concerned, are the next-to-the-last possible extrapolation of pastoral. In them the poet is no longer able to think any human being innocent, but chooses for a last implausible repository of values the pure and blameless animal: the swans have not yet bombed London. After the next war "the stinging nettle only / Will still be found to stand," and pastoral poets like Miss Pitter will write neither about shepherds nor about their sheep, but about the bare and lifeless pastures.

"Tenderness and Passive Sadness"

· ·

THE NEW YORK TIMES BOOK REVIEW, JUNE 1, 1947

Steeple Bush by Robert Frost

READING through Frost's new book, one stops for a long time at "Directive."

> *Back out of all this now too much for us,*
> *Back in a time made simple by the loss*
> *Of detail, burned, dissolved, and broken off*
> *Like graveyard marble sculpture in the weather,*
> *There is a house that is no more a house*
> *Upon a farm that is no more a farm*
> *And in a town that is no more a town.*

One climbs there along a road quarry-like with glacier-chiseled boulders, not minding the "serial ordeal" of the eye pairs that watch from forty cellar holes, not minding "the woods' excitement over you / That sends light rustle rushes to their leaves":

> *Where were they all not twenty years ago?*
> *They think too much of having shaded out*
> *A few old pecker-fretted apple trees.*

Finally on "the height / Of country where two village cultures faded / Into each other. Both of them are lost," you too are lost, "pull in your ladder road behind you," and make yourself at home with the only field left, "no bigger than a harness gall," with the shattered "playthings in the playhouse of the children." ("Weep for what little things could make them glad.") Then, passing the "house in earnest" that has become "only a belilaced cellar hole," you go to your destination, "A brook that was the water of the house, / Cold as a spring as yet so

near its source, / Too lofty and original to rage"; and at last you
find

> *. . . hidden in the instep arch*
> *Of an old cedar at the waterside*
> *A broken drinking goblet like the Grail*
> *Under a spell so the wrong ones can't find it,*
> *So can't get saved, as Saint Mark says they mustn't.*
> *(I stole the goblet from the children's playhouse.)*
> *Here are your waters and your watering place.*
> *Drink and be whole again beyond confusion.*

There are weak places in the poem, but these are nothing beside so
much longing, tenderness, and passive sadness, Frost's understanding
that each life is tragic because it wears away into the death that it at last
half welcomes—that even its salvation, far back at the cold root of
things, is make-believe, drunk from a child's broken and stolen goblet
hidden among the ruins of the lost cultures. Much of the strangeness
of the poem is far under the surface, or else so much on the surface, in
the subtlest of details (how many readers will connect the "serial
ordeal" of the eye pairs with the poem's Grail parody?), that one slides
under it unnoticing. There are no notes in the back about this Grail.

There is nothing else in *Steeple Bush* like "Directive"; probably
the nearest thing is the dry mercilessness of "The Ingenuities of Debt."
But most of the poems merely remind you, by their persistence in the
mannerisms of what was genius, that they are productions of somebody
who once, and somewhere else, was a great poet. The man who said that
he learned from Marlowe to say his prayers: "Why, this is Hell, nor
am I out of it"; who could be annoyed at a hornet for not recognizing
him as "the exception I like to think I am in everything"; who in
poems like "A Servant to Servants," "The Witch of Coös," or "Home
Burial," had a final identifying knowledge of the deprived and dispossessed, the insulted and injured, that one matches in modern poetry
only in Hardy—this poet is now, most of the time, an elder states-
man like Baruch or Smuts, full of complacent wisdom and cast-iron
whimsy. (Of course there was always something of this in the official
role that Frost created for himself; one imagines Yeats saying about
Frost, as Sarah Bernhardt said about Nijinsky: "I fear, I greatly fear,
that I have just seen the greatest actor in the world.")

Steeple Bush is no book to convert intellectuals to Frost. Yet the
ordinary "highbrow" reader is making a far greater mistake when he

neglects Frost as commonplace than the academic reader makes when he apotheosizes him, often on the basis of his most complacent or sentimental poems.

　　Frost is one of the subtlest and saddest of poets; and no other living poet has written so well about the actions of ordinary men. But anyone should know this after reading "Home Burial," "Two Witches," "A Servant to Servants," "Neither Out Far Nor In Deep," "Design," "Acquainted with the Night," "Provide, Provide," "Desert Places," "Directive," "The Gift Outright," "An Old Man's Winter Night"; or guess at it after reading

> *But now he brushed the shavings from his knee*
> *And stood the axe there on its horse's hoof,*
> *Erect, but not without its waves, as when*
> *The snake stood up for evil in the Garden.*

Corrective for Critics

THE NEW YORK TIMES BOOK REVIEW, AUGUST 24, 1947

In Defense of Reason by Yvor Winters

THIS COLLECTION of most of Winters's criticism (some *Hound and Horn* reviews, and the *Poetry* magazine article on Tudor and Elizabethan poets, are omissions one is sorry for) is a particularly good book to buy; one can put it between Empson's *Some Versions of Pastoral* and Eliot's *Selected Essays,* and feel for them the mixture of awe, affection, and disagreement that one always feels for a first-rate critical book. But the proportion of disagreement, often of incredulous and despairing disagreement, is extraordinarily high as one reads Winters: there is no critic of comparable eminence who has made so many fantastic judgments.

Winters is what Kierkegaard said *he* was—a corrective; and Winters's case for the rational, extensive, prosaic virtues that the age disliked, his case against the modernist, intensive, essentially romantic vices that it swallowed whole, have in his later criticism become a case for any academic rationalistic vices, a case against any complicated dramatic virtues. Winters's tone has long ago become that of the leader of a small religious cult, that of the one sane man in a universe of lunatics; his habitual driven-to-distraction rages against the reprobates who have evidenced their lunacy by disagreeing with him go side by side with a startled, giant admiration for the elect who in a rational moment have become his followers.

His arguments often remind one of Tolstoy's: he takes a few facts, disregards the existence of the rest, and reasons simply, clearly, and convincingly to a partial and extravagant conclusion. All his vices are cumulative: in a book like Winters's last one, *Edwin Arlington Robinson,* one walks among the ruins of criticism.

But these are the ruins—temporary, one hopes—of an extraordinary critical talent, of someone who, at his best, is one of the finest of all critics of poetry. A note like this cannot be much more than a hand pointing dumbly to Winters's virtues; but it is a pleasure to testify

to all the pleasure and insight one has gained from them, to acknowl-
edge what a genuinely educational influence he has been to everybody
except his disciples (to them he has been mesmeric).

Essentially he is an evaluative, analytical critic, concerned first of
all with the intrinsic, objective methods of the work of art, with the
quality and qualities of a particular work of art; his criticism is only
secondarily interested in how these were arrived at, in the biographical,
political and economic, genetic aspects of works of art. But these are
the regular interests of *our* critical life; consequently, many critics dismiss Winters, a few join him, as they would join the Party or the
Church, and a few more accept him as something different, partially
wrong, and valuable.

Taste—unlike the lesser qualities of the critic—can be impressive
only to the reader who has it himself; to understand what Winters's discovery of "During Wind and Rain" or Empson's discovery of "The
Sacrifice" *meant,* you have to be so far to one side of the normal curve
of distribution as to be statistically negligible. When Winters's taste
is at its best one feels that he is an immediate contact with the reality
of the poem, that his criticism has reached a level at which praise and
objection are alike superfluous; but much of the time, in whole desolate
areas, his taste can be depended upon to be valueless, since in them it
is purely dogmatic and theoretical, proceeding not from his experience
but from his standards. Winters has tried to revolutionize the tastes and
performance of the age, and his revolution has had its own terrible by-
products: Siberian labor camps full of mishandled poets, marble Under-
grounds within which a whole new Pantheon has snored in plaster.

Winters's greatest theoretical mistake is this: he takes the act of
criticism, assumes that the values involved are moral, that the act is an
act of moral judgment, and then assumes that this process of judgment
is itself the act of creation by which any work of art is produced. His
practical misvaluations, at their most extraordinary, rival the Himalayas; perhaps their most forbidding peak is the judgment which pro-
nounces Edith Wharton's *The Age of Innocence* the "finest single
flower of the Jamesian art," and finds its prose "certainly superior to
the prose of James."

But Winters's clear, independent, and serious talent has produced
criticism that no cultivated person can afford to leave unread. His
essential insights can be found in their purest form in *Primitivism and
Decadence,* but there are perceptions that match those scattered through
his later essays on Hawthorne, Melville, Poe, Dickinson, James, and
Henry Adams.

FROM *Verse Chronicle*

· ❀ ·

THE NATION, OCTOBER 18, 1947

The Age of Anxiety by W. H. Auden

THE AGE OF ANXIETY is the worst thing Auden has written since *The Dance of Death;* it is the equivalent of Wordsworth's "Ecclesiastical Sonnets." The man who, during the thirties, was one of the five or six best poets in the world has gradually turned into a rhetoric mill grinding away at the bottom of Limbo, into an automaton that keeps making little jokes, little plays on words, little rhetorical engines, as compulsively and unendingly and uneasily as a neurotic washes his hands. A poet has turned into a sack of reflexes: Auden no longer has to struggle against standard tricks, set idiosyncrasies, behavior adjustments aged into obsessive behavior—it is these that write his poems.

Most of *The Age of Anxiety* is supposed to be thought or said by four different characters, but they are only four chairs in which Auden takes turns sitting: always the same old voice saying the same old thing. *The Age of Anxiety* is "about" the Seven Ages of Man, landscapes, war, God, everything, anything; after all, if you treat everything alike, any subject is as good as any other, and you might as well give yourself room for completely free association. If a boat is torpedoed and the men die, it's just one more chance for rhetoric; all you need do is make your regular plays on words, write:

> *They swallowed and sank, ceased thereafter*
> *To appear in public; exposed to snap*
> *Judgments of sharks, to vague inquiries*
> *Of amoeboid monsters, mobbed by slight*
> *Unfriendly fry . . .*

Page after page the poem keeps saying: *Remember, the real subject of poetry is words.* One understands what Auden meant when he said, in a recent review, that all art is so essentially frivolous that he prefers it to embody beliefs he thinks false, since its frivolity would

145

degrade those he thinks true. What sounds like an indictment is a confession, and *The Age of Anxiety* is the evidence that substantiates the confession. Underneath the jokes and fantasies and sermons there is a chaotic, despairing, exhausted confusion about the poem; all its moral sentiments are solemn, hollow whistles in the dark, all its frivolity is the frivolity of a world in which everything is dying away into a senseless dream, "self in self steeped and pashed—quite. / Disremembering, disremembering all now."

Some of the rhetoric in *The Age of Anxiety* is an extravagantly accomplished and professional job, and there are even gleams of Auden, the real Auden, here and there among its manufactured, irrelevant pages; but most of it is mediocre and much of it is abominable—dreary facetiousness that would embarrass a comedian on the radio:

> *. . . Listen courteously to us*
> *Four reformers who have founded—why not?—*
> *The Gung-Ho Group, the Ganymede Club*
> *For homesick young angels, the Arctic League*
> *Of Tropical Fish, the Tomboy Fund*
> *For Blushing Brides and the Bide-a-wees*
> *Of Sans-Souci, assembled again*
> *For a Think-Fest . . .*

The critic who says what I have said about *The Age of Anxiety* is more or less in the position of the little boy who watched the emperor's new clothes go shivering by; but believe me, reader, that morning coat, that rich and modest necktie, that simple but assertive pin, are nothing but delusions of the reviewers, occupational phantasmagoria of people who are reviewing not one bad poem by Auden, but Auden. Auden was, and is potentially, one of the best poets on earth; if it weren't for this, *The Age of Anxiety* would be worth neither indignation nor dismay, but only a line or two of indifferent dismissal.

Verse Chronicle

THE NATION, MARCH 27, 1948

A Map of Verona by Henry Reed   *Forbid Thy Ravens* by
Rolfe Humphries   *Other Skies* by John Ciardi

THE ENGLISH, with Auden in America, Graves in Majorca, and
Empson in Peiping, haven't much of their own left but Thomas
and MacNeice; a well-bred, knowledgeable intention of accomplishment is likely to go a surprisingly long way with them. This would
explain their excitement over Henry Reed's *A Map of Verona*. Mr.
Reed is a rather talented, rather pleasant poet, a little on the gray,
passive, retrospective side, and a *lot* influenced by late Eliot. His typical
poem is a sober trance, full of present participles and gently effective
or ineffective phrases, about Tristram or Chrysothemis or Philoctetes
or Antigone; while I was trying to sum them all up I remembered with
joy:

> *He fell at Gettysburg or Fredericksburg,*
> *I ought to know—it makes a difference which:*
> *Fredericksburg wasn't Gettysburg, of course.*

Compared to our bad young poets Mr. Reed is a controlled, civilized,
attractive affair; but compared to the good ones—Robert Lowell and
Elizabeth Bishop, say—he is a nap after dinner.

The virtues of Rolfe Humphries's poems are obvious: they have
something to say and say it fairly effectively and very plainly; they are
good-humored, sensible, and well organized (Mr. Humphries is particularly accomplished at playing off a long line against a short); they
have none of the extravagances and obscurities of most modernist
poems. Mr. Humphries is a talented writer of interesting and sympathetic verse, but he rarely even attempts to write anything so difficult
as a good poem: he is like a high jumper who jumps five and a half
feet with easy grace, and then leaves the track meet. The immediate,
peculiar, individual rightness of a really good poem is directly opposed
to the general approximate rightness of academic poems like Mr.

Humphries's; and his have little of the scrupulous, slight offness and oddness of diction and sentiment—all the more surprising because of the exact, traditional correctness and purity of the ground against which they figure—that sometimes lift the verse of an academic poet like Bridges into poetry. (One of Bridges's lectures begins: "Little do you know how surprised you ought to be to see me here"; and the sentence—which reads exactly as if it were quoted from Bernard Haggin—has some of the firm idiosyncratic rightness or wrongness of that "Soul awful . . . uttering odious truth," John Milton.)

What Mr. Humphries's poems say is agreeable, feeling common sense, necessarily a little too easy and superficial, since it has neither the depth of the unconscious, nor that of profound thought, nor that of profound emotion, nor that of the last arbitrary abyss of fact. Reading these poems, one keeps edging away from a faint comfortable softness of idealism and sentiment and reasonable optimism; Death and Evil walk chained in their triumphs, and one is astonished at the reminiscent Rooseveltian didacticism of the conqueror:

> *Not only all that lives, but all that dies*
> *Is holy, having lived, and testifies*
> *To bravery in season, spirit, man.*
> *Face it. You must. You can.*

Academic poems must have sustained good taste, a secure decorum; a number of Mr. Humphries's poems spoil themselves by playing down to their audience, by saying in a crude and slangy sentence something disquietingly obvious. One reads that something is "O.K. for the smart and chi-chi bitches," that hell is all right to visit but that the poet wouldn't live there, "Not if you gave me all the God-damned place." Certainly a poet *can* make good poetry out of slang, provincialisms, animal noises, or anything else; but the poetry is likely to have the atmosphere, half sea fog and half coal smoke, of Corbière's poems, and not the Indian summer, Golden Mean-ish haze of Mr. Humphries's.

John Ciardi's poems are Karl Shapiro second-hand. The war poems are mostly rhetoric ("Our bombs like phallic comets scanned the air") and Dear Diary (Mr. Ciardi prints poems commemorating his twenty-seventh, twenty-eighth, twenty-ninth, and thirtieth birthdays, a poem on looking at his own photograph in uniform, a poem On Sending Home His Civilian Clothes, Reflections While Oiling a Machine Gun, a Reverie During Briefing, an elegy for himself in case he got killed, and so forth). It is extremely disappointing that a B-29 gunner shouldn't get more of the feel of what happened to him into what he writes; maybe he will later on, if he ever gets rid of all his flashy machinery. As it is, the quoted sentences of interphone conversation have a thousand times the reality of "await the rose / Blossoming in fire upon the town"—Mussolini's son's old metaphor that shocked us so much so long ago, in the days of our innocence.

FROM *Verse Chronicle*

THE NATION, MAY 8, 1948

The Ego and the Centaur by Jean Garrigue   *The Kid* by Conrad Aiken

IN JEAN GARRIGUE's early poems one found landscapes full of effectively queer details and phrases, an adulterated freshness and naïveté, and many sorts of awkwardness and weakness; this promising poetry has lost old virtues and gained new vices—as it has become more rapid, exaggerated, and easily rhetorical—until a great deal of it, by now, is a textbook of forced, automatic, and random rhetoric. One sees inside half a page: "A gauged discord, irregular and clair, / Or corsleted in ribands like a beau . . . rayed and tangled in douce ropes . . . a belle cool din . . ." Imagine Stevens's remorseful groans as he reads this; or Dylan Thomas's as he reads: "Wracked by the seas sprung of the Venus, / By the green loin hairy . . . I cleft the great spiral as the hour brimmed . . . thronged protest and pride / Mixed with the lymph and milk of my mother . . ." And *'gainst* and *'mid* and *'mong* and *'twixt* rain on the 'wildered reader thick as *O*'s. It takes a zoo to lead Miss Garrigue up from this hell of rhetoric; one goes through *The Ego and the Centaur* searching longingly for the human, faintly Moore-ish faces of the animals. What Miss Garrigue needs—as the animals prove—is subjects that she can look at, care for, and say something about: plainly she *can* write.

Conrad Aiken's *The Kid* is one of those manufactured, sponsored, "American" epics: a surprisingly crude hodgepodge of store-bought homespun, of Madison Square Garden patriotism, of Johnny Appleseed and Moby Dick and Paul Revere and the Grand Canyon, all banged out in conscientiously rough rhymes, meter, and grammar—"just like a ballad." There is something a little too musically ectoplasmic, too pretty-pretty, about Mr. Aiken's best poems; but one longs for them as one wanders, like an imported camel, through the Great American Desert of *The Kid*.

Verse Chronicle

· ·

Trial of a Poet by Karl Shapiro   *Selected Poems* by Bertolt Brecht, translated by H. R. Hays   *The Dispossessed* by John Berryman

KARL SHAPIRO'S *Trial of a Poet* has been a disappointment to everybody. The first third of the book, a commonplace and derivative autobiographical series, is a sort of bobby-soxer's *Mauberley;* the long title poem seems worse than *Essay on Rime*—one reviewer commented that it "barely makes sense"; and the separate lyrics, with several partial and one or two complete exceptions, are automatic— over the old machinery, the world and the poet look clearly past each other. One reads with familiar pleasure "In the Waxworks," or lines like:

> *Gnawing the thin slops of anxiety,*
> *Escorted by the ground swell and by gulls,*
> *In silence and with mystery we enter*
> *The territorial waters.*

But one also reads how the poet hated, in the army, "the vast / And national ignorance of the dividing line / Between the many and the few. He classed / The majority of his fellow-men as swine." Did he? This may not be the Great Refusal, but it's as big a one as most men ever get a chance to make.

Mr. Shapiro was, to begin with, an attractive, extremely *young* poet, with a style half individual and half imitative, and with the faculty of doing his best work on a fairly easy and popular level; he has made fewer demands on himself with every poem, and has sunk and sunk until one wishes that he could go back to his best book, his first, and start over from there. He is a real poet, a confused and innocent one; although his poems do not have the penetration and finality of first-rate work, a few of them are fresh, clear, and individual suc-

151

cesses. If he could distinguish between the manner of all his poems and the matter of the good ones, he might be able to get free of the rut he has ground himself down into; but this is particularly hard for a poet, largely and volubly uncritical, who has based so much of his practice on certain effects of Auden's.

Bertolt Brecht's poetry, even in translation—and some of his poems must be as hard to translate as, say, Kipling's "Shilling a Day"— is plainly the work of a good and unusual poet. Some of the dramatic force of the poems, some of the knowledge and sympathy of the poet, would translate into Esperanto. If I knew German I'd try to do Brecht justice; as it is, let me refer the reader to Hannah Arendt's excellent piece on him in a recent *Kenyon Review.* Through most of his *Selected Poems* one is touching real people and the real world—and in our time, generally, one gets to touch only a real poet. There was once a Senator Chandler who said about a book named *Onomoo, the Huron,* "The man who doesn't like it isn't fit to live"; I feel the same way about anybody who isn't very much moved by Brecht's "Concerning the Infanticide, Marie Farrar."

John Berryman is a complicated, nervous, and intelligent writer whose poetry has steadily improved. At first he was possessed by a slavishly Yeatsish grandiloquence which at its best resulted in a sort of posed, planetary melodrama, and which at its worst resulted in monumental bathos like:

> *Deep in the unfriendly city Delmore lies*
> *And cannot sleep, and cannot bring his mind*
> *And cannot bring those marvellous faculties*
> *To bear upon the day sunk down behind.*

A good critic, he had felt, understood, and remembered only too well the effects of half a dozen contemporary poets, and these effects kept cropping up in his own poems; but, without them, he could write as impersonal and nostalgic a poem as "Winter Landscape."

By the time he wrote "The Nervous Songs" he had got together many of the elements of his own style—though things like "I am the king of the dead" certainly do have a familiar ring; and his latest poetry, in spite of its occasional echoes, is as determinedly individual as one could wish. Doing things in a style all its own sometimes seems the primary object of the poem, and its subject gets a rather spasmodic and fragmentary treatment. The style—conscious, dissonant, darting; allusive, always over- or undersatisfying the expectations which it is intelligently exploiting—seems to fit Mr. Berryman's knowledge and sensibility surprisingly well, and ought in the end to produce poetry better than the best of the poems he has so far written in it, which have raw or overdone lines side by side with imaginative and satisfying ones. Here are six lines taken almost at random from the last poem in the book:

> Our *arms, our story. Every seat was sold.*
> *A crone met in a clearing sprouts a beard*
> *and has a tirade. Not a word we heard.*
>
> *Movement of stone within a woman's heart,*
> *abrupt and dominant. They gesture how*
> *fings really are. Rarely a child sings now.*

Compare these with that unforced tribute to a friend that I've already quoted. How things *have* changed! One looks forward with real curiosity and pleasure to Mr. Berryman's new poems, just as one looks back with real amusement and embarrassment to many of his old poems; but even there, among all those statues talking like a book, there were, sometimes, lines of an obscure magic:

> *Childhood speaks to me in an austere face.*
> *The Chast Mayd only to the thriving Swan*
> *Looks back and back with lecherous intent,*
> *Being the one nail known, an excrement;*
> *Middleton's grave in a forgotten place.*

B. H. Haggin

THE NATION, DECEMBER 17, 1949

Music in The Nation by B. H. Haggin

THIS is a collection of some of the best essays of one of the best critics alive. Mr. Haggin is, as anybody can see, a born critic: the reader of *Music in The Nation* gets to observe something rare and wonderful, a man who is doing exactly what he was put in the world to do. Mr. Haggin is more interested in saying precisely what he thinks about a composer or performer, in representing as accurately as possible the quality and value of what he hears, than he is in anything else whatsoever: consequently he is a sort of exemplary monster of independence, of honesty, of scrupulous and merciless frankness. His taste is traditional and classical in the best senses of the words—as you can see if you make a list of the musicians and composers he likes best and writes about most often; you cannot call it catholic, because of his real disinclination for experimentalism (in music, that is; outside of music his favorite contemporaries seem to be Picasso and Balanchine).

Inside its limits Mr. Haggin's taste has extraordinary consistency and rigor—and it is not distorted by having friends or enemies, by being part of any movement, by needing to like or dislike some work in order to prove something. Even his errors—by *errors* I mean simply those views which he doesn't persuade his reader to agree with, either in the beginning or in the end—usually seem reasonable and consistent errors, the more or less inevitable results of looking at the world from this particular point of view: "Notice the fine warp," as the lady in the antique shop said of the table. Few living critics have been so exclusively concerned with intrinsic values; have worked so unremittingly and undeviatingly to maintain the highest standards of excellence in an art.

Mr. Haggin has an unobtrusive mastery of a sort of completely organized, completely functional exposition or description that is comparatively uncommon in criticism, since it goes almost unrecognized, and is difficult and laborious to write; not many writers can say better exactly what they want to say. To have a style and never to be carried away by it—what a gift! Mr. Haggin is a witty writer, too: "Astounding that in 1912 Fry should have prophesied those paintings of Stalin Halting the Cowardly Flight of Trotsky from the Battlefield of Tsaritsin, Stalin Demonstrating to the Leningrad Academy of Sciences that E=mc², Ivan the Terrible Gently Admonishing His Son for Cutting Off the Ears of His Pet Rabbit—and their musical counterparts." These make the point as well as it could be made; and there's something additional, a good there for its own sake. Mr. Haggin writes a clear, vigorous, exact, and efficient prose—one that is as personal and characteristic as can be, without trying to be either—that can rise to surprising heights of enthusiasm or exasperation. He writes about Toscanini so that for a moment you believe that you are seeing and hearing and feeling Toscanini conduct—no one else has done half so well—and his description of *Le Baiser de la fée* must have made Balanchine himself run to the theater to make sure that it was really that good. As for exasperation: I don't know which of the virtuosi, musicologists, or American composers in these pages has the most frightening verisimilitude. And yet not one of these unfavorable essays is as notable as any of twenty or thirty favorable ones: moving and serious evocations of masterpieces, of composers and musicians at their greatest—essays full of a real forgetfulness of self, of anything at all but their subjects, that make one remember Goethe's "In the face of the great superiority of another person there is no means of safety but love."

All Mr. Haggin's unfavorable pieces seem necessary and useful: taste has to be maintained (or elevated, if it's at too low a level to make maintenance bearable), and there is no other way of doing it. His detailed, thoroughly explained, thoroughly persuasive objections to some of the great virtuoso performances of the day—those of Horowitz, Heifetz, Stokowski, and so on—must have been particularly valuable; and his pieces on the lapses and excesses of the really great have made his eulogies of their triumphs even more convincing than they would otherwise have been. His remarks about several bad critics are no more—far less—than they deserve; and his paragraphs or essays about Tovey, Dent, Turner, Virgil Thomson, Shaw, Lambert, and Sullivan are admiring and convincing enough to send many additional readers to their books. (Too unqualifiedly admiring, once: I grew up on Shaw's criticism; and neither my delight in it nor Mr. Haggin's admiration for it can make me forget passages like that wonderful one in which Shaw—after telling how Mozart bathed in the Rhine by moonlight to get those "airs from Heaven and blasts from Hell" of which *Don Giovanni* is full—implores his readers not to let this romanticism, mesmeric as it is, win them away from the everyday matter-of-fact realism of the *Ring*.)

One of the most appealing and amusing sections of *Music in The Nation* is one (indexed as Stravinsky, Igor: change in author's response to, 311) which begins: "Some of the kind of music by Stravinsky in which I used to hear only 'expertly contrived aridity and ugliness' I have recently begun to find interesting and enjoyable; and nobody could be more surprised at this than myself." Balanchine's choreography acted as a catalyst for the process, as Mr. Haggin watched and heard, again and again, *Danses Concertantes* and *Le Baiser de la fée;* and before long he found himself liking, almost as much, unaccompanied Stravinsky—and late Stravinsky at that, not the earlier he had always liked. This sort of admission of error, of change, makes us trust a critic as nothing else but omniscience could; but in this case it makes one wish, very hard, that Balanchine had written ballets to a couple of scores by Bartók: that is, it makes one feel that there is a certain amount of other modern music that Mr. Haggin would find interesting and enjoyable if he had listened to it enough, *without judgment,* to become as thoroughly familiar with it as he is with *Danses Concertantes.* This certainly hasn't been one of the great ages of music: one has a real sympathy for Mr. Haggin's lack of sympathy with it; but one can't help feeling that a critic who likes the Stravinsky that Mr. Haggin likes, and the Prokofiev First Violin Concerto, and who writes so well about *Das Lied von der Erde, ought* to like as wonderful a piece as Bartók's First Quartet.

Since *Music in The Nation* treats—with equal penetration, style, and conviction—everything from Mozart's financial circumstances to the nature and responsibilities of criticism, it is not a book of whose subject matter one is likely to tire. I've read most of these pieces, here or in *The Nation,* enough times to feel safe in saying that it is a book that particularly repays rereading. A critic like Mr. Haggin writes best about the composers he likes most: one thinks immediately of Beethoven, of Schubert (especially the late works), of Haydn, of Berlioz, and—first and last of all—of Mozart. Who else has conveyed so well the quality, range, and value of those wonderful contemporary works of art, the ballets of George Balanchine? And one can say something similar about the performances of several of those artists whom Mr. Haggin writes about again and again: Schnabel, Szigeti, Toscanini, Beecham, the Budapest Quartet, Landowska, Casals, Lotte Lehmann, Elisabeth Schumann, Aitken, Markova, Danilova. No one is likely to undervalue a critic who has written about these great artists, and their arts, with such seriousness, insight, and love.

Poetry, Unlimited

PARTISAN REVIEW, FEBRUARY 1950

The Arrivistes by Louis Simpson   *The Creaking Stair* by Elizabeth Coatsworth   *No Moat No Castle* by Donald F. Drummond   *The Broken Landscape* by John Williams   *Yoked by Violence* by John Pauker   *An Acre in the Seed* by Theodore Spencer   *The Beast in His Hunger* by Harry Brown   *Poems 1943–1949* by Francis Golffing   *Volume Two* by José Garcia Villa

THERE ISN'T a good poem in *The Arrivistes,* but Louis Simpson is as promising a new poet as I've read in some time. His poems are gay, felt, mocking, rather inexperienced, thoroughly uneven, thoroughly unexpected poems; they are not organized or thought out into successful works of art, but a few of their lines or stanzas are good, and more than a few are beautifully funny (for instance, the pseudo-Jacobean sections of "The Vagrants"). The ordinary young poet is a part of all that he has read, a summation of standard influences, as tame as can be. Mr. Simpson seems genuinely wild: sometimes he sounds like himself, a surprising creature in a surprising world, and the rest of the time he manages to make (sometimes very funny) allusions out of all his influences, so that his rhetorical education is one public joke after another. His worst mistakes, awful mistakes, somehow don't alienate you; at his best he is witty and moving, a fine amateur who ought—with luck—to turn into a good professional. He is a surprisingly *live* poet: as you read him you forget for a moment that we are the ancients. A critic can hardly resist saying to this particular poet: Whatever you do, don't pay any attention to critics—and here is a quotation to use as an amulet: "Against criticism we can neither protect nor defend ourselves; we must act in despite of it, and gradually it resigns itself to this."

The poems in Elizabeth Coatsworth's *The Creaking Stair* are, roughly, more commonplace versions of de la Mare's scary poems; all the fairy-tale, ghost-story properties in the world are in them. But sometimes these are used, not just exhibited, and once or twice they come to exact and frightening life: the ogre's maid, scrubbing the floor with her household soap of merchants' fat, finishes by praising the ogre's wife for having been

> *patience' self to me,*
> *though she could never understand*
> *the dreadful shaking of my hand*
> *skimming the broth or pouring that thick tea.*

The extra foot in the last line—no other line in the poem has five—helps to make *that thick tea* a triumph; because of the line a good many readers may feel a flash of fondness for the poet, and say to themselves: The world never understands why our hands shake so as we serve it.

Donald Drummond is one of Yvor Winters's students. Some of his verse is serious ("'Huitzilopotchi's hunger must be fed!' / The outthrust arms enforced hysteria / On the brown mass below. Priest food! / ... His eyes flashed once and dulled again. He turned / And met the Spaniard's look. He saw the smile / Tighten the bearded lips"), some of it is jocular ("The chiselled good which Yvor Winters turns / Between his fingers makes him hard to please, / And though his critics often die from burns, / His friends as often freeze"), and all of it scans—if there are any prosodists who are also Mongolian idiots, this is the verse for them to scan. But if it were possible to like Mr. Drummond better than any other poet, one would like him better than John Williams, who is a poet representative enough to have no individual characteristics whatsoever. John Pauker's *Yoked by Violence* shows more wit, skill with language, and general intelligence than these other two members of Alan Swallow's New Poetry Series; but his poems are often derivative, tastelessly mannered, and heartlessly inconsequential. These books come rather surprisingly short of the Series' intention, which is to "present, each year, three important new poets who have not previously had collections of their own." This statement, for overweening yet somehow endearing ambition, rivals one I came on in a Soviet critic: "Subjective Objectivism in music has always been Nikolai Myaskovsky's intention."

The sestets of Theodore Spencer's *An Acre in the Seed* make fairly quiet and pointed observations, in verse at its worst commonplace and at its best pleasant; usually they sound like this poet and nobody else, but some of them are based on Frost's very short poems—"Perennial," "Fair," "Adult," and "The Iris" make this plain—and one or two sound like the notes to *The Double Man.* Such poems seem to have been more congenial to Spencer than anything very sizable or intense, and represent him, I imagine, as well as he can be represented.

Goethe said that the worst thing in art is technical facility accompanied by triteness. Many an artist, like God, has never needed to think twice about anything. His works are the mad scene from *Giselle*, on ice skates: he weeps, pulls out his hair—holding his wrists like Lifar—and tells you what Life is, all at a gliding forty miles an hour. Harry Brown is this sort of poet, a model of his kind. He can do anything another poet has done, and does it; but why that poet did it he will never know. (His book is almost a synopsis of middle and late Auden, and has smooth, faithful, senseless imitations of half a dozen other poets.) If Macaulay's was a style in which you couldn't tell the truth, Mr. Brown's is a style in which you can't tell anything: the matter of the poems is no more than a vehicle for their manner, an accomplished and unimaginably unconvincing one.

Francis Golffing's *Poems 1943–1949* is one of the Cummington Press's prettiest little books. The poems are self-conscious, metallic, rather affected constructions—Mr. Golffing works so obtrusively that it is difficult to see past him to the poem. People once would have said that his vocabulary and techniques smell of the lamp; almost all the poems have the tinny glitter that makes one feel they are meant to be praised for their "strict wit." Two or three of them *are* successful as wit, if not as poetry; several of the ideas are better than their execution; and a poem about the sun ends excellently: *Changed by the fierce sympathy / That, passing across vapor, leaves it clear.* But then the reader gets to the Rilke translations at the end of the book; a wondering shudder comes over him, he is in a different universe:

> *Behind the inculpable trees*
> *slowly the old Fatality*
> *works out her silent face.*
> *Wrinkles are drawing that way . . .*
> *What down here a bird screeches*
> *bends off as a woe-line*
> *at the hard soothsaying mouth.*
>
> *O and the soon-to-be lovers*
> *smile on each other, ignorant of farewells.*
> *Over them sets and rises*
> *starlike their destiny.*

No, poetry is something written by poets or by accident.

Once upon a time, in Manila or Guadalajara, as he sat outside a convent wall and listened to the nuns preparing a confection called Angels' Milk, a little boy decided to go to New York City and become a great poet. There he wrote a book called, charmingly, *Have Come, Am Here;* after he had read the reviews of it he telegraphed to his parents, *Vici,* and said to himself, in his warm, gentle, Southern way: "What critics these mortals be!" For Edith Sitwell had said that he was "a poet with a great, even an astounding, and perfectly original gift . . . no poet now writing is more so"; Mark Van Doren had spoken of his "purest and most natural gifts . . . his power to say, quietly, the most astonishing and exalted things"; Marianne Moore had said, "Final wisdom encountered in poem after poem." Babette Deutsch wrote that his poetry was "as singular as the work of Emily Dickinson or Hopkins"; Conrad Aiken wrote that he was "the most important new poet in America in a decade"—Irwin Edman, in a generation.

For there to be great poets there must be great audiences too: the poet, sure of his, wrote *Volume Two.* He wrote a poem made of 476 commas, a poem made of 132 repetitions of the letter *O,* and a poem—called "The Emperor's New Sonnet," naturally—made of nothing at all. He wrote eighty Aphorisms like "LOVE-KNOW / LOVE-DO"; like "Imperil, me—*Mohammedan, rose!*" For a hundred and fifty pages he put a comma between each word and the next; as he says, "The result is a lineal pace of quiet dignity and movement." For instance:

> *Pale, vermouth, ultraviolet,*
> *And, tender, lambs, astray,*
> *But, if, these, keep, love, beautiful,*
> *Sweet, heavens, yes.*
>
> *If, they, keep, love, beautiful,*
> *Wych-tree, wych-bird,*
> *Any, living, whyless, do,*
> *In, that, living, kingdom, fire.*

This is a typical passage. But so is any passage. One reads a poem and asks oneself *Isn't this the poem before?*—but when one goes back and reads that, one asks oneself, *Isn't this the poem before?* But it is time for the end of my story: imagine Miss Sitwell and Mr. Van Doren and Miss Deutsch; imagine them somewhere in *Volume Two,* turning its commas slowly over on their tongues, and thinking a little complacently, a little drowsily, but with perfect truth: "If it hadn't been for *my* encouragement Mr. Villa would never have gone on to write 'The Emperor's New Sonnet.' "

I wish that I had had the wit to invent this story, a parable of the way in which critics can guide and encourage the poet to the fullest realization of his powers—but in these matters art limps trembling behind reality. I thought of calling a fairy tale of this kind *The Perfect Fool*, but then it occurred to me that it would be better to call it *The Perfect Fools*.

The Profession of Poetry

PARTISAN REVIEW, SEPTEMBER–OCTOBER 1950

Fingerboard by Marshall Schacht   *A Fountain in Kentucky* by John Frederick Nims   *Guide to the Ruins* by Howard Nemerov *Welcome to the Castle* by Alfred Hayes   *Kaire* by E. E. Cummings   *The Collected Poetry of Isaac Rosenberg*   *Poems* by Wilfred Owen

WHAT TO LEAVE OUT is the first thing the artist has to decide; a painter who "held the mirror up to nature" would spend his life on the leaves of one landscape. The work of art's fluctuating and idiosyncratic threshold of attention—the great things disregarded, the small things seized and dwelt on—is as much of a signature as anything in it. In Marshall Schacht's poems this threshold is a curve drawn with a compass: its outlines, the outlines of everything else, have the reasonable (and, in the end, maddening to the reader) simplification and conventionalization of a Grant Wood tree, of old bars of soap; they are not the silhouette of the artist, but of the procedure by which the artist found it easy to write the poem. Someone praises these poems by speaking of their "deceptive simplicity": it is this deceived and conscious "simplicity" of form and content which serves Mr. Schacht for a style—that is, instead of a style—so that he reminds one of those carefully humble, awkward, sincere persons, full of hesitations, *wells,* and *you knows,* half *jeune fille,* half Grandma Moses, whose lives are one long moral victory over their suffering and inattentive friends.

These poems seem to me the equivalent of the paintings of amateurs, of the musical performances of doctors who one evening a week play in quartets; nobody dreams of comparing their performances with those of Klee or Lehmann, so why should I compare Mr. Schacht's poems with Rilke's? (I suppose this is what the dust jacket's critic means when he says, in the style of Atticus, that "without this kind of poetry there can be no general diffusion of literary culture in any society.") I, like any society, don't enjoy this kind of poetry except in an occasional faint cotton-candy way; but I am bothered not so much by the limitations these poems set up into a style—any style is as much what you can't say as what you can—as by the sensibility they limit, which thinks that "the minor thrush" is "cause enough for major sunsets," or which writes:

> *I also note Tom's greatest novel said*
> *That he wished to be remembered with the dead*
> *Who thought and loved no more than he in bed.*

John Frederick Nims's first book of poems depressed me because it made me feel that poetry is a profession to be learned like any other—that bees, if they could read, would make the best poets; I felt as I had felt when a most distinguished critic said to me, after I had asked him what he thought of one of Mann's books: "Well, you know, the fact is, I've never really got up on Mann. I've always meant to." Mr. Nims used to write fairly synthetic, extraordinarily concentrated adaptations of those Audenesque poems of Shapiro's which give a rapid, almost blatantly effective description of the more obvious features of an American scene; he would crowd so many effects into every line that reading a stanza was like having one's mouth stuffed with pennies—and the stanza seldom had any of the individuality, the fresh animal ease, that Shapiro would have given it. In *A Fountain in Kentucky* Mr. Nims has improved a great deal: these poems are mild and human and bearable, compared to the old; but they are all spoiled by the commonplaceness, the moderately effective approximation, the undistinguished essential anonymity that spoil the work of most of the younger American poets. One never feels, "How *like* Mr. Nims," "Who else in the world would have thought of *that*," or any of the other silly exclamations that go along with a good line. One feels, instead: this is the sort of thing a man says to write poems; that adjective does pretty well—pretty well. And the *I* of the poems (as it usually is with the youngish American poets of whom I am speaking) is that composite photograph, that institutional lay figure, that poet in the street, which conceals beyond any possibility of revelation the features of the living being, the poor unprofessional animal that feeds and obeys (and unto please what end) the industrious typewriter-like double that turns out the poems. *Which of you by taking thought can add a line to a poem?* one wants to ask this *I;* and one can imagine the rightfully puzzled answer: *Why, I thought of every word of it.*

When one turns to Howard Nemerov's *Guide to the Ruins,* it is what one doesn't find that makes Mr. Nemerov seem, immediately, a more intelligent and individual poet—most of Mr. Nims's standard professional effects have been replaced by a dry plainness and hardness, a "classical" stiffness and severity. Now if Odysseus tried to swim ashore to the Sirens, it wasn't for the stretchèd meter of an antique song, but for something that sounded—as he must have said to his men afterwards—a lot like Alban Berg; and, too, Mr. Nemerov's "classicism" is just as much of a learned bedside manner (modeled, as different poems show, on Empson, Ransom, and Tate) as is Mr. Nims's mechanical gingerbread. But at least it isn't the sort of manner that stupefies the patient before he can even hear the prescription; and it is, at times, thin enough to seem a morning mist, fairly easily burned off. This book— very much a second book—shows an often vexing wit; half the poems have the decided-upon look of exercises—are possessed, if at all, by worked-out formulae of hypothetical demons; and many of them might be given the name that John Berryman—a better poet with whom Mr. Nemerov has something in common—gave to some of his: "The Nervous Songs." But the book is here and there sharp enough, dry enough, and serious enough—shows, too, enough gift for organization— to make one interested in Mr. Nemerov's future poems. He knows very well that the poet, as Goethe says, is someone who takes risks (and today most intellectuals take no risks at all—are, from the cradle, critics); but he thinks romantic and old-fashioned, couldn't believe, or hasn't heard of something else Goethe said: that the poet is essentially naïve.

Alfred Hayes is unusual because he is interested in people—most contemporary poets think them one of the causes of words—and because he has a rare ill-brokered talent for thinking up ingenious, immediately effective ideas for poems (so that one can identify his best poem merely by saying: "Oh, you know, it's that poem in *A Little Treasury of Modern Verse* that's a conceit about pigs in a slaughterhouse"). These ideas usually are worked out well enough—which is to say, not really well enough at all—in a rhetoric that is frighteningly near to becoming, or that long ago became, vulgarly effective in the way that *Death of a Salesman* or good radio sketches or imitation Hemingway stories are effective. Mr. Hayes's poems about Italy, which are poorer than his others, are unusually influenced—just as his stories are usually influenced —by Hemingway; and he is influenced, both usually and overwhelmingly, by various periods of Auden—for instance, "In the Days of the Recruiting Stations" is thoroughly like "Which Side Am I Supposed to Be On," and his poem about Heine at Paris is an amusingly faithful imitation of "Voltaire at Ferney," even down to cadences: because the last line of Auden's first stanza is *The white alps glittered. It was sum-*

mer. He was very great, the last line of Mr. Hayes's first stanza is *Marx was in England; Gautier was his friend; Goethe was dead.* This seems to suggest that there is in this world no line so bad that someone won't someday copy it. (Although the disciple's semicolons are, logically, an improvement on the original periods, they strip from the line its lucid atmosphere of Beatrix Potter; Mr. Hayes has not truly understood it, one is ready to feel: and then one looks at his *Goethe was dead*—that superb reproduction, on another plane, of the pure *statement* of *He was very great*—and decides that for a moment he did not merely understand, but *was,* that line.)

Yet in spite of all his influences—there are several others—Mr. Hayes is in some sense a fairly individual poet; in spite of all his rhetoric he is in some sense an attractive poet. For he isn't interested in putting on a slick professional performance, in showing off a learned collection of juggler's tricks; it was not of Mr. Hayes, but of hundreds of other poets, that I thought when I read, in my *Handbook of American Birds*: "Starlings are noisy at all seasons, and the song is a jumble of squeaks, rattles, wheezes, loud whistles, and imitations (often excellent) of other birds." Mr. Hayes wants to move and terrify people with what has moved and terrified him in this world—so that you respect him even when, as usually happens, two things go wrong with his procedure: when he does what he does in too crude and direct and reliable a way; and when what he has seen and been moved by, the emotional and intellectual climates of the poems, so badly lack personal distortion, the unconscious individuality which at once signs and guarantees, that the poem seems to represent faithfully and immediately a fairly common type or group, but without ever speaking—as the best poems do—for the poet and everybody. "Jael," one of the most interesting of his poems, is intended to be grand and monumental, and to a surprising extent it succeeds; but when one compares it to the best-known poem on a similar subject, Ransom's "Judith of Bethulia," one sees that in "Judith" the language itself links to the peculiarity of the past the peculiarity of the poet, and gives to the florid, Venetian, Marriage-at-Cana tableau an equivocal, particular truth that is wanting in the generalized astronomical finality of "Jael." It seems to me that Mr. Hayes can write better poems than those he usually tries to write; as a naturally effective writer, he ought to despise effectiveness, and to try for individuality, exactness, complication. At present he is like some friend, serious, sympathetic, rather gifted, who six days out of the week speaks and thinks and feels in such heartfelt clichés that he finally seems to you the myth made flesh, a generalized, breathing, statistical reality.

During the early twenties E. E. Cummings's reputation was at its highest point: at one moment, a sort of false dawn, he was more imitated, better regarded, than Eliot himself. But as people came to demand that poets, and the very chairs they sat in, be socially conscious, Mr. Cummings slowly came to seem an irrelevant and unaccountable anachronism; when poets read his verse, as it pushed on into the heart of that last undiscovered continent, e. e. cummings, they thought of this moral impossibility, this living fossil, with a sort of awed revulsion. Later, as the fortunes of unengaged art improved, as novels by E. M. Forster replaced novels about strikes, as Mr. Cummings approached a certain age—that age at which literary survivors come to the king's row, and are accepted as Fathers of the Tribe—most of his reputation returned, and he now seems one more dean of American poets. He had a sort of underground popularity even during the darkest thirties—many a good Party member had a guilty taste for Cummings or Sherlock Holmes; I think that he will remain popular for a long time, for several reasons. He is one of the most individual poets who ever lived—and, though it sometimes seems so, it is not just his vices and exaggerations, the defects of his qualities, that make a writer popular. But, primarily, Mr. Cummings's poems are loved because they are full of sentimentality, of sex, of more or less improper jokes, of elementary lyric insistence—they are the popular songs of American intellectuals. (I hope the reader won't think this a joke, but will seriously consider the similarities between the two.) That the poems are extravagantly, professedly modernist, experimental, avant-garde, is an additional attraction: the reader of modern poetry—especially the inexperienced or unwilling reader—feels toward them the same gratitude that the gallery-goer feels when, his eyes blurred with corridors of analytical cubism, he comes into a little room full of the Pink and Blue periods of Picasso. Even the poems' difficulties are of an undemanding, unaccusing sort—that of puzzles: a poem that looks like the ruins of a type-casting establishment will not elicit from the editors of *The Saturday Review of Literature* a fraction of the indignation with which they see, in Eliot, some random quotation from Pausanias.

Rilke, in his wonderful "Archaic Statue of Apollo," ends his description of the statue, the poem itself, by saying without transition or explanation: *You must change your life.* He needs no explanation. We know from many experiences that this is what the work of art does: its life—in which we have shared the alien existences both of this world and of that different world to which the work of art alone gives us access—unwillingly accuses our lives. But Mr. Cummings's poems say to us something very different: that we and the poet are so superior to the fools and pedants and reformers of the world that our only obligation is to condemn them, to draw apart into rapture—the reader is asked to wash his hands of them, and to become part of the sanctimonious anarchic ecstasy of the poem. The poet has made a separate peace; sitting among the lakes and flowers of a Swiss summer, he complacently dismisses the fools killing each other below, people who have never even realized that love is enough. I have heard only once his recording of his poem about the soldier from New York City who is killed by steel from the Sixth Avenue Elevated; but I shall never forget the firm superiority, the confident rejection of the voice as it said that you and I told him, Christ told him, Socrates told him, and he wouldn't listen; but part of the old Sixth Avenue Elevated, in a Japanese shell—*that* made him listen . . . Yes, Christ and Socrates did tell him (though it is odd to see that old soldier Socrates in this particular connection), and he didn't listen; but they told you and me and Mr. Cummings this and many other things, and we listened to few and lived by fewer. In the triumph of his poems there is one thing lacking, that slave who whispers: You too are mortal. But usually Mr. Cummings is moral about not being conventionally moral: he resembles a student of ethics who, after reading that some tribes feed the old and others eat them, decides that it is all right to do anything anywhere, that the self-expression of the knowing superior is the one true key to ethics—and from then on he looks with pharisaical impatience at those not elect, weak spirits caught in the bloody toils of morality.

The poems' relation to "Nature" is impressive in its purity and delight, but depressing in its affinity to that of picture postcards; and Love, in the poems, is so disastrously neo-primitive, has been swept so fantastically clean of complication or pain or moral significance, that it seems a kind of ecstatic chocolate soda which is at once a sin—to the world—and a final good—to us happy few. For such poems Stendhal and Proust (and anyone who was ever in love, one is tempted to say) have lived and died in vain. One is bewildered by the complacency with which the poet accepts himself and his, and rejects or doesn't even notice the existence of the rest of the world. One of his poems lives along the line like Pope's spider, but hides at the heart of its sensitivity a satisfied inaccessibility to experience—for experience is, after all, what is different from oneself. He has hidden his talent under a flower, and there it has gone on reproducing, by parthenogenesis, poem after poem after poem. Because of this his poems are, year after year, the same poems; the only true changes are technical changes, ingenious discoveries exhaustively exploited. He is like a painter who has on every canvas charming and characteristic patches, colors that are a pleasure in themselves, but who has never once managed to paint a good picture. For I can't think of a single poem of his that can be called, in the most serious meaning of the phrase, a good poem. When one asks people to name one they seem oddly at a loss, and finally mention poems like "My father moved through dooms of shall" or "Anyone lived in a pretty how town"— attractive poems which are spoiled both by filling in, the automatic repetition of technical novelties (as if you wrote a poem by discovering a novel formula and repeating it a dozen times), and by the willing shallowness of the attitude which produces them, that Renascence of Wonder of our own day. (And something as wonderfully promising as *The Enormous Room* is the most distressing disappointment of all—as though one could read *The House of the Dead* only in an adaptation by Paul Goodman and Kenneth Patchen.) Even Mr. Cummings's delectable freshness and innocence have come to seem professionally surprising in the way that, say, Mistinguette's legs are: how much care and avoidance, what cloistral resolution, have been necessary to preserve intact this stock in trade!

Yet how wonderfully individual, characteristic, original, all his poems are. (Thinking how extraordinarily true to himself he has been, how false to every other man, one is forced to remember how far from "self-expression" great poems are—what a strange compromise between the demands of the self, the world, and Poetry they actually represent.) And Mr. Cummings's poems are full of perceptions pure as those in dreams, effects of wonderful delicacy and exactness; many a flower of rank sentiment twinkles at one such dewy petals that one gobbles it up like a cow. In fact, as soon as the reader lowers the demands he makes on art—pretends that it is, at best, no more than a delightful or ecstatic or ingenious diversion—the best poems become a thorough pleasure. For Mr. Cummings is a fine poet in the sense in which Swinburne is one; but in the sense in which we call Hardy and Yeats and Proust and Chekhov poets, great poets, he is hardly a poet at all. Marshal Zhdanov said, delighting me: *There is a great big hole in the foundations of Soviet music;* well, there is a great big moral vacuum at the heart of E. E. Cummings's poetry. As Louise Bogan has written, with summary truth: "It is this deletion of the tragic that makes Cummings's joy childish and his anger petulant." What delights and amuses and disgusts us he has represented; but all that is heartbreaking in the world, the pity and helplessness and love that were called, once, the tears of things, the heart of heartlessness—these hardly exist for him.

It seems many years too late to review the poetry of Isaac Rosenberg or Wilfred Owen; but I should like to express my surprise at the common judgment that thinks both interesting "war poets," with Owen, of course, rather the better of the two. Rosenberg surely was a poet of no merit whatsoever; and Owen—in spite of passages lush as Brooke, of touching haste and inexperience, of a compulsive eagerness to push home all his points, to make his readers see beyond possibility of misunderstanding what the war was—surely was a poet in the true sense of the word, someone who has shown to us one of those worlds which, after we have been shown it, we call the real world. The best criticism of Owen I have ever read was Yvor Winters's review in an old *Hound and Horn*; it is worth looking up. One does not get a fair idea of Owen from anthologies, which always include a number of bad and sentimental poems, omit some of the best ones, and, naturally, are unable to do anything with the good passages of mediocre ones. He was occasionally a good poet—and would, surely, have become a better; I should like to finish this review by quoting lines I have often remembered, a stanza from "Exposure" and the last stanza of "The Send-Off":

Slowly our ghosts drag home: glimpsing the sunk fires, glozed
With crusted dark-red jewels; crickets jingle there;
For hours the innocent mice rejoice: the house is theirs;
Shutters and doors, all closed: on us the doors are closed,—
  We turn back to our dying.

Shall they return to beatings of great bells
In wild train-loads?
A few, a few, too few for drums and yells,
May creep back, silent, to still village wells
Up half-known roads.

Answers to Questions

MID-CENTURY AMERICAN POETS, EDITED BY JOHN CIARDI, 1950

1 (ORAL QUALITY). All my poems are meant to be said aloud; many of them are dramatic speeches or scenes.

2 (audience). I don't know whom they are written for—for the usual audience that reads poetry from age to age, I believe, and not for the more specialized audience that reads modern poetry. It seems to me that the poet's responsibility is to his subject matter, but that one of the determining conditions of the poem is the hypothetical normal audience for which he writes it. No one would say that a mathematician or scientist is chiefly or directly responsible to his readers; it is a mistake to say that a poet is.

3 (language). I try to make the language fit the poem. Since the poem is one of my actions, it will have a family resemblance to other actions and poems of mine, but I do not try to make it have one. As the cartwright in Chuang-tze says, "When I make the spokes too tight, they won't fit the wheel, and when I make them too loose, they will not hold. I have to make them just right. I feel them with my hands and judge them with my heart. There is something about it which I cannot put down in words. I cannot teach that feeling to my own son, and my own son cannot learn it from me." And he finishes as anyone would like to finish: "Therefore, at the age of seventy, I am good at making wheels."

4 (overtones). If the poem has a quiet or neutral ground, a delicate or complicated figure can stand out against it; if the ground is exaggerated and violent enough, no figure will.

5 (levels of meaning). It is better to have the child in the chimney corner moved by what happens in the poem, in spite of his ignorance of its real meaning, than to have the poem a puzzle to which that meaning is the only key. Still, complicated subjects make complicated poems, and some of the best poems can move only the best readers; this is one more question of curves of normal distribution. I have tried to make my poems plain, and most of them are plain enough; but I wish that they were more difficult because I had known more.

6 (subjects). Half my poems are about the war, half are not. Some of their usual subjects are: airplanes and their crews, animals, ballet,

carriers, children, concentration camps, the dead and dying, dreams, forests, graves, hospitals, letters, libraries, love, *Märchen,* moralities, people in extreme situations, prisoners, soldiers, the State, training camps, Western scientific and technical development—in short, *la condition humaine.* Some of these I enjoy writing about, others I could not help writing about. Ordinarily the poems are dramatic or have implied narratives; few are pure lyrics.

7 (imagery). Images seem to me means, not ends; I often reread Proust, and almost never reread Virginia Woolf.

8 (symbols). In works of art almost anything stands for more than itself; but this *more,* like Lohengrin, vanishes when it names itself.

9 (rhyme). Rhyme as an automatic structural device, automatically attended to, is attractive to me, but I like it best irregular, live, and heard.

10 (line endings). I assume that the reader will indicate line endings when he reads the poem aloud; if he doesn't he is reading it as prose.

11 (the structure of the total poem; what makes its unity?). An answer would take too many pages.

12 (meter). Most of my poems are written in ordinary iambic verse, regular or irregular according to the poem. Once upon a time I wrote accentual verse; I've used irregular anapests for special-case poems, syllabic verse for translations of Corbière, and so on.

The questionnaire also says that *Any statement you make about the ethical-philosophical relation of the poet to his writing will be most welcome.* My poems show what this relation actually is for me; what I say that it should be matters less. I *think* that I am relatively indifferent to the poem-as-performance-of-the-poet, and try to let the poem have a life of its own; the reader of the poem can know whether or not this is true.

To write in this way about one's own poetry is extremely unpleasant and unnatural. A successful poem says what a poet wants to say, and more, with particular finality. The remarks he makes about his poems are incidental when the poem is good, and embarrassing or absurd when it is bad—and he is not permitted to say how the good poem is good, and may never know how the bad poem is bad. It is better to write about other people's poetry. But to be in this anthology, one had to write about one's own; and to have you read the poems, I was willing to write this prose.

No Love for Eliot

THE NEW YORK TIMES BOOK REVIEW, NOVEMBER 18, 1951

The T. S. Eliot Myth by Rossell Hope Robbins

HERE is a methodical insensate attack by a man driven by righteous indignation. Rossell Robbins says that he has "sought to disentangle the actual Eliot, a poet of minor achievement, emotionally sterile and with a mind coarsened by snobbery and constricted by bigotry, from the myth which has exalted him into a great poet and a cultural leader." To Robbins, Eliot is not really a writer but a sort of Goebbels of Respectable Reaction—so that he says of him: "It is time to ask whether his intransigent religious and political opinions have not obtruded so much into his poetry, his drama, and his prose that Eliot should perhaps no longer be considered a man of letters but a propagandist."

Robbins even speaks of Eliot's "most recent political work, *Four Quartets.*" Robbins does not, of course, consider the poem a political work; this is only a Freudian error; but it is a truthful and revealing error. Works of art—especially Eliot's—*are* political works to Robbins, and he judges them as such. He says: "The views on life we find in his poetry, with its restricted and limited imagery, in his drama, where all his characters are unloving and unlovable, and in his essays which are unashamedly reactionary . . . derive from an obvious hatred of people . . . A writer who is avowedly anti-human."

Rossell Robbins's condemnation is graceless, pitiless, and comes to seem endless; its excesses at first shock and at last amuse the reader. He writes, for instance: "Perhaps when the man-scorning, life-hating prejudices in his work have been swept away and forgotten except as source material examples of intellectual perversity, *Old Possum's Book of Practical Cats* is the book that future generations will read and enjoy." He explains Eliot's early reputation by writing: "He was able to gain immediate note as a literary critic, for example, because there were so few critics in the earlier twentieth century in England . . . This lack of rigorous competition holds true for his poetry as well. There, too, he had few rivals."

The author's final explanation of "the Eliot myth" is this: "The current Eliot vogue is no mystery; the Eliot problem no enigma; it is the logical reflection of present-day decadence." I think this remark very man-scorning and life-hating and anti-human; people think Eliot a good poet because they like his poems, not because they are puppets of "present-day decadence." *Soviet Literature Today* always tells you you like Eliot's poetry because you are a decadent cannibal. Yet even a decadent cannibal sees more than the man who does not need to open his eyes.

No, Eliot is a fact, not a myth: a good poet; a bad dramatist; a sometimes bad and sometimes wonderful critic; a serious, limited, and often disquietingly unsatisfactory thinker about our culture. Robbins is, I find, an Englishman teaching at the Brooklyn Institute of Technology, a specialist in Middle English verse. When he writes about it he must surely tell good from bad, must show some sense of humility or humor or proportion. In writing about Eliot he does not; he is an Inquisitor. It is a shame that readers have to read a book like this, and a worse shame that Robbins had to write it: the readers are through with it after a couple of hours, but Robbins has had to live with it for years.

To Fill a Wilderness

THE NATION, DECEMBER 29, 1951

A Dictionary of Americanisms, edited by Mitford M. Mathews

IT WOULD TAKE a lexicographer to write a review of *A Dictionary of Americanisms*—this is only an appreciation. Lexicographers say very convincingly, in several reviews I have read, that the dictionary is a judicious, copious, and unusually excellent book. That they said so pleased me, its faithful reader: I have owned and lived with and read around in this dictionary for several months, long enough to have developed a strong patriotic feeling about it—I would hate to have anybody look down on it. But who is going to look down on a book that costs fifty dollars? a book whose two dignified black-and-blue volumes are so monumental that one is afraid either to lift them or to put them down on anything but the floor? a book that makes *Huckleberry Finn* look like one of the posthumous works of Jean Racine? I am not joking; this is the most American book that I have ever read. It contains most of the new words that we Americans invented, and most of the new meanings we found for the words that we already had; some are illustrated by tame, pleasant, informative little drawings, and all are illustrated—in the most satisfying profusion—by wild, wonderful, more than informative quotations from newspapers and magazines and books and letters and speeches. Here are our fathers in direct quotation.

These quotations have not lost their life with the years, and that life is—to us—a mixed blessing, something that both delights and disquiets. As we read these quotations we may see our nation's life as Yeats saw his own—as a preparation for something that never happened. The quotations dump us into a small new world that may seem to us older and larger than our own—a world of which we may seem to ourselves, in some sense, the dwarfed and scanty survivors. (I think that George Washington would be extremely afraid of the traffic on the Merritt Parkway, but I think that we would be afraid of George Washington.) The people who wrote these quotations had left a good deal in Europe, and it was impossible for them to fill a wilderness with what they had kept; they made up things fast—more than anyone else has ever made up, that fast—and as they made them they looked around with the confidence of accomplishment. If they didn't have it they could get it for you. They took their chances and the chances always worked— or if they didn't, the people they didn't work for were dead and didn't get into the quotations: all *these* words, you can see from a block away, were made by the livest of the live, men who named the plants and animals of a new world as Adam and Eve named those of Paradise, but with less hesitation. *Never explain, never excuse,* advised one of an older and uneasier race; these people explained and excused at the top of their voices, not needing to, just wanting to—it was one more thing to do, and they did everything. But they knew that they were their own excuse for being; or would have known it if they had had to stop to think about it. I sound rhetorical, but consider what I'm writing about! It would look tame to them: "I'm all brimstone, and ride the roughest rocking horse in any three of the United States," as one of them says under *Brimstone.*

Some of them remind us, sometimes, of men from Plutarch, and this is not just because they were imitating men from Plutarch. They had escaped from the scheme of things, and had set up a new one somewhere west of the sun and west of the moon. It was a kind of fault in time, a vacation from necessity; and it is hard for their descendants to have to come back to the human condition, to Europe, to the West that they had sailed west away from, and to face across Europe those Europeans who had gone east to make another people half European. As we and the Russians look at each other over Europe, how bitterly the Europeans must think, *No more colonies!* For Montezuma never sent an ambassador to the Vatican, or one bomber to bases in Tripolitania; and Genghis Khan, say what you like about him, stopped a long way east of Berlin.

Philosophers talk about a very primitive but very certain form of knowing called *knowledge by acquaintance.* As I read this dictionary (it is much too good merely to look things up in, you *read* it, and you don't complain of any lack of plot: that it is what it is and you are what you are is plot enough) I couldn't help feeling that it is just such knowledge of America that this book gives you or reminds you that you already have. It is knowledge of an America part of which has ceased to exist; but this is the echo of all of it.

On the Underside of the Stone

THE NEW YORK TIMES BOOK REVIEW, AUGUST 23, 1953

Brother to Dragons: A Tale in Verse and Voices by Robert Penn Warren

THIS IS Robert Penn Warren's best book. It is the story of a peculiarly atrocious murder that took place in the family of Charles and Lucy Lewis, the brother-in-law and sister of Thomas Jefferson. The murderers were their sons, Lilburn and Isham; the murdered man was their slave. These people, Jefferson, Lilburn's wife Laetitia, Lilburn's Negro mammy Aunt Cat, Lilburn's (and Jefferson's) cousin Meriwether Lewis, Laetitia's brother, and Warren himself speak the poem. They say what people do not say, but would say if they could. When they are through we know them, and what they have done, very thoroughly, and we give a long marveling sigh.

About Laetitia and Ishey-Boy, two of the most touching creations in American literature; about Aunt Cat, whose concluding lullaby Schubert and Mahler and Wolf together couldn't have done justice to; about that brother, about Lilburn, about the moth that lights on Lilburn's hand, even, our disbelief is suspended forever. We *were* Laetitia and Isham and Lilburn: so they are clubs we can beat Jefferson and Charles and Lucy and Meriwether Lewis and—but only half the time—Warren over the head with, when these seem to us more rhetorical and moralizing than life.

Warren's florid, massive, rather oratorical rhetoric, with its cold surprises, its accustomed accomplished continuations, its conscious echoes of Milton and Shakespeare, its unconscious echoes of Eliot and Arnold and Warren, is sometimes miraculous, often effective, and sometimes too noticeable to bear. Warren's impressive verbal gifts are less overwhelming than his dramatic gifts, one is tempted to say; but then one remembers Laetitia and the others—and the first speeches of Adam and Eve and the animals were hardly fresher, hardly more natural, hardly more unexpected, than the best of the speeches of these descendants of theirs.

Warren moralizes for effect and out of necessity: man is the animal that moralizes. Man is also the animal that complains about being one, and says that there is an animal, a beast inside him—that he is brother to dragons. (He is certainly a brother to wolves, and to pandas too, but he is father to dragons, not brother: they, like many gods and devils, are inventions of his.) The character in *Brother to Dragons* most loathingly obsessed with man's dragonish heart is a part of Warren which he calls Thomas Jefferson. The live Jefferson spoke and believed that Noble Lie of man's innocence and perfectibility which, Meriwether Lewis is made to say, "was my death."

The live Jefferson had not prepared Lewis for the ignoble truth of man's depravity; the dead Jefferson hammers it home with ignoble avidity. The dead Jefferson looks at the obscene underside of the stone and—he can do no other—licks his lips: he knows, now. Most of us know, now, that Rousseau was wrong: that man, when you knock his chains off, sets up the death camps. Soon we shall know everything the eighteenth century didn't know, and nothing it did, and it will be hard to live with us.

Brother to Dragons is written out of an awful time, about an awful, a traumatic subject: sin, Original Sin, without any Savior. The time is the subject; but the poem is a net, wide enough, high enough, deep enough, to have caught most of the world inside it—and if happiness, "a butterfly and not a gloomy bird of prey," has flown through its iron interstices as if they weren't there, it wasn't happiness Warren was in pursuit of, but the knowledge of Good and Evil.

Cruel sometimes, crude sometimes, obsessed sometimes, the book is always extraordinary: it does know, and knows sadly and tenderly, even. It is, in short, an event, a great one. There is a wonderful amount of life in it, of living beings who are free of Warren's rhetoric and moralizing, and of ours—are freed by their share in that reality or power or knowledge or glory which, as Warren says contradictorily and very humanly, is the one thing man lives by.

Malraux and the Statues at Bamberg

ART NEWS, DECEMBER 1953

The Voices of Silence by André Malraux

IT IS NO USE to tell you to read *The Voices of Silence:* if you care for art and know how to read, you have read it or will read it. And if you don't care for art but know about it instead, and have spent your life stopping up the holes in your dressing gown with the canvases of the universe—even then you will read it, so as to be able to call Malraux a phrase-making amateur standing on the shoulders of better art historians. And if you say this, there will be something in what you say. Malraux does stand head and shoulders above most writers on art, though I doubt that he gets this way simply by basing himself on them; he is an amateur—he speaks with all of the exaggeration of love and some of its errors; and he makes phrases as naturally as—or rather, considerably more naturally than—he breathes. (His last breath is going to be drawn in the Pantheon, under the subjugated eyes of Academicians, and his earlier breaths have been changed by knowing this.)

Malraux's book is a long, lyrical, aphoristic, oratorical, wonderfully illustrated Discourse on the Arts of this Earth, with space for Celtic coins, van Meegeren's Vermeers, any artist who ever was, fairy tales, religions, a history of taste, the drawings of the insane, best-sellers, the influence of Tintoretto on cameramen: it is a kind of (very elevated) Flea Market of the Absolute, with room even for a remark about paintings at the Flea Market. Malraux's intelligence, imagination, and originality manifest themselves as much in his choice of subjects as in what he has to say. His work is not art history, exactly, but a kind of free fantasia on themes from the history of art—still, a successful enough confusion of genres is a new genre, and Malraux's book, which now stands solitary as *Alice,* will probably have some dreadful descendants.

It is certainly one of the most interesting books ever written: Malraux writes a passage of ordinary exposition so that we breathe irregularly and jerk our heads from side to side, like spectators at a tennis match. He conducts an argument (and he can't even tell you that Art isn't Photography without having a fearful and dazzling argument that leaves you sorry you ever thought it was) as other people conduct a campaign, and his pages are full of speeches to the soldiers, of epigrams and aphorisms and passages of more-than-Tyrian purple, of *Te Deums,* of straw men with their bowels all over the countryside: it is as if we were getting to see a *Massacre of the Innocents* begun by Uccello, concluded by Caravaggio, and preserved for us, I do not need to say miraculously, in an armory of the Knights of Malta.

Malraux tells us hundreds of times that the artist "masters" the world, "conquers" his material, "destroys" the works of the predecessors he admires; art is a "victory" over reality, the work of art "subjugates" its spectator: the root metaphor underlying Malraux's view of art is one of conquest, of victory, power, domination. (One feels: how all the animals do order each other around!) Chardin's "seeming humility" is said to involve the model's "destruction"; Malraux says in a typical sentence: "That eternal *youngness* of mornings in the Ile-de-France and that shimmer—like the long, murmurous cadences of the *Odyssey*—in the Provençal air cannot be imitated; they must be conquered." Conquered! The sentence is worthy of Cortez, of Pizarro, of those lunatics who used to think themselves Napoleon. How do you "conquer" a shimmer in the air, the youngness of morning? We do not know how to go about it; most of us do not even know how to want to go about it. Such things cannot be imitated, Malraux is right; they must be translated. The artist translates, finds an equivalent for, makes a painting or poem or piece of music that has, that shimmer—and, often, in the purity of separation, the youngness seems to us younger, the shimmer more shimmering. Art matches the world idiom for idiom; the work of art is not a conquest of the things of the world but their apotheosis. Really Malraux knows this: as he says, the buffalo in some Cro-Magnon cave is not a different buffalo but *more* buffalo—the buffalo of the world is not subjugated beneath it, conquered by it, but realized in it.*

---

* What I had remembered Malraux as saying is quite different from what he actually says: "If the Magdalenian bison is more than a sign and also more than a piece of illusionist realism—if, in short, it is a bison *other than the real bison*—is this merely due to chance?"

This man who writes so wonderfully of Piero della Francesca, La Tour, Vermeer, of men who would have thought the word *conquest* a profanation, cannot think of the natural world except as raw material ready for the processing that is our victory and its defeat. For Malraux, at bottom, the world is a war; and anyone who writes about *The Voices of Silence,* responding to this, will tend to make his praise warm and general and his blame cold and specific. The book is, some of the time, a marvelous evocation and appreciation of the works of art it reproduces; the rest of the time it is an argument, a fight, and we fight back. We are willing to forgive most things to a writer who cares this much for painting and sculpture, and catches us up in his caring; but the life and manners of this truly vivacious book are too contagious, we forget all about forgiving, make what speeches we can to what troops we have, gnaw our moustaches, and get out our French dictionaries so as to denounce Malraux in the style to which he is accustomed.

Malraux's passion, violence, energy seem as genuine as they are habitual, though the form in which they are expressed and the emotions by which they are accompanied are often stock. I once visited a pottery where all the dogs and cats were named after characters in the *Ring,* and where all the shapes of the pots, as the potter told me, "had authority." All Malraux's sentences "have authority," but only his more timid or less-informed readers are likely to remain submissive beneath it: Malraux writes in a language in which there is no way to say "perhaps" or "I don't know," so that after a while we grow accustomed to saying it for him. But we need to say it less often than would be supposed: how many men have written about art with better taste, with more intelligence, with a keener sympathy, with a more extraordinary scope and grasp and intensity, and have alloyed these with a rhetoric so grandiose, sentiments so conventionally theatrical, and an obsession with power so radical, that a book of theirs can seem to us a miracle which we partly dislike?

When Malraux wants to assert a proposition about which he, alone among mortals, feels no doubts, he prefaces it with—and I combine two of his favorite introductory remarks—"WHO CAN FAIL TO SEE THAT, *regardless of what everybody says* . . ." But ordinarily he proves his propositions. He says, for instance, that "the ill-success of *The Night Watch* was inevitable," and goes on to show us why it was inevitable. He is completely successful: when we have finished his paragraphs we can see that the painting *had* to be disliked. If we happen to have learned that as a matter of fact it was greatly liked, and that its failure is a poetically just myth, we are troubled to see Malraux's method so powerful. The connections of European art with Christianity are more enlightening, if less surprising, than its connections with double-entry bookkeeping, so that Malraux's semi-religious determinism is a good deal better than the economic determinism which tells us that Masaccio's outlines are as firm as they are because the financial position of the rising middle class was as sound as it was. But both methods have the same fault: they are too powerful. By using either we can show just why everything necessarily was what we already know it to have been—and we can often, in the process, distort (or neglect to see closely enough or disinterestedly enough) what everything was.

We say with a sigh: "The ways of God are inscrutable." To the critic of art the ways of art are inevitable, and he explains with a smile why everything had to happen as it did. (He can explain it only after it happens, not before—but, everything has its limitations. In everyday life, a crude sphere, we call someone whose explanations have these limitations a Monday-morning quarterback.) The critic of art often does all that he can to make the ways of art inevitable, saying without any smile: "Certainly no representational painting of the first importance could be produced *now;* certainly no diatonic composition of the first importance could be produced *now.*" Schönberg said that there were a great many good pieces still to be composed in the key of C major, and his sentence is as inspiring to me, as a human being, as is Cromwell's: "I beseech you, in the bowels of Christ, believe that you may be mistaken!"

What I am saying is very obvious, and if anything is obvious enough it seems almost to give us the right to ignore it. Analysts of society or art regularly neglect what is, for the parts of it their explanation is able to take account of, and then go on the assumption that their explanation is all that there is. (If the methods of some discipline deal only with, say, what is quantitatively measurable, and something is not quantitatively measurable, then the thing does not exist for that discipline—after a while the lower right-hand corner of the inscription gets broken off, and it reads *does not exist.*) But if someone has a good enough eye for an explanation he finally sees nothing inexplicable, and can begin every sentence with that phrase dearest to all who professionally understand: *It is no accident that* . . . We should love explanations well, but the truth better; and often the truth is that there *is* no explanation, that so far as we know it is an accident that . . . The motto of the city of Hamburg is: *Navigare necesse est, vivere non necesse.* A critic might say to himself: for me to know *what* the work of art is, is necessary; for me to explain *why* it is what it is, is not always necessary nor always possible.

Let me illustrate all this by examining Malraux's treatment of six statues, three at Rheims and three at Bamberg. He writes that at Rheims the art of antiquity, of the smile, of "smoothly modeled planes, of supple garments and gestures," was at last able to be resuscitated, in order "to voice the concord between man and what transcends him, the last act of the Incarnation." He reminds the reader that "there are classical precedents for the way the Master of the Visitation treated drapery," persuades him (unnecessarily, but in sensitive and beautiful detail) that the Virgin *is* Gothic, not classical, and finishes by explaining why the sculptor was able to make the Mary and Elizabeth of this *Visitation* what they are: "When man had made his peace with God and once again order reigned in the world, the sculptors found in the art of antiquity a means of expression ready to hand. If we turn east to Bamberg, where this reconciliation was less complete, we find that its Virgin gives an impression of being much earlier than the Rheims Virgin, from which, nevertheless, it derived. Gazing with eyes still misted with fears of hell, above that miraculously apt fracture which makes her face the very effigy of Gothic death, the St. Elizabeth of Bamberg seems to contemplate her 'prototype' of Rheims across an abyss of time."

This last sentence may itself seem to us a work of art; certainly we seem to ourselves to feel more, to understand better, now that the weights and relations of these things have been shown to us, understood for us. But if we look at the Bamberg and Rheims *Visitations*, the Bamberg Rider and its "prototype" at Rheims, and read what is known about the circumstances of their making, we find that Malraux has understood for us too swiftly and too well: some of his facts are not facts at all, and—what matters far more—some of his feeling for, his seeing of, these statues has been distorted by his understanding of them, by the thesis to which the statues have been required to testify.

Certainly Bamberg was influenced by Rheims; but the Bamberg *Visitation* often is dated before the Rheims *Visitation*—which *was* the prototype? That the Rheims Virgin and St. Elizabeth look just as they look doesn't puzzle Malraux, but it puzzles everyone else: sober art historians sound like writers of detective stories as they try to account for it. Morey says, for instance: "It is not impossible that a German sculptor, schooled in the early atelier of Rheims, returned to work at Bamberg, and later joined the eclectic group which finished the façade of Rheims cathedral. This would explain the Teutonic Mary and Elizabeth of the *Visitation* at Rheims, and the general identity of style of the Elizabeth in this group with the Elizabeth of another *Visitation* in the ambulatory at Bamberg." It would explain it—unless we look at the statues. The three Bamberg statues which have "prototypes" at Rheims—the Virgin, the St. Elizabeth, and the Rider—are a family of masterpieces, as like as sister, mother, and brother; the Rheims Virgin, St. Elizabeth, and Philip Augustus vary from sublimity to pure commonplace. Philip (purse-lipped, tremulous-lidded, his face closed uncertainly, almost pedantically, about the cares of power) looks as though he were dreaming that he is the other, that Rider who—profound, ambiguous, weighing, full of a strength touching in its delicacy and forbearance, of an innate, almost awkward elegance—looks out with eyes more considering, more deeply set, more widely set than other eyes, so that we see in him one of the great expressions of man's possibility, of that grace which comes upon him too naturally for him to be aware either of its source or of its presence.

The Rheims St. Elizabeth is, as Malraux would say, a Stoic's mother that has somehow found a soul, a quiet, sad, beautiful statue which we forget as we look at the Bamberg St. Elizabeth. *Her* eyes are misted neither by "fears of hell" nor by anything else—here Malraux's taste, his mere ability to see, have been debauched by his theory—but are calmer and less changing than the stone in which they are carved. Man's ability to bear and disregard—to look out into, to look out past, anything in his world—has been expressed as well in a few other works of art, but never, I think, better: she seems to look out into that Being which has canceled out the Becoming which the Rider looks into and is.

But the two Virgins are most puzzling of all, if we want to *explain* them: how can one masterpiece be derived from another that contradicts it? The Virgin of Rheims's humanity, which Malraux describes so beautifully, is too wonderful for us to be willing to compare her unfavorably with anything, yet the Virgin of Bamberg's inhumanity (if a Fate can be called inhuman) is almost as wonderful: her reserved, brooding, slightly too full young face, with the future held uneasily in its fullness, is like the first premonition of one of Michelangelo's sibyls; as we look at the curve of this body at once extended to us and withdrawn from us, at the grave, dimpled, half-archaic smile of a troubling and ununderstandable benediction, we feel more than ever the inscrutability of God's ways and our own.

Do the Rheims figures look as they look, do the Bamberg figures look as *they* look, because at one place the "reconciliation" of God and man was "less complete"? While we read Malraux, we understand; while we look at the statues we do not understand, but we are looking at the statues.

And, much of the time, Malraux is looking with us; but a historian, a critic, cannot always stand idly looking and feeling, but must explain things. While he explains them gently and consideringly, with tact and insight and forbearance—explains them partially, only partially—*then* we may see them as we have never seen them before, but as he has. Often Malraux does this—with La Tour, for instance—but often he is a rough explainer. A little of Rheims fits into his ideological scheme perfectly, as the climax of Gothic art; the specific qualities of Bamberg and Naumburg do not, so that in spite of liking them so much that he refers to them again and again, he "filters" them out of his main argument, and regards them as belated survivals of an earlier stage of Gothic development. Similarly, he says about Vermeer (and he writes with a wonderful feeling for the depth and poetry of a painter so often called "limited" or a "jeweler") that "the depiction of a world devoid of value can be magnificently justified by an artist who treats *painting itself* as the supreme value." He goes on to say about his favorite Vermeer, *The Love Letter:* "The letter has no importance, and the woman none. Nor has the world in which letters are delivered; all has been transmuted into painting." If the picture had been called *The Visitation,* how willingly Malraux would have accepted the importance of the visit, of the woman, and of the world in which visits are made! (One feels like saying: Vermeer's canvases are as full of values as is Spinoza's *Ethics;* they might even be used as illustrations for it.) But Malraux is quite sensitive to religious and quasi-religious values, quite insensitive to others; the sciences, for him, are not much more than what has produced television sets and the atomic bomb. The quieter personal and domestic values—what St. Jerome felt for his lion instead of what he felt for his church—hardly exist for Malraux; his mind is large and public. Someone said that in the ideal dictatorship everything would be either forbidden or obligatory; in Malraux's world everything is either heroic, ignoble, or irrelevant. The world itself, for Malraux, has become a kind of rhetoric. Any religion attracts him as a work of art, a source of style, an incarnation of values, and yet you can hardly imagine his believing in one—in *one.* You can say of him what you can say of any true rhetorician: that rhetoric frees us from all claims except its own.

The Voices of Silence, if it had a denotative instead of a connotative title, might be called *Religious, Anti-Religious, and Proto-*

Religious Art. Malraux detests "the incapacity of modern civilization for giving form to its spiritual values," and says in a beautiful and heartfelt sentence: "On the whole face of the globe the civilization that has conquered it has failed to build a temple or a tomb." He goes on: "Agnosticism is no new thing: what is new is an agnostic culture. Whether Cesare Borgia believed in God or not, he reverently bore the sacred relics, and, while he was blaspheming among his boon companions, St. Peter's was being built." Whether he believes in God or not, Malraux passionately believes in the necessity of a culture's believing, and he reverently bears into the only church any longer possible to us, the Museum without Walls, the sacred relics of the religious arts of the past.

Malraux feels that European painting first embodied religious values, next embodied poetic and humanistic values, and finally rejected "*all* values that are not purely those of painting." Just as religious art distorted Nature into forms that would express the values of religion, so modern painting distorts it into forms that will express the values of painting: "the quality modern art has in common with the sacred arts," Malraux writes, "is not that, like them, it has any transcendental significance, but that, like them, it sponsors only such forms as are discrepant from visual experience . . . Our style is based on a conviction that the only world which matters is other than the world of appearances." One might suppose that in the long run "the world of appearances" would have to matter to that creator of a new world of appearances, the painter. But Malraux despises the arts of "illusionist realism," of "delectation." "When I hear the word Nature," Malraux might say, "I reach for my revolver." In his scheme of things there are earlier artists and their schemata, the new artist and his schema, and far back in the corner under a dunce's stool, cowering dully, a dwarfed Mongoloid, Nature. It is almost out of the picture; and yet Malraux is uneasy at having it there, he wants it all the way out.

The artist and Nature, as Malraux conceives them, are almost exactly like Henry James and that innocent bystander who gives James the germ of one of his stories. "Just outside Rye the other day," the man begins, "I met a—" "Stop! stop!" cries James. "Not a word more or you'll spoil it!" Most of the European artists Malraux writes about had a neurotic, lifelong compulsion to *look at things:* they made studies, made sketches, made dissections, paid models, hired maids because of the way the maids' skin took the light; some of them lived half their lives in the middle of the landscape, getting red and wrinkled with its suns, getting pneumonia from its rains—so that an unsympathetic observer can say of their style what Malraux says of Corot's, that it "tells of a long conflict with Nature (which he was apt to confound with the pleasure of visits to the country)." Nature had their deluded, heartfelt tributes, their "assertions that they were her faithful servants." "Certain masters," Malraux observes, "even claimed that this submission contributed to their talent." Some loved to say that Nature had been their master.

When they say this, Malraux of course realizes that this is not what they meant; he knows that he wouldn't let a thing like Nature be *his* master. (Actually Malraux wouldn't let anything be his master: his motto is *Vici, vici, vici.*) He explains what they did mean: "When Goya mentioned Nature as being one of his three masters he obviously meant, 'Details I have observed supply their accents to ensembles I conjure up in my imagination.'" Obviously. "When Delacroix spoke of Nature as a dictionary he meant that her elements were incoherent." What they said either meant something else, or they didn't mean what they said, or they meant what they said but just didn't know: "No great painter," Malraux concludes, "has ever talked as we would like him to talk." When van Gogh made a painting of a chair that almost pushes the chair in your face, that says like a child: *Look, there's my chair!*—at that moment, Malraux writes, "the conflict between the artist and the outside world, after smoldering for so long, had flared up at last." Malraux singularly, uniquely, inimitably sees that in this picture van Gogh had declared war on the chair. But what puzzles Malraux is: why did he, why did they all, wait so long to declare it? If only—

"Chardin's *Housewife*," writes Malraux, "might be a first-class Braque dressed-up enough to take in the spectator." "Corot," writes Malraux, "makes of the landscape a radiant still life; his *Narni Bridge, Lake of Garda,* and *Woman in Pink* are, like the *Housewife,* dressed-up Braques." If only Chardin and Corot had undressed their Braques! If only Chardin had got rid of that housewife, Corot of that landscape, the world would have had two more Braques, 1760 and 1840 would have been 1920, and Malraux wouldn't be having to persuade us to pay no attention to what Chardin and Corot said about Nature. (Somehow it never seems to occur to him to call Piero della Francesca's *Resurrection* a dressed-up Cézanne, and to imply that if Piero had only got rid of Christ and those soldiers he would have had a first-class Cézanne: religion matters.) Malraux spends so much time persuading his readers that art isn't a photographic imitation of Nature that it gives portions of his book a curiously old-fashioned look—he needs to persuade most of his readers, today, that art has *any* relation to Nature.

Of the quasi-aesthetic organization of visual perception itself—
an organization that is at the root of aesthetic organization—Malraux
is ignorant; for him Koffka, Köhler, Gombrich, and the rest might
never have existed. He understands "the world of appearances," our
perception of Nature, only as a kind of literal photograph of formless
raw material—raw material that demands the immediate transforma-
tion, the supernatural distortion, of a religious, transcendental art. (An
old sexual metaphor underlies Malraux's view of aesthetic creation: a
masculine Art forms and conquers a helpless, formless, feminine
Nature.) Malraux is willing to accept a modern art that no longer embodies religious values, if it rejects "the world of appearances," is
"discrepant from visual experience." Yet his acceptance is the provisional
acceptance we give to something that is only a transitional stage; "akin
to all styles that express the transcendental and unlike all others, our
style seems to belong to some religion of which it is unaware," "is
nearing its end," "cannot survive its victory intact." Our culture "will
certainly transform modern art"; after having "conquered and an-
nexed" the religious and transcendental arts of the past, it will see its
own art become a new religious and transcendental art of a nature we
cannot now fathom: "whether we desire it or not, Western man will
light his path only, by the torch he carries, even if it burns his hands,
and what that torch is seeking to throw light on is everything that can
enhance the power of man." (The disadvantages of so oratorical a style
of understanding as Malraux's are terribly apparent in the last sentence.) Malraux adores power, and is willing to accept the understanding that sometimes goes along with power, if that power and that
understanding are personal, aesthetic, religious; when they are the impersonal power and understanding of science, that conquers in the long
run by being submissive and observant in the short run, by first imag-
ining and then seeing whether the fact fits, Malraux has no interest in
them.

Reality is what we want it to be or what we do not want it to be,
but it is not our wanting or our not wanting that makes it so. Yet with
sufficient mastery the critic can have reality almost what he wants it—
and Malraux's temperament is very masterful. (The last time I read
The Voices of Silence I thought longingly of the submissiveness of Sir
Kenneth Clark's *The Nude*—just as, the last time I heard *Parsifal,* I
couldn't help thinking of *Falstaff.*) The soldier Descartes philosophized
while at war, in quiet winter quarters; Malraux has to philosophize in
the midst of a war which he himself is staging, a war that rages through
every season. That Malraux's is a book of "tremendous philosophical

and moral importance"—Edmund Wilson says so—I cannot believe. How could such a book have the *facility*—of thought, feeling, and expression—that this book so often has? Yet it is a book that shows better than any but a few others what art has been to man. Often Malraux writes as well about some painter or sculptor, some style or influence, some metamorphosis in taste, as anyone I have read, and his intelligence, his dramatic imagination, his passionate absorption, the sheer liveness of his experience and knowledge are extraordinary; if he is an intermittent trial, he is a continual delight. His virtues are so dazzlingly apparent that one writes at exaggerated length about his faults; but his book is a work of art, and we judge it as we judge a work of art: by its strengths.

What is worst about it, as a work of art, is the way in which some of it is written. It has thousands of arresting or moving or conclusive or exactly realizing sentences, and hundreds of sentences that are coarsely, theatrically, and conventionally rhetorical. One cannot do justice to Malraux's good writing, since there is so much of it, but one can certainly do justice to the bad. "The Oriental night of blood and doom-fraught stars" is the phrase he finds for Byzantium; he calls the world of primitive artists "a nether world of blood, and fate-fraught stars"; he writes that "neither blood, nor the dark lures of the underworld, nor the menaces of doom-fraught stars have at all times prevailed against that soaring hope which enabled human inspiration, winged with love, to confront the palpitating vastness of the nebulae with the puny yet indomitable forms of Galilean fishermen or the shepherds of Arcadia." Who would have thought those old stars had so much doom in them? Malraux says about the Dutch: "We tend to overlook that glorious page of Dutch history, and even today you will hear people talking, as of quaint figures in picture-postcards, of a nation that put up a stout resistance to Hitler's hordes, and has led the world in postwar reconstruction." This is the lingua franca of vice-presidents and major generals, the tongue in which the Dean talks to the *pompier,* and needs no translator. Malraux even ends his book, his beautiful book, with this sentence: "And that hand whose waverings in the gloom are watched by ages immemorial is vibrant with one of the loftiest of the secret yet compelling testimonies to the power and glory of being Man." Imagine—I won't say Rilke's—imagine Degas's face as he read such a sentence!

As for another author, the man who wrote *La Condition Humaine;* the man who writes about the first "retrograde" art: "Thereafter Byzantium reigned alone. The age which was discovering the sublimity of tears showed not a weeping face," and who goes on: "As much genius was needed to obliterate man at Byzantium as to discover him on the Acropolis"; the man who tells how the yielding feminine smile of the Greek statues was changed by the Asiatic sculptors into "something sterner, hewn in the cliffside: the lonely smile of the men of silence"; who says of Botticelli's figures that "knots of fine-spun lines enwrap their shining smoothness"; who writes about the end of the Middle Ages and the beginning of the Renaissance: "To restore to life that slumbering populace of ancient statues, all that was required was the dawn of the first smile upon the first mediaeval figure," ends his chapter there, and begins the next: "How very timid was that smile!"—as for the man who wrote these sentences, how does *he* feel about the man who wrote the others? We are almost willing to use the terms of Malraux's effective and misleading distinction between Michelangelo and Signor Buonarroti, Paul Cézanne and Monsieur Cézanne, and to say that it is André Malraux who is responsible for the grandeur of some of these sentences, and Monsieur Malraux, the well-known politician and man of action, who is responsible for the vulgar grandiosity of the others. But if we said so we should be making Malraux's mistake: it is the same man who is responsible for both, and it is our task to understand how this is possible. When we read what Goethe says about men we are ashamed of what we have said; when we read what he says about paintings and statues we are ashamed of what Goethe has said. It is one of the merits of Malraux's book that it shows, perhaps more forcibly and vivaciously than any other, why it is historically possible for us to feel this; or to feel as we feel when we read, in Berenson, that Uccello "in his zeal forgot local color—he loved to paint his horses pink and green—forgot action, forgot composition, and, it need scarcely be added, significance." A few pages later we read about a painter, more to be despised than pitied, who made "the great refusal," and who degenerated until "at his worst he hardly surpasses the elder Brueghel." I suppose I ought to say that it is only *our* taste these judgments appall, that after a while the wheel will have come full circle, and another age will smile at Malraux's judgments of Uccello and Brueghel, nod approvingly at Berenson's . . . Well, unhappy the age that does so! May it be further accursed!

I have talked of the faults or exaggerations of *The Voices of Silence* far too much for justice, so let me say that I have worn into sections the unbound copy I first owned and wrote about, and cannot look at my bound copy without a surge of warmth and delight: if I knew a monk I would get him to illuminate it. Who has ever picked illustrations like Malraux? He has worked hard rewriting the old version of the book: has changed, added, omitted, rearranged, more than one would have thought possible; since the phrasing has been improved and since the blank spaces that gave the old version a somewhat disjointed, aphoristic look have been done away with, it now has more of a Spenglerian weight and continuity, and less of the I-am-just-thinking-for-you air that the first version occasionally had—and had attractively, I thought. Malraux still thinks that famous Scythian deer, antlered from nose to tail, a horse, and prints it opposite Degas's for comparison; and he still believes that Schumann composed to the smell of rotten apples, but that you can't smell them in his music. Poor Schiller! I'd as soon see Eve, Newton, and Gregor Samsa deprived of their apples.

Aristotle Alive!

SATURDAY REVIEW, APRIL 3, 1954

The Languages of Criticism and the Structure of Poetry by R. S. Crane

R. S. CRANE is a distinguished scholar, the former chairman of the Department of English at the University of Chicago. His volume *The Languages of Criticism and the Structure of Poetry* is composed of five lectures which he delivered at the University of Toronto in 1952. They are lectures about the two most influential sorts of contemporary criticism, and about a very different kind, an Aristotelian kind, which would supplement and counteract these.

This word *Aristotelian* will make some of us grunt, some of us beam, and some of us exclaim, "Oh yes, now I remember—Crane's the man that's been starting that neo-Aristotelian school of criticism." So far as most of us are concerned, to hear of such a project is to hate it. We feel, more or less: "If it's a good thing to do, surely in all this time somebody would have done it"; and we remember that during a surprisingly large proportion of that time somebody *was* doing it. Mr. Crane's school of criticism comes to bat with, so to speak, two millennia against it.

But as we read we see that Mr. Crane is persuasive and judicious and reasonable, that his arguments aren't lofty sneers, or rhetoric, or appeals to prejudice, but real arguments; we dismiss this general prejudice of ours, and try to make specific judgments worthy of Mr. Crane and of ourselves. Most of us will be pleased when he warns us of his anti-Hegelian turn of mind, delighted when we see that he really does believe in seeing what great artists did, rather than in saying what they should have done. He is, most of the time, empirical. And he does not believe in some ideal form of criticism which has the virtues of all and the vices of none, but sees that the different ways of criticizing, languages of criticism, are themselves as different and contradictory as works of art are. They too have the defects of their qualities and the qualities of their defects—to want Arnold's criticism just like Hopkins's is as stupid as to want "The Scholar-Gipsy" just like "Carrion Comfort."

Mr. Crane divides modern critics of poetry into two schools: those who take an analytic, systematic interest in the language and meanings of poetry as these are differentiated from the language and meanings of prose; those who apply to poetry the insights of psychoanalysis and anthropology. Most of both sorts are New. Gazing at them from calm, distant, common-sensical eyes, Mr. Crane describes, with reflective detachment, his critics' midnight marches, routs, sieges, voyages, their all-but-mortal combats, their—I was about to say, their discoveries and victories . . . but these, alas! he does not describe. He does intelligent justice to their vices and exaggerations and absurdities—some of these pages are, in their mild, matter-of-fact way, crushing—but he neglects with methodical thoroughness the insight and imagination and affection that are so signally present in some of them, so signally absent in others. From his sensible, unfavorable, and rather unjust survey you can learn a great deal of what was wrong with the criticism of our time, and almost nothing of what was right with it.

And this is natural: Mr. Crane's analysis is, if not a vindictive one, a kind of preparatory one—he is setting the stage for his own special kind of criticism. He explains it, lists its limitations, honestly admits that it derives from a quite unorthodox interpretation of Aristotle; and then he talks, at length, with enthusiasm, about all that it would be, all that it would do for literature, criticism, education. (He can't talk about its faults because, after all, hardly any of it exists to be faulty.) Reading this celebration of the hypothetical virtues of an imaginary criticism, we smile, but it's a sympathetic smile; we all have a fellow-feeling for inventors, Utopia imaginers, and we enjoy Mr. Crane's enthusiasm and emotion—we had been troubled, earlier, by his calm tameness, his withdrawn, abstract, academic decorum. We wish him good luck with, good critics for, his new school of criticism. We wish it in a voice of perfunctory good will.

"The Poet's Store of Grave
and Gay"

THE NEW YORK TIMES BOOK REVIEW, AUGUST 15, 1954

Collected Poems by James Stephens

IT IS a real pleasure to read James Stephens's big new *Collected Poems*. I knew the old edition and one or two of the separate books, and had come across several winning poems in other places. All of them are in this book: poems of eloquent and elevated speech, of pure and extreme emotion—some of them like amusingly faithful Blake imitations, one or two like Blake; poems in which a child or an angel speaks easily enough for children and hard enough for grown-ups; poems in which some old Irish poet bewails the poet's lot, in words that will make poets smile forcedly and anti-poets give a little laugh of contrition; and some live, talking, disrespectable poems, straight off the street, that are just right to appeal to those "sensible people" about whom Stephens says: "Shops, sermons and marriage, and dear and cheap, / These make sensible people weep." (Many rich, married, shopkeeping churchgoers will enjoy these pieces too.)

Some of the poems are about the persistences of our lives, the dark permanent sea, and others are about the bright, equally permanent spray. I haven't found any new poems as good as my old favorites, but there are two or three almost as good and a lot that are direct, individual, and appealing. Seeing them all together has made me decide, a little bit ruefully, that Stephens is a better and more varied poet than I realized.

Stephens's masterpiece, I think, is a poem a great many readers must remember, "The Goat-Paths." The goats who stray day after day, in "quiet Sunniness, in sunny Quietness," along their crooked paths; who go far back into the center of the furze to stand staringly, dreamingly

In the deeper
Sunniness;
In the place
Where nothing stirs;
Quietly
In quietness;
In the quiet
Of the furze
They stand a while;
They dream;
They lie;
They stare
Upon the roving sky.

If you approach
They run away!
They will stare,
And stamp,
And bound,
With a sudden angry sound,
To the sunny
Quietude;
To crouch again
Where nothing stirs,
In the quiet
Of the furze:
To crouch them down again,
And brood,
In the sunny
Solitude.

These are real goats moving up a real hill, but are also the thoughts
and feelings that move along the crooked paths of our own being.
Readers are made to wish for a way to the still center of the mind, the
stillness above or below it, by the poet's wishing that he might be as
free as the animals to wander back into the "airy quietness," the place
where nothing stirs; and the readers' wish and the poet's merge, with
magical conclusiveness when the poem says that then

I would think
Until I found
Something

I can never find
—Something
Lying
On the ground,
In the bottom
Of my mind.

Here something very hard to say has been said so easily that—although it is the embodiment of our own longing imperfection—it has for us a look of perfect grace.

Several of Stephens's most delightful pieces are adaptations of, or poems after the manner of, older Irish poems. In "Skim-Milk" a poet says that if he does not "publish all the tale" of his grief, it is only "because my gloom gets some respite / By just a small bewailing." Then he tells how "into the forest day by day I go, / And trot beneath a load of wood that high! / Which raises on my poor old back a row / Of raw red blisters till I cry—Alack, / The rider that rides me will break my back!"

But best of all is his eloquent

Once I had books, each book beyond compare,
And now no book at all is left to me;
Now I am spied and peeped on everywhere;
And this old head, stuffed with latinity,
Rich with the poet's store of grave and gay,
Will not get me skim-milk for half a day.

Yeats or Graves could feel pleased with those last three lines; and there is no poet who would need to feel ashamed of "Egan O Rahilly." Someone, Michelangelo I think, said that you should be able to roll a good statue downhill without having the arms and legs break off; this poem could be rolled downhill, and hammered red-hot, and dropped in cold water, and nothing would happen except that the hammer would break and the water boil away:

Here in a distant place I hold my tongue;
I am O Rahilly!

When I was young
Who now am young no more
I did not eat things picked up from the shore:
The periwinkle and the tough dog-fish
At even-tide have got into my dish!

The great, where are they now! the great had said—
This is not seemly! Bring to him instead
That which serves his and serves our dignity—
And that was done.

I am O Rahilly!
Here in a distant place he holds his tongue
Who once said all his say, when he was young!

One could give a good idea of Stephens's poetry by quoting the majestic and tender "What Tomas Said in a Pub"; that best and best written of curses, "A Glass of Beer"; "To the Four Courts, Please," a description of a cab driver and his horse sad enough and truthful enough to remind you of Hardy's "No Buyers" or Chekhov's "To Whom Shall I Tell My Grief?" And poems of "natural sorrow, loss, or pain" like "Bessie Bobtail," "The Snare," and "Why Tomas Cam Was Grumpy"; one of the late poems that have, besides their content of "Eastern mysticism," a fairly individual and most highly developed rhetoric; one of the poems that are pure exclamation point; and the poem that begins, "A man said to me at the fair / —If you've got a poet's tongue / Tumble up and chant the air / That the Stars of Morning sung; / —I'll pay you, if you sing it nice, / A penny-piece.—I answered flat, / —Sixpence is the proper price / For a ballad such as that."

Stephens is such a human and appealing poet that one rather winks at his faults, which are obvious enough and extensive enough, heaven knows. At his best he could differentiate one poem from another, give it a movement and organization all its own and *sound as if he meant it.* If we judge strictly we may decide that Stephens's lifetime of writing poetry resulted in four or five good—really good—poems and a dozen or two dozen which are attractive or pleasant or unusually well put. Does that seem a poor reward? It wouldn't have seemed so to Stephens, who knew well what it means to "strictly meditate the thankless Muse," and who wrote—how could you say it better?—that Egan O Rahilly "meditated misery / And cared it into song—strict care, strict joy!"

The Little Cars

VOGUE, SEPTEMBER 15, 1954

SOMEDAY, driving along the highway, you will see the traffic begin to change. Among the lanes of ordinary cars, streaming by like big, sedate, efficient hens, two or three little dyed Easter chicks of cars will appear—then half a dozen, dozens, hundreds. The exhausts of the small engines make a sharp, bright, crackling sound (if you lean closer you will hear their owners saying, "Listen to that exhaust!") or else a little bubbling roar, the sound a child makes playing with a bubble pipe.

Even the cars' horns, when they honk them, have an old-fashioned squawk, as if somebody had made the noise by squeezing a bulb; now and then the car of some see-er of foreign lands, or advertisement-prone stay-at-home, passes to the note of a Bermuda carriage bell. A few of the cars have a sleek, nasty look, as if they wanted to go a hundred and fifty and despised traffic, but the rest have a gay, light, irresponsible air— they are perfect meringues of cars. They seem all for fun and hardly at all for transportation; the ordinary automobiles alongside look like a vocation with a pension at the end, and the little ones like a vacation.

Their drivers, mostly, are bright as they. Like birds, they run to crests: a rainbow, converted into billed caps, crowns their brown, bouncy, white-toothed faces. They wear stocking caps, hoods, tam-o'-shanters, fast hats like a skier's or a brownie's; now and then there goes by, in stern, exotic navy, a beret—goes by, one among ten thousand, a deer-stalker of Harris tweed. You see someone, rarely, in just hair: if his, crew-cut; if hers, platinum. (One magnificent creature—my children call her *The Dish*—has, besides everything else, spun-aluminum hair inches and inches long, and flourishes alongside Phil Hill's pit crew; some people have never noticed Phil Hill, his Ferrari, or his pit crew, but only The Dish.) And there are turtleneck sweaters, terry-cloth coveralls, halters figuring on a ground of goose-flesh; you may even see, as I have seen, a husband, a wife, and their four-year-old in Churchill shelter-suits of red plush, the three of them looking like dyed polar bears. Of course, a lot of the drivers are solid citizens not worth a first glance, men who provoke from the others—and from me—a marveling,

"What's the world coming to when people like that drive MG's?" But they wave to them just the same; everybody waves to everybody. If there were fewer of them, you would think them the happy few.

What's happening? What are all these? They are sports cars. Where are they going? To the races. Horse races? Yachts? Indianapolis? No, no, they wouldn't be caught dead there. They're going to the sports-car races—the Road Races, as *they* say, even if the cars are racing on airport runways half a mile from the nearest road. They're going to Pebble Beach or Palm Springs or Watkins Glen or Torrey Pines, and there they will all—race each other? No. Oh, a few will; when you see a car with bad paint, cycle fenders, bucket seats, and a grim mechanical look, that one's going to race; some of the stock jobs will be racing too. But these cars you see are mostly just audience. The rest of the audience comes in regular-sized cars, and the sports-car drivers look pityingly at them in their "Detroit XX iron," and they look longingly or amusedly at the little cars. Shrouded in parachutes, the real race cars—the noble and important ones—go by on trailers: if you've just paid $16,000 for a new Ferrari at Modena, and have flown it to this country so as not to waste several weeks of its competitive life, you're not likely to take it through traffic on its own wheels. And the chances are your trailer went by yesterday, and you yourself sat up all last night with your car and four mechanics after saying to your friends in a stern, level voice—I've heard it said—"That car is a sick car."

If, won over by the shining eyes of their drivers, someone follows the little cars to their races, he will see something he doesn't see every day, or every year either. On roads winding among the cliffs and beaches of some seaside park, on country lanes frequented only by hermits and farmers, on the streets and runways of some accursed airport far out in the middle of a boiling plain, people from the Sports Car Club of America have come with snow fences, hay bales, and ticket sellers, and radar timers, and have made themselves a pastoral, ephemeral racecourse. The whole scene looks surprisingly like one of those Degas landscapes of racing in the eighties. Thousands of cars are parked out in the fields—at Torrey Pines, in fields of rosemary—and thousands more are parked all along the course, just behind the snow fencing. (Twenty or thirty thousand people come to Torrey Pines, a hundred thousand to Golden Gate, two hundred thousand to Elkhart Lake.) People are sitting in or on or in the shade of their cars biting chicken legs, and passing one another pickles, and wishing they'd brought more to drink; people are standing in big bunches buying hot dogs, beer, soft drinks, and they too are wishing they'd brought more to drink and less to wear. The brown people are getting black and the white people are getting red; it is hot, hot, hot. People are slipping into the pit area, and being escorted out of the pit area, and hanging their babies in papoose blankets on the back side of the snow fence, and taking naps, and looking at girls in bathing suits, and being escorted away from the hay bales and escape roads they've been sitting on, and getting into vivacious arguments with their natural enemies the police. But, most of all, they cross the road. How they cross the road! Like chickens, road-race audiences had rather cross the road than do anything else in the world, and the announcer either is saying to them in the voice of Moses, "There are twenty-five people on the course at Turn Four! Send the motorcycle policemen to Turn Four! This race positively cannot begin till we get the course clear at Turn Four!" or else is telling everybody benignly, "The course is open. You may cross the course!"

All this goes on for two days; meanwhile, the cars race. The course, ordinarily, is a couple of miles long; the road, ordinarily, is a narrow bumpy road full of the most harrowing curves—right-angle, hairpin, reverse curves going downhill and banked the wrong way. (At Torrey Pines, the first turn, a bad one after a mile straightaway, has a big sign saying only: *Turn No. 1. WOW!*) The shortest races last fifteen minutes, the longest two or three hours. All the drivers are amateurs. They make nothing out of the races, and spend a good deal—often, an amazing lot—on cars, mechanics, pit crews, repairs, replacements. Some of the drivers are novices baring their teeth for their first race, but others are skillful, just short of Fangio and Ascari and Farina, the great drivers who race, in Europe, on courses like these, sometimes in sports cars and sometimes in one-man Grand Prix cars. A sports car has to have a door, a seat for a passenger, headlights, fenders, half a dozen things; a Grand Prix car is the pure fleeting Idea of a car.

Now I should tell you what the races are like, but of course that's impossible; I could as well tell you in a paragraph or two what football is like, or tennis, or a Balanchine ballet, or what it used to be like to watch Danilova or Vines. The best drivers race with dazzling skill, individuality, and aesthetic expressiveness: Phil Hill corners like—like Youskevitch or Tanaquil Le Clercq, and once won Pebble Beach without a clutch, shifting simply by ear. Drivers like these—Hill, Fitch, Walters, Spears—show extraordinary judgment, courage, experience, and native talent; and they show them on demand, in a tenth of a second, hundreds of times in an hour, under conditions of the utmost difficulty. Often they show them in a heartbreaking way, when a wonderful driver in a mediocre car gets beaten by a competent driver in a wonderful car; road races, like so many things, have a lowest common denominator of money, plain money. But sometimes, by taking every turn a little faster than it ought to be taken, by using to the utmost his own superiority of talent and experience, a first-rate driver in a second-rate car can win a race that he never should have entered—and these are the best of all races.

As for the worst . . . it's hard to choose. Most works of art are, necessarily, bad, and so are most races; one suffers through the many for the few. Ladies' races, on the West Coast, are Sleeping Beauty affairs won by Josie von Neumann, her long black hair streaming in the wind; 500 c.c. cars are abject skeletal objects that could skitter under your dining-room table, and one of their races is like a Marathon of water spiders. Motorcycle races—forty copies of Superman going by with a terrible sound, hunched over their handle bars like tailors on magic bicycles—are rarest of all, but worst of all; worse even than stock Jaguar races, where every turn is torture, the brakes are always screaming, and the inside rear wheel is always just about to lift. The ideally awful race, I think, would be between ladies, stock Jaguars, 500 c.c. cars, motorcycles, and Edith Sitwell.

If you go to a road race be sure to sit at a good curve: that is, a bad curve at the end of a straightaway. When a car comes into a turn too fast, it either leaves the road (there to lead a life of its own among weeds and bushes and hay bales) or else "spins out"—spins, like a top or a planet, on its own axis. A good turn, when it gets a bad oil slick, may have three or four cars spinning out at the same instant, a sight that—as the English car advertisements say—"must be seen to be appreciated." So sit at a good curve, borrow four or five extra Thermos bottles, and, if you can, go in a sports car; when we go in our Oldsmobile we feel like bears at *Phèdre*—good bears, honest bears, but bears. When, at sunset of the second day, the races are over, the sports-car drivers blink, shake themselves, and go back to Life.

A Poet's Own Way

Poems: 1923–1954 by E. E. Cummings

E. E. CUMMINGS'S *Poems 1923–1954* contains "all the poems from all the collections of verse he has published to date." I've read these six hundred poems before, I think, and now I've read all six hundred again; and it seemed to me, as always, that Cummings is one of the most individual and American of poets, a man who has found his own one way and stuck to it with obstinate courage and integrity. There is a great deal of the world in the book, and a great deal more of one man. This formidable collection is going to get much praise and several prizes, and will be for many readers a veritable feast: all this year and next, people will be rising from the book stuffed, their ribs sore with laughter, their wits sharpened with typographical puzzles, their eyes shining with big lyric tears. "Good old Cummings!" they'll say. "There's nobody like him."

And I will nod: it's so. And then I will sit there dumbly, a stranger at a feast which, to me, is not a feast at all but a picnic—a picnic which goes on for yard after yard, mile after mile, of hot dogs, rat cheese, soda crackers, boiled ham curled into imitation rose petals, valentines, jokes and favors from the Jokes and Magic Shop, warm chain-store beer. Here and there, I have to admit—I'm eager to admit—one comes on real wild flowers, the realest and brightest of chipmunks, a portable phonograph playing a wonderful popular song, a gold lock of a drunk girl's hair; and the sun sets behind the picnic, and the moon rises before it, like things from the *Iliad* or things from a nickel postcard.

It's a picnic which has its points—and what would life be without picnics? What I'm objecting to is calling it a Lucullan feast and Cummings the American Brillat-Savarin. "E. E. Cummings has achieved a permanent place among the great poets of this age," says his dust jacket; has he, or has he a place off at the side, a special place all his own, among the good poets of the age? If Cummings is a great poet, what are you going to call Eliot and Frost? Rilke? Let's say together: "Great me no greats," and leave this grading to posterity.

So many critics have been more than just to Cummings's virtues— who could overlook so much life, individuality, charm, freshness, ingenuity?—that I should like to be unjust about his faults. Some of his sentimentality, his easy lyric sweetness I enjoy in the way one enjoys a rather commonplace composer's half-sweet, half-cloying melodies, but much of it is straight ham, straight corn. All too often Cummings splits man into a delicate unique Ariel, drifting through dew like moonlight, and into a Brooklyn Caliban who says, to prostitutes, dese, dem and dose. Some of all that Sex is there to shock, but more of it is there for its own sweet sake. And there is so much love—love infinite and eternal; love in the movie moonlight, after the prop champagne—that one values all the more the real love affair in Cummings's play *Him*.

To Cummings words are things, exciting things excitingly manipulable: he sits at the Muse's door making mobiles. He is a magical but shallow rhetorician who specializes in turning inside out, fooling around with the rhetoric of popular songs, advertisements, bad romantic poetry. He invents a master stroke, figures out the formula for it, and repeats it fifty times. The best rhetoric is less interested in itself, more interested in what it describes, than Cummings's.

Some of Cummings's humor is genuinely funny, some is crude and expected. He is, alas! a monotonous poet. Everything a poem does is, to old readers, expected. "Type Four," they murmur. "Well done!" Then they yawn. "Change in all things is sweet," said Aristotle; "They must often change who would be constant in happiness or wisdom," said Confucius; "Change the name of Arkansas? Never!" said Senator James Kimbrough Jones. Would that Cummings had listened to Aristotle and Confucius.

What I like least about Cummings's poems is their pride in Cummings and their contempt for most other people; the difference between the *I* and *you* of the poems, and other people, is the poems' favorite subject. All his work thanks God that he is not as other men are; none of it says, "Lord, be merciful to me, a sinner."

"Very Graceful Are the Uses of Culture"

HARPER'S, NOVEMBER 1954

Thirty Years by J. P. Marquand   *A Study of History,* Vols. VII, VIII, IX, X, by Arnold J. Toynbee   *The Long Ships* by Frans G. Bengtsson   *The Collected Poems of Wallace Stevens   Tactical Exercise* by Evelyn Waugh   *The Tastemakers* by Russell Lynes   *The View from Pompey's Head* by Hamilton Basso   *The Huge Season* by Wright Morris   *The Literary Situation* by Malcolm Cowley   *The Big Ball of Wax* by Shepherd Mead   *Leopards and Lilies* by Alfred Duggan   *Reunion* by Merle Miller   *The Youth's Companion,* edited by Lovell Thompson   *The Saturday Evening Post Treasury*

THIRTY YEARS is a book of J. P. Marquand's articles and stories. Most of them are about the Wars and the Army, Harvard and Boston, a New England prep school, the Far East, marriage, and the Mulligatawny Club, an American enclave in the Bahamas. The earliest stories—"Good Morning, Major," "High Tide," "Rainbows"—are very bad but very interesting, since they show you a Marquand who had not yet become the skillful, attractively mannered creator of *Ming Yellow* and Mr. Moto. Marquand is a reporter, a good reporter, with troubles of his own, bad troubles: since as a general thing the troubles get into the fiction and not into the articles, the fiction has underneath it a personal compulsion—that of a wish-fantasy, a daydream, a nightmare— that the mild objective articles lack. The Marquand of the articles is usually not much more than a competent, sensible, pleasant photographer, though occasionally there is an arresting detail of the world, an engaging splinter of Marquand's own carefully wooden and commonplace and representative being. When, at Iwo Jima, all the amphibious vehicles leave the LST's, Marquand thinks that "it's like all the cats in the world having kittens." The wife of the governor of Ascension Island says to him: "Oh, hardly. Hugo and I are never lonely . . . And then Hugo is governor of St. Helena. We spend six months there. It's very gay in St. Helena." And when Marquand tells the story of Paul and Virginia to an angry general to get the general to drink a bottle of Scotch, he is at his most charming: great, and very graceful, are the uses of culture.

A man, to Marquand, is a nexus of institutions, the half-unwilling, half-imaginary point at which Harvard, the Stock Exchange, and the Army intersect. He has one soldier say: "You're not in school any longer. Can't you forget it?" The other answers, à la Marquand: "Why should I? I'm always thinking about school"; and the first soldier reflects that war *is* like school, wonders whether "school and war do not go together." Marquand himself says in a speech: "Most people obviously believe that Harvard is the greatest and freest institution in the world," and finishes the speech with: "Let us not say it elsewhere, but perhaps we all are more fascinating and a little better than other people." This was said with a smile, and with a grain of irony, and to an audience a little better for it than other people, an audience of Harvard men, but Marquand's heart was in what he said. He is in love with—or anyway, married to—the institutions of this world, and that is why he can observe them so carefully: he has, by now, all the grounds for the divorce he will never quite get, all the facts for the biography he will never quite write except in its authorized form; and when, in the end, he is laid away, by schoolfellows, he will be able to remember in detail everything that he is missing.

And how easily he might have missed it all! how easily America, with all its buffalo and Elks and Indians, might not have had any Oxford, any Académie française, any *Almanach de Gotha* for Marquand to observe! If you reply, like James or Hawthorne, that America doesn't have them for Marquand or anybody else to observe, there is always the retort: "And what's wrong with Harvard and the National Academy of Arts and Letters and the Social Register?"—the retort, "And what's wrong with the Pentagon, the Senate, and General Motors?" No, the institutions are here for him to observe, and he is inside them observing: to Marquand there is something romantic, something miraculous, about both facts. As for the men whose shadows these institutions are—the men who make and break states, corporations, and academies—in Marquand's books they are a little gray, a little ghostly, except in so far as their organizations give them bone and hue.

But it *is* romantic, miraculous almost, that Marquand should be here, straight out of *The Age of Innocence,* to observe this new age of *adjusting to one's group,* and *sharing the experience of one's generation,* and getting divorced because the president of one's corporation doesn't approve of one's wife, and all the rest of it. Why doesn't General Motors give Marquand a few hundred thousand dollars, keep him around the office—the offices—for a year or two, and then let him write the great American novel, about General Motors? Of course, it would be the same novel he's always written, but that's all right too, isn't it?—what's good enough for the rest of the country is good enough for General Motors.

As a writer Marquand is somewhat short on talent, imagination, brute ability, but is long on care, observation, directed curiosity, and is longest of all on personal involvement, subjective compulsion. Most of his books, under their veneer of patiently observed objective detail, seem versions of the same subjective fable, one designed to say to him and also to us: "You were right to do as you did; or if not right, still, you had no choice; or if you had a choice, still, it's the choice all of us necessarily make wrong: life's life. If only—but it doesn't matter. And . . . and it was all so long ago." The fable is told in a series of flashbacks, of sighs as elegiac, nostalgic, and wistfully submissive—as mannered and un-varying—as a Puccini opera. These flashbacks are not optional technique, but compulsory content: because of them the hero never has to make, in close-up, a clear choice to kiss or kill—the choices are always ob-scured by the haze of the past, of rueful and lyric recollection.

At the proper distance of time everything looks inevitable: we do not judge, but feel about, what we did, and the possibility of doing or choosing differently seems naïve, one more of youth's illusions. A Marquand character says: "I was faced by one of those uncomfortable moments of illumination when life is clear and simple, and, con-sequently, grim." But usually, to a Marquand character, life is obscure and complicated, and, consequently, elegiac. Marquand characters—the "real" Marquand characters, those we think like Marquand—love noth-ing so much as saying: "No matter how you try, you can't really under-stand anything; no matter what you do, you can't really change any-thing." Marquand's coat of arms ought to have in the middle a man saying *It doesn't matter* because it matters so much that there is nothing else for him to say.

This "real" Marquand character is the hero of the books' persistent fable. A man a little different—and consequently a little on the outside—looks with half-superior, half-inferior understanding at those entirely un-different others who *are* the inside. This man has a chance to break out of it all and be a different failure: a female chance, generally, one as mesmeric and unreliable as life; and he refuses this chance, or accepts it only to regress, as soon as he gets a chance to be the same success the others are: a female chance, generally, as monotonous and inescapable as life. Lying alongside Eve's spare necessary shape, the man dreams of the Lilith he left—and, waking in the darkness, he sighs that he was right to leave her, and that life is life.

Browning said, "The sin I impute to each frustrate ghost / Is the unlit lamp and the ungirt loin"; we learn from Marquand that it wasn't a sin but a necessary evil. No wonder that our age and nation and species are grateful to him! Besides, there has always been something attractive about Marquand: we like somebody who succeeds with such bad conscience, and who seems to wish that he had had the nerve to be a failure or, better still, something to which the terms *success* and *failure* don't apply—as when Mallory said, about Everest: "Success is meaningless here." This small uneasy institution set down at the intersection of so many great ones, this little newsstand among the skyscrapers, looking up at them with a wistful accepting sigh—what if he *has* made as much money as some of them? It isn't money that is the legal tender of our dreams: the dreamer would trade all his royalty statements for one thaler of fairy gold. We leave Marquand with one of his own sighs: if only his good angel had been a person, and not an institution . . .

The concluding volumes of Toynbee's *A Study of History* have at last been published. I never dreamed of owning any, and now four, patriarchal in gold and black and wine buckram, sit before me as I write; if I owned all ten I would sit inside them like St. Jerome, and not be seen by man for months. I began reading *A Study of History* on a cold, snowy, Ohio evening in the year 1937, and I've been reading it, off and on, ever since. If reading Proust is the best of vocations, reading Toynbee is the most delightful of avocations. All the historians in hell, from Herodotus to Spengler, have been spending their spare time, these last years, reading Toynbee; they say to the newly dead, "And Toynbee? *You haven't read Toynbee!*" For *A Study of History,* errors, idiosyncrasies, and all, is an immortal masterpiece. How I know this I don't know: the muse of history must have possessed me, since I am far too ignorant to make the judgment myself. No book convinces one better of one's own ignorance; I don't know enough to criticize it, don't know enough, really, to appreciate it.

But I love it just the same, and would give a good deal to convince those of you who haven't read it (and reading the one-volume condensation is no more like reading *it* than reading *Lamb's Tales* is like reading Shakespeare) of the exquisite, inimitable, almost interminable enjoyment you can get from reading *A Study of History.*

These new volumes deal with Universal States; Universal Churches; Heroic Ages; Contacts between Civilizations in Space (Encounters between Contemporaries); Contacts between Civilizations in Time (Renaissances); Law and Freedom in History; The Prospects of the Western Civilization; The Inspirations of Historians; and, in conclusion, there is Toynbee's odd and endearing account of the origins and development of his own work. After reading these 2,700 pages I am still too dazed and, so to speak, enlarged, to say what my favorite parts are, or to compare them with such old favorites as the accounts of Sparta and the Ottoman Empire; my eyes are still blurred, my ears echoing, with that strange, stiff-robed, grandly conventional, innocently monumental style. Hokusai called himself the old man mad about painting; Toynbee could call himself the old man mad about metaphor —metaphors dead for many centuries are revived by his impartial trust, and go slowly by, their draperies billowing in the wind of Time. For as you read *A Study of History* the air of all the earth, of all the ages, is circulating around you; it is, if ever a book was, ecumenical.

Frans G. Bengtsson is a Swedish "poet, essayist, historian, and novelist." His *The Long Ships* is two books, really. The first half—the story of how a young man given to poetry gets kidnapped while defending his mother's sheep, and becomes a Viking, a galley slave, the commander of the Moor Almansur's bodyguard, one of the leaders of the biggest Danish raid on England, and, finally, the husband of King Harald Bluetooth's prettiest daughter—this is one of the funniest, most knowing, and most delightful historical novels I have ever read. It's quite worthy of going on Toynbee's list of the historical novels he's enjoyed most; if you like sagas or *I, Claudius,* be sure to read *The Long Ships.* The second half of the book, the story of how Orm settles on the frontier, prospers, and voyages to Russia to dig up some buried treasure, is on a lower level—one reads it with much loyalty and some pleasure. But in the first half even the little poems are straight out of the sagas; Orm, tied, guarded, and about to be slaughtered, says to the other Vikings: *At home in the house / That saw me grow / Would I were seated now / Eating sour milk and bread.* And this is how an invalid got his hair combed at Harald's court by Harald's daughter:

Ylva had some difficulty in attending to Orm, because he was unable to sit up, but she supported his body with her arm and used him carefully, and emerged from her task with credit, for he got no lye in his eyes or mouth and yet became clean and fine. Then she seated herself on the head of his bed, put his head between her knees, and began to comb him. She asked him if he was uncomfortable, but Orm had to admit that he was not. She found difficulty in passing the comb through his hair, for it was thick and coarse, and very tangled as a result of the washing; but she persevered patiently with the task, so that he thought he had never in his life been better combed.

. . . She drew her comb slowly through a tuft of Orm's hair which she had just untangled, and held it up against the daylight to examine it closely.

"I do not understand how this can be," she said, "but there does not appear to be a single louse in your hair."

"That is not possible," said Orm. "It must be a bad comb."

She said that it was a good louse-comb, and scraped his head so that his scalp burned, but still she could find no louse.

"If what you say is true, then I am sick indeed," said Orm, "and things are even worse than I had feared. This can only mean that my blood is poisoned."

The Collected Poems of Wallace Stevens contains all the poetry of one of the greatest of living poets. I have before this written about both his best poems and his worst, but on occasion (and a book like this is truly an occasion) a critic can behave like posterity, which memorializes—which memorizes—the good, and which looks by the bad with a sweet uncaring smile. One might as well argue with the Evening Star as find fault with so much wit and grace and intelligence; such knowledge of, feeling for, other times and places, and our own; such an overwhelming and exquisite command both of the words and of the rhythms of our language; such charm and irony, such natural and philosophical breadth of sympathy, such dignity and magnanimity. (Toynbee often has the calm and generosity of a visitor from a better age, and you feel that Stevens would like nothing better than to be such a traveler through time.) Little of Stevens's work has the dramatic immediacy, the mesmeric, involving humanity, of so much of Yeats's and Frost's poetry: his poems, if they were ideally successful, might resemble the paintings of Piero della Francesca. But some of these cool, clear, airy poems, which tower above us in the dazzling elegance, the "minute brilliance," of yachts or clouds, ought to be sailing over other heads many centuries from now.

Evelyn Waugh is a man born to write *Candide;* and after he had written it and called it *Decline and Fall*—it is, surely, one of the funniest books in English—he went on writing and became at last a professional inventor of atrocities, a very witty, very sadistic-masochistic, and very unreliable one. The Waugh hero, characteristically, is a stiff, numb, gentlemanly lay figure in the chamber of horrors of the Present, the torture chamber of the Future.

In *Tactical Exercise,* the toccata which gives his new collection its name, Waugh tells the story of an orphan pyromaniac in the State of the Future. After burning down the air base at which he is stationed, he finds a loved home in the country manor, torn from a "maimed V.C.," which the State uses to rehabilitate its criminals. Unwillingly rehabilitated, he becomes an official in the Department of Euthanasia, the only institution which flourishes in that bad time; falls in love with a ballet dancer with a long golden beard, the result of the de-sexing operation which, as is customary, she has undergone. When she learns that, beard or no, she is about to have a baby, she has a second operation, which removes beard and skin together, replacing them by a plastic mask ideal as a base for greasepaint. That loved beard gone, the hero burns down the loved home-prison, killing all the criminals; and he himself, the only surviving example of rehabilitation, is sent out on a lecture tour with a pretty mistress.

In all these stories things go wrong—vulgarly, basely wrong—with a magician's ingenuity, a star's fidelity: the stew the natives feed the hero is, always, the heroine. The reader, instead of getting avidly indignant over the age, the State, and people, only says: "I know your methods, Waugh." Waugh writes as he does, not because the world is what it is, but because Waugh is what he is—another sign that he is a real writer. This book has little of his best writing, though "Work Suspended" is an attractive, unusually personal novelette. But in this world bursting with sin and sorrow, how can we spend our time licking our lips over the ingenious imaginary enormities that *bad* people keep showering on one gray guiltless figure? Waugh's moral imagination is so one-sided that it has become a crippled, macabre joke.

Most of Russell Lynes's *The Tastemakers* is a careful and interesting history, with fine illustrations, of American taste in houses, furniture, pictures, and sculpture, and of the people who made it what it was. (A favorite nineteenth-century way of getting a man to buy a chair was to call it *sincere,* something I didn't know and won't forget.) Lynes leaves out novels, poems, plays, music, dancing: this one-sided selection of facts makes his conclusions one-sided, I think. Part of *The Tastemakers* is his very well-known essay on Lowbrows, Middlebrows, and High-brows. This is an essay I heartily enjoyed and thoroughly disbelieved. When you're told exactly what lowbrows, middlebrows, and highbrows eat, drink, love, think, and wear, you laugh and like it; but pretty soon you begin to notice that neither you nor I nor Russell Lynes—nor any-body else with any sense and opinions of his own—fits into the categories very well, and you decide that this pigeonholing is wit, not thought. We're always told, quite correctly, that we must judge a man as a man, and not as a Negro, a Turk, or a Jew. To judge him as a lowbrow, a highbrow, a middlebrow—to force all that we can into one of these pigeonholes into which, after all, so little of a man will go—seems to me an analogous sin.

I read *The View from Pompey's Head,* like almost all these books, in galleys. (Galleys are thirty-six, or forty-eight, or seventy-two inches long—they grew longer as I grew older. I thought of how Gilbert Highet, year in and year out, had dealt with these paper anacondas without a word, and it seemed to me that this department of *Harper's* should be called *The New Laocoön.*) Along with this proof there was a marvelous sentence: "This is Hamilton Basso's big novel, an important and extremely salable book that he has been on the verge of writing for the last decade and a half." I felt for Hamilton Basso, and for Hamilton Basso's publishers, and for the society which puts such sentences into people's heads—a society which Hamilton Basso views with a somewhat unacquiescing, somewhat Marquandish eye.

Pompey's Head is a small Southern city to which a New York lawyer in early middle age is summoned home by an unfortunate and unbelievable subplot about a Wolfe-ish writer whose wicked wife has accused a Perkins-ish publisher of Stealing Royalties. Pompey's Head, and the lawyer, and the girls he used to go with, and the little girl, grown now, whom he falls in love with, and the wife he left behind him, a clear, clean, crisp, Vassar, PTA, AAUW type calculated to scare Europe, Asia, and Africa into the middle of the Indian Ocean—all these are quite believable and rather interesting. This is a medium-sized novel, not a big one, but it is in a mild way enjoyable; you feel that it is, except for that subplot, the best its writer can do, and a decent enough thing to be doing, and you extend to it the qualified respect it deserves.

The Huge Season is a much better book, and a much bigger dis-appointment. Wright Morris is a "real writer" in a way, to a degree, that Hamilton Basso never is: he knows a great deal more about just what people said and felt and did at a certain time, or would say and feel and do at any time, and he has more of a gift for words, more cultivation, more imagination. My wife and I read *The Huge Season* at the same time, and would read parts aloud to each other, ask *Where are you now?*, say, *Wait till you get to the chapter about So-and-So:* we were really interested—and, when we got to the end, really disappointed. The alternating chapters, one in the late twenties, the other in the early fifties, seem designed to lead up to some revelation which will explain and justify everything, and so end the book. But though the book pretends to End, it only stops: instead of a revelation there is only (as Wells said) a mouse on the altar, and a queer, hysterical, writerish little mouse at that.

But I hope that such news of the end won't keep anybody from reading the book; it is, most of the time, an appealing story by a talented and attractive writer. There is something engaging and shelterable about him, so that you want to spread your wings over his faults or, at least, run off into a hedge to draw the hunters away from them. His characters, except for the author-character, are not a lot more than skin deep; some of the book is romantic and confused, about liberals, Hemingway heroes, and the twenties, in a partly touching, partly distressing way; its author, in spite of his real talents, is a little commonplace, a little lacking in personal force, unintended individuality. But just the same, read the book: the best parts are fresh and live enough to make the worst parts an honorable disappointment.

First one gets works of art, then criticism of them, then criticism of the criticism, and, finally, a book on *The Literary Situation,* a book which tells you all about writers, critics, publishing, paperbacked books, the tendencies of the (literary) time, what sells and how much, what writers wear and drink and want, what their wives wear and drink and want, and so on. Malcolm Cowley has plainly enjoyed writing his—as a review would say—readable, informative, and entertaining book: his style, which is usually rather doughy and matter-of-course, is in this book a good deal more animated. *The Literary Situation* is less objective than its informing, summarizing manner would indicate—its author would give all that he has, and more, to get us back to the twenties and thirties, times when he swam more freely in a tide running his own way. His book rather depressed me, since it is such a thoroughgoing example of what Tocqueville called—Cowley quotes the sentence—"the trading spirit in literature."

One of the most popular sorts of science fiction, these last few years, has been the cautionary Utopia. *The Big Ball of Wax* shows you a society which is all business, advertising, and "mass entertainment media," and shows you what happens to it when something is invented which allows you not simply to see, but to be, the television program you are watching. Shepherd Mead's book is sometimes quite funny and sometimes quite crude; the best thing about it is his vivid and detailed knowledge—he is a vice-president—of business ways and advertising speech.

Alfred Duggan's *Leopards and Lilies* is the competent and well-informed, moderately interesting, somewhat unimaginative history of an awful woman and a nice soldier in the days of bad King John. After Merle Miller's *Reunion,* I welcomed it. *Reunion* is the book you would get if you put in Mammoth Cave, to write a novel, every radio and television and scenario writer who ever lived. As you read it you begin to have the nightmarish feeling that sensibility and morality, nice people, good writers, are simply a fable agreed upon, a myth the Real World doesn't believe in any longer.

From Emerson to Twain, most of our great American writers wrote, and wrote well, for *The Youth's Companion;* the extremely interesting new anthology of their contributions is alloyed by the extensive comments of the editor, Lovell Thompson, who writes about them in patronizing magazinese. *The Saturday Evening Post Treasury,* though it contains a number of good things, gets worse, gets almost indistinguishably commonplace, as it approaches the fifties. It seemed to me that the articles written for those dead children who read *The Youth's Companion* were usually more thoughtful and demanding, and of more literary merit, than the articles written for the grown-ups who read the *Post* today.

A Literary Tornado

· ❀ ·

THE NEW YORK TIMES BOOK REVIEW, APRIL 17, 1955

Selected Poems by Roy Campbell

ROY CAMPBELL is what anybody would call a man of action. He has been a horse trader, "a professional bullfighter and wandering circus performer in Provence, a fisherman off the southern coast of France, a soldier in both wars, [he has] fought with Franco . . ." I was reminded among others of the life of R. B. Cunninghame Graham, a man of action who wrote some good and highly individual stories about horses, and Spain, and the Africa in which Roy Campbell was born; and of the poet Oliver St. John Gogarty, who typified for Yeats the man of action. These people's works are full of life, of their lives. But when I looked for the life in Campbell's poems all I could find was literature.

It is, mostly, a kind of literature that was very popular from 1820 to 1840. Byron created it, Shelley wrote some of it, Goethe admired it, everybody read it; after a while Byron deserted it for *Don Juan*. It is named *Childe Harold, Manfred, Mazeppa;* Shelley's "The Cloud" is close to it. In it the poet identified himself with, makes himself over into, some overwhelming, rhetorical, melodramatic force of nature. One of the transcendentalists is supposed to have looked out the window and said, "Look, I'm snowing"; in the same way, the poet thundered and lightened and avalanched for his readers.

Roy Campbell's poems do this, and do it just as it used to be done, word for word, rhythm for rhythm: he is the Byron not of our days but of Byron's. We read: "And when, by the hate of the hurricane blown, / It doubles its forces with fibers that groan, / Exulting I ride in the tower of my pride / To feel that the strength of the blast is my own." We read: "Yawn, you great gaps: you starred abysses, yawn / To swill the fiery vintage of the dawn: / Nature's grim forces heavy with their sleep / Rise up in red rebellion from the deep . . . / Let old Corruption on his spangled throne / Tremble to hear! The jagged rifts of stone / Roar for his mangled carrion: old Earth / Writhes in the anguish of a second birth." It is hard to believe that it is we who are reading this, and not our great-great-grandfathers. When we come across echoes of Rimbaud's drunken boats and Baudelaire's digging skeletons it surprises us as much as if we had seen them in Shelley or Byron.

It is a very bad-tempered Byron who writes these poems; his heart no longer bleeds, but only barks and bites. Never was there an angrier poet! And, rather engagingly, he tells you so. He speaks of "the cold infernal hates / Whose company I love the best," and tells how early he began "to wear his liver on his sleeve, / To snarl and be an angry man." It is natural for him to write satires, but it is hard for us to enjoy them: his jokes are sledge-hammer, his rhythms rocking-horse, and Time or Oblivion or his lines have killed off most of his enemies. (He loves to tell them, in the accents of *English Bards and Scotch Reviewers,* that they are stupid and homosexual and smell bad.) It is nicer when he comments about Professor Drennan's verse: "Who forced the muse to this alliance? / A man of more degrees than parts— / The jilted Bachelor of Science / And Widower of Arts." When he is at all quiet or contemporary I like him best; but usually he is what Edith Sitwell calls him, "a literary tornado."

If the damned, blown willy-nilly around the windy circle of hell, enjoyed it and were proud of being there, they would sound very much as he sounds. It isn't life, one thinks sadly, it's bad temper and reading Byron and Shelley that have produced his poetry: so it is only when we hate everybody, or feel we would sell our souls for a new *Manfred,* that his poems are much of a joy to us.

A Matter of Opinion

THE NEW YORK TIMES BOOK REVIEW, MAY 29, 1955

Predilections by Marianne Moore

Now for a few dollars the book buyer can have for his own most of what Marianne Moore has written about Wallace Stevens and William Carlos Williams and Ezra Pound, W. H. Auden and T. S. Eliot and Henry James—about old days on *The Dial,* and writing in general, and Jean Cocteau and Pavlova and the Sitwells' father. *Predilections* is a modest, original, perceptive book, full of quotations and moral truth. Even its faults seem individual and endearing.

It is particular appreciation, not general criticism: Marianne Moore has managed to find many good and a few wonderful ways to show how things are good. She does justice to a writer's special qualities by minute description, by quotation—she has, as all readers of her poetry know, a great gift for discovering lines that sound marvelous or marvelously like Marianne Moore—and by poetic, apothegmatic, truthful compliments that must leave the complimented flushed for days. (For instance, she says of Wallace Stevens's poems: "They embody hope that in being frustrated becomes fortitude.") Usually her pieces disapprove of a quality by leaving it unmentioned. Occasionally they suggest dislike in imaginative or aphoristic form, as when an admiring review of *The Infernal Machine* ends:

"Aware that imagination with Jean Cocteau is no appurtenance but an ichor, as it was shown to be in *Le Sang d'un Poête,* one has, nevertheless, the sense of something submerged and estranged, of a somnambulist with feet tied, of a musical instrument in a museum, that should be sounding; of valor in a fairy tale, changed by hostile enchantment into a frog or carp that cannot leave its pool or well. In myth there is a principle of penalty: Snow White must not open the door of the dwarfs' house when the peddler knocks. Pandora must not open the box, Perseus must not look at the Gorgon except in his shield; and M. Cocteau, in refusing to be answerable to any morality but his own, is in the Greek sense impious and unnatural."

Could even Cocteau feel better his own essence, or express it in a style more magically his own? This criticism of a poet is itself a poem, and it is the imagination that consents to it.

One often comes across lines or passages of poetry, of Marianne Moore's poetry, in this book's prose:

> *now, tropic*
> > *pinks and yellows,*
> *avocado*
> > *and Kuniyoshi cabouchon*
> *emerald-greens, the blent*
> > *but violent*
> *excellence of ailanthus*
> > *silk-moths and metallic*
> *breast-feathers, as o-*
> > *pen and unpretending as Rousseau's*
> *Snake-Charmer and Sleeping*
> > *Gipsy, combine in an impression of incandescence.*

The reader may complain that Marianne Moore's poetry would hardly have so many rhymes—that's so, but this is her prose.

Miss Moore is particularly good about Stevens, Williams, Pound, and James; she talks of them with familiar love, as if she and they made up—I suppose they do—one wonderful family. She is best of all about writing: she says that "when we think we don't like art it is because it is artificial art"; that "originality is in any case a by-product of sincerity"; that "humility is an indispensable teacher, enabling concentration to heighten gusto. There are always objectors, but we must not be sensitive about not being liked or not being printed . . . The thing is to see the vision and deny it; to care and admit that we do."

Predilections, like Marianne Moore's other books, is purely and individually and imaginatively faithful to the truth as she has seen it.

A Dylan Thomas Collection

· ·

NEW YORK POST, JUNE 5, 1955

Adventures in the Skin Trade by Dylan Thomas

ADVENTURES IN THE SKIN TRADE is an imaginative and individual book. The best things in it are magical, and the worst things are full of phrases and ideas that could have occurred only to Dylan Thomas. Most of these stories I read in 1939, when I was reviewing *The World I Breathe,* and I've occasionally reread such favorites as "The Enemies" and "The Burning Baby"; this time I decided that readers grow old, but that the stories are as young as ever.

Writers grow old, too: *Adventures in the Skin Trade,* the 80-page "novel-in-progress" which begins this collection of stories, is written by the middle-aged, humorous, broadcasting Thomas about the adolescent, daydreaming, purely poetic Thomas. The story tells what happens to a young poet just come to London: nothing happens, nothing ever happens, the story complains.

Yet, all the time it's complaining, the story can't resist making the most grotesque and unlikely things happen to the poet. We see him naked in a stranger's bathtub, a beer bottle stuck fast on his finger—he's unconscious, too, because of the glass of eau de cologne he's just gulped down. Who gave it to him? A girl. And so the story goes. A lot happens, the poet complains that nothing ever happens, and the poet is uneasy whenever anything does happen.

The reader may retort that this is pretty much like life and very much like poets, and I don't disagree. But it is disappointing to have Thomas on such specially warm terms with the young Thomas—particularly disappointing after *Under Milk Wood,* where Thomas is on specially warm terms with the whole world, and can transform a Welsh town into a Garden of Eden of his own, live, green, and beyond either good or evil.

There Thomas loves the live things merely for their living; feels, always: "How else would you want something to act except according to its nature?" In *Under Milk Wood* Thomas plays no favorites: even the good appeal to him.

The early stories play no favorites either, since Thomas has let nothing but favorite things into the stories. He says about one of his characters what could be said of him: "The gardener loved the Bible . . . He would sit with a candle in his shed, reading of the first love and the legend of apples and serpents. But the death of Christ on a tree he loved most."

Many of these stories are, so to speak, Bible stories for readers of Grimm and Freud; they are told in terms of Wales and childhood, dreams and the body—the terms of Thomas's poems. Their sentences are grave, pure, and sure; are in a strange, somewhat mannered way, natural.

The worst of the stories are rich rank marshes of phrases and images, marvelous to look at, hard to wade through; the best are beautiful, touching, and entirely magical myths or fairy tales or wish fantasies of an imagination different from any other in our time. Stories like "The Enemies" and "The Burning Baby," like "The Dress," "The School for Witches," and "The Followers," are things it would be sad not to get to read.

Here is the beginning of one story: "Early one morning, under the arc of a lamp, carefully, silently, in smock and rubber gloves, old Doctor Manza grafted a cat's head on to a chicken's trunk. The cat-headed creature, in a house of glass, swayed on its legs; though it stared through the slits of its eyes, it saw nothing; there was the flutter of a strange pulse under its fur and feathers, and, lifting its foot to the right of the glass wall, it rocked again to the left."

The witch watches the old preacher as he nears her house: "But as he climbed over the craggy edges and down the side of the hill, he lost his place in Mrs. Owen's crystal. A cloud displaced his black hat, and under the cloud walked a very old phantom, a shape of air with stars all frozen in its beard, and a half-moon for a smile. Mr. Davies knew nothing of this as the stones scratched his hands. He was old, he was drunk with the wine of the morning, but the stuff that came out of his cuts was a human blood."

If you like Grimm, or Hoffmann, or Kafka, you will like some of these stories, I think; and people who can really write something, really imagine something, are not so common that we can let even their odd or slight works go unread.

Speaking of Books

THE NEW YORK TIMES BOOK REVIEW, JULY 24, 1955

I HAVE trouble knowing what to do at parties. Prisoners tame mice, or make rings out of spoons: I analyze people's handwriting— Pierre Emmanuel taught me, saying: "It will help you"—or else ask you to tell me what you read when you were a child. (People speak un- usually well of the books of their childhood, don't they? Or is this one more life-giving illusion?) I love to see a hard eye grow soft over *Little Women,* or *The Black Arrow,* or *Grandma Elsie*—yes, Elsie Dinsmore became a grandmother. And, I've found, there's no children's book so bad that I mind your having liked it: about the tastes of dead children there is no disputing.

The live grown-ups are different. Readers, real readers, are always telling other readers what to read; and according to what it is, they use a different tone—they know that they are about to be judged. "Always speak your mind and base men will avoid you," Blake said. Always say what you like and readers who know what they should like will look at you silently and then tell you what you should like, too. Once I told a critic—since he was standing in a railway station, wearing a cream- colored corduroy suit, he looked remarkably like that Disraeli-ish figure, dressed all in newspapers, whom you see in *Through the Looking-Glass* —about a wonderful novel named *The Man Who Loved Children.* (I've been getting people to read it for ten years, with the most dazzling re- sults; so many have bought it for themselves that Simon and Schuster wrote one a letter, saying: "Would you be kind enough to tell us how you happened to order this particular book? In recent years there has been a small but steady demand for it.") A sort of despairing contempt filled the critic's eyes, and he cried: "But—but—but that's absurd! That isn't a good novel, it couldn't be! I haven't read it, but I know the sort of author she is, and it couldn't be. Why, she's a Stalinist!"

This may have been a great injustice to Christina Stead, and it was a small injustice to me: if we jump on readers who recommend to us some unlikely thing they've liked, they get apologetic—soon the gentler ones will only say to themselves softly, in bed that night: "I wish I'd told him about *The Man Who Loved Children*." But there is a Pope in the breast of each of us whom it is hard to silence. Long ago a lady said to me, when I asked her the composers she liked: "Dvořak." I said before I could stop myself: "Dvořak!" How many times, and with what shame, I've remembered it! And now I like Dvořak and Tchaikovsky and, even, the creator of the "Weihnachtsbaum," the "Vallée d'Obermann," and the "Hungarian Rhapsodies" which Edith Farnadi plays so beautifully— that banal and individual genius, Liszt.

"Liszt!" I know, I know; it was because of the "Liszt!" that I used that periphrasis, those adjectives—I should have told you that my favorite quartet is Opus 130 (with the "Grosse Fugue" as the last move- ment, of course) in a very different tone. And yet, what good tone is there for Beethoven and Shakespeare and Spinoza and Proust and Rilke? They are no better, and we no better thought of, for our admiration; but still we admire. And when I recommend the second book of *The Excur- sion*, or speak of Wordsworth as one of the three or four greatest of English poets, I don't mind having the remark thought either a truism or an absurdity: I feel Matthew Arnold's approving breath at my shoulder, and see out before me, smiling bewitchingly, the nations of the not-yet-born.

I regularly recommend Saltykov-Shchedrin's *The Golovlyov Family;* it makes me feel like Chaliapin just to say it. And recommend- ing Kant's *The Critique of Judgment*, reader, is its own reward. A fresh, candid tone is best. Strauss told conductors to play *Elektra* "as if it were *A Midsummer Night's Dream*—like fairy music"; that is how I recommend *The Critique of Judgment*.

May I finish by recommending—in no tone—some books for summer reading? Giraudoux's *Electra;* Bemelmans's *Hotel Splendide;* *Kim;* Saint-Simon's *Memoirs;* Elizabeth Bishop's *North & South;* the new edition of A. L. Kroeber's textbook of anthropology, and Ralph Linton's *The Study of Man;* Turgenev's *A Sportsman's Sketches;* Colette's *Julie de Carneilhan* and *The Last of Chéri;* Pirandello's *Henry IV;* Freud's *Collected Papers;* Peter Taylor's *The Widows of Thornton;* Isak Dinesen's *Out of Africa;* Goethe's aphorisms; Blake's *The Mar- riage of Heaven and Hell;* Gerard Manley Hopkins's *Letters to Robert Bridges;* Rilke's *The Notebooks of Malte Laurids Brigge*, and Chekhov's plays, stories, letters—anything.

Recent Poetry

THE YALE REVIEW, SUMMER 1955

The Collected Poems of Edith Sitwell   Collected Poems by James Stephens   *The Dark Is Light Enough* by Christopher Fry   *A Spring Journey and Other Poems* by James Kirkup   *Selected Poems* by Mark Van Doren   *The Scarecrow Christ and Other Poems* by Elder Olson   *Water Ouzel and Other Poems* by William H. Matchett   *Poems: Collected and New* by Rolfe Humphries   *The Middle Voice* by Constance Carrier   *Songs for Eve* by Archibald MacLeish   *The Shield of Achilles* by W. H. Auden

W HEN ANYONE reads and writes about a great many books of poetry—and I am reviewing twice as many as usual, since the spring issue was all Wallace Stevens*—he is uneasy at liking so few of the books. He feels, just as the poets and their readers feel, that he should like many more: it seems only right, only human. And yet really he should be uneasy at liking as many as he does. Posterity won't. Our age's eight or ten great, twenty or twenty-five good, forty or fifty talented poets—what has posterity to do with these illusions of ours? As little as we have to do with the illusions of 1855; those poets whose names we do not recognize, whose poems we have never even seen. Whether we live in the Athens of Pericles or the England of Elizabeth I, there is one law we can be sure of: there are only a few good poets alive. And there follows from it another law, about critics: if a man likes a great many contemporary poets, he is, necessarily, a bad critic.

But even if all this is true—and it seems to me unarguably true—saying so doesn't make me feel any better about not liking more of the books. Somewhere in the depths of my being, as in yours, there is something that keeps saying, *Praise, praise;* part of me wants to take as its rule of life, of criticism even, *Love, or be silent;* when I can write

---

* "The Collected Poems of Wallace Stevens," *The Yale Review,* Spring 1955; included in *The Third Book of Criticism.*—Ed.

in dazzled bliss about Hardy or Yeats or Whitman or Hopkins or Frost
or Eliot or Dickinson or Stevens or Moore or Thomas or Auden or
Williams or Ransom or such—when I can quote, or admire, or appreciate, beautiful or witty or moving poems by Pound or Lawrence or
Graves or Lowell or Stephens or Bridges or Muir or Elizabeth Bishop
or Owen or Tate or MacNeice or Warren or Shapiro or Katherine Hoskins or Roethke or such, I feel that I am behaving as man (who
shudders in awe, and delights most in that shudder) behaves when he
is truly man; and when I tell you what troubles me about MacLeish,
and that Edith Sitwell isn't a very good poet, I feel that I'm only behaving like the Devil, that accuser, that Spirit who Denies. Disliking what
is bad is only the other face of liking what is good; but what a dark,
dank, grudging, graceless face, one endeared neither to gods nor men!
And the good, in poetry, is always a white blackbird, an abnormal and
unlikely excellence; all that deserves our respect in ordinary life—the
consistent, adequate, responsible norm of behavior—gains only our
indifference, here. It is unpleasant, discouraging, unnatural to have
to go on saying, about each shining new blackbird: *But it's black;* I do
it, but I hate doing it; I'd rather be telling you about the miraculous
poems, rather be saying with wide eyes, like Gogarty: "If you knew
where I had been / Or half the joys I'd had, / You never would
leave me alone"—had rather be ending, as Gogarty's "O Boys! O Boys!"
so magically ends:

> *For no one believes in joys,*
> *And Peace on Earth is a joke,*
> *Which, anyhow, telling destroys;*
> *So better go on with your work:*
> *But Boys! O Boys! O Boys!*

That Edith Sitwell should be considered a great poet is puzzling. She
began as a real poet of a humble but stylish kind: her early poems, like
so many of the ballets or paintings or compositions of the twenties,
made fashionable, satiric, amusing use of romantic and Victorian
clichés, of grandiose rhetoric, of all sorts of outmoded melodramatic
machinery. As she grew older she became serious, solemn even, and
wished to say serious and solemn things: she used the same rhetorical
machinery, but now she used it seriously. (A clown always makes the
soberest Hamlet, one you can hardly tell from Polonius.) Her quite
fantastic theories about what sounds do in verse, her absorption in her
overwhelming new subjects, her sincere belief that she is a dedicated
priestess of art—these must have kept her from realizing how gro-

tesque and pretentious her style of writing had become: her phrases
delude her, I think, exactly as they delude most of her readers. They
are meant to have an apocalyptic grandeur, but they sound as if Madame Blavatsky (just after reading Yeats and the Prophetic Books
and an anthology of Christian mysticism) had written them for a
Society of Latter-day Druids. *Are* characteristic late passages like "the
azoic azure / Calls to the sphinxes of the silence and the unburied
sapphires / Staring across lion-breasted sands in the great deserts, /
And to the azoic heart (where Time, that Medusa, reigns, turns all to
stone)— / To the orange-flower, the oragious hair of youth that cool
airs lift" better than characteristic early passages like "Cried the navy-
blue ghost / Of Mr. Belaker / The allegro Negro cocktail-shaker,
/ 'Why did the cock crow, / Why am I lost, / Down the endless
road to Infinity tossed?' " Are Edith Sitwell's serious—which is to say,
solemn and melodramatic and grotesquely rhetorical—poems as good
as the best of her light verse? of Betjeman's? of Belloc's? I fancy that
the best Betjeman, or "Lord Lundy," or the most charming of Edith
Sitwell's Diaghilev pastorals, will be read when her later poems are an
almost forgotten curiosity.

No one calls James Stephens great, and he long ago stopped
being fashionable, but at his best he is a fine poet. I reviewed his *Collected Poems,* at some length, in *The New York Times;* instead of repeating myself, let me recommend poems. Some of his best are "The
Goat Paths," "Egan O Rahilly," "What Tomas Said in a Pub," "The
Snare," "To the Four Courts, Please," "A Glass of Beer," "Skim Milk,"
"Strict Care, Strict Joy," and "The Market"; some beguiling Irish poems
are "The Geraldine's Cloak," "Blue Blood," "O Brudair," and "Odell";
and child poems like "Midnight" or "The Road," Blake poems like "In
Waste Places," are certainly worth reading. His poems wear their
faults on their sleeve; but they have in them so much warmth and
pain and humor, so many of the concerns of human beings like ourselves, that it is natural for us to be attracted to them.

Poets do not think Christopher Fry a poet, I've noticed, just as
soldiers don't think someone in a suit of armor a soldier. But *The Lady's
Not for Burning* has an adolescent, narcissistic, systematically irresponsible charm that doesn't prepare you for as lame and joyless a play as *The
Dark Is Light Enough.* Even the verse sounds as if the poet could
barely make himself write it; as you read, any contemporary poetic play
seems a kind of forlorn hope, and it is hard to believe that Giraudoux's
Electra, The Words upon the Window-Pane, Blood Wedding, and *The
Infernal Machine* really exist.

James Kirkup is a calm, mild, small-scale poet of some real merit. Almost all earlier poetry seems equally close to him, equally available: he can write flat Herbert, flat Cowper, and flat School of Auden with the same ease and self-possession, and can really say something—a small, personal, imaginative something—in all three. If you went in a time machine to a ruined city just on the other side of some great deluge, and had tea with the pale, devout, unexpectedly well-adjusted proprietor of a little antique shop, he might sound as Kirkup sounds. At his worst he writes Coronation Odes worthy of a curate; at his best he gives one true "News of the Other World":

It is not merely the stirring of a windless veil,
The jumpy table, the keys leaping from their locks,
The dragging footsteps on the vanished stair;
Nor yet the rain of clothes-pegs, cotton-reels; the pail
Kicked round the empty yard, and the domestic shocks
Of crockery, pots and fenders flying through the air.

For these are surely the last distracted signals
Of one grown desperate with our obtuseness,
One who must, to greet us, hit us with a chair
Because our fumbling wits are gross denials
Of the spirit. And we, who are so subtle, guess
Blankly at the meaning of our lifted hair.

Mark Van Doren seems to me someone who almost became a good poet—"The Amber Sunstream" is an impressive poem, and a good many of the poems he wrote during the early thirties have attractive parts—but whose poetry has been spoiled by a terrible regularity, methodicalness, habitualness both of perception and of expression. It is as if he asked himself: *Is this good?* but meant, without knowing it: *Is this the way I always do it?* He is very easily satisfied. Take this ballad stanza, for instance: "I love your face as hot as this. / Put me down though, and creep. / My father! He would strangle you, / I think, like any sheep." Would a poet with much knowledge of what he has written leave in that *any sheep,* and *creep,* and *I think?* I was attracted by many of his subjects; I was interested to find him ("As if a cabinet became alive / And the recesses in it, the small curios, / Burned with an equal being, the huge world / Let him come in; made itself little and patient . . .") actually being influenced by Rilke; I finished his *Selected Poems* with a feeling of uneasy depression—how few of them are really written, really *made!*

Elder Olson's poems seem to know the world only through literature. They are best when he deliberately assumes a manner and the
properties that go with it—a period piece like his "Shepherd and
Clown" is delightful in the way that a less individual "Classical Symphony" would be delightful; but when he writes a poem in his own
style it is a stagy, exaggerated mixture of other people's poetry. William Matchett is enjoyable in a poem about Dylan Thomas, a poem
about an old woman going out to see the spring, but his poems seem
at a *very* early stage in a poet's career—too early, really, for a publisher to print him and a critic to judge him. Rolfe Humphries's *Poems:
Collected and New* are the work of a graceful and accomplished poet;
they are marred by some ordinary didacticism and some extraordinary
lapses in taste and temper; and they are, always, a little too easy and
commonplace, a little too close to what is called magazine verse. True
poets, so to speak, turn down six things and take the seventh;
Humphries always takes the fifth or sixth. Constance Carrier is,
plainly, a woman of good will and good sense; she writes carefully
and thoughtfully; what she says is earnest and reasonable and commonplace enough to make you feel that the norm or mean or median of
all members of the PTA, of the AAUW, of the League of Women
Voters, is there before you, scanned and scrubbed and shining. If only
she were one of our acknowledged legislators! Everybody must have
wished at some time that poetry were written by nice ordinary people
instead of poets—and, in a better world, it may be; but in this world
writers like Constance Carrier are the well oysters that don't have the
pearls.

It seems to me that Archibald MacLeish has made overpowering
demands upon his own delicate lyric talent. Didn't he have much the
same relation to Pound and Eliot (not to speak of Apollinaire) that
Mary Cassatt had to Degas, and didn't he do to his gift what she would
have done to hers, if she had tried to rival Degas and Daumier and
Delacroix all at once? He has made himself into a kind of Mann-like
figure, and much of what he has written has been striking in the way
effective political rhetoric is striking. It is natural that he should have
talked so much about poetry's being public speech, but isn't his own
best poetry private speech like "You, Andrew Marvell," a poem beautiful in just the way a painting by Georgia O'Keeffe is beautiful? Many
of his poems suffer from something akin to "metaphysical pathos":
they are almost more conscious of the impressiveness of what they say
than of what they say. The poem is, almost, a by-product of the attitude of the poet, and the attitude is a consciously impressive, almost

institutional one: the poet is at ease on Parnassus, and writes poems there. Yet I liked parts of *Songs for Eve* better than I did the three or four new books before it. The sharp, bright, sometimes quite interesting, sometimes quite mannered series of poems about the Garden of Eden is pleasant to read, and would be even pleasanter to believe: the poet has made Eve the heroine who brought Eternity into time, who transformed an animal into Man, by breaking the law she was right to break. *O felix culpa!*

"A culture is no better than its woods," Auden writes. Fortunately for him, a book of poetry can be better than its poems. Two-thirds of *The Shield of Achilles* is non-Euclidean needlepoint, a man sitting on a chaise longue juggling four cups, four saucers, four sugar lumps, and the round-square: this is what great and good poets do when they don't bother even to try to write great and good poems, now that they've learned that—it's Auden's leitmotif, these days—art is essentially frivolous. But a little of the time Auden is essentially serious, and the rest of the time he's so witty, intelligent, and individual, so angelically skillful, that one reads with despairing enthusiasm, and enjoys Auden's most complacently self-indulgent idiosyncrasy almost as one enjoys Sherlock Holmes's writing *Victoria Rex* on the wall in bullet holes. After a couple of decades of moralizing us to the top of our bent, Auden has finally—in half the poetry of these last two books—given up morality: "In my Eden," he writes now, "each observes his compulsive rituals and superstitious tabus but we have no morals." And Auden's old, superstitious, compulsive readers—I'm one—are that way, almost necessarily, about Auden: you can't argue with a hog, a Senator, the Epicurean Gods, or the retired Talleyrand—we don't judge Auden, we just enjoy him. (He's over on the other side of Judgment, in a wordy, worldly Limbo of his own.) As we read that "in my Eden a person who dislikes Bellini has the good manners not to get born," we just say, "I'm glad I like Bellini"; when we read that "I stand in Eden again, welcomed back by the krum-horns, doppions, sordumes of jolly miners and a bob major from the Cathedral (romanesque) of St. Sophie (*Die Kalte*)," we murmur only: "What orchestration! Nothing like it since Mahler!" It is, in a sense, a waste of great, the greatest powers; but who wastes powers if he can keep from wasting them? Better for us to smile back, wondering, at the last of the great English eccentrics. Yeats said that he had had everything he wanted, done what he had meant to do, and still was haunted by Plato's ghost crying, "What then?" Auden, it's plain, is never haunted by Rilke's. But now I'm doing what Auden's readers don't do, I'm moralizing.

A third of *The Shield of Achilles* consists of seven poems about Winds, Woods, Mountains, Lakes, Islands, Plains, and Streams: these exercises in viewing landscape quasi-morally are learned, masterly, charming, complicatedly self-delighting, trivial. "Lakes" ends: "It is unlikely I shall ever keep a swan / Or build a tower on any small tombolo, / But that's not going to stop me wondering what sort / Of lake I would decide on if I should. / Moraine, pot, oxbow, glint, sink, crater, piedmont, dimple . . . ? / Just reeling off their names is ever so comfy." Comfy, that's it! just reading the poems is ever so comfy.

"The Shield of Achilles," an impressive, carefully planned, entirely comfortless poem, is the best thing in the book's miscellaneous middle third. "The Truest Poetry Is the Most Feigning" (the most wishful title eyes e'er saw or pen e'er wrote) is done according to a formula Auden's become fond of: be as cynical as you can for a couple of pages and then, in a couple of lines, tell people it was all for the deepest and highest ethical and religious reasons. *Lie to them, do as you please, tell them anything,* this poem tells poets, with knowing contempt, and then finishes about the poet, about Man: "What but tall tales, the luck of verbal playing, / Can trick his lying nature into saying / That love, or truth in any sense, / Like orthodoxy, is a reticence?" I know that I ought to respond, "True, true! I'll never tell the truth again. Anybody like to join me in some tall tales and verbal playing?" But what I really say is—but I'll be reticent. The poem made me think of this rhetorical question: "If a shoemaker doesn't stick by his last, will he stick by anything else?" If Auden thought a little worse of himself, and a little better of poetry, how different Auden and his poetry would be!

And yet, how witty, how elegant, how altogether charming the best parts of this very poem are! When the poet, converting his love song to the Triple Goddess into an ode to Mussolini, is made to change *Goddess of wry-necks and wrens* into *Great Reticulator of the fens,* I am wax, I am putty. In spring, Auden says, "leaves by the miles hide tons of / Pied pebbles that will soon be birds." When our Mother, Earth, "joins girl's-ear lakes / To bird's-foot deltas with lead-blue squiggles she makes, / Surely, a value judgment, / 'Of pure things Water is the best.'" At this point, reading "Ode to Gaea," I've no more morals, I murmur only, "Now who else on all this earth—" whether they write poems or don't write poems, poets are best.

And in the last third of the book, a sequence about the crucifixion, there are certainly some real poems. The best two are reprinted from *Nones.* This new book is, essentially, a kind of appendix to *Nones,* a still later stage of this very late poetry of Auden's. *Nones* means "the office of the church said at the ninth hour, three in the afternoon." In the real dark day or white night of the soul, Auden seems to feel, it is always three o'clock in the afternoon: you can see everything that is there, which is what was there, which is what will be there—there is nothing else to see, and you do not see it; it is the hour when you used to despair and, now, take your nap. It is the hour of an accustomed disenchantment, of an anticlimax which smiles indifferently at its own old absurd climaxes: as Auden says, "The wind has dropped and we have lost our public." The public is still there, of course, but Auden has become surprisingly indifferent to it. The most professional magician is the one who gets bored with magic, who at last really has nothing up his sleeve, not even his arm; the most professional orator is the one who gets tired of pleasing and moving his audiences—and who, then, does as *he* pleases, talking slowly and steadily and unemotionally, with learned fantastic elaboration, reversing or inverting half his old devices, delighted that the fools no longer cheer, no longer cry. At this hour, Auden says, we cannot "remember why / We shouted or what about / So loudly in the sunlight this morning . . . We are left alone with our feat." The word *feat* is as calm and deadly as the "dead calm" of this hour; the feat, we realize as we go on into "Nones," is the crucifixion. But this is a crucifixion without cross, Christ, crowd—everything is already over; nobody is left in the stadium but the janitors picking up the cushions and Coca-Cola bottles. The poem gives us "the plain sense of things," a residuum. It is a strange poem to have been written by everybody's *enfant terrible,* by the man who wrote that he supposed "My friends will say until I turn my toes up . . . why *doesn't* Wystan ever grow up?" Wystan has grown up; has grown old—as old as Talleyrand, as Disraeli, as that "tired old diplomat" who's become a stock figure in the poems. People used to resent Eliot's "Why should the aged eagle stretch his wings?" but Auden has got over on the shady side of so much, has become so convincingly old, so irrevocably, inexorably middle-aged, that we wouldn't resent his telling us that he is the Wandering Jew. And the change in the Auden of the poems prepares us for the change in the everyday Auden, who is no longer a lank, towheaded, slouching boy, but who looks at you with a lined, sagging, fretful, consciously powerful old lion's face.

Auden said in 1940, "For I relapse into my crimes, / Time and again have slubbered through / With slip and slapdash what I do, / Adopted what I would disown, / The preacher's loose immodest tone." He said this, and it was so; and for five or six years afterwards it kept on being so. During the last half of the thirties he had preached, with slip and slapdash, the Popular Front; during the first half of the forties he preached, with as much slip and as much slapdash, as many tricks and as much talent, his own idiosyncratic version of Barth and Niebuhr and Kierkegaard. He disapproved of his crimes, perhaps, but how he enjoyed committing them! And yet one day he stopped enjoying it; he was tired. How much of his moralizing, and stained-glass attitudes, and Moving Rhetoric, he also began to be tired of! In fact, disingenuous creature that he is, he began sometimes to pretend that there was nothing to *be* tired of—began to pretend that he had always been on the other side, the side of the resistance, in the great war between Morality and Fun, between Doing as We Ought and Doing as We Please. He began to specialize (whenever he wasn't regressing into sermons) in witty and scornful denunciations of "pompous Apollo" and all his works; *he* was—had always been—on the side of Hermes, god of thieves and businessmen.

One of Housman's poems tells how, long ago, "couched upon her brother's grave / The Saxon got me on the slave"—and how now, along the "marches of my breast," the "truceless armies yet / Trample, rolled in blood and sweat; / They kill and kill and never die / And I think that each is I." Auden is writing about a war which has gone on for many years along the marches of *his* breast; often the Unconscious, the Original, the Inside Auden must have smiled mockingly, demonically, at what the Conscious Outside was telling everybody else to do—smiled, and gone about its living. In many of these last poems the Conscious and Moral Auden is, quite consciously and immorally, coming to terms with the Unconscious Auden by going along with it, letting it have its way—and not just in life, where we can do and gloss over anything, but in poems, which are held against us by us and everyone else. Perhaps Auden had always made such impossibly exacting moral demands on himself and everybody else partly because it kept him from having to worry about more ordinary, moderate demands; perhaps he had preached so loudly, made such extraordinarily sweeping gestures, in order to hide himself from himself in the commotion. But he seems, finally, to have got tired of the whole affair, to have become willing to look at himself *without doing anything about it,* not even shutting his eyes or turning his head away. In some of the best of his later poems he accepts himself for whatever he is, the world for whatever it is, with experienced calm; much in these poems is accurate just as observed, relevant, inescapable fact, not as the journalistic, local-color, in-the-know substitute that used to tempt Auden almost as it did Kipling. The poet is a man of the world, and his religion is of so high an order, his morality so decidedly a metamorality, that they are more a way of understanding everybody than of making specific demands on anybody. Auden, in most of this last book, lies back in himself as if he were an unmade bed, and every line in his sleepy, placid face seems to be saying: *But whoever makes beds?*

Auden has become the most professional poet in the world; there is a matter-of-course mastery behind the elaborate formality, the colloquial matter-of-factness, of these last two books—after reading "Under Sirius" another poet is likely to feel, "Well, back to my greeting cards." But to be the most professional poet in the world is not necessarily to be the best: Minerva says, "But *you* don't need *me*." Auden is using extraordinary skill in managing a sadly reduced income. There is a tiredness and flatness about much of *Nones,* a comfortable frivolity about much of *The Shield of Achilles,* that give the accuracy and truthfulness and virtuosity of the best poems a lonely, disquieting ring. (And it is strange to see, among so many strongly individual poems, three successful ones—"A Household," "The Chimeras," and "Cattivo Tempo"—that are characteristic less of Auden than of Graves.) These best poems are a triumph—mitigated, as triumphs are. One is delighted at the slower and drier excellence that has replaced the somewhat flashy and ambiguous excellence of what Auden wrote during the later part of the thirties, the earlier part of the forties; but has Auden ever again written quite so well as he was writing at the beginning of the thirties, in *Poems* and *Paid on Both Sides?* He wrote, then, some of the strongest, strangest, and most original poetry that anyone has written in this century; when old men, dying in their beds, mumble something unintelligible to the nurse, it is some of those lines that they will be repeating.

Recent Poetry

THE YALE REVIEW, AUTUMN 1955

Birthdays from the Ocean by Isabella Gardner　*The Gentle Weight Lifter* by David Ignatow　*Selected Poems* by Lincoln Fitzell　*The Salt Garden* by Howard Nemerov　*Wilderness Stair* by Ben Belitt　*Collected Poems* by Stephen Spender

ISABELLA GARDNER is a fresh, individual, irregularly appealing poet with one great and several small faults. The great: she almost never, as yet, manages to write good poems. The small: she thinks random technical mannerisms (long intentionally lumbering doggerel lines, words split in two to form rhymes, sounding and insensible plays on words) personal form; she is extremely self-conscious; her poems are puddings full of raw suet, rhetorical zwieback, things too underdone or overdone to seem homogeneous parts of one work of art; she is bewitched by all tricks, properties, allusions, gewgaws, doodads—any bright found object that can assure her that she, too, vividly and peculiarly exists. She needs to be assured but we, her readers, don't; the poems themselves are evidence of an actual existence, a wild being that grieves, exults, and takes its chances. Many young poets, nowadays, are insured against everything. For them poetry is a game like court tennis or squash racquets—one they learned at college—and they play it with propriety, as part of their social and academic existence; their poems are occasional verse for which life itself is only one more occasion. Wasn't it one of these poets who said, the other day: "I accept the university"? and wasn't it a Professor of Poetry who replied: "By God, he'd better!"?

Miss Gardner is very different: to her the world is a costume party for which she has just breathlessly overdressed herself, and these poems are her starry, tinselly, gold-leafy entrance into it. One likes her less for her little laughs, little gestures, than for the life they overlay: rouge is never as bright as the blood it covers. *Birthdays from the Ocean* might better be called *Portrait of the Poet as a Young Woman;* it has the charm of a diary, since Miss Gardner is good at making differentiated personal episodes out of poems. She is in all her poems, and Dylan Thomas (or Marianne Moore, or John Crowe Ransom, or anything or anybody she remembers just then) is in a good many of them. A poem with most of her virtues is:

TO THOREAU ON REREADING "WALDEN"

"I long ago lost a hound, a bay horse, and a turtle-dove."
"There too, as everywhere, I sometimes expected the visitor who never comes."
—HENRY THOREAU

Your passion was ever plural, apart
from that one twig ("the twig") you never found.
Herds of birds and fishes, stars in droves
received your taut and tender gaze
but gills beaks planets can't reciprocate
and gratefully you prayed their praise.
You loved the faces in the fire, Thoreau,
the goldgreen pickerel, the huddling snow.
I too love these, and O love you, fierceheart,
and yet were you, like Lazarus, to rise,
you would look everywhere but in my eyes.
You'd hear the loud spring ice the greening ground,
but not the caller knocking at your gate
nor the nickering in your maple groves
nor the howling for home of the hound.
You did not listen to the turtle-dove
(singular bird) sing on your lintel: LOVE
and now no visitor will come to crowd
your peace. You have dried safely in your shroud.

The best thing about this poem, I think, is the truth of what it says; the way in which it says it is often undistinguished. *Taut and tender, prayed their praise,* the glib *gills beaks planets can't reciprocate,* the sadly usual *and O love you,* the almost amusingly commonplace *like Lazarus* are a few of the more noticeable flaws in a direct, somewhat ingenuous, somewhat mannered poem, one that wears its organization and its alliteration and its poetry on its sleeve. It, like the other poems she's written, interests you in Miss Gardner and the poems she will write. And yet—when we read *I long ago lost a hound, a bay horse, and a turtle-dove,* and what follows this in Thoreau, there is in his prose a wild free imagination, an unexpected poetry, that Miss Gardner's poem is entirely without.

David Ignatow's poems are quiet, observant, matter-of-fact comments on ordinary urban life—or, more surprisingly, on Oedipus and Odysseus and Bathsheba and such—made by a man who seems individually sensitive and morally imaginative yet also, in a rather favorable sense, the man in the street. William Carlos Williams calls him "a first-rate poet . . . to whom language is like his skin," but really he's an unratable poet to whom language is like William Carlos Williams's skin. His methods are simple Williams, and his language—not at all rhetorical, close to an easy natural prose, but not prosaic—is that of a loving disciple. His temperament, unfortunately, lacks the heights and depths of Williams's. One respects and likes this poet, but one reads the poems with a mild blurred feeling of seeing them and not seeing them, a clear daze like water or late evening air; one isn't sure, sometimes, whether one is reading a new poem or rereading an old— one isn't even sure that one cares. The poems are sand that has almost been fused into glass; one feels, always, the lack of some last heat or pressure, concentration and individualization, that would have turned a photograph into a painting, a just observation into a poem. There is something humble and matter-of-course about the poems' methods: they are content, always, with an honest penny; and after a while the reader sees, rather in dismay, that it's bills he's interested in. A poem like "Promenade" gives a fairly good idea of David Ignatow's humane, unaffected, and unexciting poetry:

> *His head split in four parts,*
> *he walks down the street—pleasant*
> *with shady trees and a sun softened*
> *by leaves touching it. He walks,*
> *a revolving turret for a head,*
> *from each slit of which he looks guardedly:*
> *the enemy approaches or he approaches*
> *the enemy. At any moment the chatter of differences*
> *will break out; the four parts of his skull*
> *revolve slowly, seeking the time.*

> *In there they do not know of each other,*
> *sealed off by steel walls. They are safer*
> *together, singly and apart; and shouting,*
> *angry or in pain, have only themselves*
> *to listen; while overhead, ignored in the walk,*
> *are the leaves, touching each other and the sun.*

Poets go on Quests: and some of them meet an enchanter who says to them, "You have all met an enchanter who has transformed you into obscure romantic animals, but you can become clear and classical and human again if you will only swallow these rules." The poets swallow them, and from that moment they are all Henry Wadsworth Long-fellow, a wax one—from that moment they wander, grave weighing shades, through a landscape each leaf of which rhymes, and scans, and says softly: "And the moral of *that* is . . ."

The enchanter, of course, is Yvor Winters, and the poet, this time, is Lincoln Fitzell. In a few poems he still laughs and errs in the sunlight, like ordinary men, because, like ordinary men, he knows no better. But in most of these quatrains he is a moral, metrical machine, and moves through a graded universe on sententious inexorable feet:

> *We breathe the scent of quiet sun*
> *Still in this grove where suitors run,*
> *Where lips are warmly pressed to part,*
> *And leaves are stirred above the heart.*
>
> *Now twining fingers twist a beam*
> *Of starlight branched from leafy gleam,*
> *And clasped by Spring, the moon's light breeze*
> *Glows bright as stars of bliss we seize.*
>
> *As honor diamonds the dust,*
> *So love clings like the sparkling gust*
> *That shivers deep the silvered glade,*
> *Till arms unclasp in fragrant shade.*
>
> *Now lean and closely read her eyes*
> *That throne the night in splendid skies,*
> *That know the dark has warmth to give,*
> *And beauty lifts its love to live.*

Where poems have hearts, an iamb is beating, here.

Does the muse come to men with a ruler, a pair of compasses, and a metronome? Is it all right to say anything, no matter how commonplace and pompous and cliché, as long as you're sober, and say what the point is, and see that it scans? If you adopt the phrasing and scansion of Pope's dunces, will that make you a second Pope? The worst thing about poems like this is that they are so unnaturally silly: this is a learned imbecility, a foolishness of the schools, and ordinary common sense, ordinary human nature, will dismiss it with Johnson's "Clear your mind of cant," or with his "Sir, a man might write such stuff forever, if he would *abandon* his mind to it."

The Salt Garden, Howard Nemerov's third book of poems, is very much the best of the three. The earlier books were the products of intelligence and talent, but they were tight, dry, and uneasy—you were always conscious of omissions, abstentions, aversions, of the poet's looking for some way to write and some subject to write about, and ending, always, with something people could call ironic. (Whenever people use such words as *dialectical, metaphysical, dry, conceit, ironic* about a new poem of Mr. Nemerov's, he can tell that he has gone back to his old ways.) As you read *The Salt Garden* you are impressed with how much the poet has learned, how well he has developed: you can see where he found out how to do some of the things he does—he isn't, as yet, a very individual poet—and you can see that they were the right places for him. Behind the old poems there was a poet trying to write poetry; behind these new ones there is a man with interests and experiences of his own—that is, a poet who has learned to write poetry. In his best poems his language and rhythms have a natural, normal vigor, a quality that makes you think, "Yes, a lot of good English poetry feels like this." When he is speaking of the "deep woods" of this New World of ours, without hermits, hunting kings, the woodcutter's or the witch's house—before history, really—he says that here in the forest the mind

> *uneasily rests, as if a beast,*
> *Being hunted down, made tiredness and terror*
> *Its camouflage and fell asleep, and dreamed,*
> *At the terrible, smooth pace of the running dogs,*
> *A dream of being lost, covered with leaves,*
> *And hidden in a death like any sleep . . .*

He looks at the "unlegended land" whose "common splendors are comparable only to / Themselves," and then moves on through history and legend, deciding, always, that that too hasn't happened here— that if we want it to happen we ourselves will have to make it happen—and finishes:

> *Most probably*
> *Nothing will happen. Even the Fall of Man*
> *Is waiting, here, for someone to grow apples;*
> *And the snake, speckled as sunlight on the rock*

In the deep woods, still sleeps with a whole head
And has not begun to grow a manly smile.

These last three lines are what the fairy tale calls a wonderful wonder,
a marvelous marvel; I keep saying them over for the way they sound
and move. The snake is alive, and the past is latent in him. (And now
I want to say, as much in surprise as in complaint: How did phrases
like *the Fourth, or Disney, Dimension*—or for that matter, like the
Frost-ish *this / Place is too old for history to know / Beans about*—
get into a poem like this?)

I'd like to quote an ingenious and moving poem named "And I
Only Am Escaped Alone to Tell Thee," or some beautiful or thoughtful parts of "The Quarry" or "The Pond" or "Truth," but perhaps I
had better let a short poem, "The Cuckoo King," stand for all of them:

My head made wilderness, crowned of weed
And marigold, the world my witching bride
And the half of my kingdom lying in the seed,
I reap the great root of a planted pride.

All earth broken under the harrow's heel,
I through my comely kingdom went a-riding
Out where the bearded grass climbed to rebel
And the tall stalking flower fired from hiding.

The world, O my daughter in the crooked nest,
Bridles with lust, that you by force betray
Me, weed and marigold, to the naked crest
Where castles fall; but I will make this hay
In husbandry beneath the rebel's height,
Though all the hairs of my head stand upright.

That *world, O my daughter in the crooked nest* is pure Thomas (almost the only Thomas in the book) but, like the future, it works. The
poem has a kind of emblematic force, as if it were a King of Spades
painted for *The White Goddess.* And now I must talk about the
specter which is haunting this particular book: middle and late Yeats;
you find half of Yeats's pet words and rhythms, his rhetorical use of the
word *maybe,* even. And whenever Mr. Nemerov sees a gull he starts to
sound like "The Wild Swans at Coole": "Sweet are their bitter cries, /
As their fierce eyes are sweet; in their mere greed / Is grace, as they
fall splendidly to feed. / And sometimes I have seen them as they
glide / Mysterious upon a morning sea . . ." This last is a reminis-

cence of Yeats's "But now they drift on the still water / Mysterious, beautiful," of course, but doesn't it also echo Bridges's lines about the frigates he saw from the summer house on the mound, as they glided murderously over a calm sea? (I'm far from books, and go by memory alone.) And the poet says, about another gull, that he had "thought that image of the wild / Wave where it beats the air / Had come, brutal, mysterious"; the poem in which these lines occur, "The Salt Garden," is what a composer would call "Yeatsiana."

And is this so bad? No—Yeats has spoiled some of the poems, but has helped the poetry. It's odd that the poet should need or wish or consent to this much help this late; perhaps it is because he is a late blooming, youthful-seeming poet from whom one can expect, soon, poems even better than the best two or three in this book.

I have never understood why I could feel so little interest in Ben Belitt's work—he is a writer of skill, force, and intelligence—but I have decided, after reading and rereading *Wilderness Stair,* that it is because he is not a poet but a rhetorician. He is very much influenced by that very rhetorical poet Hart Crane—"Tourist and Turtle" and "Battery Park: High Noon" are faithful imitations—but where Crane, at his best, uses rhetoric to say something, Mr. Belitt says something to use rhetoric. Underneath all his writing there is the settled determination to use certain words, to take certain attitudes, to produce a certain atmosphere; what he is seeing or thinking or feeling has hardly any influence on the way he writes. The reader can reply, ironically, "That's what it means to have a style"; but few people have so much of one, or one so obdurate that you can say of it, "It is a style that no subject can change." (You cannot say this with perfect truth—one poem, "The Spool," is a kind of transcript tempered with adjectives—but as a wise man has written, "In all pointed sentences, some degree of accuracy must be sacrificed to conciseness.")

Let me illustrate Mr. Belitt's style with several examples—the book itself is the best illustration: "I have willed the event, / At length, and confront the violent shape, / And break, on the pyx of my lap, / In the old, paschal posture, the obscene Innocent. / The pure vocation of that younger rage— / Godhead, little with woe— / Must bend to the stone of my knees and take its wage / And measure that murderous anvil, for the blow . . ." "What stayed, was the wish to praise / In a causeless occasion. / The wasp in the through-shine, by the unreal window, / Above scarabs, in the termite's detonation, / Snored on the blind glaze, brightened a shard, / And opened the hallowing summer of its pulses . . ." "O lost and mythic scene, /

Move yet within this frame! / This is the angel, whether gem or flower — / Leaven and gum and flint— / Recalled from carbon in explicit power, / Whose massive slumber wears the pure impress / Of old renewal and first fruitfulness, / Pledging the fern's shape in primordial tinder . . ." "When we rose on the smoke of the sacrifice, vaunting our famine, / Fasted and absolute, crackling the crystals of salt, / They broke the abysses and showed us the bladders of salmon / Sowing the deluge like pollen. Their benevolence altered / The zenith's unsparing progressions and the span of the sickle . . ." The first eight lines are supposed to be said by Mary to the body of Christ in her lap; the next six are David and Goliath; the next eight are part of a description of the Battery; the next five are supposed to be said by Alyosha Karamazov. I cannot tell the masks from the face. And I keep coming to *the lewd cornucopia's helix, the vehement interim, the agonist's warlock shared in a multitude of shadow, combustion's vehement heart;* to poems beginning *In jackal country, in the gum and umber, / That bird broke blank to the eyebeam* or *They splay at a bend of the road, rifles slung, the / shadows minimal;* to *spilth* and *cusp* and *coronal, leaven* and *paradigm* and *shibboleth, strict* and *formal* and *rigours, clabbered* and *hasped* and *scanted* and *cozened, phosphor* and *quartz* and *shard:* it is as if Medusa had had as many heads as the Hydra. Ah, memories of other days! some of this rhetoric is as evocative as waists around the knees, spoke wheels, cloche hats. But only its datedness is endearing; such languages and attitudes are intended, whether or not the writer realizes it, to cow the reader. The poem says something, but who cares what? What matters is the style's permanent statement that it is strict, that it is elevated, that it is profound: that the reader is being judged. In Lifemanship, impressing other people with your own superior culture is called Rilking; this rhetoric is always Rilking. Marianne Moore speaks, in an astonishing phrase, of Shakespeare's "well-nested effects of helpless naturalness"; as one reads poems like these one longs for something helpless, something natural, something human, but everything is marble. Imported marble. There are mistakes in the rhetoric—phrases wearyingly like Crane and the common rhetorical practice of the thirties—but it is the rhetoric itself which is the real mistake.

A good deal of Stephen Spender's *Collected Poems* is, in an easy way, attractive and appealing, but one finishes it thoughtful and depressed. The young poet wrote better than the middle-aged one, and that's saddening; and, young or middle-aged, the poet never writes quite so well as one could wish—after almost any of his poems, something inside one whispers meanly, "Very nice. And—wouldn't you say?—a little soft." When the muse first came to Mr. Spender he looked so sincere that her heart failed her, and she said: "Ask anything and I will give it to you," and he said: "Make me sincere."

If you look at the world with parted lips and a pure heart, and will the good, won't that make a true and beautiful poem? One's heart tells one that it will; and one's heart is wrong. There is no direct road to Parnassus. The most lyric and sentimental of Mr. Spender's poems combine all the best words and all the best intentions: the reader is so conscious of what they are meant to be that it seems cruel and uncalled-for to notice what they are. If Mr. Belitt is the sort of poet who seems, always, just about to use the word *glozed*—actually he never does—Mr. Spender is the sort who seems, always, just about to say *O life!* and to tell you that *these young suns, like singing roses, are the flesh of fire,* or that *this young flesh is the rose's sun, like singing fire,* or any of the other combinations. (That a poem beginning *I think continually of those who were truly great* should ever have been greeted with anything but helpless embarrassment makes me ashamed of the planet upon which I dwell.) Many readers respond to such poetry as if it were music—they shut their eyes, feel a good blur come over them, and don't think any more; after they have come to, they say that the poet is the Shelley of our days. These aren't very good days for a Shelley—or, anyway, for a Shelley of our days—as Mr. Spender knows; part of the time he is fighting against his softer self, and the rest of the time he just lets himself go.

It isn't Mr. Spender but a small, simple—determinedly simple—part of Mr. Spender that writes the poems; the poet is a lot smarter man than his style allows him to seem. (If he were as soft and sincere and sentimental as most of his poems make him out to be, the rabbits would have eaten him for lettuce, long ago.) He is a shrewd, notably competent literary journalist, but all his prose intelligence and worldliness, everything that a stage American would call "technological know-how," is kept out of the poems. Most of what poets call "technique" is kept out of the writing of the poems; he is an awkward poet who has become, if anything, more awkward. (Is there anyone else who would say, translating Rilke, that Orpheus' lyre had "grown ingrown" into his hand?)

Yet in spite of all this, and more, Mr. Spender is sometimes a good poet—not very good, but good; sometimes your heart goes out to him, and you say with an uneasy smile, "Better a soft heart than a hard one, better a thousand well-intentioned tears than none, better a simpleton on the side of the angels than a savant in the ranks of hell." Some of the anthology pieces—"The Express" and "The Landscape Near an Aero-

drome"—are not much more than anthology pieces, and some of the
most interesting poems, such as "The Living Values," have enough
wrong with them to make you look at Mr. Spender's rewriting and wish
that someone else could rewrite *it*; but the best poems of the thirties—
especially the poems about the Spanish Civil War such as "Port Bou"
and "Thoughts During an Air Raid"—are moving and individual poems.
When I read:

> *I assure myself the shooting is only for practice*
> *But I am the coward of cowards. The machine-gun stitches*
> *My intestines with a needle, back and forth;*
> *The solitary, spasmodic, white puffs from the carbines*
> *Draw fear in white threads back and forth through my body . . .*

this doesn't seem that sincere sincerity the poet specializes in, but honest
observation; and when I read the early

> *Moving through the silent crowd*
> *Who stand behind dull cigarettes,*
> *These men who idle in the road,*
> *I have the sense of falling light.*
>
> *They lounge at corners of the street*
> *And greet friends with a shrug of shoulder*
> *And turn their empty pockets out,*
> *The cynical gestures of the poor.*
>
> *Now they've no work, like better men*
> *Who sit at desks and take much pay*
> *They sleep long nights and rise at ten*
> *To watch the hours that drain away.*
>
> *I'm jealous of the weeping hours*
> *They stare through with such hungry eyes*
> *I'm haunted by these images,*
> *I'm haunted by their emptiness . . .*

the poem seems true and puzzlingly immediate, touches me without
reaching out to touch me; and the ending of "Song" is pure and absolute:

> *Oh, but supposing that I climb*
> *　　Alone to a high room of clouds*
> *Up a ladder of the time*
> *And lie upon a bed alone*
> *　　And tear a feather from a wing*

And listen to the world below
And write round my high paper walls
Anything and everything
Which I know and do not know!

"A Footnote," "Seascape," "Polar Exploration," "Ultima Ratio Regum,"
the MacNeice-ish "Epilogue to a Human Drama" are poems I would be
sorry not to have read. Mr. Spender is the best of the poets I have been
reviewing. If he were a young poet a critic could read him with
pleasure and excitement, and dream of poems to come. As it is, his poems
show how a native, almost constitutional limitation of approach, at first
welcomed as the poet's "gift," then fought against, then despairingly
returned to, can prevent the normal development of a poet. *Normal*: it
has a sad ring. An oculist once told Shaw that he had normal eyesight;
Shaw felt a natural disappointment, and exclaimed: "You mean I see
just as other people do?" "Oh no," said the oculist; "only one man in
ten has normal eyesight." Only one poet in a hundred has a normal
development.

And now I come to what are, surely, two of the best books of
poetry of our time: Robert Graves's *Collected Poems* and Elizabeth
Bishop's *Poems*. They arrived too late for me to review them, but next
issue I will have a whole essay about the two*—meanwhile, I can say
about them, as an advertisement would: "If you want to read some of
the poems your great-great-grandchildren will be reading, these are the
books for you to buy."

* "Graves and the White Goddess," *The Yale Review,* Winter 1956 (Part
I) and Spring 1956 (Part II); included in *The Third Book of Criticism.*
Elizabeth Bishop's *Poems* was reviewed in *Harper's,* October 1955.—Ed.

The Year in Poetry

HARPER'S, OCTOBER 1955

Under Milk Wood by Dylan Thomas   *The Collected Poems of Wallace Stevens*   *The Poems of Emily Dickinson*   *Poems* by Elizabeth Bishop   *Collected Poems* by Robert Graves   *The Shield of Achilles* by W. H. Auden   *Collected Poems* by Stephen Spender   *Birthdays from the Ocean* by Isabella Gardner   *The Salt Garden* by Howard Nemerov   *Poets of Today, II* by Louis Simpson

M RS. JACKSON has asked me to write a short piece about the year's poetry—"something to make people rush out to the bookstores," as she said. I wish that I could. Elizabeth Bishop's *Poems*, Robert Graves's *Collected Poems* are worth a long walk through sand, worth reading by the light of a bottle of lightning bugs, worth more than anybody is ever likely to pay for them—and yet, short of having a hypnotist tell people it's 1855, or that the poems are really Robert Ruark, I don't know any way to get many people to buy or read them. Let me start with two recommendations that may have a better chance:

Dylan Thomas's *Under Milk Wood* and Wallace Stevens's *Collected Poems* were published late last year; both poets are dead, now. We put up statues of poets, once they're dead, or buy their houses, but the only way we can really do anything for them is to read them. Reading *Under Milk Wood* is a piece of easy and magical piety, since it is as good a celebration of A Day in My Home Town—this one is a Welsh fishing village—as anybody is ever likely to write. Thomas describes the things and people of Llareggub, and then lets them speak for themselves, and everything that all of them say is living almost beyond life: it would be hard for any work of art to communicate more directly and funnily and lovingly what it is like to be alive. To Thomas life is not a means to anything, but an outrageous and indefensible—who needs to defend it?—end; because the people of Llareggub are hopelessly, helplessly human, he loves them without qualification. If Falstaff, safe in Arthur's bosom, had begun longing for the things of this earth, and had looked back and written his own *Midsummer Night's Dream,* he would have got something like *Under Milk Wood.* And just to make sure that this last work of his would be able to mesmerize anybody at all, Thomas put most of its poetry into prose: whether you can read poetry or not, read modern poetry or not, you can read *Under Milk Wood.*

With Stevens's *Collected Poems* it's different: you have to be able to read poetry—modern poetry, sometimes. But now that Stevens has gone to join Whitman and Dickinson and Melville—how pleasant it would be to hear him telling them, with delicacy and firmness, exactly what he thinks of them, the last world, and the next!—oughtn't all of us to read his poems? If we had been contemporaries of Whitman and Dickinson and Melville, and had got rid of them with, "All this modern Victorian poetry just doesn't make sense to me," wouldn't the angels have had the right to laugh or weep at us? and if we get rid of Stevens with the same sentence, haven't they the same right? The angels would naturally be on the side of Stevens, since he had something of their own detachment, elevation, and magnanimity. His representations of human existence are far-ranging, imaginative, and profoundly individual: they come together into a world of his own, one that makes us see a little differently the world we all share. His last poems, *The Rock,* show better than any other poems, perhaps, what the world looks like as we leave it. I wish that I could quote the long "To an Old Philosopher in Rome," a poem that is the poet's own requiem; let me quote instead "The Brave Man," a poem that can serve as a symbol of what we lost when Stevens died, and what we kept:

> *The sun, that brave man,*
> *Comes through boughs that lie in wait,*
> *That brave man.*
>
> *Green and gloomy eyes*
> *In dark forms of the grass*
> *Run away.*
>
> *The good stars,*
> *Pale helms and spiky spurs,*
> *Run away.*
>
> *Fears of my bed,*
> *Fears of life and fears of death,*
> *Run away.*

That brave man comes up
From below and walks without meditation,
That brave man.

Fifty-three years after the death of Queen Victoria, it has become
possible to read Emily Dickinson's poems as she wrote them, and not
as her guides, relatives, and friends wished that she had written them:
Thomas H. Johnson and the Belknap Press of the Harvard University
Press have brought out in three big volumes, noted, chronologically arranged, and accurate to the last variant, misspelling, and grammatical
error, *The Poems of Emily Dickinson.* Now and then—I know I
shouldn't admit this—I am glad of what the people did to the poems:
for instance, *signed away / What portion of me I / Could make as-
signable,* in the poem that begins *I heard a fly buzz when I died;* but
usually Emily Dickinson's own ways are better, even when there is a
dash every second word and an exclamation point every third. This is,
truly, a marvelous book: the reader finishes speechless, and laughing,
and shaking his head in helpless wonder. He has read some great poems,
and some good ones, and some arch and silly and *terrible* ones, poems
that would make a bureau blush; all the absolutes and intensives and
eccentricities of an absolutely intense eccentric have passed over him like
a train of avalanches, and left him a couple of hundred feet deep in
Knowledge.

He has learned all there is to know about one woman: here she
is. Her poetry is the diary or autobiography—though few diaries or
autobiographies compare with it for intentional and, especially, unin-
tentional truth—of an acute psychologist, a wonderful rhetorician, and
one of the most individual writers who ever lived, one of those best
able to express experience at its most nearly absolute. How much truth
and how many lies, what vanity and blasphemy and agony and monotony, there are in these three volumes! You live with the poems—or
rather, with the poet—in almost intolerable intimacy. After finishing
thirteen hundred pages of this magnificent and impossible little Queen
of Calvary, God's spoiled, lonely, only child, you say *Never again,*
laugh, and start out all over again. The poems are haunted by their
daemonic, ridiculously human, entirely immortal maker.

Sometimes when I can't go to sleep at night I see the family of the
future. Dressed in three-tone shorts-and-shirt sets of disposable Papersilk,
they sit before the television wall of their apartment, only their eyes
moving. After I've looked a while I always see—otherwise I'd die—a

pigheaded soul over in the corner with a book; only his eyes are moving, but in them there is a different look.

Usually it's Homer he's holding—this week it's Elizabeth Bishop. Her *Poems* seems to me one of the best books an American poet has ever written: the people of the future (the ones in the corner) will read her just as they will read Dickinson or Whitman or Stevens, or the other classical American poets still alive among us. I have been reading most of Elizabeth Bishop's poems—two-thirds were printed in *North and South,* a book long out of print—for ten years; I've read my many favorites many hundreds of times, and they seem better and fresher, more nearly perfect, than they ever did. They are quiet, truthful, sad, funny, most marvelously individual poems; they have a sound, a feel, a whole moral and physical atmosphere, different from anything else I know. And I don't know of any other poet with so high a proportion of good poems: at least half are completely realized works of art. They are honest, modest, minutely observant, masterly; even their most complicated or troubled or imaginative effects seem, always, personal and natural, and as unmistakable as the first few notes of a Mahler song, the first few patches of a Vuillard interior. (The poems are like Vuillard or even, sometimes, Vermeer.) Occasionally you meet someone and feel in astonished joy: "Well, this is what people ought to be like"; this is what poems ought to be like.

I won't quote, since I'd want to quote many pages; I hope you'll read for yourself "The Man-Moth," "Roosters," "The Weed," "The Fish," "Love Lies Sleeping," "The Monument," "Anaphora," "The Prodigal," "Little Exercise," "Rain Towards Morning," "Invitation to Miss Marianne Moore," "Faustina, or Rock Roses"—or, almost as good, "From the Country to the City," "The Map," "The Imaginary Iceberg," "The Colder the Air," "Wading at Wellfleet," "The Gentleman of Shalott," "Large Bad Picture," "The Unbeliever," "Sleeping Standing Up," "Jeronimo's House," "Over 2000 Illustrations and a Complete Concordance," the first and fourth "Songs for a Colored Singer," "A Summer Dream," "At the Fishhouses," "A Miracle for Breakfast," "Varick Street," "O Breath," "The Shampoo."

This is a ridiculously long list, but if I went back over it I'd make it longer. And have I not one fault to find? Some of the later poems are too exclusively descriptive—and there are fifty-four poems in the book, not several hundred.

There are several hundred in Robert Graves's *Collected Poems.* Some are extraordinary, many are masterly, all are like nothing else ever written: a man who liked poetry and didn't get these poems would be a foolish man indeed. I am in the middle of writing a long essay about them,* and feel a real repugnance toward crowding them into a paragraph or two: may I simply recommend them? In them many things—some of them most unusual things—are well felt, well seen, well imagined, and well expressed.

If you would like to see the most accomplished poet alive doing as he pleases, buy W. H. Auden's *The Shield of Achilles.* A few of the poems are good, and all of them are brilliant, self-indulgent, marvelously individual: if Auden sometimes loses faith in something as frivolous as poetry, he never loses it in something as serious as Auden. *Nones* was a better book, but this one is worth reading; Auden's laundry list would be worth reading—I speak as one who's read it many times, all rhymed and metered. After all—this is the point people rarely make—when Homer nods it's quite a performance.

Stephen Spender is, I think, an open, awkward, emotional, conscientiously well-intentioned, and simple-minded poet. To like his poems as much as we shouldn't, we need to respond to what they are meant to be, not to what they are—and it is surprisingly easy to do this.

Most of his virtues and vices cluster around the word *sincere.* One likes his *Collected Poems* neither for their development (most of his experience and intelligence are excluded from the poems, so any great development is impossible) nor for their general excellence, but for a few touching, truthful poems that seem the products of observation, moral insight, and inspiration.

Isabella Gardner's *Birthdays from the Ocean* is a trickily mannered but appealing and unusual book. The poems have enough personal charm to make you forget their influences and self-consciousness, but not enough to make you forget that they are never, quite, good poems. Howard Nemerov is younger than his age, and full of Yeats, and not very individual as yet, but there are several good poems in *The Salt Garden*—for instance, "The Deep Woods," "The Cuckoo King," "And I Only Am Escaped Alone to Tell Thee"—and one finishes it pleased with what he has done and very much interested in what he is going to do.

Louis Simpson (*Poets of Today, II*) is a slighter but unusually attractive poet; he has a personal irony, an easy and natural lyric charm, that are rare today—his half-dozen best poems make you wish that he would write much more than he does.

* See note on page 241.—Ed.

None of these three poets, however, seems to me as original and highly developed a poet as Katherine Hoskins, an extraordinary writer whose work still hasn't been published in a regular book.

There were other books in the past year which many people liked very much, and which I cared for less—anything I could say about them would hardly get you to a bookstore. Ben Belitt *(Wilderness Stair)* is an accomplished rhetorician in the style of Hart Crane; Constance Carrier *(The Middle Voice)* is a writer of thoughtful, goodhearted, well-meaning, commonplace poems; Roy Campbell *(Selected Poems)* imitates Byron and Shelley storm scenes, and is a sledge-hammer satirist besides; David Ignatow *(The Gentle Weight Lifter)* is an observant, appealing, unemphatic disciple of William Carlos Williams; and Lincoln Fitzell *(Selected Poems)* is a faithful—if only there were any other kind!— disciple of Yvor Winters, and usually sounds like an Academy of Arts and Letters' own Anthem.

All in all, it was a fine year.

Love and Poetry

· ·

MADEMOISELLE, FEBRUARY 1956

Children of the future Age
Reading this indignant page,
Know that in a former time
Love! sweet Love! was thought a crime.

So BLAKE WROTE, long ago; and long ago, back in what my daughter calls the Gay Twenties; back when a girl's waist was at her knees and her hat brim at her eyes and she wasn't a girl at all but a flapper; back when, day after day, I stared speechlessly at the head one desk up and one desk over, with its pilot's helmet of shining red hair—back then, long ago, I read what Blake had written.

I had just finished H. G. Wells's *Men Like Gods,* a magazine serial of beings who never were and, I guess, never will be: the good and naked people of the future. As I read Blake's stanza, I saw those shining children of the future Age gazing in perplexed wonder at this page from the criminal, miserable past. It seemed to me that I, like Blake, was one of them; under the Keds and khaki riding trousers and ribbed brown cotton stockings in which the past had clothed me, I was naked and I shone. I didn't think it queer that, 150 years after Blake, the future still hadn't come, so that Blake and it and I were still stuck miserably in the dark, perpetually present past; I didn't ask myself: What past or present or future ever made a little boy wear tennis shoes, riding trousers, and brown cotton stockings? When, at a hotel, I was allowed to order anything I pleased for breakfast and got a chocolate éclair and a strawberry milk shake, I didn't think that queer either.

It seemed to me that I did only two things: the things people made me do, and reasonable things. And how many of the reasonable things were Thought A Crime! The future in which, naked, shining, I was to sit eating my éclair, drinking my milk shake, and staring across the aisle at Joyce Meek for all eternity, with nobody minding, not even Joyce Meek—the future in which we would all live so, in liberty, in the reasonable working out of our desires—that was the world to which I belonged; if I had had a watch it would have ticked: Come quick, O world, come quick, come quick!

That world never came, of course; tomorrow never comes; the children of the future are only you. And it is tempting to someone on the side of poetry to tell you that it is always the arbitrary, contingent Past in which we live; that the bright, rational Future is only the illusion of youth, of that hopeful, romantic potentiality that existence always thwarts; that it is the poet, and not the social worker or marriage counselor, who is our true guide to love and marriage, since he writes about the real, cater-cornered past in which Achilles and Swann and you and I live and love, and not about that projected, upright future in which the mean marries the median and they have four siblings and live happily ever after.

But to say so would be false. The dark past and the bright future and the lightless and timeless Unconscious lie side by side, in unchanging contradiction, within the poet's stories and pictures and songs and poems, just as they do in our lives—the poems repeat in their own structure the structure of existence, and have, consequently, a representative truth. A poet was the first psychoanalyst, the poet who wrote, "Sooner murder an infant in its cradle than nurse unacted desires"; wrote, "Energy is the only life . . . and Reason is the bound or outward circumference of Energy. Energy is Eternal Delight"; wrote, "What is it men in women do require? / The lineaments of Gratified Desire. / What is it women do in men require? / The lineaments of Gratified Desire"; wrote,

> *"Love seeketh not Itself to please,*
> *Nor for itself hath any care,*
> *But for another gives its ease,*
> *And builds a Heaven in Hell's despair."*
>
> *So sung a little Clod of Clay*
> *Trodden with the cattle's feet,*
> *But a Pebble of the brook*
> *Warbled out these metres meet:*
>
> *"Love seeketh only Self to please,*
> *To bind another to Its delight,*
> *Joys in another's loss of ease*
> *And builds a Hell in Heaven's despite."*

And if the first psychoanalyst was the poet William Blake, the second— he who said that he had only rediscovered, systematized, what the poets had found out before him—was surely a poet of a strange and penetrating kind, the poet Sigmund Freud; any essay on love and marriage and poetry might well ask for itself the blessing of one of the most loving and most married of mortals, a husband and father who could describe with lyric humor the very tables and chairs, keys and sewing baskets of a household, and finish by calling it "a little world of happiness, of silent friends and emblems of honorable humanity."

So much of the poetry of the past is poetry about love—once readers expected love poems from poets almost as they expected sermons from preachers—that our eyes are still dazzled, our ears still ringing, with the bright blur of "O thou weed, / Who art so lovely fair and smell'st so sweet / That the sense aches at thee"; of "With thee conversing I forget all time"; of "Make the violent wheels / Of Time and Fortune stand; and great Existence, / The Maker's Treasury, now seem not to be / To all but my approaching friend and me"; of "They flee from me that sometime did me seek / With naked foot stalking within my chamber"; of "Then tell, O tell, how thou didst murder me!"; of "Stay for me there! I will not fail / To meet thee in that hollow vale"; of

> *Ay me! ay me! with what another heart*
> *In days far-off, and with what other eyes*
> *I used to watch—if I be he that watched—*
> *The lucid outline forming round thee; saw*
> *The dim curls kindle into sunny rings;*
> *Changed with thy mystic change, and felt my blood*
> *Glow with the glow that slowly crimson'd all*
> *Thy presence and thy portals, while I lay,*
> *Mouth, forehead, eyelids, growing dewy-warm*
> *With kisses balmier than half-opening buds*
> *Of April, and could hear the lips that kiss'd*
> *Whispering I knew not what of wild and sweet,*
> *Like that strange song I heard Apollo sing*
> *While Ilion like a mist rose into towers.*

Today it is a private preoccupation, and not a public expectation, that love poems are written to satisfy; and if these are hardly more common than poems about lovelessness, the distortions and frustrations of love—"Portrait of a Lady," "Prufrock," "Gerontion," and *The Waste Land* are, in one sense, a long personal poem on the subject—still, such poets as Hardy, Rilke, Yeats, Frost, Lawrence, and Graves have written in our century love poems that can compare with almost any of the love poems of the past. And, too, the last hundred or so years have produced all those unprecedentedly magnificent extensive treatments of that extensive process, love, by such poets (in the larger sense of the word) as Proust, Tolstoy, Chekhov, Emily Brontë, a hundred more. Even in the free, the rational, the impossible future, won't Shakespeare and Proust and Goethe tell us more than any *Textbook of Modern Marriage,* no matter how colorful its graphs, anatomical its diagrams, inclusive its tables? When the mean marries the median and they go home and sit down beside the firepl—beside the radiant heating unit in the wallboard, won't it still be Elizabeth Barrett Browning's *Sonnets from the Portuguese* that he puts on the tape recorder for her?

And even if the tomorrow of our dreams and predictions never comes, our todays already are changing so fast that the people of a photograph are old-fashioned before its paper can yellow, and the middle-aged live in an unpredicted future. You who read are the children of an age in which Love is a third the Crime it was, and a third an Industry, and a third a Right, the right of youth. (And youth too has become the right, the almost obligatory right, of anybody younger than Marlene Dietrich: the sexy grandma has replaced the foxy grandpa, and stores sell or will soon sell matching grandmother-and-granddaughter sets, so that the milkman can murmur, "I took you for her sister.") The good and two-thirds naked children of the future blaze out at one, in panties and girdles or all ungirdled, from every other advertisement—for Sex Sells, sells anything; and as one looks at what is sold, and the associated flesh that sells it, one sees that the greatest power, and the sweetest—Eros, builder and destroyer of cities—is for these not joy, not necessity, but only the policy of the firm. O Future, here around me now, in which junior-high-school girls go steady with junior-high-school boys, marry in high school and repent at college! Or rather, do not repent but begin with assured hope the life in which, without father, mother, aunt, or servant, alone with their little boys and little girls and an electric dishwasher, they await the day when these steady-going children of theirs marry, set out for college, and leave the still-young parents alone forever with the washer . . . You cannot have your cake and eat it too? We have changed all that. Romeo's and Juliet's parents sit with a social worker and a marriage broker—ah no, marriage counselor—until the well-counseled Montagues, the well-worked-over Capulets ship the children off to the University of Padua, where, with part-time jobs, allowances from both families, and a freezer full of TV Dinners, they live in bliss with their babies. And the moral is: *The course of true love ever did run smooth; Why should I make it at home when the store makes it better?; Love is the piece that finishes every puzzle.*

If England is a nation of shopkeepers, surely our own country is a nation of homemakers—of homemakers and their consorts. Blake wrote:

> *I went to the Garden of Love,*
> *And saw what I never had seen:*
> *A Chapel was built in the midst,*
> *Where I used to play on the green.*
>
> *And the gates of this Chapel were shut,*
> *And "Thou shalt not" writ over the door;*
> *So I turn'd to the Garden of Love*
> *That so many sweet flowers bore;*
>
> *And I saw it was filled with graves,*
> *And tomb-stones where flowers should be:*
> *And Priests in black gowns were walking their rounds,*
> *And binding with briars my joys and desires.*

The anguish that vibrates in the rhymes of those last two lines is not an obsolescent anguish: under the surface, the first green Garden and the last black one are what they were. But instead of *Thou shalt not,* now, there is *Nobody else does, and surely my little girl wouldn't want to be different from everybody else;* the angel with the flaming sword has put down his sword and taken up his card index and whispers: *Adjust, adjust—when there is not one left that I can tell from another, Paradise will have come again.*

And love, which is nourished on difficulties and prohibitions—which grows as rankly in caves in the dark, or under fig leaves, as in sunlight—how does love thrive on this bland, salt-free, even-caloried diet, the diet of a good invalid? For love *is* a crime, if something that is stronger than society itself, something in which the deluded, absolute desire of the individual triumphs over, forgets the existence of all public considerations, is a crime; and our American attempt to base society itself upon the crime, to have or pretend to have all marriages, marriages of love and none the loveless works of expedience—this attempt is as audacious as our attempt to have or pretend to have no one poor and everyone equal. Our audacity, like love itself, is partly an ideal and partly a delusion; and, I have to confess, I sympathize with each part. It is only human to be deluded so; without such delusions is humanity possible? Eighteenth-century warfare, historians say, was one of the greatest triumphs of Western civilization; and how much greater a triumph or discovery or invention is the Love! sweet Love! of Blake's stanza, the romantic love that so many cultures know nothing of . . . If

Antony and Cleopatra is actually, as it seems to me, the supreme literary expression of our culture, this is the most fitting and appropriate of actualities.

Samuel Johnson could speak, with marvelous contempt, of "wretched unidea'd girls"; but he could also call love "that passion which he who never felt never was happy," and could declare, with superb conclusiveness: "Marriage has many pains but celibacy has no pleasures." My heart—my poor representative Western heart—goes out to him, just as it goes out to Darwin when, deciding between a married and a single life, the great scientist writes in his diary: "What is the use of working without sympathy from near and dear friends? Who are near and dear friends to the old, except relatives? My God, it is intolerable to think of spending one's whole life like a neuter bee working, working, and nothing after all. —No, no won't do. —Imagine living all one's days solitarily in smoky, dirty London house— Only picture to yourself a nice soft wife on a sofa, with good fire and books and music perhaps— Marry, marry, marry. Q.E.D."

A nice soft wife on a sofa, with good fire and books and music perhaps: this is the poetry of marriage; what bachelor can hear it without a pang, what husband hear it without wanting to leave his nasty hard typewriter, light the fire, put *Verklärte Nacht* on the phonograph and sit with his wife—his nice soft wife—on the sofa? Love makes poets of us all. When Richard Garnett writes: "Eros is the wisest of the gods, because the oldest, and because there is nothing from which he does not learn," he is as truly a poet as is Rilke when he writes: "Love consists in this, that two solitudes protect and touch and greet one another." The solitude that another solitude greets, protects, and touches —learns, by love—is no longer able to believe in its own solitariness, and hears with perplexed wonder the voices that tell it that each of us is, now and forever, alone.

"Do what you will, this life's a fiction / And is made up of Contradiction," Blake wrote. I can't believe the first line, can't help believing the second. Love, and the marriages and poems which grow out of love, contain these vital contradictions in concentrated form. Love makes less than sense and much more than sense—says to us, like the universe: "Do I contradict myself? Well then I contradict myself."

Love removes none of the contradictions of our lives but, by adding one more, induces us to accept them all; transfigured by it, we had rather be loved than right—are willing, even, to be happy. Whether it moves the sun and the other stars we cannot tell, but that it moves the men and women and children and cats and dogs among whom we live we can hardly doubt. The house not built upon it, blessed by it, is founded upon the sand. We can call Eros the best and the worst of the gods, and the strangest, and the strongest. And yet often it is not bad at all, but sweet and dear and shining; and when it *is* bad, dark, nameless, turns upon us its

> *. . . soft unchristened smile*
> *That shadows neither love nor guile,*
> *But shameless will and power intense*
> *In secret sensuous innocence—*

is it so bad, always, even then? Our lives question and explain what they need only accept.

With Berlioz, Once Upon a Time . . .

· ·

THE NEW YORK TIMES BOOK REVIEW, APRIL 15, 1956

Evenings with the Orchestra by Hector Berlioz, translated and edited by Jacques Barzun

FEW OF US listen to the music of writers. Rousseau and Samuel Butler wrote operas, Gerard Manley Hopkins wrote songs, but we hardly know or care—just as we don't care much for the operations of amateur surgeons, unless these are performed at sea. The books of composers are different. Many of us read—thank Fortune for having been allowed to read—the memoirs of Berlioz or Ethel Smythe, the criticism of Schumann, the letters of Mozart or Richard Strauss. Some of us enjoy reading the reminiscences of Chaliapin or Rimsky-Korsakov, of students of Liszt or Leschetizky, of eighteenth-century organists who once saw Haydn plain. In heaven we'll get to read Mahler's autobiography, Liszt's, Scarlatti's. Meanwhile, here on earth, Jacques Barzun has made a new translation of Berlioz's *Evenings with the Orchestra*.

Once upon a time, in an imaginary French city, there was an opera house whose orchestra played great music with joy and love and awe; the other nine-tenths of the time a few of the more stolid and conscientious musicians sawed away, while the rest ate, talked, slept, or listened to Hector Berlioz (or to a *Doppelgänger* or imaginary playmate or identical twin of his named Corsino). Berlioz and Corsino quote Vergil and Shakespeare to the musicians, make up historical or utopian romances for them, tell them the dazzling awful truth about claques, tenors, opera in London, contemporary music, the public. All of this constitutes the substance of *Evenings with the Orchestra*.

It is full of knowledge, penetration, good sense, individual wit, stock humor, justifiable exasperation, understanding exaggeration, emotion and rhetoric of every kind. Sometimes *Evenings* gives us the feelings of the brave, unlucky, lovable man who wrote the *Memoirs,* sometimes it gives us the knowledge of the Father of Orchestration, the Primal Conductor, and sometimes it gives us something of the genius of the composer who, in *Nuits d'été,* created the French art song, and who lives both in a few masterpieces of his own and in the many compositions which, without him, would be a little different.

But on some of the rainier evenings the author simply performs for us as a writer, and on those evenings we may wish that the "always original" Berlioz—Heine called him this—had been original enough to ask his dear friend Heine to write the pieces for him.

How Berlioz hated writing! He tells how for three days, locked in his room, his brain "ready to burst," his veins "burning," he tried to write a newspaper article; how his pistols "looked at me with round eyes"; how he smashed his "innocent guitar," how he wept until "the salt tears seemed slightly to soothe me"; how his little boy called timidly through the door, "Father, won't you be friends?" The two fell asleep together, and the next morning Berlioz "succeeded, I know not how, in writing I know not what on I know not whom. It is fifteen years since then! . . . and my punishment continues still . . . To employ one's time, intelligence, courage, and patience at this labor, with the certainty of not even being allowed to serve art by destroying a few abuses, removing prejudices, enlightening opinion!"

Not many people have known more about music and the performance of music than Berlioz knew; few more oddly original, oddly conventional, overpoweringly romantic, obstinately classical minds have existed.

Harmony, Discord, and Taste

THE NEW YORK TIMES BOOK REVIEW, JUNE 17, 1956

The Listener's Musical Companion by B. H. Haggin

IT'S a soothing, enchanting name: *The Listener's Musical Companion.*
Children used to have *The Youth's Companion;* stars have dark companions; and now those of us who mark our Schwann record catalogues
monthly, have three-year subscriptions to *High-Fidelity,* and tune in only
to Good Music Stations and the Red Sox, can have as our companion
the ageless, light-bringing B. H. Haggin. The boy Haggin—as all the
readers who buy him, swear by him, swear at him will remember—used
to see Nijinsky; for all I know the baby Haggin sat on Liszt's knee, and
disliked it—the index of this book skips from Lipatti to London; there's
no Liszt, not even his name.

The adult Haggin has been redeeming *The Nation* with his quite
inimitable criticism since the middle thirties. Yet his clear, troubled,
rapturous spirit is as young as ever; he speaks of the Good with the same
transfigured, self-forgetful eloquence, of the Bad with the same helpless, incredulous indignation. "Morality," Freud was fond of saying, "is
self-evident"; and Haggin has the shameless honesty of the true critic—
he couldn't lie to you if he tried. When Haggin praises, with revelatory
lucidity, in his own firm choice English, the composers and performers
you love best, he sounds to you like the music of the spheres; and when
he says, about other composers and performers you love best, that they
fuss, pout, pound, and in general just don't make sense to him, you want
to kill him.

And that's the way it ought to be. The critic, as Haggin says, "is a
mind operating not with impersonal esthetic principles but with personal
sensitiveness, perception, and taste . . . I am bound to report what I hear
and the reader then is free to find what I say to be true or not true for
him." We don't always think what Haggin thinks, but we do always
know what he thinks. And he is as consistent as a ruler; after we have
set up an equation between his taste and ours, we can almost predict our
own responses from his. Since he doesn't like Bartók or Berg (except

Wozzeck) or Elliot Carter or *Elektra* or *Ariadne auf Naxos,* I myself have to discount him about modern music, the way I discount Virgil Thomson about anything French; but when he writes about Schubert, Berlioz, Mussorgsky, Haydn, Mozart, Beethoven, about Toscanini, Schnabel, Szigeti—about dozens of other composers and performers— he is hard to beat. And if you need someone to buy records for your desert island, Haggin is the man.

This delightfully printed, conveniently arranged book talks candidly and intelligently, with discrimination and affection, about an extraordinary number of things: most of the great and good composers, many of the great and good musicians; all the compositions Haggin loves most, all the recorded performances he likes best; musical forms and meanings; different kinds of performance; criticism and critics—Berlioz, Shaw, Turner, Tovey, Thomson. Since Haggin is one of the best, most courageous, and most individual critics alive, this is a unique book, one that will be a help and joy to many people.

Recent Poetry

THE YALE REVIEW, SPRING 1956

Journey to Love by William Carlos Williams   *The Second Man* by Louis O. Coxe   *Poems* by Robert Conquest   *Something of the Sea* by Alan Ross   *As If* by John Ciardi   *A Letter to Li Po* by Conrad Aiken   *Some Phases of Love* by P. D. Cummins   *The Diamond Cutters* by Adrienne Cecile Rich

JOURNEY TO LOVE is a warm, thoughtful, sympathetic book; many things in it are beautiful, and everything in it is beautifully human. If one compares it with Williams's best work, that seems concentrated, final, exactly realized, in a way that this does not; these poems are, in comparison, reflective, very personal revery. But anyone who likes Williams's poetry will want to read them, and parts of them are as memorable as the beginning of "Asphodel, That Greeny Flower": *Of asphodel, that greeny flower, / like a buttercup / upon its branching stem— / save that it's green and wooden— / I come, my sweet, / to sing to you. / We lived long together / a life filled, / if you will, / with flowers. So that / I was cheered / when I came first to know / that there were flowers also / in hell. / Today / I'm filled with the fading memory of those flowers / that we both loved, / even to this poor / colorless thing— / I saw it / when I was a child— / little prized among the living / but the dead see, / asking among themselves: / What do I remember / that was shaped / as this thing is shaped?*

Several of these poets are what one might call poets of faithful emulation. They write in someone else's person, since they have not yet found a style and subject that will suggest their own. Yvor Winters's poems about Theseus or Sir Gawain and the Green Knight, Robert Lowell's poems about Civil War monuments have been obsessing models for Louis O. Coxe. Most of the poems in *The Second Man* are based so directly upon poems like these—and, besides, exhibit so rigid a monotony, so soldered and galvanized a form—that they seem to the reader not an individual response to the world but only an able, repeated academic exercise. Robert Conquest and Alan Ross are poets who write extraordinarily faithful imitations of the poems Auden wrote during the late thirties. Often the reader can remember the particular poem, the particular line, that is responsible for some passage of theirs. Robert Conquest is the better of the two; indeed, Alan Ross has written almost the worst line I ever saw in a poem: "But the *Zeitgeist* had a kind of *ethos*."

The most notable thing about John Ciardi's *As If* is a kind of crude power. The hesitations, reticences, and inabilities of the poetic nature—for to be able to say what it does say is to be unable to say everything else—are unknown to natures of such ready force, natures more akin to those of born executives, men ripe for running things. This writer uses Stevens's, or Shapiro's, or half a dozen other poets' tricks and techniques as easily, and with as much justification, as a salesman would use a competitor's sales talk—it works, doesn't it? But he doesn't use the styles as delicately and helplessly as these poets used them—after all, he *can* help himself, has helped himself. He resembles, as a poet, what Helene Deutsch calls "persons of the 'as if' type, because in every new object-relation they live *as if* they were really living their own life and expressing their own feelings, opinions, and views." He is much at his best as a translator, where his native force can put on a more sensitive and individual mask—his translation of the *Inferno* has more narrative power, strength of action, than any other I know.

I like the poems called *A Letter to Li Po* better than anything Conrad Aiken has written in the last fifteen years. They are not so good as the best things he wrote during the thirties, but they are accomplished and often beautiful verse, a little closer to their subject—and with a more individuating subject—than most of his work. The rhyming (if you like rhymes, and I do) is a pleasure in itself. But alas, with the best will in the world (I *like* liking poetry; would, if I could, like more), I can say little else that is favorable, and have to go on to some qualifications that will take all the heart out of what I have already said.

Aiken is a kind of Midas: everything he touches turns to verse. Reading his poems is like listening to Delius—one is experiencing an unending undifferentiating wash of fairly beautiful sounds—or like watching a fairly boring, because almost entirely predictable, kaleidoscope; a kaleidoscope all of whose transmutations are veiled, misty, watered down. These are the metamorphoses of a world where it is always raining, where everything *blurs* into everything else, where the easy, automatic, lyric, elegiac, nostalgic tone of the verse turns everything into itself, as the diffused, salon photography of the first part of this century turned everything into salon photographs. Aiken is always saying that we are this, that, the other—the evening, the moon, the stars, the universe—but how rarely he *makes* us into any of them! *What* his verse says, what it says it about, seems hardly to matter. Sometimes he says new things, sometimes he says old Aikenisms (*now the subaqueous evening / Exemplary as the unalterable moon,* or *the tiger dream relinquishes / The traumatic heart*), sometimes he says poetic truisms older than "Know thyself" (*O unknown love / unknown and treacherous as that sky above / and as my own heart is / what is the meaning of your kiss?*—I didn't invent this, I didn't find it in "June Moon," I'm quoting it from *A Letter to Li Po*), just as some eighteenth-century symphonist uses his own new melodies, his own old melodies, all his age's oldest melodies, with professional, indifferent ease. Aiken has an immediately recognizable style, and yet somehow it seems no more than a fairly high common denominator of all such styles. Most of his work is an easy, approximate revery; it is a planet without continents, islands, icecaps—all is sea. And yet some of his poems come as close to being good poems, without ever quite being so, as any I know.

P. D. Cummins's poems are poems about love and abnormal psychology, difficult processes of the spirit; they are sincere and intense and, very plainly, have come out of personal experience. They are marred or, often, ruined by a conventionally, obtrusively Poetic language and structure.

And now I have so little space, and so much enthusiasm, for Adrienne Cecile Rich's *The Diamond Cutters* that I can only make boiling and whistling noises like a teakettle. It is absurd to try to do justice in a couple of paragraphs to one of the best young poets in years; may I simply recommend this limpid book, full of Mozartean melodies, airs at which the reader murmurs, "I had not known that poetry was so easy"—may I simply recommend the poet now and write about her at length in the summer, along with Elizabeth Bishop?

Five Poets

THE YALE REVIEW, AUTUMN 1956

The Diamond Cutters by Adrienne Cecile Rich   *Section: Rock Drill. 85–95 de los Cantares* by Ezra Pound   *Exiles and Marriages* by Donald Hall   *Green Armor on Green Ground* by Rolfe Humphries   *Villa Narcisse* by Katherine Hoskins

ADRIENNE CECILE RICH is an enchanting poet; everybody seems to admit it; and this seems only right. Everybody thinks young things young, Sleeping Beauty beautiful—and the poet whom we see behind the clarity and gravity of Miss Rich's poems cannot help seeming to us a sort of princess in a fairy tale. Her scansion, even, is easy and limpid, close to water, close to air; she lives nearer to perfection (an all-too-easy perfection, sometimes—there are a few of Schubert's pieces that are better the first time than they ever are again, and some of Miss Rich's poems are like this) than ordinary poets do, and her imperfections themselves are touching as the awkwardness of anything young and natural is touching. The reader feels that she has only begun to change; thinks, "This young thing, who knows what it may be, old?" Some of her poems are very different from the others, some of her nature is very far from the rest of it, so that one feels that she has room to live in and to grow out into; liking her for what she is is a way of liking her even better for what she may become.

On the third page of *The Diamond Cutters* one comes to "Pictures by Vuillard"; comes to *the wild pear-tree, / The broken ribbons of the green-and-gold / Portfolio, with sketches from an old / Algerian campaign; the placid three / Women at coffee by the window, fates / Of nothing ominous, waiting for the ring / Of the postman's bell.* By these, by *the cores of fruit* left on the luncheon plates, *we are led back where we have never been,* to a world where nothing is tragic, where everything stays at its still, summer-shaded noon. But, asks the poem, what good is this to us, *the destined readers of Stendhal,* who *scarcely think of sighing / For afternoons that found us born too late? Our prudent envy rarely paces spying / Under those walls, that lilac-shaded gate. / Yet at this moment, in our private view, / A breath of common peace, like memory, / Rustles the branches of the wild pear-tree— / Air that we should have known, and cannot know.*

This is beautiful enough, individual enough, and truthful enough, loves Vuillard well enough (and oh, that *breath of common peace*! how much of its old power Wordsworth's *common* has kept!), to make a reader unwilling to remark, as he needs to: "Stendhal! *That* perpetually enchanted being, always riding off, young, uniformed, on a spring morning into possibility!" Surely Miss Rich means *destined readers of Sartre and "The Sentimental Education."* This is an awkward crude way of defining the class, just as Miss Rich's way is a glib crude way; the *destined readers,* poor unhappy few, need more of the imagination and devotion that the poet has brought to the Vuillard. (When you call people *we* you find it easy to be unfair to them, since you yourself are included in the condemnation.) When the poet is being a Vuillard-looker she is magical and heartfelt; when she is briefly acting the part of a destined-Stendhal-reader she is rhetorical: *we . . . in monstrous change such consolations find / As restless mockery sets before the mind / To deal with what must anger and appall.* Yes, that's in the poem too: when our princess does the meanest chores—and filling out an unfelt portion with reliable rhetoric is a mean one—she sounds for an instant like any Academician. Nor does her "Pictures by Vuillard" contain any intimation of the frozen pictures, exact, photographic, almost academic, that testified during his later years to the boredom and passiveness that had always waited unpainted over at the side of those Victorian rose windows, small bourgeois paradises, that he half witnessed, half created. These are miracles free to us, but that the painter paid for—paid for with part of himself; and when that part was gone the poetry of objects, by the light of common day, became their prose.

Some of Miss Rich's ordinary subjects are the past against the present, museums and their contents, Europe and its contents, youth and middle age, morality. Now and then her reader longs for fewer, or at least odder, morals; reading "O let your human memory end / Heavy with thought and act. / Claim every joy of paradox / That time would keep intact" is like getting one of Auden's old carbons for Christmas. But usually her moralizing is part of her own particular life, and usually her influences are a surprise and delight. Think of a young poet, an *intellectual,* who can be influenced by Kipling and Frost! When one reads "Our fathers in their books and speech / Have made the matter plain: / The green fields they walked in once / Will never grow again," one can turn to the very poem, "Our Fathers Also." "The

Perennial Answer" is typical neurotic-violent Frost—with one touch of
Robert Lowell—and "Autumn Equinox" is almost the best Frost-
influenced poem I've ever read. It is the monologue, one leaf-raking
afternoon, of an old professor's old wife. Once, young, shy, stiff-collared,
he had seemed to her "superb in his refusal / To read aloud from
Bryant to the ladies / Assembled on the boarding-house piazza /
Among the moth-wings of a summer evening." But after some still years
of "a life annual, academic," she buys loud curtains, weeps in the moonlight, half asleep, and answers her husband's "Are you ill, unhappy? Tell
me what I can do," with "I'm sick, I guess. I thought that life is different than it is." She sees, but finds no way to change, "the lines of
grievous love upon his face." Nothing happens. They "finish off not
quite as we began": he reading Dryden's *Satires* by the window, like a
mended piece of clockwork, she piling leaves in baskets. Old, patient,
staid, calm-sleeping as the dead, they have learned to "wake and take
the day for what it is," she has learned to make her terrible minimal
complaint about life: "Even autumn / Can only carry through what
spring began."

The girl of "Living in Sin" had not expected that in the studio
"morning light / So coldly would delineate the scraps / Of last night's
cheese and blank sepulchral bottles; / That on the kitchen shelf
among the saucers / A pair of beetle-eyes would fix her own— /
Envoy from some black village in the mouldings." This envoy and his
fellow, the milkman under whose tread, at dawn, "each separate stair
would writhe," are as real as, no more real than, her childhood's "great
black bears who seemed more blue than black, / More violet than
blue against the dark— / Where are you now? upon what track /
Mutter your muffled paws, that used to tread / So softly, surely, up the
creakless stair?" Anticipation and actuality, scenery and whatever it is
that living transforms scenery into—the poems feel and express both;
and if some part of one wants the poet less ideally normal than she is,
the poems more nearly final than they are—for none of them are
quite what I have heard Wallace Stevens call "permanent poetry"—one
repeats to oneself her "Who sleeps, and dreams, and wakes, and sleeps
again / May dream again." The secondary elaboration of those dreams,
her poems, has been so successful that no trace of their original obscurity
remains; both the point the poems are making and the way in which
they are making it are plain to both reader and writer. Her poetry so
thoroughly escapes all of the vices of modernist poetry that it has escaped
many of its virtues too. (Beside her, Shakespeare, for instance, seems
very complicated and modern and obscure.) She tells us how at

Versailles "the cry of closing rings / For us and for the couples in the wood / And all good children who are all too good," and begs the children to "be wild today." It seems to me that she herself is, often, a good poet who is all too good—one who can afford to be wild tomorrow; meanwhile, today, she is also an endearing and delightful poet, one who deserves Shakespeare's favorite adjective, *sweet*.

A few passages of Pound's new *Cantos* have a pure and characteristic beauty: "The waves rise, and the waves fall / But you are like the moonlight: always there!"; "Had Crab such crystal, winter were as a day"; "The viper stirs in the dust, / the blue serpent / glides from the rock pool / and they take lights now down to the water / the lamps float from the rowers / the sea's claw drawing them outwards." Some lines have an easy elegance, a matter-of-fact reality; the bare look and motion of the words, sometimes, is a delight. A great deal of the book is interesting in the way an original soul's indiscriminate notes on books and people, countries and centuries, are interesting; all these fragmentary citations and allusions remind you that if you had read exactly the books Pound has read, known exactly the people Pound has known, and felt about it exactly as Pound has felt, you could understand the *Cantos* pretty well. Gertrude Stein was most unjust to Pound when she called that ecumenical alluder a village explainer: he can hardly even tell you anything (unless you know it already), much less explain it. He makes notes on the margin of the universe; to tell how just or unjust a note is, you must know that portion of the text yourself.

Meaning seems to him—as morality seemed to Freud—self-evident, something the family naturally knows; and he makes family jokes about it, witty or ingeniously farfetched allusions that are a delight to us insiders, a puzzle to the barbarians outside. (Pound does not want readers, really, but disciples, since he has the Greek feeling that wisdom is a way of life that disciples can share, and that reading is not a short cut to. As a result he has more disciples, almost, than readers.)

For instance, Pound says all at once—he has been talking about San Bertrand and Montréjeau—"Elder Lightfoot is not downhearted, / Elder Lightfoot is cert'nly / not / downhearted, / He observes a design in the Process"; and that is the end of Elder Lightfoot, the poem deserts him for "Miss Ida by the bars in the jail house" and "Carrière show in Paris." Here Pound is making fun, in what seems to me an amusing way, of Eliot and part of the *Four Quartets*. How do I know? I just know—as, more often, I just don't know, when the languages or ideographs or hieroglyphics (yes, these *Cantos* have hieroglyphics; next year Minoan B) or historical periods are ones I know nothing or little about. But here I'm better off, and smile, and say to explain the smile: Eliot is a deacon, and *Elder* is Pound's Br'er Rabbit Version of that; *Lightfoot* resembles Possum and pussyfooting, and goes well with all the Original Chameleon in Eliot, the part that seeks safety in conformity, apparent identity; *process* and *design* and *pattern* are used over and over in the *Four Quartets*—to *observe* a design *in* the Process is as solemnly ludicrous as is the parody of the troops' *Are we downhearted? No*; the tone is Pound's regular tone for making fun of Eliot; and so on.

But when I read passages like "pou éul cheu / pu erh[4] / 'O nombreux officiers / Imperator ait. / Iterum dico / T AI MEOU 1637 / 1562 / OU TING 1324 / 1265 / cognovit aerumnas / TSOU KIA reigned 33 years / wei / tcheng / tcheu / XV:II koung / naught about just contribution / invicem docentes siu M.2835 / hsü, in the first tone / kiaó, chiao,[1-4]"—the Chinese words are accompanied by twelve ideographs—I bring little knowledge to the reading and carry away little knowledge from the reading. Yet, finishing, I seem to know—how I don't know—that all the Latin, Chinese, and Ancient History in the world wouldn't make me think such a passage good poetry, good organization, or standing firm in the middle. Form, Kenneth Burke says, is a satisfied expectation; here, as in so much of the *Cantos,* it is only our uneasy expectation of disorder, of an idiosyncratic hodgepodge, that is satisfied.

If we pick an average passage, one neither at a height of lyricism nor a depth of carbon-copying, we get something like

> *Marse Adams done tol' 'em.*
> *The Major done told 'em*
> > *(having a First Folio (Shx) in his lock-box*
> *could afford waiting to see it.*
> > *"Every . . . etc. . .*
> *downright corruption." "To the consumer."*
> > *Waal, they bust the abundance*
> *and had to pay Europe,*
> > *an' Anatole tol' 'em:*
> > *"no export? No need to make war."*
> > *Ile des Pinguins,*
> *So that Perry "opened" Japan.*
> *Use of foreign coin until 1819.*
> > *Exception Spanish milled dollars,*
> *every dealer occupied in exporting them, page 446*

their exclusion an unconstitutional fraud ...
A currency of intrinsic value FOR WHICH
They paid interest to NOBODY

page 446
column two

("Thirty Years," Benton)
Is suppressed in favour of fluctuation,
this country a thoroughfare.
OBEUNT 1826, July 4.
Not battlements, but that the land go to the settlers,
Tariff! Monsieur de Tocqueville
may pass in Europe for American history.
Macon, Guilford ...

We cannot help noticing that this, like so much of the *Cantos,* doesn't have the connections and omissions, the concentration, that a work of art has: Pound throws in everything—the numbers of the pages, even. Pound has said that poetry ought to be as well written as prose; is this? Aren't good notes, even, more organized than *this*? When we finish reading it we have the approximate understanding that such a passage invites, but we have none of the aesthetic enjoyment we get from a poem, a story, a well-written passage of exposition. We do feel a pale pleasure at encountering so unexpectedly, back among the library stacks, this minstrel-show shrewdness, and think with a smile: "Uncle Ezra done tol' 'em." But here it is information, not lack of information, that gets in the way of the reader: if I had never read Tocqueville I might enjoy Pound's putting him in his place—as it is, I think, "You may not understand Tocqueville, but Tocqueville would have understood *you*."

Many writers have felt, like Pound: Why not invent an art form that will permit me to put all my life, all my thoughts and feelings about the universe, directly into a work of art? But the trouble is, when they've invented it it isn't an art form. The *Cantos* are a "form" that permits Pound not even to try to write poetry; but since he is a poet, a wonderful one, he sometimes still writes it. The *Cantos* are less a "poem containing history" than a heap containing poetry, history, recollections, free associations, obsessions. Some of the poetry is clearly beautiful, some of the history live: Pound can pick out, make up, a sentence or action that resurrects a man or a time. Many of Pound's recollections are as engaging as he is; his warmth, delight, disinterestedness, honest indignation help to make up for his extraordinary misuse of extraordinary powers, for everything that makes the *Cantos* a kind of *reductio ad absurdum*. His obsessions, at their worst, are a moral and intellectual disaster, and make us ashamed for him:

> *Democracies electing their sewage*
> *till there is no clear thought about holiness*
> *a dung flow from 1913*
> *and, in this, their kikery functioned, Marx, Freud*
> *   and the american beaneries*
> *Filth under filth . . .*

What is worst in Pound and what is worst in the age have conspired to ruin the *Cantos,* and have not quite succeeded. I cannot imagine any future that will think it a good poem; but, then as now, scholars will process it, anthologies present one or two of its beauties, readers dig through all that blue clay for more than a few diamonds.

The worst poems, perhaps, are those that confirm us in our own commonplaceness. (Even a few lines of Shakespeare or Rilke or Wordsworth—"Hang there like fruit, my soul, / Till the tree die"; Hermes' saying to Eurydice, "He has turned round," and Eurydice's replying, "Who?"; "There's not a breathing of the common wind / That will forget thee; thou hast great allies; / Thy friends are exultations, agonies, / And love, and man's unconquerable mind"—are enough to convince us of our own unalterable inferiority; but, our real being a part of the lines, we no longer care.) Donald Hall's poems are very commonplace, but they are so complacent about themselves that they shock us into awareness of their commonplaceness. But there is nothing in Rolfe Humphries's poems to arouse him from his comfortable slumbers, us from ours; he is, I think, the ideal poet of committees, academies, poetry societies—he writes the poetry that everybody would write, if everybody could write poetry.

Green Armor on Green Ground is, mostly, twenty-four poems in the twenty-four official meters of Welsh poetry. (Didn't Mr. Humphries like any meter well enough to write two poems in it? ill enough to write none? No.) The twenty-four poems have maddened Horace Gregory into calling them *dull,* and he is right: these are not poems to read but exercises to scan. Poems begin in the Unconscious; the methodical improvisations of laureates begin and end in the habitually unattended-to, in that common portion of our being that is so stock, conventional, inexorably predictable, that we are no longer able to notice it—before we know, the peas are shelled, the socks are darned, the silver's on the table. It was not Mr. Humphries but Habit that wrote these poems, it was not I but Habit that read them; while Habit wrote and Habit read, Mr. Humphries and I were scanning, rhyming, counting, in preparation for the bank examiner's semi-annual audit.

The best of these verses are some smooth firm King Arthur stories in "free meters"; they are too expectedly poetic to be quite poems, but are more the composite photographs that the Muses' official doubles inspire. And they are not, alas! very Welsh—Mr. Humphries hasn't a real vocation for being Welsh. (Some of the Welsh aren't Welsh: Ernest Jones, for instance.) Sometimes Mr. Humphries does glower, sometimes he is glib, but the Higher Glibness, those heavenly smells and hellish smiles poured over us warm as mother's milk while the poet is stealing our change purse—for these we have to go to the real Sons and Daughters of Owen Glendower.

When I first read *Villa Narcisse* I was so delighted with the good lines and poems, the existence of a new and individual poet, that I hardly cared about anything else. Now that I have read the poems a great many times, that *anything else* casts a spoiling shadow over much of the book; yet my feeling of Mrs. Hoskins's individuality is stronger than ever—reading the poems is like reading the diary of someone whom you partly like, partly are troubled by, but could under no circumstances confuse with anyone else in the world. The poet of the poems, the Narcissus of *Villa Narcisse*—who may be, of course, fairly like or fairly unlike Mrs. Hoskins herself—is cultivated and a lady; fond of Europe and the past, "the sweetness of the old regime," uneasy about America and the present; exceptional in her self-knowledge, self-distrust; full of memories of a neurotic, "freakish" Southern childhood and the black warm-spoken angels that attended it; drawn toward Donne and Gide, Mediterranean and Jacobean things; noticing animals, children, servants, women—unfamous mothers, long-haired disregarded housewives; conscious of the ways and graces—especially the slightly threadbare graces —of lives, and obsessed by what lies beneath them: nightmare, deceit, betrayal, lust, the "dream-learned, dream-pervasive sorrow," "blithe corruption." I once heard a mother say, "I'm sure that it's a very good poem, dear, but I wish that *my* little girl hadn't written it"; a reader fond of the poet of *Villa Narcisse* may feel that about some of the poems. Her poetry is more notable for personal truth, emotional and dramatic penetration, than for impeccable taste, extraordinary creative powers, dazzling skill. She is most skillful, perhaps, when working more or less in the manner of her favorite time; "To the Patron," the address to the reader with which her book begins, is as accomplished as it is personal:

On this staled stretch of beach,
  The double fork
As long as some men's sunny shadows reach,
  Its curving fingers worked
Round emptiness, arms closed or manacled;
  The tender knife,
Blunt blade and heavy heft, in half a life-
  Time's blowing sands half-held
  Are useless artifacts
  Of a mis-adventurer,
  A lonely mariner,
    North-tossed, storm-wracked.

  Yet I've heard tell, Below
    This bitter gray
Lie waters mild and blue that lip the low
    Lain lands to sunny bays.
And happy boatmen singing sail and plunder
    Them—arms wide
And plunged their curious fingers over boatside—
    Of salt-encrusted wonders.
    And the glad knife leaps
    In hard and skilful palms
    To work the watery farms
      Of Chesapeake.

  Master, sweet gentleman,
    Subscribe my voyage.
Take some stock in those exacter lands
    And in my mute tools' rage
For use. Profit by my indenture there.
    Thou needst not go
Nor new ship lend. Search what imperfect, shallow
    Vessel needs repair;
    A-leak, with ragged sheets
    And stripped of parts, no ship,
    That now drifts derelict
      Beyond belief.

Yet the poet who can say, "At night it's like another planet"; who can begin a poem, "How generous are the poor / In things! / Their sagging door / 's a-swing— / Shove in, son— to any poorer yet"; who

can begin another, "How small the world! Thus two, in wide disdain /
Remark where Norumbega's / Shrunk from a continent and mountain
chain / To a Charles' side / Canoe ride," can mar as moving and
original a poem as "An Evening of Death" with ordinary rhetoric like
"Hot thought-beasts crackle through the underbrush / Of all their
minds and drink at flowing fires"; can half spoil as good an idea as "The
Sisters" by an obviousness and one-sidedness strange in a complicated
and individual mind. Sometimes the poems are a little raw or precious,
sometimes their form is oblique, ragged, a size too small; yet they are
always part of a most private life, are never mere social behavior. They
are true to that other self, "Cousin to Tobit's journey-friend," who "formless broods in violet / Over the pale / And crackling pennants of
the corn / Before a rain"; who "is most / The some times when I
wholly am"; whom the poet finally addresses as

> *O, seldom, suave, whose merest fig-*
>   *frond hand on blue*
> *'s a good these apple eaters fear-*
>   *fully refuse;*
>
> *Magnolia grandiflora, you*
>   *Are no cozy*
> *Sickness that a train could cure*
>   *But farther, huge.*

And she is true, always, to her memories of how "the child awakes to
find the day / Half done and shadows everywhere"; how child and
gardener, "small pink / And giant black," go along the rows together,
"gnarled hand circling tender, teaching"; how he has

>   *trapped a rat and, swinging*
> *From his other hand, she's pleaded,*
>   *Hoped and joked for dear life*
> *To the laundry . . . But, bruise bare toes*
> *Or puny fists, water will mount*
> *And rat climb high and nothing stop*
> *That laughter. Then the rat shrieked, then the child.*
>
> *Mother! carved in calm, a softness*
> *Lights thy lap, thy thimble flickers*
>   *Light birds to the mirror—*
> *Mother!'s sorry . . . The sobbing room*

Stands still and taut to dark, of glass
And of a shape down there that carries
Shadows in each hand into the shadows.

These quotations must have made the reader exclaim, impatient with my qualifications and objections: "But this poetry has imagination and taste and reality; comes—very plainly—out of an individual's life. What more do you want? Are you insatiable?" Yes, I am insatiable; and the poems do so plainly come out of a special life that I have come to have for them the defensiveness that you have for the work of a relative or friend—I long to see the poet armored in dozens of perfect poems, and am uneasy at those that have, in Miss Rich's words, "the incompleteness of a natural thing." But of course I know, just as the reader does, that it is only a poet's good poems that matter—and Mrs. Hoskins's need neither solicitude nor praise, only a reader.

Songs of Rapture,
Songs of Death

THE NEW YORK TIMES BOOK REVIEW, NOVEMBER 25, 1956

Selected Writings of Jules Laforgue, edited and translated by William Jay Smith

WILLIAM JAY SMITH has selected and translated fifty of Laforgue's poems, two stories, much criticism and correspondence, and has linked them with sensible, informative pieces of criticism and appreciation. Mr. Smith's translation of Laforgue's most arresting story, "Hamlet," is incomparably better than Frances Newman's; his translation of the early "Funeral March for the Death of the Earth" is a little better than Laforgue; and he is good with Laforgue's last, best poems.

He is a good translator; but where Laforgue is concerned, a good translation isn't good enough. Putting Laforgue into English, ordinarily, is like transcribing "The Girl with the Flaxen Hair" for brass band. Laforgue's negligent, improvisatory elegance—his first fine unrecapturable rapture—goes over into no English but Eliot's, and even Eliot's has a grimness that would have troubled the lovable Laforgue.

Jules Laforgue was born in 1860 and died, of tuberculosis, in 1887. He spent almost a fifth of his brief life in Berlin—he detested it—where he was reader to the Empress of Germany. Two months after leaving Berlin he married the "very thin and very English" Leah Lee; eight months after, he was dead. His wife barely survived him. The fairly thin and very French Laforgue had begun as a "tragic Buddhist" who lived on "two eggs and a glass of water a day," and wrote of "The Sobbing of the Earth," of "all the misery, the filth of the planet adrift in the innocent heavens"; he ended as a "dilettante Buddhist" who, after having "eaten of the fruit of the Unconscious," wrote of "The Flowers of Good Will," and combined with his own wit, charm, and youth "a great deal of glorious pessimism." He had, as he says of someone else, "a beautiful soul / Of the sort they don't manufacture any longer nowadays"; and it was not simply the optimism of tuberculosis that made him write to his sister, two weeks before he died: "The least little page is successful, and I haven't an enemy, do you realize how rare a thing that is?"

As one reads Laforgue's poetry one is conscious, always, that Eliot is a little ahead and Corbière a little behind. Reading "Costumed in white, I'll play the swan, / After us the Deluge, O my Leda!" one is back in "Le Poète contumace"; reading "I have known them, known them all," or any of a hundred lines, one is ahead in "Prufrock." And yet Laforgue is as different from Corbière as even Laforgue wanted us to believe; and Eliot has completely metamorphosed Laforgue, even when he takes him over word for word. Laforgue's *Last Poems* are not, as Martin Turnell says, "the most important single poem published in Europe since the seventeenth century," nor is his Hamlet "more profound than Shakespeare's . . . tenderer, and wittier, and more charming, and wiser," as Frances Newman says. Yet his poetry is individual enough, endearing enough, to make far wiser critics say slightly less extravagant things; somebody (William Jay Smith, perhaps) should translate all or almost all of Laforgue's poems, and print them *with the French*.

Poems selected for us Americans might well include "Albums," the poem in which Laforgue decides that it is the "Far-West et les Prairies" that are his true home; there, scalped of Europe, a Desperado speaking "l'argot californien," he will learn to hunt, to fish, to relish whisky, venison, "les Etats Mormons," and "la Loi de Lynch"; a milch cow and some "petits-enfants" will sweeten his old age; and if even there the Infinite comes to vex him, in the shape of the "Condor des Montagnes-Rocheuses," he will be able to invent for himself and for the pasteurized peoples of this Age of Gold a new religion, a Code "social, empirique et mystique."

Ah, if only he and Leah Laforgue *had* come to San Francisco, and if Eliot had come to them from St. Louis, and if—and if! Perhaps Laforgue needed us; surely we needed Laforgue; as it is we have come together only in the pages of "Prufrock" and "Portrait of a Lady," both of us looking beautiful but heartbreaking.

In Pursuit of Beauty

THE NEW YORK TIMES BOOK REVIEW, MARCH 10, 1957

A Swinger of Birches: A Portrait of Robert Frost by Sidney Cox

THIS is an old friend's portrait of Robert Frost. The portrait's content is quotations, paraphrases, anecdotes, praise: its form is a guided tour's, a trudging from beauty to beauty. Frost says, "Lyrics ought to be dramatic. A poem ought to be something going on"—and so ought such a book as this.

Frost's introduction (to a book he's "just stolen a look" over the edge of) speaks of his dead friend Sidney Cox with affection, calls him "a great teacher"; but he cannot resist remembering how "very teasably young" Cox was at their first meeting: "It wasn't the last time he had to make allowances for me. He worked at it devotedly . . . He seemed worried at first lest it should appear I didn't seek him as much as he sought me. He respected me very highly. And he was more serious about such things than I." Cox knew this; he tells you, soberly, himself uninfected, that Frost "thought of poetry—and behaved, sometimes, as if he thought of life—as a prank"; and he quotes Frost about "play for mortal stakes," but doesn't mention his last awing word on play, "Directive."

It is satisfying to be given so many of the metaphors, prejudices, and discoveries of the best poet alive. Different readers will like different things; I particularly like what Frost says about the need for "doubleness," for "form that falsifies no ambiguities." On meeting and providing for ambiguities, he says, depend charm, integrity, and worth. He says: "We shall be judged finally by the delicacy of our feeling of when to stop short . . . A little of anything goes a long way in art." This is as true and troubling as von Hofmannsthal's "Good taste is the ability continuously to counteract exaggeration"; both are sayings that an age of excess will immediately repress.

Frost says, arrestingly, that he has "almost never experienced ecstasy"; Cox remembers his telling students that the aesthetic range "is from exquisite beauty, through elegant beauty, homely beauty, rough beauty, terrible beauty, mean beauty, to vile beauty. He had never been able to go on to vile beauty, he said. He knew his limits." After trying to fit in "The Subverted Flower" and "The Pauper Witch of Grafton," I have wondered whether Frost's limits know him as well as he knows them. "Eyes seeking the response of eyes / Bring out the stars, bring out the flowers" is his version of Freud's "Without love there is no understanding"; but he also says about people, "Damn them, damn them all . . . but we must forget that." "You have to live by shedding" is his account of the river of Lethe on whose banks we live.

Yet he has made it impossible for us ever to get rid of some of those "actual experiences" upon which, he says, each of his poems is based. Because of Frost a little boy, "his cheek smeared with apple-sand," is an actual experience of our own—actual enough for us not to be afraid of his last demand on us: "How do I know whether a man has come close to Keats in reading Keats? The closeness—everything depends on the closeness."

Go, Man, Go!

MADEMOISELLE, MAY 1957

"COME, Muse, let's sing of rats!" one eighteenth-century poem begins; the Department of Physical Education of one Midwestern university offers courses called "Beanbag I" and "Beanbag II." Writing on so insignificant a subject as sports cars makes me feel like a rat poet, a beanbag professor, and I have to reassure myself with Samuel Johnson's "Nothing is too insignificant for so insignificant a creature as man."

But part of me does not need reassuring; part of me, like part of you, feels, Cars, cars! Nor do we feel this simply because we are Americans. Alfa Romeo test drivers go at a hundred miles an hour through the streets of Milan while the pedestrians and the traffic policemen applaud; England has two prosperous weekly magazines in which ladies write lives of their eleven-year-old Austins, and sports reporters tell by how many seconds a thirty-year-old Bentley beat a thirty-five-year-old Bugatti in a vintage race at Brighton. Cars are some of the things we share with the rest of the world, the rest of the ages: a man polishing his Mercedes is the last link in a chain that goes back to Achilles patting his divine steeds Balius and Xanthus—or, at least, that's what I tell myself as I polish my Mercedes.

People love cars. Looking at them driving off fast in every direction, a Thoreau or Emerson might ask: "From what are they all escaping?" The answer is, "Themselves"; if only they'd stayed home and cultivated those selves they wouldn't need to escape from them. "It is because our own eyes are so dull that the chromium on our cars shines so," the Thoreau or Emerson would continue. All this is one of those demeaning truths to which we say, "It's so. It's so," and walk away muttering, "Thank God *something* shines!" Nor should the word "escape" frighten us: most selves are good things to escape from— happy the man who has become, for a moment, selfless!

Proust says about people: No matter how ugly and old and odd you are, there is always someone whose ideal love you would be if only he could find you. It's true of cars. Steam cars, electrics like little parlors with cut-glass bud vases, touring cars ten feet high whose side curtains are of many-windowed isinglass, whose tops can be erected by three men in two hours and, once up, can shelter half a circus—you all have someone to bid for you shining-eyed, to take you home and, after many nights and many days, restore you to your original, authentic, mint condition. If we were like cars someone would marry us at the age of forty for our patent-leather fenders curved like a wave, our mahogany toolboxes, our gleaming brass lanterns and radiators and Motometers, our "mother-in-law seats" out in the open behind the rear wheels, our tires whose treads spell "Nonskid"; for the Russian fur coats and fur trousers and leather face masks in which our passengers rode in winter; for our varnished artillery-spoke wheels higher than a man's heart— four, six, eight of them. Yes, there *was* an Octoauto, and Elbert Hubbard was paid to say of it: "It is figured out on a reasonable basis that by the use of eight wheels eight times the ordinary service is obtainable."

Ah, advertisements of yesteryear! One could read, in 1910: "Protect your car against theft. Locks may be picked or jimmied. But no thief ever attempted to steal a car with a man at the wheel. Bosco's collapsible rubber driver is so lifelike and terrifying that nobody a foot away can tell it isn't a real, live man. When not in use, this marvelous device is simply deflated and put under the seat. Price $15."

These collapsible rubber drivers, like the real, live ones, are un-restorable; but the cars they drove still glitter in Glidden Tours or at antique-car meets, where they look as improbably magnificent as old uniforms, engraved tournament armor. As loved, as collected are the classic cars: the Duesenbergs, Hispano-Suizas, Isotta-Fraschinis, Mercedes, Pierce-Arrows, Packards, Rolls-Royces, Bugattis of the twenties and thirties. Is stepping into *your* car "like stepping into a palace"? Does *your* car have a 180-inch wheel base; an engine four feet seven inches long; a top speed of 140; a price of $30,000; a guarantee for the life-time of the owner? The Bugatti Royale had them all.

In England they still race such cars. In Italy they race everything: two-hundred-mile-an-hour Ferraris, jeeps, scooters, economy cars whose engine the mechanic lifts from the trunk with one hand. On dirt or asphalt ovals we Americans race stock cars, jalopies, midgets, one-man Indianapolis racers; out on dry lakes and salt flats the lakesters and streamliners go record-hunting; at the drag strips souped-up stock cars, home- or garage-made dragsters spend their Sundays seeing which can accelerate fastest.

At a *concours d'élégance* a car is judged for its beauty, authenticity, perfection of maintenance; your 1899 De Dion Bouton may be disqualified because it has a 1901 mudguard or because, when the judge ran his white-gloved finger along the underside of the axle, it came away stained with a butterfly's blood. In rallies you drive over some labyrinth of iced roads—or, in summer, over the Alps—at a required 41.5 mph, while your navigator sweats and figures; at a hill climb—well, you can imagine what people do at a hill climb. But unless you're Beatrix Potter I don't think you can imagine what they do at trials. Over little rivers, through marshes, up grassy hillsides and monolithic crags— stalling, miring down, balancing with front wheels in air, capsizing— go hippity-hop, hippity-hop, little bicycle-wheeled baby-buggy cars driven, mostly, by middle-aged couples: husbands with clear, sparkling eyes and round, rosy cheeks; wives lying across the hood to keep the car's nose down but still managing to look like Mopsy, Flopsy, and Cottontail after they'd found good homes and a husband with a hobby. And behind, sober-faced, attentive, decorously applauding, as natural and unquestioning as the willows they stand or sit on shooting sticks among, are the watchers of the trials. Ah, England!

And, best of all, there are sports cars. The sports-car driver—the enthusiast, as he calls himself—is someone whose eyes get starry whenever he sees a sign saying "Winding road"; he corners all day and then drifts off into that country where no road is straight. Speed is only speed; it is the curves and hills, up-shifts and down-shifts, motions made just fast enough and just small enough that transform the indifferent inhabitant of a car into a Driver. A Driver wants a car light and low; wants big, well-cooled brakes, quick, precise steering; wants the kind of suspension and weight distribution that will make the car absolutely stable—"rock-steady," the enthusiast says—on curves and at high speed; wants four or more gears; wants the car, generally, open or openable, so that as he drives along country lanes he's out among, down among weeds and rabbits and Nature; wants a rigid, compact car that handles like a racer—and is, consequently, the safest thing on the road. And he wants it beautiful; the enthusiast may not be able to tell Gothic from Romanesque, Soutine from Giotto, but he can talk for half an hour about the aesthetic inferiority of the TF to the TC.

Some sports cars are fast, some surprisingly slow; some are closed and luxurious, some as open and luxurious as an orange crate. A few of the most famous makers are Alfa Romeo, Mercedes, Ferrari, Lancia, Maserati, Jaguar, Aston Martin, Frazer Nash, OSCA, Bristol, Porsche, BMW; as these names are read out to the enthusiast, drums roll and in the distance the shining trumpets blow. And for every enthusiast with a sports car, sports cars, there are dozens with the wrong-sized pocket-book, the wrong-sized family and a '53 Ford; these buy the magazines, read the books, go to the races, daydream, dream.

Enthusiasts can be divided into two classes, those who say, "It corners like it was on rails," and those who say, "She corners as if she were on rails, old boy!" One of these last may even wear string gloves, leather-palmed, a Norfolk jacket and a Sherlock Holmes hat—or as *he* would say, a deerstalker; if he does, there is nothing you can do. All enthusiasts say that their cars do *an honest hundred* (*honest* as opposed to *indicated*—the average speedometer is 10 percent fast); that closing the car's door is *like closing a bank vault* (usually this is an exaggeration, but in the case of my Mercedes it is almost literally true: if you'll come listen to me close my car door I'll come listen to you close your bank vault). All enthusiasts speak in approving or longing tones of things like overhead cams, knock-off hubs, sprung weight, oversquare engines, "light" or "positive" steering, independent suspension, dry sump lubrication, flat cornering, close-ratio gearboxes, wire wheels. All look down their noses at automatic transmissions, power steering, long wheel bases, unsprung weight, roll, L-head engines, chromium, over-hang, "Detroit iron." If a sports car jars their teeth out they say: "It hath [*hath* because their teeth are gone] a *firm* ride," and then they mourn the fact that it doesn't have the *classical,* the *coal-cart* ride of the sports cars of yesteryear.

Enthusiasts treasure even the squeal of the pig; one of their commoner phrases is, "What a note!" Racing cars or sports cars that mean business—are real bombs—ought, as the rpm's go up, to make a hard, screaming sound. A noise like tearing silk is particularly prized; Bugattis are famous for it. A car friend of mine wrote to Cook Laboratories proposing that they make a record of the sounds of loved and famous marques (you call a make a marque); as his wife and he, my wife and I sit comfortably drinking cocoa, we cry, "Listen to that TC!" or else with a "Say, what's that?" run out to the porch. Often it's a truck. I know about the Colonel's lady and Judy O'Grady, but why should trucks and sports cars sound the same?

About sports cars even a lot of learning goes a little way. You must learn—well, more than most people would ever want to learn. You must learn not to confuse a Nash-Healey with a Frazer Nash, an Austin-Healey, an Aston Martin. Don't mix up Delahayes, Delages, De Dions—a De Dion isn't even a car any more but a kind of rear axle, and you need to know what kind. As for Farinas: Pinin is the best contemporary car designer, Nino is the racing-driver, and Stabilimento isn't a man but an establishment—it makes bodies. You mustn't confuse initials: TC's, TD's, and TF's are different—words can't express *how* different—MG's; these having nothing to do with AC's, nor with HRG's, nor with BMW's—Frazer Nashes once were British BMW's, and EMW's are Soviet Zone BMW's, and . . . but surely you don't want me to go on.

Or if you do, read *Road and Track.* Fortunate the man who has four years of *Road and Track* stacked under the bed! In them there are articles about, pictures of sports-car races, Grand Prix races, classic cars, the latest bodies from Ghia and Bertone and Vignale, the last special some mute inglorious Dr. Porsche has made in a friend's garage—these and Le Mans, the Targa Florio, the Nurburgring, Fangio and Moss and Gonzales, Kling, Trintignant, the Marquis de Portago: *all the live murmur of a summer's day,* as the poet says.

There is a bliss in stamp collecting that only stamp collectors know. As the enthusiast sits at the stop light in his Grand Prix Bugatti, converted for road use by the addition of a couple of bicycle fenders, he gets a stare of wondering contempt from the engineer of the leviathan beside him, a stare that says, "Some car! It's the size of a coaster wagon, it hasn't even got Hydra-Matic, in a year more it'll be old enough to vote. Why don't you get wise to yourself and buy a real car?"

A few thousand of these stares and the enthusiast begins composing a look of his own. A friend of mine, a rhetorician and MG owner from way back, once put the look into words, and the words went:

"Someday as your Cadillac Imperial drives you along the highway —the days when you drove it are long gone by—look down from your high window, your power-operated window, at the couple below you, there at the stop light. They are different from you, very different . . . and yet they look happy. You have a tail twelve feet long, with fins as high as their windshield; you have a trunk large enough to hold their little bug of a car and the tugs you use to park your own; you billow along on springs so custardy-smooth, tires so supercushioning that you need power steering just to turn your steering wheel. You have acquired, to move you from place to place, a two-and-a-half-ton estate on wheels: here and there about your grounds, on the broad expanse of a deck or fender, one sees objects of art or utility, in finest chromium, placed there by the hand of a master landscape gardener. If Rousseau could see you he would scratch his fur hat and murmur: 'Man was born free, yet everywhere we see him in Cadillacs.'

"Why should every driver need a machine to shift gears for him? I need one about as much as I need a machine to eat strawberries for me. My MG has, just under my hand, a little black lever that goes from gear to gear like a Nuremberg egg the goblins have made for me on special order—and I'm in the gear *I* want to be in, not the one a mentally deficient mechanical brain has decided I'd be better off in. And when I want to go around a corner I don't need sea room and some sailors singing 'Blow the Man Down' to haul away until the steering wheel's come full circle and the corner's negotiated—I move my hand six inches and we're in the next street. Curves? Hah! There *are* no curves in an MG!"

We used to have an MG. People laughed at us, but it was worth it. "It'd be a nice little car to collect eggs under the barn in," a farmerly man said to us at a stop light. We smiled up at him. "Look, Mother," a little boy said. "Don't point at the people in the car," his mother said. "It's not a car, it's an MG," he said. We smiled up at him. Children would come to us and beg for rides—children love MG's; Schatzel, our dachshund, would come and jump up in the MG and hope. Other MG drivers would wave to us, and we would wave to them; when, waking in the night, I'd hear the distant snarl of an MG shifting gears, I would know that out there in the darkness was somebody who wanted to wave to me.

We called our MG Little Teakettle—anyway, we called it that once—because of the noise it made at an honest fifty-nine miles an hour: a sleepy bubbling sound, inexpressibly contenting. Ours was black, a classic black, but we'd painted the wheels and grille and dash a beautiful mermaid's-eye blue; people would look admiringly at it, though none so admiringly as we. When we would see an MG that had had nothing done to it we would shake our heads, sorrowing, and say: "Stock."

Even in snowstorms the children would say, "Oh, *no,* let's take the MG"; the smaller would sit on a pillow over the racing brake, the larger would fit herself, segment by segment, into the well, and off we went, as happy as anchovies. Snow-covered expanses were always hard for us to resist; we'd drive over the abandoned golf course at the college, get stuck in snow-covered ditches, and call to the girls sledding, who would come and push us out. And in summer, driving a few blocks to the beach, we've carried three grown-ups—one a grandmother—two children, a dachshund, two kittens named Jason and Medea, a picnic basket, an air mattress, a beach umbrella, and an inner tube.

Now, of course, we have the Mercedes. Ours is a sports car; white, with red leather; so beautiful we still walk away from it backward. Imitate Phil Hill as you will: no wheel lifts. Drive onto the shoulder at sixty: nothing happens. Leaning back in our leather armchairs, warmed, ventilated, serene, Mary and I sigh luxuriously. "Isn't it *nice* we have our beautiful car!" our little Beatrice sighs from the back seat—if seat it can be called; and Alleyne, fitted against her like a jigsaw puzzle, makes a loving, loyal, strangled sound.

When we got the car we bought four cases of Pilsner Urquell, the Only Genuine Pilsner; it'd hardly be right for the drivers of a Mercedes to drink domestic beer, do you think? I have a German general's leather overcoat I bought in Austria; it weighs forty pounds and is warm as a summer blanket, and in it I look so—so lifelike and terrifying that a foot away nobody can tell it isn't a real, live general. When I wear it and Mary wears a Garbo- or lady-spy-type trench coat and we speed along, all sleek and white and low, with little Negro children calling to us, sweet as song sparrows, "Go, man, go!"—why, then we feel like Toad in *The Wind in the Willows* when he saw his first car: "Glorious, stirring sight! The poetry of motion! The *real* way to travel! Here today—in next week tomorrow! . . . And to think I never even *knew!* All those wasted years that lie behind me, I never knew, never even *dreamt!* That swan, that sunbeam, that thunderbolt!" And when we park our swan, our sunbeam, our thunderbolt, the passers-by go round and round it wide-eyed, open-mouthed, and ask us what it is, and we tell them. Only the other day a man came up to the car, and looked, and looked, and finally said: "Is that a homemade car?" After a minute my wife said no, and he said, turning to leave us: "There's a guy on the Burlington Road that makes cars like that for people."

We mean to keep it till we die. And yet we keep reading the used-car advertisements in the *Times* and *Road and Track* and *The Autocar:* we can't help thinking how nice it would be to have another Mercedes. A 300SL, for instance, has fuel injection and gull-wing doors, and with a high-speed axle will do 167. It's not that I *want* to do 167, but it'd be a nice thing to have in reserve for Judgment Day. And 540K's! They really are the classic car to end all classic cars—why, children could have a bobsled race down the front fenders, and the ignition keys weigh half a pound and look as if they'd been designed by Dürer for a draw-bridge.

And—and we keep meeting our MG. It's had a wreck, and the left front fender's gone. It was the fault of the lady in the other car, and her insurance company is paying for a new fender, but just the same, we can't help thinking, *we'd* have dodged her. That poor rusty crumpled fender! Maybe we should have kept the MG—lots of families that hardly care about cars at all have two cars. If I had a 300SL and Mary had the 190SL and Alleyne—Alleyne's had a driving course and could have the 540K—no, that wouldn't do, they didn't teach her to shift gears; but the MG would be just the right size for Beatrice, when she gets a little older and needs a car. And then there're the cats and Schatzel . . .

Cars, cars!

Against Abstract Expressionism

ART NEWS, SUMMER 1957

A DEVIL'S ADVOCATE opposes, as logically and forcibly as he can, the canonization of a new saint. What he says is dark, and serves the light. The devil himself, if one can believe Goethe, is only a sort of devil's advocate. Here I wish to act as one for abstract expressionism.

Continued long enough, a quantitative change becomes qualitative. The latest tradition of painting, abstract expressionism, seems to me revolutionary. It is not, I think, what it is sometimes called: the purified essence of that earlier tradition which has found a temporary conclusion in painters like Bonnard, Picasso, Matisse, Klee, Kokoschka. It is the specialized, intensive exploitation of one part of such painting, and the rejection of other parts and of the whole.

Earlier painting is a kind of metaphor: the world of the painting itself, of the oil-and-canvas objects and their oil-and-canvas relations, is one that stands for—that has come into being because of—the world of flesh-and-blood objects and their flesh-and-blood relations, the "very world, which is the world / Of all of us,—the place where, in the end, / We find our happiness or not at all." The relation between the representing and the represented world sometimes is a direct, mimetic one; but often it is an indirect, farfetched, surprising relation, so that it is the difference between the subject and the painting of it that is insisted upon, and is a principal source of our pleasure. In the metaphors of painting, as in those of poetry, we are awed or dazed to find things superficially so unlike, fundamentally so like; superficially so like, fundamentally so unlike. Solemn things are painted gaily; overwhelmingly expressive things—the Flagellation, for instance—painted inexpressively; Vollard is painted like an apple, and an apple like the Fall; the female is made male or sexless (as in Michelangelo's *Night*), and a dreaming, acquiescent femininity is made to transfigure a body factually

285

masculine (as in so many of the nude youths on the ceiling of the Sistine Chapel). Between the object and its representation there is an immense distance: within this distance much of painting lives.

All this sums itself up for me in one image. In Georges de La Tour's *St. Sebastian Mourned by St. Irene* there is, in the middle of a dark passage, a light one: four parallel cylinders diagonally intersected by four parallel cylinders; they look like a certain sort of wooden fence, as a certain sort of cubist painter would have painted it; they are the hands, put together in prayer, of one of St. Irene's companions. As one looks at what has been put into—withheld from—the hands, one is conscious of a mixture of emotion and empathy and contemplation; one is moved, and is unmoved, and is something else one has no name for, that transcends either affect or affectlessness. The hands are truly like hands, yet they are almost more truly unlike hands; they resemble (as so much of art resembles) the symptomatic gestures of psychoanalysis, half the expression of a wish and half the defense against the wish. But these parallel cylinders of La Tour's—these hands at once oil-and-canvas and flesh-and-blood; at once dynamic processes in the virtual space of the painting, and spiritual gestures in the "very world" in which men are martyred, are mourned, and paint the mourning and the martyrdom— these parallel cylinders are only, in an abstract expressionist painting, four parallel cylinders: they are what they are.

You may say, more cruelly: "If they are part of such a painting, by what miracle have they remained either cylindrical or parallel? In this world bursting with action and accident—the world, that is, of abstract expressionism—are they anything more than four homologous strokes of the paintbrush, inclinations of the paint bucket; the memory of four gestures, and of the four convulsions of the Unconscious that accompanied them? . . . We need not ask—they are what they are: four oil-and-canvas processes in an oil-and-canvas continuum; and if, greatly daring, we venture beyond this world of the painting itself, we end only in the painter himself. A universe has been narrowed into what lies at each end of a paintbrush."

But ordinarily such painting—a specialized, puritanical reduction of earlier painting—is presented to us as its final evolution, what it always ought to have been and therefore "really" was. When we are told (or, worse still, shown) that painting "really" is "nothing but" this, we are being given one of those definitions which explain out of existence what they appear to define, and put a simpler entity in its place. If this is all that painting is, why, what painting was was hardly painting. Everyone has met some of the rigorously minded people who carry this process of reasoning to its conclusion, and value Piero della Francesca and Goya and Cézanne only in so far as their paintings are, in adulterated essence, the paintings of Jackson Pollock. Similarly, a few centuries ago, one of those mannerist paintings in which a Virgin's face is setting after having swallowed alum must have seemed, to a contemporary, what a Donatello Virgin was "really" intended to be, "essentially" was.

The painting before abstract expressionism might be compared to projective geometry: a large three-dimensional world of objects and their relations, of lives, emotions, significances, is represented by a small cross section of the rays from this world, as they intersect a plane. Everything in the cross section has two different kinds of relations: a direct relation to the other things in the cross section, and an indirect—so to speak, transcendental—relation to what it represents in the larger world. And there are also in the small world of the picture process many absences or impossible presences, things which ought to be there but are not, things which could not possibly be there but are. The painter changes and distorts, simplifies or elaborates the cross section; and the things in the larger world resist, and are changed by, everything he does, just as what he has done is changed by their resistance. Earlier painters, from Giotto to Picasso, have dealt with two worlds and the relations between the two: their painting is a heterogeneous, partly indirect, many-leveled, extraordinarily complicated process. Abstract expressionism has kept one part of this process, but has rejected as completely as it could the other part and all the relations that depend on the existence of this other part; it has substituted for a heterogeneous, polyphonic process a homogeneous, homophonic process. One sees in abstract expressionism the terrible aesthetic disadvantages of directness and consistency. Perhaps painting can do without the necessity of imitation; can it do without the possibility of distortion?

As I considered some of the phrases that have been applied to abstract expressionism—revolutionary; highly non-communicative; non-representational; uncritical; personal; maximizing randomness; without connection with literature and the other arts; spontaneous; exploiting chance or unintended effects; based on gesture; seeking a direct connection with the Unconscious; affirming the individual; rejecting the external world; emphasizing action and the process of making the picture—it occurred to me that each of them applied to the work of a painter about whom I had just been reading. She has been painting only a little while, yet most of her paintings have already found buyers, and her friends hope, soon, to use the money to purchase a husband for the painter. She is a chimpanzee at the Baltimore Zoo. Why should I have said to myself, as I did say: "I am living in the first age that has ever bought a chimpanzee's paintings"? It would not have occurred to me to buy her pictures—it would not have occurred to me even to get her to paint them; yet in the case of action painting, is it anything but unreasoning prejudice which demands that the painter be a man? Hath not an ape hands? Hath not an animal an Unconscious, and quite a lot less Ego and Superego to interfere with its operations?

I reminded myself of this as, one Saturday, I watched on Channel 9 a chimpanzee painting; I did not even say to myself, "I am living in the first age that has ever televised a chimpanzee painting." I watched him (since he was dressed in a jumper, and named Jeff, I judged that he was a male) dispassionately. His painting, I confess, did not interest me; I had seen it too many times before. But the way in which he painted it! He was, truly, magistral. He did not look at his model once; indeed, he hardly looked even at the canvas. Sometimes his brush ran out of paint and he went on with the dry brush—they had to remind him that the palette was there. He was the most active, the most truly sincere, painter that I have ever seen; and yet, what did it all produce?—nothing but that same old abstract expressionist painting . . .

I am joking. But I hope it is possible to say of this joke what Goethe said of Lichtenberg's: "Under each of his jokes there is a problem." There is an immense distance between my poor chimpanzee's dutiful, joyful paintings and those of Jackson Pollock. The elegance, force, and command of Pollock's best paintings are apparent at a glance—are, indeed, far more quickly and obviously apparent than the qualities of a painter like Chardin. But there is an immense distance, too, between Pollock's paintings and Picasso's; and this not entirely the result of a difference of native genius. If Picasso had limited himself to painting the pictures of Jackson Pollock—limited himself, that is, to the part of his own work that might be called abstract expressionism— could he have been as great a painter as he is? I ask this as a typical, general question; if I spoke particularly I should of course say: If Picasso limited himself in anything he would not be Picasso: he loves the world so much he wants to steal it and eat it. Pollock's anger at things is greater than Picasso's, but his appetite for them is small; is neurotically restricted. Much of the world—much, too, of the complication and contradiction, the size and depth of the essential process of earlier painting—is inaccessible to Pollock. It has been made inaccessible by the provincialism that is one of the marks of our age.

As I go about the world I see things (people; their looks and feelings and thoughts; the things their thoughts have made, and the things that neither they nor their thoughts had anything to do with making: the whole range of the world) that, I cannot help feeling, Piero della Francesca or Brueghel or Goya or Cézanne would paint if they were here now—could not resist painting. Then I say to my wife, sadly: "What a pity we didn't live in an age when painters were still interested in the world!" This is an exaggeration, of course; even in the recent past many painters have looked at the things of this world and seen them as marvelously as we could wish. But ordinarily, except for photographers and illustrators—and they aren't at all the same—the things of our world go unseen, unsung. All that the poet must do, Rilke said, is praise: to look at what is, and to see that it is good, and to make out of it what is at once the same and better, is to praise. Doesn't the world need the painter's praise any more?

Malraux, drunk with our age, can say about Cézanne: "It is not the mountain he wants to realize but the picture." All that Cézanne said and did was not enough to make Malraux understand what no earlier age could have failed to understand: that to Cézanne the realization of the picture necessarily involved the realization of the mountain. And whether we like it or not, notice it or not, the mountain is still there to be realized. Man and the world are all that they ever were—their attractions are, in the end, irresistible; the painter will not hold out against them long.

The Taste of the Age

THE SATURDAY EVENING POST, JULY 26, 1958

WHEN WE LOOK at the age in which we live—no matter what age it happens to be—it is hard for us not to be depressed by it. The taste of the age is, always, a bitter one. "What kind of a time is this when one must envy the dead and buried!" said Goethe about his age; yet Matthew Arnold would have traded his own time for Goethe's almost as willingly as he would have traded his own self for Goethe's. How often, after a long day witnessing elementary education, School Inspector Arnold came home, sank into what I hope was a Morris chair, looked around him at the Age of Victoria, that Indian Summer of the Western World, and gave way to a wistful, exacting, articulate despair!

Do people feel this way because our time is worse than Arnold's, and Arnold's than Goethe's, and so on back to Paradise? Or because forbidden fruits—the fruits forbidden us by time—are always the sweetest? Or because we can never compare our own age with an earlier age, but only with books about that age?

We say that somebody doesn't know what he is missing; Arnold, pretty plainly, didn't know what he was having. The people who live in a Golden Age usually go around complaining how yellow everything looks. Maybe we too are living in a Golden or, anyway, Gold-Plated Age, and the people of the future will look back at us and say ruefully: "We never had it so good." And yet the thought that they will say this isn't as reassuring as it might be. We can see that Goethe's and Arnold's ages weren't as bad as Goethe and Arnold thought them: after all, they produced Goethe and Arnold. In the same way, our times may not be as bad as we think them: after all, they have produced us. Yet this too is a thought that isn't as reassuring as it might be.

A Tale of Two Cities begins by saying that the times were, as always, "the best of times, the worst of times!" If we judge by wealth and power, our times are the best of times; if the times have made us willing to judge by wealth and power, they are the worst of times. But most of us still judge by more: by literature and the arts, science and philosophy, education. (Really we judge by more than these: by love and wisdom; but how are we to say whether our own age is wiser and more loving than another?) I wish to talk to you for a time about what is happening to the audience for the arts and literature, and to the education that prepares this audience, here in the United States.

In some ways this audience is improving, has improved, tremendously. Today it is as easy for us to get *Falstaff* or *Boris Godunov* or *Ariadne auf Naxos,* or Landowska playing *The Well-Tempered Clavichord,* or Fischer-Dieskau singing *Die Schöne Müllerin,* or Richter playing Beethoven's piano sonatas, as it used to be to get Mischa Elman playing *Humoresque.* Several hundred thousand Americans bought Toscanini's recording of Beethoven's Ninth Symphony. Some of them played it only to show how faithful their phonographs are; some of them played it only as the stimulus for an hour of random, homely rumination. But many of them really listened to the records—and, later, went to hear the artists who made the records—and, later, bought for themselves, got to know and love, compositions that a few years ago nobody but musicologists or musicians of the most advanced tastes had even read the scores of. That there are sadder things about the state of music here, I know; still, we are better off than we were twenty-five or thirty years ago. Better off, too, so far as the ballet is concerned: it is our good fortune to have had the greatest influence on American ballet the influence of the greatest choreographer who ever lived, that "Mozart of choreographers," George Balanchine.

Here today the visual arts are—but I don't know whether to borrow my simile from the Bible, and say *flourishing like the green bay tree,* or to borrow it from Shakespeare and say *growing like a weed.* We are producing paintings and reproductions of paintings, painters and reproductions of painters, teachers and museum directors and gallery-goers and patrons of the arts, in almost celestial quantities. Most of the painters are bad or mediocre, of course—this is so, necessarily, in any art at any time—but the good ones find shelter in numbers, are bought, employed, and looked at like the rest. The people of the past rejected Cézanne, Monet, Renoir, the many great painters they did not understand; by liking and encouraging, without exception, all the painters they do not understand, the people of the present have made it impossible for this to happen again.

Our society, it turns out, can use modern art. A restaurant, today, will order a mural by Miró in as easy and matter-of-fact a spirit as, twenty-five years ago, it would have ordered one by Maxfield Parrish. The president of a paint factory goes home, sits down by his fireplace— it *looks* like a chromium aquarium set into the wall by a wall-safe company that has branched out into interior decorating, but there is a log burning in it, he calls it a fireplace, let's call it a fireplace too—the president sits down, folds his hands on his stomach, and stares relishingly at two paintings by Jackson Pollock that he has hung on the wall opposite him. He feels at home with them; in fact, as he looks at them he not only feels at home, he feels as if he were back at the paint factory. And his children—if he has any—his children cry for Calder. He uses thoroughly advanced, wholly non-representational artists to design murals, posters, institutional advertisements: if we have the patience (or are given the opportunity) to wait until the West has declined a little longer, we shall all see the advertisements of Merrill Lynch, Pierce, Fenner, and Smith illustrated by Jean Dubuffet.

This president's minor executives may not be willing to hang a Kandinsky in the house, but they will wear one, if you make it into a sport shirt or a pair of swimming trunks; and if you make it into a sofa, they will lie on it. They and their wives and children will sit on a porcupine, if you first exhibit it at the Museum of Modern Art and say that it is a chair. In fact, there is nothing, nothing in the whole world that someone won't buy and sit in if you tell him that it is a chair: the great new art form of our age, the one that will take anything we put in it, is the chair. If Hieronymus Bosch, if Christian Morgenstern, if the Marquis de Sade were living at this hour, what chairs they would be designing!

Our architecture is flourishing too. Even colleges have stopped rebuilding the cathedrals of Europe on their campuses; and a mansion, today, is what it is, not because a millionaire has dreamed of the Alhambra, but because an architect has dreamed of the marriage of Frank Lloyd Wright and a silo. We Americans have the best factories anyone has ever designed; we have many schools, post offices, and public buildings that are, so far as one can see, the best factories anyone has ever designed; we have many delightful, or efficient, or extraordinary houses. The public that lives in the houses our architects design—most houses, of course, are not designed, but just happen to a contractor—this public is a broad-minded, tolerant, adventurous public, one that has triumphed over inherited prejudice to an astonishing degree. You can put a spherical plastic gas tower on aluminum stilts, divide it into rooms, and quite a few people will be willing to crawl along saying, "Is this the floor? Is this the wall?"—to make a down payment, and to call it home. I myself welcome this spirit, a spirit worthy of Captain Nemo, of Rossum's Universal Robots, of the inhabitants of the Island of Laputa; when in a few years some young

American airmen are living in a space satellite part way to the moon, more than one of them will be able to look around and think: "It's a home just like Father used to make," if his father was an architect.

But in the rest of the arts, the arts that use words—

But here you may interrupt me, saying: "You've praised or characterized or made fun of the audience for music, dancing, painting, furniture, and architecture, yet each time you've talked only about the crust of the pie, about things that apply to hundreds of thousands, not to hundreds of millions. Most people don't listen to classical music at all, but to rock-and-roll or hillbilly songs or some album named Music To Listen To Music By; they've never seen any ballet except a television ballet or some musical comedy's last echo of *Rodeo*. When they go home they sit inside chairs like imitation-leather haystacks, chairs that were exhibited not at the Museum of Modern Art but at a convention of furniture dealers in High Point; if they buy a picture they buy it from the furniture dealer, and it was the furniture dealer who painted it; and their houses are split-level ranch-type rabbit warrens. Now that you've come to the 'arts that use words,' are you going to keep on talking about the unhappy few, or will you talk for a change about the happy many?"

I'll talk about the happy many; about the hundreds of millions, not the hundreds of thousands. Where words and the hundreds of thousands are concerned, plenty of good things happen—though to those who love words and the arts that use them, it may all seem far from plenty. We do have good writers, perhaps more than we deserve—and good readers, perhaps fewer than the writers deserve. But when it comes to tens of millions of readers, hundreds of millions of hearers and viewers, we are talking about a new and strange situation; and to understand why this situation is what it is, we need to go back in time a little way, back to the days of Matthew Arnold and Queen Victoria.

II

We all remember that Queen Victoria, when she died in 1901, had never got to see a helicopter, a television set, penicillin, an electric refrigerator; yet she *had* seen railroads, electric lights, textile machinery, the telegraph—she came about midway in the industrial and technological revolution that has transformed our world. But there are a good many other things, of a rather different sort, that Queen Victoria never got to see, because she came at the very beginning of another sort of half-technological, half-cultural revolution. Let me give some examples.

If the young Queen Victoria had said to the Duke of Wellington: "Sir, the Bureau of Public Relations of Our army is in a deplorable state," he would have answered: "What is a Bureau of Public Relations, ma'am?" When he and his generals wanted to tell lies, they had to tell them themselves; there was no organized institution set up to do it for them. But of course Queen Victoria couldn't have made any such remark, since she too had never heard of public relations. She had never seen, or heard about, or dreamed of an advertising agency; she had never seen—unless you count Barnum—a press agent; she had never seen a photograph of a sex slaying in a tabloid—had never seen a tabloid. People gossiped about her, but not in gossip columns; she had never heard a commentator, a soap opera, a quiz program. Queen Victoria—think of it!—had never heard a singing commercial, never seen an advertisement beginning: *Science says . . .* and if she *had* seen one she would only have retorted: "And what, pray, does the Archbishop of Canterbury say? What does dear good Albert say?"

When some comedian or wit—Sydney Smith, for example—told Queen Victoria jokes, they weren't supplied him by six well-paid gag writers, but just occurred to him. When Disraeli and Gladstone made speeches for her government, the speeches weren't written for them by ghost writers; when Disraeli and Gladstone sent her lovingly or respectfully inscribed copies of their new books, they had written the books themselves. There they were, with the resources of an empire at their command, and they wrote the books themselves! And Queen Victoria had to read the books herself: nobody was willing—or able—to digest them for her in *Reader's Digest,* or to make movies of them, or to make radio or television programs of them, so that she could experience them painlessly and effortlessly. In those days people chewed their own food or went hungry; we have changed all that.

Queen Victoria never went to the movies and had an epic costing eight million dollars injected into her veins—she never went to the movies. She never read a drugstore book by Mickey Spillane; even if she had had a moral breakdown and had read a Bad Book, it would just have been *Under Two Flags* or something by Marie Corelli. She had never been interviewed by, or read the findings of, a Gallup Poll. She never read the report of a commission of sociologists subsidized by the Ford Foundation; she never Adjusted herself to her Group, or Shared the Experience of her Generation, or breathed a little deeper to feel herself a part of the Century of the Common Man—she *was* a part of it for almost two years, but she didn't know that that was what it was.

And all the other people in the world were just like Queen Victoria.

Isn't it plain that it is all *these* lacks that make Queen Victoria so old-fashioned, so finally and awfully different from us, rather than the fact that she never flew in an airplane, or took insulin, or had a hydrogen bomb dropped on her? Queen Victoria in a DC-7 would be Queen Victoria still—I can hear her saying to the stewardess: "We do not wish Dramamine"; but a Queen Victoria who listened every day to *John's Other Wife, Portia Faces Life,* and *Just Plain Bill*—that wouldn't be Queen Victoria at all!

There has been not one revolution, an industrial and technological revolution, there have been two; and this second, cultural revolution might be called the Revolution of the Word. People have learned to process words too—words, and the thoughts and attitudes they embody: we manufacture entertainment and consolation as efficiently as we manufacture anything else. One sees in stores ordinary old-fashioned oatmeal or cocoa; and, side by side with it, another kind called Instant Cocoa, Instant Oats. Most of our literature—I use the word in its broadest sense—is Instant Literature: the words are short, easy, instantly recognizable words, the thoughts are easy, familiar, instantly recognizable thoughts, the attitudes are familiar, already-agreed-upon, instantly acceptable attitudes. And if all this is true, can these productions be either truth or—in the narrower and higher sense—literature? The truth, as everybody knows, is sometimes complicated or hard to understand; is sometimes almost unrecognizably different from what we expected it to be; is sometimes difficult or, even, impossible to accept. But literature is necessarily mixed up with truth, isn't it?—our truth, truth as we know it; one can almost define literature as the union of a wish and a truth, or as a wish modified by a truth. But this Instant Literature is a wish reinforced by a cliché, a wish proved by a lie: Instant Literature—whether it is a soap opera, a Broadway play, or a historical, sexual best-seller—tells us always that life is not only what we wish it, but also what we think it. When people are treating him as a lunatic who has to be humored, Hamlet cries: "They fool me to the top of my bent"; and the makers of Instant Literature treat us exactly as advertisers treat the readers of advertisements—humor us, flatter our prejudices, pull our strings, show us that they know us for what they take us to be: impressionable, emotional, ignorant, somewhat weak-minded Common Men. They fool us to the top of our bent—and if we aren't fooled, they dismiss us as *a statistically negligible minority.*

An advertisement is a wish modified, if at all, by the Pure Food and Drug Act. Take a loaf of ordinary white bread that you buy at the grocery. As you eat it you know that you are eating it, and not the blotter, because the blotter isn't so bland; yet in the world of advertisements little boys ask their mother not to put any jam on their bread, it tastes so good without. This world of the advertisements is a literary world, of a kind: it is the world of Instant Literature. Think of some of the speeches we hear in political campaigns—aren't they too part of the world of Instant Literature? And the first story you read in *The Saturday Evening Post,* the first movie you go to at your neighborhood theater, the first dramatic program you hear on the radio, see on television—are these more like *Grimm's Tales* and *Alice in Wonderland* and *The Three Sisters* and *Oedipus Rex* and Shakespeare and the Bible, or are they more like political speeches and advertisements?

The greatest American industry—why has no one ever said so?—is the industry of using words. We pay tens of millions of people to spend their lives lying to us, or telling us the truth, or supplying us with a nourishing medicinal compound of the two. All of us are living in the middle of a dark wood—a bright Technicolored forest—of words, words, words. It is a forest in which the wind is never still: there isn't a tree in the forest that is not, for every moment of its life and our lives, persuading or ordering or seducing or overawing us into buying this, believing that, voting for the other.

And yet, the more words there are, the simpler the words get. The professional users of words process their product as if it were baby food and we babies: all we have to do is open our mouths and swallow. Most of our mental and moral food is quick-frozen, pre-digested, spoon-fed. E. M. Forster has said: "The only thing we learn from spoon-feeding is the shape of the spoon." Not only is this true—pretty soon, if anything doesn't have the shape of that spoon we won't swallow it, we can't swallow it. Our century has produced some great and much good literature, but the habitual readers of Instant Literature cannot read it; nor can they read the great and good literature of the past.

If Queen Victoria had got to read the *Reader's Digest*—awful thought!—she would have loved it; and it would have changed her. Everything in the world, in the *Reader's Digest*—I am using it as a convenient symbol for all that is like it—is a palatable, timely, ultimately reassuring anecdote, immediately comprehensible to everybody over, and to many under, the age of eight. Queen Victoria would notice that Albert kept quoting, from Shakespeare—that the Archbishop of Canterbury kept quoting, from the Bible—things that were very different from anything in the *Reader's Digest.* Sometimes these sentences were not reassuring but disquieting, sometimes they had big words or hard thoughts in them, sometimes the interest in them wasn't human, but literary or divine. After a while Queen Victoria would want Shakespeare and the Bible—would want Albert, even—digested for her beforehand by the *Reader's Digest.* And a little further on in this process of digestion, she would look from the *Reader's Digest* to some magazine the size of your palm, called *Quick* or *Pic* or *Click* or *The Week in TV,* and a strange half-sexual yearning would move like musk through her veins, and she would—

But I cannot, I will not say it. You and I know how she and Albert will end: sitting before the television set, staring into it, silent; and inside the set, there are Victoria and Albert, staring into the television camera, silent, and the master of ceremonies is saying to them: "No, I think you will find that *Bismarck* is the capital of North Dakota!"

But for so long as she still reads, Queen Victoria will be able to get the Bible and Shakespeare—though not, alas! Albert—in some specially prepared form. Fulton Oursler or Fulton J. Sheen or a thousand others are always rewriting the Bible; there are many comic-book versions of Shakespeare; and only the other day I read an account of an interesting project of rewriting Shakespeare "for students":

Philadelphia, Pa. Feb. 1. (AP)

Two high school teachers have published a simplified version of Shakespeare's "Julius Caesar" and plan to do the same for "Macbeth." Their goal is to make the plays more understandable to youth.

The teachers, Jack A. Waypen and Leroy S. Layton, say if the Bible can be revised and modernized why not Shakespeare? They made 1,122 changes in "Julius Caesar" from single words to entire passages. They modernized obsolete words and expressions and substituted "you" for "thee" and "thou."

Shakespeare had Brutus say in Act III, Scene I:

Fates, we will know your pleasures;
That we shall die, we know; 'tis but the time
And drawing days out, that men stand upon.

In the Waypen-Layton version, Brutus says:

We will soon know what Fate decrees for us.
That we shall die, we know. It's putting off
The time of death that's of concern to men.

Not being Shakespeare, I can't find a comment worthy of this, this project. I am tempted to say in an Elizabethan voice: "Ah, wayward Waypen, lascivious Layton, lay down thine errant pen!" And yet if I said this to them they would only reply earnestly, uncomprehendingly, sorrowfully: "Can't you give us some *con*structive criticism, not *de*structive? Why don't you say *your* errant pen, not *thine?* And *lascivious!* Mr. Jarrell, if you *have* to talk about that type subject, don't say *lascivious* Layton, say *sexy* Layton!"

Even Little Red Ridinghood is getting too hard for children, I read. The headline of the story is CHILD'S BOOKS BEING MADE MORE SIMPLE; the story comes from New York, is distributed by the International News Service, and is written by Miss Olga Curtis. Miss Curtis has interviewed Julius Kushner, the head of a firm that has been publishing children's books longer than anyone else in the country. He tells Miss Curtis:

"Non-essential details have disappeared from the 1953 Little Red Ridinghood story. Modern children enjoy their stories better stripped down to basic plot—for instance, Little Red Ridinghood meets wolf, Little Red Ridinghood escapes wolf. [I have a comment: the name Little Red Ridinghood seems to me both long and non-essential—why not call the child Red, and strip the story down to Red meets wolf, Red escapes wolf? At this rate, one could tell a child all of Grimm's tales between dinner and bedtime.]

" 'We have to keep up with the mood of each generation,' Kushner explained. 'Today's children like stories condensed to essentials, and with visual and tactile appeal as well as interesting content.'

"Modernizing old favorites, Kushner said, is fundamentally a matter of simplifying. Kushner added that today's children's books are intended to be activity games as well as reading matter. He mentioned books that make noises when pressed, and books with pop-up three-dimensional illustrations as examples of publishers' efforts to make each book a teaching aid as well as a story."

As one reads one sees before one, as if in a vision, the children's book of the future: a book that, pressed, says: *I'm your friend;* teaches the child that Crime Does Not Pay; does not exceed thirty words; can be used as a heating pad if the electric blanket breaks down; and has three-dimensional illustrations dyed with harmless vegetable coloring matter and flavored with pure vanilla. I can hear the children of the future crying: "Mother, read us another vanilla book!"

But by this time you must be thinking, as I am, of one of the more frightening things about our age: that much of the body of common knowledge that educated people (and many uneducated people) once had, has disappeared or is rapidly disappearing. Fairy tales, myths, proverbs, history—the Bible and Shakespeare and Dickens, the *Odyssey* and *Gulliver's Travels*—these and all the things like them are surprisingly often things that most of an audience won't understand an allusion to, a joke about. These things were the ground on which the people of the past came together. Much of the wit or charm or elevation of any writing or conversation with an atmosphere depends upon this presupposed, easily and affectionately remembered body of common knowledge; because of it we understand things, feel about things, as human beings and not as human animals.

Who teaches us all this? Our families, our friends, our schools, society in general. Most of all, we hope, our schools. When I say *schools* I mean grammar schools and high schools and colleges—but the first two are more important. Most people still don't go to college, and those who do don't get there until they are seventeen or eighteen. "Give us a child until he is seven and he is ours," a Jesuit is supposed to have said; the grammar schools and high schools of the United States have a child for ten years longer, and then he is—whose? Shakespeare's? Leroy S. Layton's? The *Reader's Digest*'s? When students at last leave high school or go on to college, what are they like?

III

College teachers continually complain about their students' "lack of preparation," just as, each winter, they complain about the winter's lack of snow. Winters don't have as much snow as winters used to have: things are going to the dogs and always have been. The teachers tell one another stories about The Things Their Students Don't Know—it surprises you, after a few thousand such stories, that the students manage to find their way to the college. And yet, I have to admit, I have as many stories as the rest; and, veteran of such conversations as I am, I am continually being astonished at the things my students don't know.

One dark, cold, rainy night—the sort of night on which clients came to Sherlock Holmes—I read in a magazine that winters don't have as much snow as winters used to have; according to meteorologists, the climate *is* changing. Maybe the students are changing too. One is always hearing how much worse, or how much better, schools are than they used to be. But one isn't any longer going to grammar school, or to high school either; one isn't, like Arnold, a school inspector; whether one believes or disbelieves, blames or praises, how little one has to go on! Hearing one child say to another: "What does E come after in the alphabet?" makes a great, and perhaps unfair, impression on one. The child may not be what is called a random sample.

Sitting in my living room by the nice warm fire, and occasionally looking with pleasure at the rain and night outside—how glad I was that I wasn't in them!—I thought of some other samples I had seen just that winter, and I wasn't sure whether they were random, either. That winter I had had occasion to talk with some fifth-grade students and some eighth-grade students; I had gone to a class of theirs; I had even gone caroling, in a truck, with some Girl Scouts and their Scout-mistress, and had been dismayed at all the carols I didn't know—it was a part of my education that had been neglected.

I was not dismayed at the things the children hadn't known, I was overawed; there were very few parts of their education that had not been neglected. Half the fifth-grade children—you won't, just as I couldn't, believe this—didn't know who Jonah was; only a few had ever heard of King Arthur. When I asked an eighth-grade student about King Arthur she laughed at my question, and said: "Of course I know who King Arthur was." My heart warmed to her *of course*. But she didn't know who Lancelot was, didn't know who Guinevere was; she had never heard of Sir Galahad. I realized with a pang the truth of the line of poetry that speaks of "those familiar, now unfamiliar knights that sought the Grail." I left the Knights of the Round Table for history: she didn't know who Charlemagne was.

She didn't know who Charlemagne was! And she had never heard of Alexander the Great; her class had "had Rome," but she didn't remember anything about Julius Caesar, though she knew his name. I asked her about Hector and Achilles: she had heard the name Hector, but didn't know who he was; she had never heard of "that other one."

I remembered the college freshman who, when I had asked her about "They that take the sword shall perish with the sword," had answered: "It's Shakespeare, I think"; and the rest of the class hadn't even known it was Shakespeare. Nobody in the class had known the difference between faith and works. And how shocked they had all been—the Presbyterians especially—at the notion of predestination!

But all these, except for the question of where E comes in the alphabet, had been questions of literature, theology, and European history; maybe there *are* more important things for students to know. The little girl who didn't know who Charlemagne was had been taught, I found, to conduct a meeting, to nominate, and to second nominations; she had been taught—I thought this, though farfetched, truly imaginative—the right sort of story to tell an eighteen-months-old baby; and she had learned in her Domestic Science class to bake a date pudding, to make a dirndl skirt, and from the remnants of the cloth to make a drawstring carryall. She could not tell me who Charlemagne was, it is true, but if I were an eighteen-months-old baby I could go to her and be sure of having her tell me the right sort of story. I felt a senseless depression at this; and thought, to alleviate it, of the date pudding she would be able to bake me.

I said to myself about her, as I was getting into the habit of saying about each new eighth-grade girl I talked to: "She must be an exception"; pretty soon I was saying: "She *must* be an exception!" If I had said this to her teacher she would have replied: "Exception indeed! She's a nice, normal, well-adjusted girl. She's one of the drum majorettes and she's Vice-President of the Student Body; she's had two short stories in the school magazine and she made her own formal for the Sadie Hawkins dance. She's an *exceptionally* normal girl!" And what could I have answered? "But she doesn't know who Charlemagne was"? You can see how ridiculous that would have sounded.

How many people cared whether or not she knew who Charlemagne was? How much good would knowing who Charlemagne was ever do her? Could you make a dirndl out of Charlemagne? make, even, a drawstring carryall? There was a chance—one chance in a hundred million—that someday, on a quiz program on the radio, someone would ask her who Charlemagne was. If she knew, the audience would applaud in wonder, and the announcer would give her a refrigerator; if she didn't know, the audience would groan in sympathy, and the announcer would give her a dozen cartons of soap powder. Euclid, I believe, once gave a penny to a student who asked: "What good will studying geometry do me?"—studying geometry made *him* a penny. But knowing who Charlemagne was would in all probability never make her a penny.

Another of the eighth-grade girls had shown me her Reader. All the eighth-grade students of several states use it; it is named *Adventures for Readers*. It has in it, just as Readers used to have in them, *The Man Without a Country* and *The Legend of Sleepy Hollow* and *Evangeline,* and the preface to *Adventures for Readers* says about their being there: "The competition of movies and radios has reduced the time young children spend with books. It is no longer supposed, as it once was, that reading skills are fully developed at the end of the sixth grade . . . Included are *The Man Without a Country, The Legend of Sleepy Hollow,* and *Evangeline.* These longer selections were once in every eighth grade reading book. They have disappeared because in the original they are far too difficult for eighth grade readers. Yet, they are never presented for other years. If they are not read in the eighth grade, they are not read at all. In their simplified form they are once more available to young people to become a part of their background and experience."

I thought that in the next edition of *Adventures for Readers* the editors would have to substitute for the phrase *the competition of movies and radios,* the phrase *the competition of movies, radios, and television:* I thought of this thought for some time. But when I thought of Longfellow's being *in the original* far too difficult for eighth-grade students, I—I did not know what to think. How much more difficult everything is than it used to be!

I remembered a letter, one about difficult writers, that I had read in *The Saturday Review.* The letter said: "I have been wondering when somebody with an established reputation in the field of letters would stand tiptoe and slap these unintelligibles in the face. Now I hope the publishers will wake up and throw the whole egotistical, sophist lot of them down the drain. I hope that fifty years from now nobody will remember that Joyce or Stein or James or Proust or Mann ever lived."

I knew that such feelings are not peculiar to our own place or age. Once while looking at an exhibition of Victorian posters and paintings and newspapers and needlework, I had read a page of the London *Times,* printed in the year 1851, that had on it a review of a new book by Alfred Tennyson. After several sentences about what was wrong with this book, the reviewer said: "Another fault is not particular to *In Memoriam;* it runs through all Mr. Tennyson's poetry— we allude to his obscurity." And yet the reviewer would not have alluded to Longfellow's obscurity; those Victorians for whom everything else was too difficult still understood and delighted in Longfellow. But Tennyson had been too obscure for some of them, just as Longfellow was getting to be too obscure for some of us, as our "reading skills" got less and less "fully developed."

This better-humored writer of the London *Times* had not hoped that in fifty years nobody would remember that Tennyson had ever lived; and this is fortunate, since he would not have got his wish. But I thought that the writer to *The Saturday Review* might well get, might already be getting, a part of his wish. How many people there were all around him who did not remember—who indeed had never learned—

that Proust or James or Mann or Joyce had ever lived! How many of them there were, and how many more of their children there were, who did not remember—who indeed had never learned—that Jonah or King Arthur or Galahad or Charlemagne had ever lived! And in the end all of us would die, and not know, then, that anybody had ever lived: and the writer to *The Saturday Review* would have got not part of his wish but all of it.

And if, in the meantime, some people grieved to think of so much gone and so much more to go, they were the exception. Or, rather, the exceptions: millions and millions—tens of millions, even— of exceptions. There were enough exceptions to make a good-sized country; I thought, with pleasure, of walking through the streets of that country and having the children tell me who Charlemagne was.

I decided not to think of Charlemagne any more, and turned my eyes from my absurd vision of the white-bearded king trying to learn to read, running his big finger slowly along under the words . . . My samples weren't really random, I knew; I was letting myself go, being exceptionally unjust to that exceptionally normal girl and the school that had helped to make her so. She was being given an education suitable for the world she was to use it in; my quarrel was not so much with her education as with her world, and our quarrels with the world are like our quarrels with God: no matter how right we are, we are wrong. But who wants to be right all the time? I thought, smiling; and said goodbye to Charlemagne with the same smile.

Instead of thinking, I looked at *The New York Times Book Review;* there in the midst of so many books, I could surely forget that some people don't read any. And after all, as Rilke says in one of his books, we are—some of us are—*beaten at / By books as if by perpetual bells;* we can well, as he bids us, *rejoice / When between two books the sky shines to you, silent.* In the beginning was the Word, and man has made books of it.

I read quietly along, but the review I was reading was continued on page 47; and as I was turning to page 47 I came to an advertisement, a two-page advertisement of the Revised Standard Version of the Bible. It was a sober, careful, authorized sort of advertisement, with many testimonials of clergymen, but it was, truly, an advertisement. It said:

"In these anxious days, the Bible offers a practical antidote for sorrow, cynicism, and despair. But the King James version is often difficult reading.

"If *you* have too seldom opened your Bible because the way it is written makes it hard for you to understand, the Revised Standard Version can bring you an exciting new experience.

"Here is a Bible so enjoyable you find you pick it up twice as often . . ."

Tennyson and Longfellow and the Bible—what *was* there that wasn't difficult reading? And a few days before that I had torn out of the paper—I got it and read it again, and it was hard for me to read it—a Gallup Poll that began: "Although the United States has the highest level of formal education in the world, fewer people here read books than in any other major democracy." It didn't compare us with minor autocracies, which are probably a lot worse. It went on to say that "fewer than one adult American in every five was found to be reading a book at the time of the survey. [Twenty years ago, 29 percent were found to be reading a book; today only 17 percent are.] In England, where the typical citizen has far less formal schooling than the typical citizen here, nearly three times as many read books. Even among American college graduates fewer than half read books."

It went on and on; I was so tired that, as I read, the phrase *read books* kept beating in my brain, and getting mixed up with Charlemagne: compared to other major monarchs, I thought sleepily, fewer than one-fifth of Charlemagne reads books. I read on as best as I could, but I thought of the preface to *Adventures for Readers,* and the letter to *The Saturday Review,* and the advertisement in *The New York Times Book Review,* and the highest level of formal education in the world, and they all went around and around in my head and said to me an advertisement named *Adventures for Non-Readers:*

"In these anxious days, reading books offers a practical antidote to sorrow, cynicism, and despair. But books are often, in the original, difficult reading.

"If *you* have too seldom opened books because the way they are written makes them hard for you to understand, our Revised Standard Versions of books, in their simplified, televised form, can bring you an exciting new experience.

"Here are books so enjoyable you find you turn them on twice as often."

I shook myself; I was dreaming. As I went to bed the words of the eighth-grade class's teacher, when the class got to *Evangeline,* kept echoing in my ears: "We're coming to a long poem now, boys and girls. Now don't be babies and start counting the pages." I lay there like a baby, counting the pages over and over, counting the pages.

Poets, Critics, and Readers

· ❀ ·

THE AMERICAN SCHOLAR, SUMMER 1959

PEOPLE often ask me: "Is there any poet who makes his living writing poetry?" and I have to say: "No." The public has an unusual relationship to the poet: it doesn't even know that he is there. Our public is a rich and generous one; if it knew that the poet was there, it would pay him for being there. As it is, poets make their living in many ways: by being obstetricians, like William Carlos Williams; or directors of Faber and Faber, like T. S. Eliot; or vice-presidents of the Hartford Accident and Indemnity Company, like Wallace Stevens. But most poets, nowadays, make their living by teaching. Kepler said, "God gives every animal a way to make its living, and He has given the astronomer astrology"; and now, after so many centuries, He has given us poets students. But what He gives with one hand He takes away with the other: He has taken away our readers.

Yet the poet can't help looking at what he has left, his students, with gratitude. His job may be an impossible one—there are three impossible tasks, said Freud: to teach, to govern, and to cure—but what is there so grateful as impossibility? and what is there better to teach, more nearly impossible to teach, than poems and stories? As Lord Macaulay says: "For how can man live better / Than facing fearful odds / For the poems of his fathers—"

I seem to have remembered it a little wrong, but it's a natural error. And, today, when we get people to read poems—to read very much of anything—naturally and joyfully, to read it not as an unnatural rightness but as a natural error: what people always have done, always will do—we do it against fearful odds. I can't imagine a better way for the poet to make his living. I certainly can't imagine his making his living by writing poems—I'm not *that* imaginative. I'm used to things as they are.

But there is a passage in Wordsworth that I read, always, with a rueful smile. He is answering the question, *Why write in verse?* He gives several reasons. His final reason, he writes, "is all that is *nec-*

essary to say upon this subject." Here it is, all that it is *necessary* to say upon this subject: "Few persons will deny, that of two descriptions, either of passions, manners, or characters, each of them equally well executed, the one in prose and the other in verse, the verse will be read a hundred times where the prose is read once."

One sees sometimes, carved on geology buildings: *O Earth, what changes thou hast seen!* When a poet finishes reading this passage from Wordsworth, he thinks in miserable awe: *O Earth, what changes thou hast seen!* Only a hundred and fifty years ago *this* is what people were like. Nowadays, of course, the prose will be read a thousand times where the verse is read once. And this seems to everybody only natural; the situation Wordsworth describes seems unnatural, improbable, almost impossible. What Douglas Bush writes is true: we live in "a time in which most people assume that, as an eminent social scientist once said to me, 'Poetry is on the way out.'" To most of us verse, any verse, is so uncongenial, so exhaustively artificial, that I have often thought that a man could make his fortune by entirely eliminating from our culture verse of any kind: in the end there would *be* no more poems, only prose translations of them. This man could begin by publishing his Revised Standard Version of *Mother Goose:* without rhyme, meter, or other harmful adulterants; with no word of anything but honest American prose, prose that cats and dogs can read.

A friend of mine once took a famous Italian scholar on a tour of New Haven. She specialized in objects of art and virtue—samplers, figureheads, paintings of women under willows, statues of General Washington—but no matter what she showed him, the man would only wave his hand in the air and exclaim: *Ridickalus!* And shouldn't we feel so about things like *Mother Goose?*

> *Early to bed and early to rise*
> *Makes a man healthy, wealthy, and wise.*

Ridickalus! Why say it like a rocking horse? why make it jingle so? and *wise*—who wants to be wise?

> *Which sibling is the well-adjusted sibling?*
> *The one that gets its sleep.*

That is the way the modern *Mother Goose* will put it. I don't expect the modern *Mother Goose* to be especially popular with little children, who have not yet learned not to like poetry; but it is the parents who buy the book.

Isn't writing verse a dying art, anyway, like blacksmithing or buggy-making? Well, not exactly: poets are making as many buggies as ever—good buggies, fine buggies—they just can't get anybody much to ride in them. As for blacksmithing: I read the other day that there are twice as many blacksmith shops in the United States as there are bookstores. Something has gone wrong with that comparison too. No, I'm doing what poets do, complaining; and if I exaggerate a little when I complain, why, that's only human—surely you want me to exaggerate a little, in my misery. Goethe says, when he is talking about slum children: "No person ever looks miserable who feels that he has the right to make a demand on you." This right is not anything that anyone can confer upon himself; it is the public, society, all of us, that confer this right. If the poet looks miserable, it is because we have made him feel that he no longer has the right to make a demand on us. It is no longer a question of what he wants, or of what he ought to be given— he takes what he gets, and complains about getting it, and he hears the echo of his complaint, and then the silence settles around him, a little darker, a little deeper.

What does he want? To be read. Read by whom? critics? men wise enough to tell him, when they have read the poem, what it is and ought to be, what its readers feel and ought to feel? Well, no. A writer cannot learn about his readers from his critics: they are different races. The critic, unless he is one in a thousand, reads to criticize; the reader reads to read.

Freud talks of the "free-floating" or "evenly-hovering" attention with which the analyst must listen to the patient. Concentration, note-taking, listening with a set—a set of pigeonholes—makes it difficult or impossible for the analyst's unconscious to respond to the patient's; takes away from the analyst the possibility of learning from the patient what the analyst doesn't already know; takes away from him all those random guesses or intuitions or inspirations which come out of no-where—and come, too, out of the truth of the patient's being. But this is quite as true of critics and the poems that are *their* patients: when one reads as a linguist, a scholar, a New or Old or High or Low critic, when one reads the poem *as a means to an end,* one is no longer a pure reader but an applied one. The true reader "listens like a three years' child: / The Mariner hath his will." Later on he may write like a sixty-three-year-old sage, but he knows that in the beginning, unless ye be converted, and become as little children, ye shall not enter into the kingdom of art. Hofmannsthal says, with awful finality: "The world has lost its innocence, and without innocence no one creates or enjoys a work of art"; but elsewhere he says more hopefully, with entire and not with partial truth, that each of us lives in an innocence of his own which he never entirely loses.

Is there a public for poetry that is still, in this sense of the word, innocent? Of course, there are several publics for poetry—small, benighted, eccentric publics—just as there are publics for postage stamps and cobblers' benches; but this is such a disastrous change from the days of *Childe Harold* and *In Memoriam* and *Hiawatha,* when the public for poetry was, simply, the reading public, that you can see why poets feel the miserable astonishment that they feel. The better-known poets feel it more than the lesser-known, who—poor things—lie under the table grateful for crumbs, pats, kicks, anything at all that will let them be sure they really exist, and are not just a dream someone has stopped dreaming. A poet like Auden says that nobody reads him except poets and young men in cafeterias—his description of the young men is too repellent for me to repeat it to you.

Literally, Auden is wrong: we read Auden, this is no cafeteria; but, figuratively, Auden is right—the poet's public's gone. Frederick the Great translated Voltaire, and trembled as the poet read the translation; Elizabeth—Elizabeth the First—and Henry the Eighth and Richard the Lion-Hearted wrote good poems and read better; and I cannot resist quoting to you three or four sentences from Frans Bengtsson's novel *The Long Ships,* to show you what things were like at the court of Harald Bluetooth, King of Denmark in the year 1000. A man gets up from a banquet table: "His name was Björn Asbrandsson, and he was a famous warrior, besides being a great poet to boot . . . Although he was somewhat drunk, he managed to improvise some highly skilful verses in King Harald's honor in a meter known as töglag. This was the latest and most difficult verse-form that the Icelandic poets had invented, and indeed the poem was so artfully contrived that little could be understood of its content. Everybody, however, listened with an appearance of understanding, for any man who could not understand poetry would be regarded as a poor specimen of a warrior; and King Harald praised the poet and gave him a gold ring."

Auden is a descendant of just such poets as this one; but if Auden, when he next visits the University of your state, makes up an incomprehensible poem, in a difficult new meter, in honor of the President of the University, will all its football players pretend they understand the poem, so as not to be thought poor specimens of football players? and will the President give Auden a gold ring?

In the days when his readers couldn't read, the poet judged his public by his public: the gold ring or the scowl the king gave him was as concrete as the labored, triumphant faces of his hearers. But nowadays King Harald and his warriors are represented by a reviewer, next year, in *The New York Times;* a critic, nine years later, in *The Sewanee Review.* "Ah, better to sing my songs to a wolf pack on the Seeonee than to a professor on the *Sewanee!*" the poet blurts, baring his teeth; but then—what choice has he?—he lets the Reality Principle do its worst, and projects or extends or extrapolates a critic or two, a dozen reviewers, into the Public; into Posterity. Critics, alas! are the medium through which the poet darkly senses his public. Nor is it altogether different for the public: Harald and his Vikings, lonely in their split-levels, do not even remember the days when, as they listened, they could look into one another's faces and know without looking what they would find there. Now they too look into the *Times;* wish that they could replace that scowl with a gold ring, that gold ring with a scowl; reconstruct from the exclamations on dust jackets, quotations in advertisements, the fierce smiles on the faces of the warriors.

So if we are to talk about the poet and his poems and his public, what each is to the others, we must spend much of our time—too much of our time—talking about his critics. Criticism is necessary, I suppose; I know. Yet criticism, to the poet, is no necessity, but a luxury he can ill afford. Conrad cried to his wife: "I don't want criticism, I want praise!" And it is praise, blame, tears, laughter, that writers want; when Columbus comes home he needs to be cheered for finding a new way to India, not interned while the officials argue about whether it is Asia, Africa, or Antarctica that he has discovered. Really, of course, it's America—and if they agreed about it this would be helpful to Columbus; he could say to himself, in awe: "So it was America I discovered!" But how seldom the critics do agree! A gray writer seems black to his white critics, white to his black critics: the same poem will seem incomprehensible modernistic nonsense to Robert Hillyer, and a sober, old-fashioned, versified essay to the critics of some little magazine of advanced tastes. Ordinary human feeling, the most natural tenderness, will seem to many critics and readers rank sentimentality, just as a kind of nauseated brutality (in which the writer's main response to the world is simply to vomit) will seem to many critics and readers the inescapable truth. We live in a time in which Hofmannsthal's "Good taste is the ability continuously to counteract exaggeration" will seem to most readers as false as it seems tame. "Each epoch has its own sentimentality," Hofmannsthal goes on, "its specific way of overemphasizing strata of emotion. The sentimentality of the present is egotistic and unloving; it exaggerates not the feeling of love but that of the self."

Everyone speaks of the "negative capability" of the artist, of his ability to lose what self he has in the many selves, the great self of the world. Such a quality is, surely, the first that a critic should have; yet who speaks of the negative capability of the critic? how often are we able to observe it? The commonest response to the self of a work of art is the critic's assertion that he too has a self. What he writes proves it. I once saw, in an essay by a psychoanalyst, the phrase *the artist and his competitor, the critic.* Where got he that truth? Out of an analysand's mouth? I do not know; but that it is an important and neglected truth I do know. All mediators become competitors: the exceptions to this rule redeem their kind.

Critics disagree about almost every quality of a writer's work; and when some agree about a quality, they disagree about whether it is to be praised or blamed, nurtured or rooted out. After enough criticism the writer is covered with lipstick and bruises, and the two are surprisingly evenly distributed. There is *nothing* so plain about a writer's books, to some critics, that its opposite isn't plain to others. Kafka is original? Not at all, according to Edmund Wilson. A fine critic of poetry, Ezra Pound, writes: "In [the writer So-and-So] you have an embroidery of language, a talk *about* the matter, not presentation; you have grace, richness of language, etc., as much as you like, but you have nothing that isn't replaceable by something else, no ornament that wouldn't have done just as well in some other connection, or that for which some other figure of rhetoric or fancy couldn't have served, or which couldn't have been distilled from literary antecedents." About whom is Pound speaking? About Shakespeare. Anyone who has read at all widely has come across thousands of such judgments, and it is easy for him to sympathize with the artist when the artist murmurs: "We wish to learn from our critics, but it is hard for us even to recover from them. A fool's reproach has an edge like a razor, and his brother's praise is small consolation. Critics are like bees: one sting lasts longer than a dozen jars of honey."

The best thing ever said about criticism—I am not, now, speaking as a critic—was said, as is often the case, by Goethe: "Against criticism we can neither protect nor defend ourselves; we must act in despite of it, and gradually it resigns itself to this." The great Goethe suffered just as we little creatures do, and he spoke about it, as we don't, in imperishable sentences: "All great excellence in life or art, at its first recognition, brings with it a certain pain arising from the strongly felt inferiority of the spectator; only at a later period, when we take it into our own culture, and appropriate as much of it as our capacities allow, do we learn to love and esteem it. Mediocrity, on the other hand, may often give us unqualified pleasure; it does not disturb our self-satisfaction, but rather encourages us with the thought that we are as good as another . . . Properly speaking, we learn only from those books we cannot judge. The author of a book that I am competent to criticize would have to learn from me." Goethe says over and over: "Nothing is more terrible than ignorance in action . . . It is a terrible thing when fools thrive at the expense of a superior man." You and I will agree— and then we will have to decide whether we're being thriven at the expense of, or thriving. Goethe says in firm doggerel: "However clear and simple be it / Finder and doer alone may see it." No, Goethe didn't have too much use for critics, since he thought that critics weren't of too much use.

And why am I quoting all this to you? have critics hurt me so that I want to pull down the temple upon their heads, even if I too perish in the ruins?—for I too am a critic. No, it's not that; critics have done their best for me, and their best has been, perhaps, only too good; when I myself criticize, I am willing for you to believe what I say; but I am trying to explain why it is that critics are of so little use to writers, why it is that they are such a poor guide to the opinions of the next age—and I am explaining in an age which has an unprecedented respect for, trust in, criticism.

All of us have read pieces of criticism—many pieces of criticism—which seem worthy both of delighted respect and cautious trust. All of us have read criticism in which the critic takes it for granted that what he writes about comes first, and what he writes comes second—takes it for granted that he is writing as a reader to other readers, to be of use to them; criticism in which the critic works, as far as he is able, in the spirit of Wordsworth's "I have endeavored to look steadily at my subject." All of us have some favorite, exceptional critic who might say, with substantial truth, that he has not set up rigid standards to which a true work of art must conform, but that he has tried instead to let the many true works of art—his experience of them—set up the general expectations to which his criticism of art conforms; that he has tried never to see a work of art as mere raw material for criticism, data for generalization; that he has tried never to forget the difference between creating a work of art and criticizing a work of art; and that he has tried, always, to remember what Proust meant when he said, about writers like Stendhal, Balzac, Hugo, Flaubert, the great creators called "romantics": "The classics have no better commentators than the 'romantics.' The romantics are the only people who really know how to read the classics, because they read them as they were written, that is to say, 'romantically' and because if one would read a poet or a prose writer properly one must be, not a scholar, but a poet or a prose writer." It might be put a little differently: if one would read a poet or a prose writer properly one must be, not a scholar or a poet or a prose writer, but a reader: someone who reads books as they were written, that is to say, "romantically." Proust's grandmother was not a poet or a prose writer, but she read Madame de Sévigné properly. To be, as she was, a reader, is a lofty and no longer common fate.

The best poetry critic of our time, T. S. Eliot, has said about his criticism: "I see that I wrote best about poets whose work had influenced my own, and with whose poetry I had become thoroughly familiar, long before I desired to write about them, or had found the occasion to do so . . . The best of my literary criticism . . . is a by-product of my private poetry-workshop." But perhaps something of this sort is always true: perhaps true criticism is something, like sincerity or magnanimity, that cannot be aimed at, attained, directly; that must always be, in some sense, a by-product, whether of writing or reading, of a private poetry-workshop or a private reading-room.

We all realize that writers are inspired, but helpless and fallible beings, who know not what they write; readers, we know from personal experience, are less inspired but no less helpless and fallible beings, who half the time don't know what they're reading. Now, a critic is half writer, half reader: just as the vices of men and horses met in centaurs, the weaknesses of readers and writers meet in critics. A good critic—we cannot help seeing, when we look back at any other age—is a much rarer thing than a good poet or a good novelist. Unless you are one critic in a hundred thousand, the future will quote you only as an example of the normal error of the past, what everybody was foolish enough to believe then. Critics are discarded like calendars; yet, for their year, with what trust the world regards them!

Art is long, and critics are the insects of a day. But while he survives, it is the work of art he criticizes which is the critic's muse, or daemon, or guardian angel: it is a delight to the critic to think that sometimes, in moments of particular good fortune, some poem by Rilke or Yeats or Wordsworth has hovered above him, whispering what to say about it in his ear. And, in the moments of rash ambition which can come even to such humble—rightly humble—things as critics, the critic can imagine some reader, in the midst of his pleasure at a poem or story the critic has guided him to, being willing to think of some paragraph of the critic's work in terms of a sentence of Goethe's: "There is a sensitive empiricism that ultimately identifies itself with the object and thereby becomes genuine theory."

In other moments the critic can imagine the reader's thinking of him in terms of a paragraph that Proust once wrote. That miraculous writer and great critic, distressed at someone's having referred to Sainte-Beuve as one of the "great guides," exclaimed: "Surely no one ever failed so completely as did he in performing the functions of a guide? The greater part of his *Lundis* are devoted to fourth-rate writers, and whenever, by chance, he does bring himself to speak of somebody really important, of Flaubert, for instance, or Baudelaire, he immediately atones for what grudging praise he may have accorded him by letting it be understood that he writes as he does about them simply because he wants to please men who are his personal friends . . . As to Stendhal, the novelist, the Stendhal of *La Chartreuse,* our 'guide' laughs out of court the idea that such a person ever existed, and merely sees in all the talk about him the disastrous effects of an attempt (foredoomed to failure) to foist Stendhal on the public as a novelist . . . It would be fun, had I not less important things to do, to 'brush in' (as Monsieur Cuvillier Fleury would have said), in the manner of Sainte-Beuve, a 'picture of French literature in the nineteenth century,' in such a way that not a single great name would appear and men would be promoted to the position of outstanding authors whose books today have been completely forgotten."

A portion of any critic, as he reads these sentences, turns white; and if another portion whispers, "Ah, but *you* needn't be afraid; certainly *you're* not as bad a critic as Sainte-Beuve," it is not a sentence to bring the color back into his cheeks, unless he blushes easily.

Wordsworth said, as Proust said after him, that "every writer, in so far as he is great and at the same time *original,* has the task of creating the taste by which he is to be enjoyed: so is it, so will it continue to be." But *taste,* he goes on to say, is a vicious and deluding word. (And surely he is right; surely we should use, instead, a phrase like *imaginative judgment.*) Using such a word as *taste* helps to make us believe that there is some passive faculty that responds to the new work of art, registering the work's success or failure; but actually the new work must call forth in us an active power analogous to that which created it—the reader "cannot proceed in quiescence, he cannot be carried like a dead weight," he must "exert himself" to feel, to sympathize, and to understand. *"There,"* as Wordsworth says, "lies the true difficulty." He is right: *there* lies the difficulty for us, whether we are critics or readers; so is it, so will it continue to be.

You may say, "Of course this is true of great and original talents, but how does it apply to the trivial, immature, and eccentric writers with whom our age, like any other, is infested?" It applies only in this way: some of these trivial, immature, and eccentric writers *are* our great and original talents. The readers of Wordsworth's age said, "Of course what he says is true of great and original talents, but it is absurd when applied to a trivial and eccentric creature like Wordsworth"; and the critics of Wordsworth's age, applying the standards of the age more clearly, forcibly, and self-consciously, could condemn him with a more drastic severity. The readers read to read, the critics read to judge—both were wrong, but the critics were more impressively and rigorously and disastrously wrong, since they confirmed most readers in their dislike of Wordsworth and scared most of the others out of their liking.

We all see that the writer cannot afford to listen to critics when they are wrong—though how is he, how are we, to know when they are wrong? Can he afford to listen to them when they are right?—though how is he, how are we, to know when they are right? and right for this age or right for the next?* The writer cannot afford to question his own essential nature; must have, as Marianne Moore says, "the courage of his peculiarities." But often it is this very nature, these very peculiarities—originality always seems peculiarity, to begin with—that critics condemn. There must be about the writer a certain spontaneity or naïveté or somnambulistic rightness: he must, in some sense, move unquestioning in the midst of his world—at his question all will disappear.

And if it is slighter things, alterable things which the critics condemn, should the poet give in, alter them, and win his critics' surprised approval? "No," says Wordsworth, "where the understanding of an

---

* "When the great innovation appears, it will almost certainly be in a muddled, incomplete, and confusing form. To the discoverer himself it will be only half-understood; to everybody else it will be a mystery. For any speculation which does not at first glance look crazy, there is no hope."

F. L. Dyson, *Innovation in Physics*

author is not convinced, or his feelings altered, this cannot be done without great injury to himself: for his own feelings are his stay and support, and, if he set them aside in this one instance, he may be induced to repeat this act till his mind shall lose all confidence in itself, and become utterly debilitated. To this it may be added, that the critic ought never to forget that he is himself exposed to the same errors as the Poet." Let me repeat this: we ought never to forget that the critic is himself exposed to the same errors as the poet. We all know this— yet, in a deeper sense, we don't know it. We all realize that the poet's beliefs are, first of all, *his:* our books show how his epoch, his childhood, his mistresses, and his unconscious produced the beliefs; we know, now, the "real" reasons for his believing what he believed. Why do we not realize what is equally true (and equally false)?—that the critic's beliefs are, first of all, *his;* that we can write books showing how his epoch, his mistresses, and his unconscious produced the beliefs; that we can know, now, the "real" reasons for his believing what he believed. The work of criticism is rooted in the unconscious of the critic just as the poem is rooted in the unconscious of the poet. I have had the pleasure and advantage of knowing many poets, many critics, and I have not found one less deeply neurotic than the other.

When the critic is also an artist—a T. S. Eliot—we find it easier to remember all this, and to distrust him; but when the critic is an Irving Babbitt—that is to say, a man who, tenanted by all nine of the muses, still couldn't create a couplet—we tend to think of his beliefs as somehow more objective. "Surely," we feel, "a man with so little imagination couldn't be making up something—couldn't be *inspired.*" We are wrong. Criticism is the poetry of prosaic natures (and even, in our time, of some poetic ones); there is a divinity that inspires the most sheep-like of scholars, the most tabular of critics, so that the man too dull to understand *Evangeline* still can be possessed by some theory about *Evangeline,* a theory as just to his own being as it is unjust to *Evangeline*'s. The man is entitled to his inspiration; and yet . . . if only he would leave out *Evangeline!* If only he could secede from Literature, and set up some metaliterary kingdom of his own!

The poet *needs* to be deluded about his poems—for who can be sure that it is delusion? In his strongest hours the public hardly exists for the writer: he does what he ought to do, has to do, and if afterwards some Public wishes to come and crown him with laurel crowns, well, let it! if critics wish to tell people all that he isn't, well, let them—he knows what he is. But at night when he can't get to sleep it seems to him that it is what he is, his own particular personal quality, that he is being disliked for. It is this that the future will like him for, if it likes him for anything; but will it like him for anything? The poet's hope is in posterity, but it is a pale hope; and now that posterity itself has become a pale hope . . .

The writer—I am still talking about the writer-not-yet-able-to-go-to-sleep—is willing to have his work disliked, if it's bad; is ready to rest content in dislike, if it's good. But which is it? *He* can't know. He thinks of all those pieces of his that he once thought good, and now thinks bad; how many of his current swans will turn out to be just such ducklings? All of them? If he were worse, would people like him better? If he were better, would people like him worse? If—

He says to himself, "Oh, go to sleep!" And next morning, working at something the new day has brought, he is astonished at the night's thoughts—he does what he does, and lets public, critics, posterity worry about whether it's worth doing. For to tell the truth, the first truth, the poem is a love affair between the poet and his subject, and readers come in only a long time later, as witnesses at the wedding . . .

But what would the ideal witnesses—the ideal public—be? What would an ideal public do? Mainly, essentially, it would just read the poet; read him with a certain willingness and interest; read him imaginatively and perceptively. It needs him, even if it doesn't know that; he needs it, even if he doesn't know that. It and he are like people in one army, one prison, one world: their interests are great and common, and deserve a kind of declaration of dependence. The public might treat him very much as it would like him to treat it. It has its faults, he has his; but both "are, after all," as a man said about women, "the best things that are offered in that line." The public ought not to demand the same old thing from the poet whenever he writes something very new, nor ought it to complain, *The same old thing!* whenever he writes something that isn't very new; and it ought to realize that it is not, unfortunately, in the writer's power to control what he writes: something else originates and controls it, whether you call that something else the unconscious or Minerva or the Muse. The writer writes what he writes just as the public likes what it likes; he can't help himself, it can't help itself, but each of them has to try: most of our morality, most of our culture are in the trying.

We readers can be, or at least can want to be, what the writer himself would want us to be: a public that reads a *lot*—that reads widely, joyfully, and naturally; a public whose taste is formed by acquaintance with the good and great writers of many ages, and not simply acquaintance with a few fashionable contemporaries and the fashionable precursors of those; a public with broad general expectations, but without narrow particular demands, that the new work of art must satisfy; a public that reads with the calm and ease and independence that come from liking things in themselves, for themselves.

This is the kind of public that the poet would like; and if it turned out to be the kind of public that wouldn't like him, why, surely that is something he could bear. It is not his poems but poetry that he wants people to read; if they will read Rilke's and Yeats's and Hardy's poems, he can bear to have his own poems go unread forever. He *knows* that their poems are good to read, and that's something he necessarily can't know about his own; and he knows, too, that poetry itself is good to read—that if you cannot read poetry easily and naturally and joyfully, you are cut off from much of the great literature of the past, some of the good literature of the present. Yet the poet could bear to have people cut off from all that, if only they read widely, naturally, joyfully in the rest of literature: much of the greatest literature, much of the greatest poetry, even, is in prose. If people read this prose—read even a little of it—generously and imaginatively, and felt it as truth and life, as a natural and proper joy, why, that would be enough.

A few months ago I read an interview with a critic; a well-known critic; an unusually humane and intelligent critic. The interviewer had just said that the critic "sounded like a happy man," and the interview was drawing to a close; the critic said, ending it all: "I read, but I don't get time to read at whim. All the reading I do is in order to write or teach, and I resent it. We have no TV, and I don't listen to the radio or records, or go to art galleries or the theater. I'm a completely negative personality."

As I thought of that busy, artless life—no records, no paintings, no plays, no books except those you lecture on or write articles about—I was so depressed that I went back over the interview looking for some bright spot, and I found it, one beautiful sentence: for a moment I had left the gray, dutiful world of the professional critic, and was back in the sunlight and shadow, the unconsidered joys, the unreasoned sorrows, of ordinary readers and writers, amateurishly reading and writing "at whim." The critic said that once a year he read *Kim;* and he read *Kim,* it was plain, at whim: not to teach, not to criticize, just for love—he read it, as Kipling wrote it, just because he liked to, wanted to, couldn't help himself. To him it wasn't a means to a lecture or an article, it was an end; he read it not for anything he could get out of it, but for itself. And isn't this what the work of art demands of us? The work of art, Rilke said, says to us always: *You must change your life.* It demands of us that we too see things as ends, not as means—that we too know them and love them for their own sake. This change is beyond us, perhaps, during the active, greedy, and powerful hours of our lives; but during the contemplative and sympathetic hours of our reading, our listening, our looking, it is surely within our power, if we choose to make it so, if we choose to let one part of our nature follow its natural desires. So I say to you, for a closing sentence: *Read at whim! read at whim!*

The Woman at the Washington Zoo

· ❀ ·

UNDERSTANDING POETRY, EDITED BY CLEANTH BROOKS AND
ROBERT PENN WARREN, THIRD EDITION, 1960

*Critics fairly often write essays about how some poem was written;
the poet who wrote it seldom does. When Robert Penn Warren
and Cleanth Brooks were making a new edition of* Understanding
Poetry, *they asked several poets to write such essays. I no longer remembered much about writing "The Woman at the Washington Zoo"
—a poem is, so to speak, a way of making you forget how you wrote
it—but I had almost all the sheets of paper on which it was written,
starting with a paper napkin from the Methodist Cafeteria. If you had
asked me where I had begun the poem I'd have said: "Why, Sir, at the
beginning"; it was a surprise to me to see that I hadn't.*

*As I read, arranged, and remembered the pages it all came back
to me. I went over them for several days, copying down most of the
lines and phrases and mentioning some of the sights and circumstances
they came out of; I tried to give a fairly good idea of the objective
process of writing the poem. You may say, "But isn't a poem a kind of
subjective process, like a dream? Doesn't it come out of unconscious
wishes of yours, childhood memories, parts of your own private emotional life?" It certainly does: part of them I don't know about and the
rest I didn't write about. Nor did I write about or copy down something
that begins to appear on the last two or three pages: lines and phrases
from a kind of counterpoem, named "Jerome," in which St. Jerome is
a psychoanalyst and his lion is at the zoo.*

*If after reading this essay the reader should say: "You did all that
you could to the things, but the things just came," he would feel about
it as I do.*

Late in the summer of 1956 my wife and I moved to Washington. We
lived with two daughters, a cat, and a dog, in Chevy Chase; every day I

would drive to work through Rock Creek Park, past the zoo. I worked across the street from the Capitol, at the Library of Congress. I knew Washington fairly well, but had never lived there; I had been in the army, but except for that had never worked for the government.

Some of the new and some of the old things there—I was often reminded of the army—had a good deal of effect on me: after a few weeks I began to write a poem. I have most of what I wrote, though the first page is gone; the earliest lines are:

> *any color*
> *My print, that has clung to its old colors*
> *Through many washings; this dull null*
> *Navy I wear to work, and wear from work, and so*
> *And so to bed*   *To bed*
> *With no complaint, no comment—neither from my chief,*
> *nor*
> *The Deputy Chief Assistant, from his chief,*
> *Nor*   *nor*
> *From Congressmen, from their constituents—*
> *thin*
> *Only I complain; this poor worn serviceable . . .*

The woman talking is a near relation of women I was seeing there in Washington—some at close range, at the Library—and a distant relation of women I had written about before, in "The End of the Rainbow" and "Cinderella" and "Seele im Raum." She is a kind of aging machine part. I wrote, as they say in suits, "acting as next friend"; I had for her the sympathy of an aging machine part. (If I was also something else, that was just personal; and she also was something else.) I felt that one of these hundreds of thousands of government clerks might feel all her dresses one dress, a faded navy-blue print, and that dress her body. This work or life uniform of hers excites neither complaint, nor comment, nor the mechanically protective *No comment* of the civil servant; excites them neither from her "chief," the Deputy Chief Assistant, nor from his, nor from any being on any level of that many-leveled machine: all the system is silent, except for her own cry, which goes unnoticed just as she herself goes unnoticed. (I had met a Deputy Chief Assistant, who saw nothing remarkable in the title.) The woman's days seem to her the going-up-to-work and coming-down-from-work of a worker; each ends in *And so to bed,* the diarist's conclusive unvarying entry in the daybook of his life.

These abruptly opening lines are full of duplications and echoes, like what they describe. And they are wrong in the way in which beginnings are wrong: either there is too much of something or it is not yet there. The lines break off with *this worn serviceable*—the words can apply either to her dress or to her body, but anything so obviously suitable to the dress must be intended for the body. *Body that no sunlight dyes, no hand suffuses,* the page written the next day goes on; then after a space there is *Dome-shadowed, withering among columns, / Wavy upon the pools of fountains, small beside statues . . .* No sun colors, no hand suffuses with its touch, this used, still-useful body. It is subdued to the element it works in: is shadowed by the domes, grows old and small and dry among the columns, of the buildings of the capital; becomes a reflection, its material identity lost, upon the pools of the fountains of the capital; is dwarfed beside the statues of the capital—as year by year it passes among the public places of this city of space and trees and light, city sinking beneath the weight of its marble, city of graded voteless workers.

The word *small,* as it joins the reflections in the pools, the trips to the public places, brings the poem to its real place and subject—to its title, even: next there is *small and shining,* then (with the star beside it that means *use, don't lose*) *small, far-off, shining in the eyes of animals;* the woman ends at the zoo, looking so intently into its cages that she sees her own reflection in *the eyes of animals, these wild ones trapped / As I am trapped but not, themselves, the trap . . .* The lines have written above them *The Woman at the Washington Zoo.*

The next page has the title and twelve lines:

This print, that has kept the memory of color
Alive through many cleanings; this dull null
Navy I wear to work, and wear from work, and so
To bed (with no complaints, no comment: neither from my
        chief,
The Deputy Chief Assistant, nor her chief,
Nor his, nor Congressmen, nor their constituents
        ~~*wan*~~
—Only I complain); this ~~plain~~, worn, serviceable
        sunlight
Body that no ~~sunset~~ dyes, no hand suffuses
But, dome-shadowed, withering among columns,
Wavy beneath fountains—small, far-off, shining

~~wild~~
In the eyes of animals, these beings trapped
As I am trapped but not, themselves, the trap . . .

Written underneath this, in the rapid, ugly, disorganized handwriting
of most of the pages, is *bars of my body burst blood breath breathing—
lives aging but without knowledge of age / Waiting in their safe
prisons for death, knowing not of death;* immediately this is changed
into two lines, *Aging, but without knowledge of their age, / Kept safe
here, knowing not of death, for death*—and out at the side, scrawled
heavily, is: *O bars of my own body, open, open!* She recognizes herself
in the animals—and recognizes herself, also, in the cages.

Written across the top of this page is *2nd and 3rd alphabet.* Streets
in Washington run through a one-syllable, a two-syllable, and a three-
syllable (Albermarle, Brandywine, Chesapeake . . .) alphabet, so that
people say about an address: "Let's see, that's in the second alphabet,
isn't it?" It made me think of Kronecker's "God made the integers, all
else is the work of man"; but it seemed right for Washington to have
alphabets of its own—I made up the title of a detective story, *Murder
in the Second Alphabet.* The alphabets were a piece of Washington that
should have fitted into the poem, but didn't; but the zoo was a whole
group of pieces, a little Washington, into which the poem itself fitted.

Rock Creek Park, with its miles of heavily wooded hills and valleys,
its rocky stream, is like some National Forest dropped into Washington
by mistake. Many of the animals of the zoo are in unroofed cages back
in its ravines. My wife and I had often visited the zoo, and now that we
were living in Washington we went to it a great deal. We had made
friends with a lynx that was very like our cat that had died the spring
before, at the age of sixteen. We would feed the lynx pieces of liver or
scraps of chicken and turkey; we fed liver, sometimes, to two enormous
white timber wolves that lived at the end of one ravine. Eager for the
meat, they would stand up against the bars on their hind legs, taller than
a man, and stare into our eyes; they reminded me of Akela, white with
age, in *The Jungle Books,* and of the wolves who fawn at the man
Mowgli's brown feet in "In the Rukh." In one of the buildings of the
zoo there was a lioness with two big cubs; when the keeper came she
would come over, purring her bass purr, to rub her head against the bars
almost as our lynx would rub his head against the turkey skin, in rapture,
before he finally gulped it down. In the lions' building there were two
black leopards; when you got close to them you saw they had not lost

the spots of the ordinary leopards—were the ordinary leopards, but spotted black on black, dingy somehow.

On the way to the wolves one went by a big unroofed cage of foxes curled up asleep; on the concrete floor of the enclosure there would be scattered two or three white rats—stiff, quite untouched—that the foxes had left. (The wolves left their meat, too—big slabs of horse meat, glazing, covered with flies.) Twice when I came to the foxes' cage there was a turkey buzzard that had come down for the rats; startled at me, he flapped up heavily, with a rat dangling underneath. (There are usually vultures circling over the zoo; nearby, at the tennis courts of the Sheraton-Park, I used to see vultures perched on the tower of WTTG, above the court on which Defense Secretary McElroy was playing doubles—so that I would say to myself, like Peer Gynt: "Nature is witty.") As a child, coming around the bend of a country road, I had often seen a turkey buzzard, with its black wings and naked red head, flap heavily up from the mashed body of a skunk or possum or rabbit.

A good deal of this writes itself on the next page, almost too rapidly for line endings or punctuation: *to be and never know I am   when the vulture buzzard comes for the white rat that the foxes left   May he take off his black wings, the red flesh of his head, and step to me as man—a man at whose brown feet the white wolves fawn—to whose hand of power / The lioness stalks, leaving her cubs playing / and rubs her head along the bars as he strokes it.* Along the side of the page, between these lines, two or three words to a line, is written *the animals who are trapped but are not themselves the trap   black leopards   spots, light and darkened, hidden except to the close eyes of love, in their life-long darkness, so I in decent black, navy blue.*

As soon as the zoo came into the poem, everything else settled into it and was at home there; on this page it is plain even to the writer that all the things in the poem come out of, and are divided between, color and colorlessness. Colored women and colored animals and colored cloth—all that the woman sees as her own opposite—come into the poem to begin it. Beside the typed lines are many hurried phrases, most of them crossed out: *red and yellow as October maples   rosy, blood seen through flesh in summer   colors wild and easy natural   leaf-yellow cloud-rose leopard-yellow, cloth from another planet   the leopards look back at their wearers, hue for hue   the women look back at the leopard.* And on the back of the vulture's page there is a flight of ideas, almost a daydream, coming out of these last phrases: *we have never mistaken you for the others   among the legations one of a differ-*

ent architecture   women, saris of a different color   envoy   impassive
clear bulletproof glass   lips, through the clear glass of a rose sedan
color of blood   you too are represented on this earth . . .

One often sees on the streets of Washington—fairly often sees at
the zoo—what seem beings of a different species: women from the
embassies of India and Pakistan, their sallow skin and black hair
leopard-like, their yellow or rose or green saris exactly as one imagines
the robes of Greek statues before the statues had lost their colors. It was
easy for me to see the saris as cloth from another planet or satellite; I
have written about a sick child who wants "a ship from some near
star / To land in the yard and beings to come out / And think to
me: 'So this is where you are!' " and about an old man who says that it
is his ambition to be the pet of visitors from another planet; as an old
reader of science fiction, I am used to looking at the sun red over the
hills, the moon white over the ocean, and saying to my wife in a sober
voice: "It's like another planet." After I had worked a little longer, the
poem began as it begins now:

> *The saris go by me from the embassies.*
>
> *Cloth from the moon. Cloth from another planet.*
> *They look back at the leopard like the leopard.*
>
> *And I . . . This print of mine, that has kept its color*
> *Alive through so many cleanings; this dull null*
> *Navy I wear to work, and wear from work, and so*
> *To my bed, so to my grave, with no*
> *Complaints, no comment: neither from my chief,*
> *The Deputy Chief Assistant, nor his chief—*
> *Only I complain; this serviceable*
> *Body that no sunlight dyes, no hand suffuses*
> *But, dome-shadowed, withering among columns,*
> *Wavy beneath fountains—small, far-off, shining*
> *In the eyes of animals, these beings trapped*
> *As I am trapped but not, themselves, the trap,*
> *Aging, but without knowledge of their age,*
> *Kept safe here, knowing not of death, for death*
> *—Oh, bars of my own body, open, open!*

It is almost as if, once all the materials of the poem were there, the
middle and end of the poem made themselves, as the beginning seemed
to make itself. After the imperative *open, open!* there is a space, and
the middle of the poem begins evenly—since her despair is beyond

expression—in a statement of accomplished fact: *The world goes by my cage and never sees me.* Inside the mechanical official cage of her life, her body, she lives invisibly; no one feeds this animal, reads out its name, pokes a stick through the bars at it—the cage is empty. She feels that she is even worse off than the other animals of the zoo: they are still wild animals—since they do not know how to change into domesticated animals, beings that are their own cages—and they are surrounded by a world that does not know how to surrender them, still thinks them part of itself. This natural world comes through or over the bars of the cages, on its continual visits to those within: to those who are not machine parts, convicts behind the bars of their penitentiary, but wild animals—the free beasts come to their imprisoned brothers and never know that they are not also free. Written on the back of one page, crossed out, is *Come still, you free;* on the next page this becomes:

> *The world goes by my cage and never sees me.*
> *And there come not to me, as come to these,*
> *The wild ~~ones~~ beasts, sparrows pecking the llamas' grain,*
> *Pigeons ~~fluttering to~~ settling on the bears' bread,*
>   *turkey-buzzards*
> ~~*Coming with grace first, then with horror* Vulture~~
>   ~~*seizing*~~
> *Tearing the meat the flies have clouded . . .*

In saying mournfully that the wild animals do not come to her as they come to the animals of the zoo, she is wishing for their human equivalent to come to her. But she is right in believing that she has become her own cage—she has changed so much, in her manless, childless, fleshless existence, that her longing wish has inside it an increasing repugnance and horror: the innocent sparrows *pecking* the llamas' grain become larger in the pigeons *settling on* (not *fluttering to*) the bears' bread; and these grow larger and larger, come (with grace first, far off in the sky, but at last with horror) as turkey buzzards seizing, no, *tearing* the meat the flies have clouded. She herself is that stale leftover flesh, nauseating just as what comes to it is horrible and nauseating. The series *pecking, settling on,* and *tearing* has inside it a sexual metaphor: the stale flesh that no one would have is taken at last by the turkey buzzard with his naked red neck and head.

Her own life is so terrible to her that, to change, she is willing to accept even this, changing it as best she can. She says: *Vulture* [it is a euphemism that gives him distance and solemnity], *when you come for the white rat that the foxes left* [to her the rat is so plainly herself that she does not need to say so; the small, white, untouched thing is more accurately what she is than was the clouded meat—but, also, it is euphemistic, more nearly bearable], *take off the red helmet of your head* [the bestiality, the obscene sexuality of the flesh-eating death-bird is really—she hopes or pretends or desperately is sure—merely external, *clothes,* an intentionally frightening war garment like a Greek or Roman helmet], *the black wings that have shadowed me* [she feels that their inhuman colorless darkness has always, like the domes of the inhuman city, shadowed her; the wings are like a black parody of the wings the Swan Brothers wear in the fairy tale, just as the whole costume is like that of the Frog Prince or the other beast-princes of the stories] *and step* [as a human being, not fly as an animal] *to me as* [what you really are under the disguising clothing of red flesh and black feathers] *man*—not the machine part, the domesticated animal that is its own cage, but man as he was first, still must be, is: the animals' natural lord,

> *The wild brother at whose feet the white wolves fawn,*
> *To whose hand of power the great lioness*
> *Stalks, purring . . .*

And she ends the poem when she says to him:

> *You know what I was,*
> *You see what I am: change me, change me!*

Here is the whole poem:

THE WOMAN AT THE WASHINGTON ZOO

> *The saris go by me from the embassies.*
>
> *Cloth from the moon. Cloth from another planet.*
> *They look back at the leopard like the leopard.*
>
> *And I . . .*
>   *This print of mine, that has kept its color*
> *Alive through so many cleanings; this dull null*
> *Navy I wear to work, and wear from work, and so*
> *To my bed, so to my grave, with no*
> *Complaints, no comment: neither from my chief,*
> *The Deputy Chief Assistant, nor his chief—*
> *Only I complain; this serviceable*
> *Body that no sunlight dyes, no hand suffuses*
> *But, dome-shadowed, withering among columns,*
> *Wavy beneath fountains—small, far-off, shining*

In the eyes of animals, these beings trapped
As I am trapped but not, themselves, the trap,
Aging, but without knowledge of their age,
Kept safe here, knowing not of death, for death
—Oh, bars of my own body, open, open!

The world goes by my cage and never sees me.
And there come not to me, as come to these,
The wild beasts, sparrows pecking the llamas' grain,
Pigeons settling on the bears' bread, buzzards
Tearing the meat the flies have clouded . . .
                          Vulture,
When you come for the white rat that the foxes left,
Take off the red helmet of your head, the black
Wings that have shadowed me, and step to me as man,
The wild brother at whose feet the white wolves fawn,
To whose hand of power the great lioness
Stalks, purring . . .
                       You know what I was,
You see what I am: change me, change me!

Four Shakespeare Plays

HIFI / STEREO, AUGUST 1961

The Winter's Tale; Henry IV, Part One; Henry IV, Part Two; and *The Two Gentlemen of Verona,* recorded by the Cambridge University Marlowe Society and Professional Players

THE Marlowe Society and Professional Players (the Players come out ahead) have recorded three more of the works of Shakespeare for London Records. The stereophonic sound really helps: when a high voice downstage left is talking to a bass voice in deepest right field, you have no trouble telling which is which. *The Winter's Tale* is certainly worth buying. Hear *Henry IV* before you buy it—a better one may be along soon. And the best *Two Gentlemen of Verona* ever made would still not be worth buying.

    The Winter's Tale seems to me the best of the plays that come after *Antony and Cleopatra;* the mastery and objective perfection of the writing remind one of—perhaps helped to produce—Milton's *Comus.* The play is a sexual pastoral the real subject of which is the emotional connection between one generation and the next: the Oedipus complex. This deliberately improbable pastoral combines a concentrated, altogether incomparable treatment of jealousy with the most idealized and Arcadian of love affairs. The "perilous stuff" with which *Hamlet* and so many other plays had been charged is no longer perilous in *The Winter's Tale;* is, so to speak, neurosis recollected in tranquillity: The King of Sicily's sudden, unmotivated jealousy of his queen (it is slow and thoroughly motivated in Shakespeare's source) results in the regrettable, quite accidental, entirely unintended death of the son whom he loves, mocks, and is mirrored by ("Looking on the lines / Of my boy's face, methoughts I did recoil / Twenty-three years, and saw myself unbreech'd, / In my green velvet coat, my dagger muzzled, / Lest it should bite its master, and so prove, / As ornaments oft do, too dangerous"); in the apparent death of the boy's mother, whom the king wishes to have burned as a witch; and in the exposure in the wilderness, like Oedipus, of that newborn "female bastard" whom the king believes the "issue" (the thirty-times-repeated key word of the play) of his queen and his "brother" the King of Bohemia. Even the oracle at Delphi cannot convince the king of his wife's innocence: "There is no truth at all in the oracle," he cries. But told a line later of his son's death, he instantly speaks of his own "injustice," confesses "I have too much believed mine own suspicion," and after the news of his queen's heartbroken death becomes a legendarily constant, kind, and remorseful man for the next eighteen years—years the play immediately skips, in order that the son (of the brother King of Bohemia) who takes the dead son's place can be allowed, this time, to love and marry the daughter who takes the dead mother's place. When the first intolerable situation is transferred to the next generation, with Florizel taking the place of his dead son, Perdita taking the place of his dead wife, the king accepts it; and he is rewarded by the miraculous resurrection of his wife. No dream could have handled it all with more tact. Or with more sophistication: those who like to laugh at "the sea-coast of Bohemia" ought to remember that the queen's father is the Emperor of Russia, that she is vindicated by the oracle of Apollo at Delphi, and that the lifelike statue of her is "newly performed by that rare Italian master Julio Romano." A tiara from Cartier's and a commission of investigation from the United Nations would not seem out of place in the play; the Unconscious *is* timeless.

The Winter's Tale is much the best acted of these plays. The King of Sicily is sometimes excellent, often good, now and then unaccountably commonplace; he delivers flatly a line about his dead queen's eyes— "Stars, stars, / And all eyes else dead coals!"—with which a teletype machine ought to be able to bring down the house. His queen, the best but also the sweetest of women, is acted rather as an institution of virtue by a lady with a voice on the bass side of alto, so that the part is given an unfortunate flavor of the Statue of Liberty. Her daughter Perdita is all parted lips and dewy candor, and her lover's manly and irreproachable devotion (Florizel is, roughly, the ideal son-in-law) is entirely believable. Some of the courtiers are worthy of a fairy tale, in their delicate and supercilious grandeur, but it is hard for them to equal all the characters who pronounce *s* as *z*, the sweet homely country folk who inhabit this pastoral. The old shepherd, Perdita's foster father, is particularly winning; he sounds like a stuffed bear, like an animal cracker, like all Hardy's country characters rolled into one. That operator Autolycus is all he ought to be, and Paulina—a scold with a heart of gold—will awake in any hearer memories of his childhood.

For most of us, Part One and Part Two of *Henry IV* are two

pedestals for one Falstaff. Falstaff himself is even better in Part Two, but the political sections fall off a little. The prose of both parts is prose as good as anybody has ever written, but the verse—compared to verse of the miraculous exactness and mastery of that in *The Winter's Tale*—seems rather repetitively and approximately effective. It works, works wonderfully sometimes, but it is rarely as poetic as the prose that enshrines, incarnates, that "sweet Jack Falstaff, kind Jack Falstaff, true Jack Falstaff, valiant Jack Falstaff," the sweet, round, invincible old baby to whom the world is still, somehow, child's play. Way down at the bottom of each of us, or floating above each of us like a captive balloon, there is a fat part named Falstaff. "Banish plump Jack and you banish all the world," says plump Jack; and when Prince Hal gets rid of the Falstaff inside him, when he transforms that end-in-himself, Falstaff, into a poor means, he transforms himself into that finally public character, that institution, Henry V. It is he who dies of an aborted heart, not Falstaff who dies of a broken one. Falstaff die of a broken heart!—as well expect the autumnal equinox to die of one! "I'll be damned for never a king's son in Christendom," that "latter spring" Falstaff has already cried; his slogan was always the primordial "Nothing can happen to *me!*"

The best words ever written about Falstaff were written, about humor in general, by Freud: "Like wit and the comic, humor has in it a *liberating* element. But it has also something fine and elevating . . . the ego's victorious assertion of its own invulnerability. It insists that it is impervious to wounds dealt by the outside world, in fact, that these are merely occasions for affording it pleasure . . . By its repudiation of the possibility of suffering, it takes its place in the great series of methods devised by the mind of man for evading the compulsion to suffer—a series which begins with neurosis and culminates in delusions, and includes intoxication, self-induced states of abstraction, and ecstasy . . . This humorous attitude asseverates the invincibility of one's ego against the real world and victoriously upholds the pleasure principle, yet all without quitting the ground of mental sanity." It adopts "the attitude of an adult towards a child, recognizing and smiling at the triviality of the interests and sufferings which seem to the child so big . . . Its meaning is: 'Look here! this is all that this seemingly dangerous world amounts to. Child's play—the very thing to jest about!' "

No actor's Falstaff will satisfy us. But the Marlowe Society really should have got a bigger and lighter man. "By this corrupt flesh and light blood," Falstaff could cry, "you've made me into a middleweight!

—and one with a nasal and insistent, a classed, a *classifiable* voice!" This *Henry IV* founders on the class structure of present-day English speech; a couple of record sides and you feel that the battle of Waterloo was lost in the classrooms of Cambridge. *Did* Henry V, Richard the Lion-Hearted, sound like Noel Coward as an undergraduate? Most of these armored barons have the voices of *rentiers,* of people trying to make sure no one takes away from them what they've inherited, not of people who got it for themselves in the first place. Both Prince Hal and Poins sound as if they were being played by Prince John of Lancaster, some sober-blooded boy fallen into a kind of male green-sickness and meticulosity. They talk with jolly unctuous assertion, laugh before and after each new piece of facetiousness, and sound like a Girl Scout troop pretending to get drunk in a saloon. But Hotspur is a blessed exception; *he* sounds as if he'd been sent down from Cambridge for trying to burn down Cambridge. Henry IV, like many of the older professionals the Marlowe Society has borrowed, is knowingly efficient; Owen Glendower, though he ought really to be done by Dylan Thomas, is a fishy pleasure; and most of the country comics are good, though Justice Shallow, with his falsetto trills à la Edward Everett Horton, beats them all. Bardolph sounds like a large fireworks cannon for Guy Fawkes Day; Pistol is pure bombast; Mistress Quickly and Doll Tearsheet, taken all in all— and how else would you take them?—are a sweet pair of (as *The Winter's Tale* puts it) "lower messes," a joy to God and man; and Falstaff's page pipes up bravely as the first buttercup of spring, straight from the pages of *When We Were Very Young.*

Modjeska could make people cry by reciting the alphabet in Polish —but would it have worked for Poles? Listening to *The Two Gentlemen of Verona* you long for it to be in Polish, Esperanto, baby talk, but it keeps on English and you keep on understanding every word. Even the man who writes the program notes calls it "this apprentice piece," and it is—to be candid—an absurdly bad play. How miraculous that the greatest of writers should have begun like this! The jokes are like the jokes in dreams: they have the structure of jokes but are not funny; the plot has the concentrated implausible irrelevance of a plot summary in an encyclopedia. The Marlowe Society performs as well as it deserves to be performed their act of definitive piety. The sixth record side is filled with *A Lover's Complaint,* a meandering ornamental narrative recited with overmastering gentility by a gentleman and a lady—a real gentleman and a real lady. You feel that the two of them, left alone on an island for twenty years, would end up with a set of doilies.

On Preparing to Read
Kipling

THE BEST SHORT STORIES OF RUDYARD KIPLING, 1961

MARK TWAIN said that it isn't what they don't know that hurts people, it's what they do know that isn't so. This is true of Kipling. If people don't know about Kipling they can read Kipling, and then they'll know about Kipling: it's ideal. But most people already do know about Kipling—not very much, but too much: they know what isn't so, or what might just as well not be so, it matters so little. They know that, just as Calvin Coolidge's preacher was against sin and the Snake was for it, Kipling was for imperialism; he talked about the white man's burden; he was a crude popular—immensely popular—writer who got popular by writing "If," and "On the Road to Mandalay," and *The Jungle Book,* and stories about India like Somerset Maugham, and children's stories; he wrote, "East is East and West is West and never the twain shall meet"; he wrote, "The female of the species is more deadly than the male"—or was that Pope? *Somebody* wrote it. In short: Kipling was someone people used to think was wonderful, but we know better than that now.

People certainly didn't know better than that then. "Dear Harry," William James begins. (It is hard to remember, hard to believe, that anyone ever called Henry James *Harry,* but if it had to be done, William James was the right man to do it.) "Last Sunday I dined with Howells at the Childs', and was delighted to hear him say that you were both a friend and an admirer of Rudyard Kipling. I am ashamed to say that I have been ashamed to write of that infant phenomenon, not knowing, with your exquisitely refined taste, how you might be affected by him and fearing to *jar.* [It is wonderful *to have the engineer / Hoist with his own petard.*] The more rejoiced am I at this, but why didn't you say so ere now? He's more of a Shakespeare than anyone yet in this generation of ours, as it strikes me. And seeing the new effects he lately brings in in *The Light That Failed,* and that Simla Ball story with Mrs. Hauksbee in the *Illustrated London News,* makes one sure now that he is only at the beginning of a rapidly enlarging career, with indefinite growth before him. Much of his present coarseness and jerkiness is youth only, divine youth. But *what* a youth! Distinctly the biggest literary phenomenon of our time. He has such human entrails, and he takes less time to get under the heartstrings of his personages than any-one I know. On the whole, bless him.

"All intellectual work is the same,—the artist feeds the public on his own bleeding insides. Kant's *Kritik* is just like a Strauss waltz, and I felt the other day, finishing *The Light That Failed,* and an ethical address to be given at Yale College simultaneously, that there was no *essential* difference between Rudyard Kipling and myself as far as that sacrificial element goes."

It surprises us to have James take Kipling so seriously, without reservations, with Shakespeare—to treat him as if he were Kant's *Kritik* and not a Strauss waltz. (Even Henry James, who could refer to "the good little Thomas Hardy"—who was capable of applying to the Trinity itself the adjective *poor*—somehow felt that he needed for Kipling that coarse word *genius,* and called him, at worst, "the great little Kipling.") Similarly, when Goethe and Matthew Arnold write about Byron, we are surprised to see them bringing in Shakespeare—are surprised to see how unquestioningly, with what serious respect, they speak of Byron, as if he were an ocean or a new ice age: "our soul," wrote Arnold, "had *felt* him like the thunder's roll." It is as though mere common sense, common humanity, required this of them: the existence of a world figure like Byron demands (as the existence of a good or great writer does not) that any inhabitant of the world treat him some-how as the world treats him. Goethe knew that Byron "is a child when he reflects," but this did not prevent him from treating Byron exactly as he treated that other world figure Napoleon.

An intelligent man said that the world felt Napoleon as a weight, and that when he died it would give a great *oof* of relief. This is just as true of Byron, or of such Byrons of their days as Kipling and Heming-way: after a generation or two the world is tired of being their pedestal, shakes them off with an *oof,* and then—hoisting onto its back a new world figure—feels the penetrating satisfaction of having made a mistake all its own. Then for a generation or two the Byron lies in the dust where we left him: if the old world did him more than justice, a new one does him less. "If he was so good as all that, why isn't he still famous?" the new world asks—if it asks anything. And then when another generation or two are done, we decide that he wasn't altogether a mistake people made in those days, but a real writer after all—that if we like *Childe Harold* a good deal less than anyone thought of liking it then, we like *Don Juan* a good deal more. Byron *was* a writer, people just didn't realize the sort of writer he was. We can feel impatient with Byron's world for liking him for the wrong reasons, and with the succeeding world for disliking him for the wrong reasons, and we are glad that our world, the real world, has at last settled Byron's account.

Kipling's account is still unsettled. Underneath, we still hold it against him that the world quoted him in its sleep, put him in its headlines when he was ill, acted as if he were God; we are glad that we have Hemingway instead, to put in *our* headlines when his plane crashes. Kipling is in the dust, and the dust seems to us a very good place for him. But in twenty or thirty years, when Hemingway is there instead, and we have a new Byron-Kipling-Hemingway to put in our news programs when his rocket crashes, our resistance to Hemingway will have taken the place of our resistance to Kipling, and we shall find ourselves willing to entertain the possibility that Kipling *was* a writer after all—people just didn't realize the sort of writer he was.

There is a way of traveling into this future—of realizing, now, the sort of writer Kipling was—that is unusually simple, but that people are unusually unwilling to take. The way is: to read Kipling as if one were not prepared to read Kipling; as if one didn't already know about Kipling—had never been told how readers do feel about Kipling, should feel about Kipling; as if one were setting out, naked, to see something that is there naked. I don't entirely blame the reader if he answers: "Thanks very much; if it's just the same to you, I'll keep my clothes on." It's only human of him—man is the animal that wears clothes. Yet aren't works of art in some sense a way of doing without clothes, a means by which reader, writer, and subject are able for once to accept their own nakedness? the nakedness not merely of the "naked truth," but also of the naked wishes that come before and after that truth? To read Kipling, for once, not as the crudely effective, popular writer we know him to be, but as, perhaps, the something else that even crudely effective, popular writers can become, would be to exhibit a magnanimity that might do justice both to Kipling's potentialities and to our own. Kipling did have, at first, the "coarseness and jerkiness" and mannered vanity of youth, human youth; Kipling did begin as a reporter, did print in newspapers the *Plain Tales from the Hills* which ordinary readers— and, unfortunately, most extraordinary ones—do think typical of his work; but then for half a century he kept writing. Chekhov began by writing jokes for magazines, skits for vaudeville; Shakespeare began by writing *Titus Andronicus* and *The Two Gentlemen of Verona*, some of the crudest plays any crudely effective, popular writer has ever turned out. Kipling is neither a Chekhov nor a Shakespeare, but he is far closer to both than to the clothing-store-dummy-with-the-solar-topee we have agreed to call Kipling. Kipling, like it or not, admit it or not, was a great genius; and a great neurotic; and a great professional, one of the most skillful writers who have ever existed—one of the writers who have used English best, one of the writers who most often have made other writers exclaim, in the queer tone they use for the exclamation: "Well, I've got to admit it really is *written*." When he died and was buried in that foreign land England, that only the Anglo-Indians know, I wish that they had put above his grave, there in *their* Westminster Abbey: "It really was *written*."

Mies Van Der Rohe said, very beautifully: "I don't want to be interesting, I want to be good." Kipling, a great realist but a greater inventor, could have said that he didn't want to be realistic, he wanted to get it right: that he wanted it not the way it did or—statistics show—does happen, but the way it really would happen. You often feel about something in Shakespeare or Dostoevsky that nobody ever said such a thing, but it's just the sort of thing people would say if they could—is more real, in some sense, than what people do say. If you have given your imagination free rein, let things go as far as they want to go, the world they made for themselves while you watched can have, for you and later watchers, a spontaneous finality. Some of Kipling has this spontaneous finality; and because he has written so many different kinds of stories—no writer of fiction of comparable genius has depended so much, for so long, on short stories alone—you end dazzled by his variety of realization: so many plants, and so many of them dewy!

If I had to pick one writer to invent a conversation between an animal, a god, and a machine, it would be Kipling. To discover what, if they ever said, the dumb would say—this takes real imagination; and this imagination of what isn't is the extension of a real knowledge of what is, the knowledge of a consummate observer who took no notes, except of names and dates: "If a thing didn't stay in my memory I argued it was hardly worth writing out." Knowing what the peoples, animals, plants, weathers of the world look like, sound like, smell like, was Kipling's métier, and so was knowing the words that could make someone else know. You can argue about the judgment he makes of something, but the thing is there. When as a child you first begin to read, what attracts you to a book is illustrations and conversations, and what scares you away is "long descriptions." In Kipling illustration and conversation and description (not long description; read, even the longest of his descriptions is short) have merged into a "toothsome amalgam" which the child reads with a grown-up's ease, and the grown-up with a child's wonder. Often Kipling writes with such grace and command, such a combination of experienced mastery and congenital inspiration, that we repeat with Goethe: "Seeing someone accomplishing arduous things with ease gives us an impression of witnessing the impossible." Sometimes the arduous thing Kipling is accomplishing seems to us a queer, even an absurd thing for anyone to wish to accomplish. But don't we have to learn to consent to this, with Kipling as with other good writers?—to consent to the fact that good writers just don't have good sense; that they are going to write it their way, not ours; that they are never going to have the objective, impersonal rightness they should have, but only the subjective, personal wrongness from which we derived the idea of the rightness. The first thing we notice about *War and Peace* and *Madame Bovary* and *Remembrance of Things Past* is how wonderful they are; the second thing we notice is how much they have wrong with them. They are not at all the perfect work of art we want— so perhaps Ruskin was right when he said that the person who wants perfection knows nothing about art.

Kipling says about a lion cub he and his family had on the Cape: "He dozed on the stoep, I noticed, due north and south, looking with slow eyes up the length of Africa"; this, like several thousand such sentences, makes you take for granted the truth of his "I made my own experiments in the weights, colors, perfumes, and attributes of words in relation to other words, either as read aloud so that they may hold the ear, or, scattered over the page, draw the eye." His words range from gaudy effectiveness to perfection; he is a professional magician but, also, a magician. He says about stories: "A tale from which pieces have been raked out is like a fire that has been poked. One does not know that the operation has been performed, but everyone feels the effect." (He even tells you how best to rake out the pieces: with a brush and Chinese ink you grind yourself.) He is a kind of Liszt—so isn't it just empty bravura, then? Is Liszt's? Sometimes; but sometimes bravura is surprisingly full, sometimes virtuosos are surprisingly plain: to boil a potato perfectly takes a chef home from the restaurant for the day.

Kipling was just such a potato boiler: a professional knower of professionals, a great trapeze artist, cabinetmaker, prestidigitator, with all the unnumbered details of others' guilds, crafts, mysteries, techniques at the tip of his fingers—or, at least, at the tip of his tongue. The first sentences he could remember saying as a child had been haltingly translated into English "from the vernacular" (that magical essential phrase for the reader of Kipling!), and just as children feel that it is they and not the grown-ups who see the truth, so Kipling felt about many things that it is the speakers of the vernacular and not the sahibs who tell the truth; that there are many truths that, to be told at all, take the vernacular. From childhood on he learned—to excess or obsession, even—the vernaculars of earth, the worlds inside the world, the many species into which place and language and work divide man. From the species which the division of labor produces it is only a step to the animal species which evolutionary specialization produces, so that Kipling finds it easy to write stories about animals; from the vernaculars or dialects or cants which place or profession produces (Kipling's slogan is, almost, "The cant *is* the man") it is only a step to those which time itself produces, so that Kipling finds it easy to write stories about all the different provinces of the past, or the future (in "As Easy as A.B.C."), or Eternity (if his queer institutional stories of the bureaucracies of Heaven and Hell are located there). Kipling was no Citizen of the World, but like the Wandering Jew he had lived in many places and known many peoples, an uncomfortable stranger repeating to himself the comforts of earth, all its immemorial contradictory ways of being at home.

Goethe, very winningly, wanted to have put on his grave a sentence saying that he had never been a member of any guild, and was an amateur until the day he died. Kipling could have said, "I never saw the guild I wasn't a member of," and was a professional from the day he first said to his ayah, in the vernacular—not being a professional myself, I don't know what it was he said, but it was the sort of thing a man would say who, from the day he was sixteen till the day he was twenty-three, was always—"luxury of which I dream still!"—shaved by his servant before he woke up in the morning.

This fact of his life, I've noticed, always makes hearers give a little shiver; but it is all the mornings when no one shaved Kipling before Kipling woke up, because Kipling had never been to sleep, that make me shiver. "Such night-wakings" were "laid upon me through my life," Kipling writes, and tells you in magical advertising prose how lucky the wind before dawn always was for him. You and I should have such luck! Kipling was a professional, but a professional possessed by both the Daemon he tells you about, who writes some of the stories for him, and the demons he doesn't tell you about, who write some others. Nowadays we've learned to call part of the unconscious *it* or *id;*

Kipling had not, but he called this Personal Demon of his *it*. (When he told his father that *Kim* was finished his father asked: "Did *it* stop, or you?" Kipling "told him that it was It.") "When your Daemon is in charge," Kipling writes, "do not try to think consciously. Drift, wait, and obey." He was sure of the books in which "my Daemon was with me . . . When those books were finished they said so themselves with, almost, the water-hammer click of a tap turned off." (Yeats said that a poem finishes itself with a click like a closing box.) Kipling speaks of the "doom of the makers": when their Daemon is missing they are no better than anybody else; but when he is there, and they put down what he dictates, "the work he gives shall continue, whether in earnest or jest." Kipling even "learned to distinguish between the peremptory motions of my Daemon, and the 'carry-over' of induced electricity, which comes of what you might call mere 'frictional' writing." We always tend to distrust geniuses about genius, as if what they say didn't arouse much empathy in us, or as if we were waiting till some more reliable source of information came along; still, isn't what Kipling writes a colored version of part of the plain truth?—there is plenty of supporting evidence. But it is interesting to me to see how thoroughly Kipling manages to avoid any subjective guilt, fallible human responsibility, so that he can say about anything in his stories either: "Entirely conscious and correct, objectively established, independently corroborated, the experts have testified, the professionals agree, it is the consensus of the authorities at the Club," or else: "I had nothing to do with it. I know nothing about it. *It* did it. The Daemon did it all." The reader of Kipling—this reader at least—hates to give all the credit to the Professional or to the Daemon; perhaps the demons had something to do with it too. Let us talk about the demons.

One writer says that we only notice what hurts us—that if you went through the world without hurting anyone, nobody would even know you had been alive. This is quite false, but true, too: if you put it in terms of the derivation of the Principle of Reality from the primary Principle of Pleasure, it does not even sound shocking. But perhaps we only notice a sentence if it sounds shocking—so let me say grotesquely: Kipling was someone who had spent six years in a concentration camp as a child; he never got over it. As a very young man he spent seven years in an India that confirmed his belief in concentration camps; he never got over this either.

As everybody remembers, one of Goya's worst engravings has underneath it: *I saw it.* Some of Kipling has underneath: *It is there.* Since the world is a necessary agreement that it isn't there, the world answered: *It isn't,* and told Kipling what a wonderful imagination he had. Part of the time Kipling answered stubbornly: *I've been there (I am there* would have been even truer), and part of the time he showed the world what a wonderful imagination he had. Say *Fairy tales!* enough to a writer and he will write you fairy tales. But to our *Are you telling me the truth or are you reassuring yourself?*—we ask it often of any writer, but particularly often of Kipling—he sometimes can say truthfully: *Reassuring you;* we and Kipling have interests in common. Kipling knew that "every nation, like every individual, walks in a vain show— else it could not live with itself"; Kipling knew people's capacity not to see: "through all this shifting, shouting brotheldom the pious British householder and his family bored their way back from the theaters, eyes-front and fixed, as though not seeing." But he himself had seen, and so believed in, the City of Dreadful Night, and the imperturbable or delirious or dying men who ran the city; this City outside was the duplicate of the City inside; and when the people of Victorian Europe didn't believe in any of it, except as you believe in a ghost story, he knew that this was only because they didn't *know*—he knew. So he was obsessed by—wrote about, dreamed about, and stayed awake so as not to dream about—many concentration camps, of the soul as well as of the body; many tortures, hauntings, hallucinations, deliria, diseases, night-mares, practical jokes, revenges, monsters, insanities, neuroses, abysses, forlorn hopes, last chances, extremities of every kind; these and their sweet opposites. He feels the convalescent's gratitude for mere existence, that the world is what the world was: how blue the day is, to the eye that has been blinded! Kipling praises the cessation of pain and its more blessed accession, when the body's anguish blots out for a little "Life's grinning face . . . the trusty Worm that dieth not, the steadfast Fire also." He praises man's old uses, home and all the ways of home: its Father and Mother, there to run to if you could only wake; and praises all our dreams of waking, our fantasies of return or revenge or insensate endurance. He praises the words he has memorized, that man has made from the silence; the senses that cancel each other out, that man has made from the senselessness; the worlds man has made from the world; but he praises and reproduces the sheer charm of—few writers are so purely charming!—the world that does not need to have anything done to it, that is simply there around us as we are there in it. He knows the joy of finding exactly the right words for what there are no words for; the satisfactions of sentimentality and brutality and love too, the "exquisite tenderness" that began in cruelty. But in the end he thanks God most for the small drugs that last—is grateful that He has not laid on us "the yoke of too long Fear and Wonder," but has given us Habit and Work: so that his Seraphs waiting at the Gate praise God

> *Not for any miracle of easy Loaves and Fishes*
> *But for doing, 'gainst our will, work against our wishes,*
> *Such as finding food to fill daily emptied dishes . . .*

praise him

> *Not for Prophecies or Powers, Visions, Gifts, or Graces*
> *But the unregardful hours that grind us in our places*
> *With the burden on our backs, the weather in our faces.*

"Give me the first six years of a child's life and you can have the rest" are the first words of *Something of Myself,* Kipling's reticent and revealing autobiography. The sentence exactly fits and exactly doesn't fit. For the first six years of his life the child lived in Paradise, the inordinately loved and reasonably spoiled son of the best of parents; after that he lived in the Hell in which the best of parents put him, and paid to have him kept: in "a dark land, and a darker room full of cold, in one wall of which a white woman made naked fire . . . a woman who took in children whose parents were in India." The child did not see his parents again for the next six years. He accepted the Hell as "eternally established . . . I had never heard of Hell, so I was introduced to it in all its terrors . . . I was regularly beaten . . . I have known a certain amount of bullying, but this was calculated torture—religious as well as scientific . . . Deprivation from reading was added to my punishments . . . I was well beaten and sent to school through the streets of Southsea with the placard 'Liar' between my shoulders . . . Some sort of nervous breakdown followed, for I imagined I saw shadows and things that were not there, and they worried me more than the Woman . . . A man came down to see me as to my eyes and reported that I was half-blind. This, too, was supposed to be 'showing-off,' and I was segregated from my sister—another punishment—as a sort of moral leper."

At the end of the six years the best of parents came back for their leper ("She told me afterwards that when she first came up to my room to kiss me good-night, I flung up an arm to guard off the cuff that I had been trained to expect"), and for the rest of their lives they continued to be the best and most loving of parents, blamed by Kipling for nothing, adored by Kipling for everything: "I think I can truthfully say that those two made up for me the only public for whom then I had any regard whatever till their deaths, in my forty-fifth year."

My *best of parents* cannot help sounding ironic, yet I do not mean it as irony. From the father's bas-reliefs for *Kim* to the mother's "There's no Mother in Poetry, my dear," when the son got angry at her criticism of his poems—from beginning to end they are bewitching; you cannot read about them without wanting to live with them; they were the best of parents. It is *this* that made Kipling what he was: if they had been the worst of parents, even fairly bad parents, even ordinary parents, it would all have made sense, Kipling himself could have made sense out of it. As it was, his world had been torn in two and he himself torn in two: for under the part of him that extenuated everything, blamed for nothing, there was certainly a part that extenuated nothing, blamed for everything—a part whose existence he never admitted, most especially not to himself. He says about some of the things that happened to him during those six years: "In the long run these things and many more of the like drained me of any capacity for real, personal hatred for the rest of my life." To admit from the unconscious something inadmissible, one can simply deny it, bring it up into the light with a *No;* Kipling has done so here—the capacity for real, personal hatred, real, personal revenge, summary fictional justice, is plain throughout Kipling's work. Listen to him tell how he first began to write. He has just been told about Dante: "I bought a fat, American-cloth-bound notebook and set to work on an *Inferno,* into which I put, under appropriate tortures, all my friends and most of the masters." (Why only *most?* Two were spared, one for the Father and one for the Mother.) Succinct and reticent as *Something of Myself* is, it has room for half a dozen scenes in which the helpless Kipling is remorselessly, systematically, comprehensively humiliated before the inhabitants of his universe. At school, for instance: "H—— then told me off before my delighted companions in his best style, which was acid and contumelious. He wound up with a few general remarks about dying as a 'scurrilous journalist' . . . The tone, matter, and setting of his discourse were as brutal as they were meant to be—brutal as the necessary wrench on the curb that fetches up a too-flippant colt." Oh, necessary, entirely necessary, we do but torture in education! one murmurs to these methodical justifications of brutality as methodical, one of authority's necessary stages. Here is another master: "Under him I came to feel that words could be used as weapons, for he did me the honor to talk at me plentifully . . . One learns more from a good scholar in a rage than from a score of lucid and laborious drudges; and to be made the butt of one's companions in full form is no bad preparation for later experiences. I think this 'approach' is now discouraged for fear of hurting the soul of youth, but in essence it is no more than rattling tins or firing squibs under a colt's nose. I remember nothing save satisfaction or envy when C—— broke his precious ointments over my head." Nothing? Better for Kipling if he had remembered—not remembering gets rid of nothing. Yet who knows? he may even have felt—known that he felt—"nothing save satisfaction and envy," the envying satisfaction of identification. As he says, he was learning from a master to use words as weapons, but he had already learned from his life a more difficult lesson: to know that, no matter how the sick heart and raw being rebel, it is all for the best; in the past there were the best of masters and in the future there will be the best of masters, if only we can wait out, bear out, the brutal present—the incomprehensible present that someday we shall comprehend as a lesson.

The scene changes from England to India, school to Club, but the action—passion, rather—is the same: "As I entered the long, shabby dining-room where we all sat at one table, everybody hissed. I was innocent enough to ask: 'What's the joke? Who are they hissing?' 'You,' said the man at my side. 'Your damn rag has ratted over the Bill.' It is not pleasant to sit still when one is twenty while all your universe hisses you." One expects next a sentence about how customary and salutary hissing is for colts, but for once it doesn't come; and when Kipling's syntax suffers as it does in this sentence, he is remembering something that truly is not pleasant. He even manages somewhat to justify, somehow to justify, his six years in Hell: the devils' inquisitions, after all, "made me give attention to the lies I soon found it necessary to tell; and this, I presume, is the foundation of literary effort . . . Nor was my life an unsuitable preparation for my future, in that it demanded constant wariness, the habit of observation and attendance on moods and tempers; the noting of discrepancies between speech and action; a certain reserve of demeanor; and automatic suspicion of sudden favors." I have seen writers called God's spies, but Kipling makes it sound as if they were just spies—or spies on God. If only he could have blamed God—his Gods—a little consciously, forgiven them a little unconsciously! could have felt that someone, sometimes, doesn't *mean* something to happen! But inside, and inside stories, everything is meant.

After you have read Kipling's fifty or seventy-five best stories you realize that few men have written this many stories of this much merit, and that very few have written more and better stories. Chekhov and Turgenev are two who immediately come to mind; and when I think of their stories I cannot help thinking of what seems to me the greatest lack in Kipling's. I don't know exactly what to call it: a lack of dispassionate moral understanding, perhaps—of the ability both to understand things and to understand that there is nothing to do about them. (In a story, after all, there is always something you *can* do, something that a part of you is always trying to make you do.) Kipling is a passionate moralist, with a detailed and occasionally profound knowledge of part of things; but his moral spectrum has shifted, so that he can see far down into the infrared, but is blind for some frequencies normal eyes are sensitive to. His morality is the one-sided, desperately protective, sometimes vindictive morality of someone who has been for some time the occupant of one of God's concentration camps, and has had to spend the rest of his life justifying or explaining out of existence what he cannot forget. Kipling tries so hard to celebrate and justify true authority, the work and habit and wisdom of the world, because he feels so bitterly the abyss of pain and insanity that they overlie, and can do—even will do—nothing to prevent.

Kipling's morality is the morality of someone who has to prove that God is not responsible for part of the world, and that the Devil is. If Father and Mother were not to blame for anything, yet what did happen to you could happen to you—if God is good, and yet the concentration camps exist—then there has to be *someone* to blame, and to punish too, some real, personal source of the world's evil. (He finishes "At the End of the Passage" by having someone quote: "There may be Heaven, there must be Hell. / Meanwhile there is our life here. Well?" In most of his stories he sees to it that our life here is Heaven and Hell.) But in this world, often, there is nothing to praise but no one to blame, and Kipling can bear to admit this in only a few of his stories. He writes about one source of things in his childhood: "And somehow or other I came across a tale about a lion-hunter in South Africa who fell among lions who were all Freemasons, and with them entered into a conspiracy against some wicked baboons. I think that, too, lay dormant until the Jungle Books began to be born." In Chekhov or Turgenev, somehow or other, the lions aren't really Freemasons and the baboons aren't really wicked. In Chekhov and Turgenev, in fact, most of the story has disappeared from the story: there was a lion-hunter in South Africa, and first he shot the lions, and then he shot the baboons, and finally he shot himself; and yet it wasn't *wicked*, exactly, but human—very human.

Kipling had learned too well and too soon that, in William James's words: "The normal process of life contains moments as bad as any of those which insane melancholy is filled with, moments in which radical evil gets its innings and takes its solid turn. The lunatic's visions of horror are all drawn from the material of daily fact. Our civilization is founded on the shambles, and each individual existence goes out in a lonely spasm of helpless agony. If you protest, my friend, wait till you arrive there yourself!" Kipling had arrived there early and returned there often. One thinks sadly of how deeply congenial to this torturing obsessive knowledge of Kipling's the First World War was: the death and anguish of Europe produced some of his best and most terrible stories, and the death of his own son, his own anguish, produced "Mary Postgate," that nightmarish, most human and most real daydream of personal revenge. The world *was* Hell and India underneath, after all; and he could say to the Victorian, Edwardian Europeans who had thought it all just part of his style: "You wouldn't believe me!"

Svidrigailov says: "We are always thinking of eternity as an idea that cannot be understood, something immense. But why must it be? What if, instead of all this, you suddenly find just a little room there, something like a village bath-house, grimy, and spiders in every corner, and that's all eternity is . . . I, you know, would certainly have made it so deliberately." Part of Kipling would have replied to this with something denunciatory and biblical, but another part would have blurted eagerly, like somebody out of *Kim:* "Oah yess, that is dam-well likely! Like a dak-bungalow, you know." It is an idea that would have occurred to him, down to the last *deliberately.*

But still another part of Kipling would suddenly have seen—he might even later have written it down, according to the dictates of his Daemon—a story about a boy who is abandoned in a little room, grimy, with spiders in every corner, and after a while the spiders come a little nearer, and a little nearer, and one of them is Father Spider, and one of them is Mother Spider, and the boy is their Baby Spider. To Kipling the world was a dark forest full of families: so that when your father and mother leave you in the forest to die, the wolves that come to eat you are always Father Wolf and Mother Wolf, your real father and real mother, and you are—as not even the little wolves ever quite are—their real son. The family romance, the two families of the Hero, have so predominant a place in no other writer. Kipling never said a word or thought a thought against his parents, "both so entirely comprehending that except in trivial matters we had hardly need of words"; few writers have made authority so tender, beautiful, and final—have had us miserable mortals serve better masters; *but* Kipling's Daemon kept bringing Kipling stories in which wild animals turn out to be the abandoned Mowgli's real father and mother, a heathen Lama turns out to be the orphaned Kim's real father—and Kipling wrote down the stories and read them aloud to his father and mother.

This is all very absurd, all very pathetic? Oh yes, that's very likely; but, reader, down in the darkness where the wishes sleep, snuggled together like bats, you and I are Baby Spider too. If you think *this* absurd you should read Tolstoy—all of Tolstoy. But I should remark, now, on something that any reader of Kipling will notice: that though he can seem extraordinarily penetrating or intelligent—inspired, even—he can also seem very foolish or very blind. This is a characteristic of the immortals from which only we mortals are free. They oversay everything. It is only ordinary readers and writers who have ordinary common sense, who are able to feel about things what an ordinarily sensible man should. To another age, of course, our ordinary common sense will seem very very common and ordinary, but not sense, exactly: sense never lasts for long; instead of having created our own personal daydream or nightmare, as the immortals do, we merely have consented to the general daydream or nightmare which our age accepted as reality—it will seem to posterity only sense to say so, and it will say so, before settling back into a common sense of its own.

In the relations of mortals and immortals, yesterday's and today's posterities, there is a certain pathos or absurdity. There is a certain absurdity in my trying to persuade you to read Kipling sympathetically— who are *we* to read or not read Kipling sympathetically? part of me grunts. Writing about just which writers people are or are not attracted to, these years—who was high in the nineteenth, who's low in the twentieth—all the other stock-market quotations of the centuries, makes me feel how much such things have to do with history, and how little with literature. The stories themselves are literature. While their taste is on my tongue, I can't help feeling that virtue is its own reward, that good writing will take care of itself. It is a feeling I have often had after reading all of an author: that there it is. I can see that if I don't write this about the stories, plenty of other writers will; that if you don't read the stories, plenty of other readers will. The man Kipling, the myth Kipling is over; but the stories themselves—Kipling—have all the time in the world. The stories—some of them—can say to us with the calm of anything that has completely realized its own nature: "Worry about yourselves, not us. *We're* all right."

And yet, I'd be sorry to have missed them, I'd be sorry for you to miss them. I have read one more time what I've read so often before, and have picked for you what seem—to a loving and inveterate reader, one ashamed of their faults and exalted by their virtues—fifty of Kipling's best stories.

In the Vernacular

IN THE VERNACULAR: THE ENGLISH IN INDIA, 1963

KIPLING was born in Bombay, in 1865. His earliest memories were memories of the native servants who took care of the little boy and his sister—of being "sent into the dining-room after we had been dressed, with the caution 'Speak English now to Papa and Mamma.' So one spoke 'English,' haltingly translated out of the vernacular idiom that one thought and dreamed in." Kipling's memory of going with his bearer Meeta "into little Hindu temples where being below the age of caste, I held his hand and looked at the dimly-seen, friendly Gods," will seem as appropriate to a reader, in one way, as his memory of the Parsee Towers of Silence will seem in another: "Near our little house on the Bombay Esplanade were the Towers of Silence, where their Dead are exposed to the waiting vultures on the rim of the towers, who scuffle and spread wings when they see the bearers of the Dead below. I did not understand my Mother's distress when she found 'a child's hand' in our garden, and said I was not to ask questions about it. I wanted to see that child's hand." A reader cannot help smiling at the last sentence: that child's hand was something Kipling never got over wanting to see, and for the rest of his life he managed either to see it, to dream that he saw it, or to pretend to his readers that he had seen it. Another language, other gods, other deaths: his life gave him these from the beginning.

When he was five he was given another life. The loved, spoiled child, the delight of his family and servants, was taken to "a dark land, and a darker room full of cold, in one wall of which a white woman made naked fire, and I cried aloud with dread, for I had never before seen a grate. Then came a new small house smelling of aridity and emptiness, and a parting in the dawn with Father and Mother, who said that I must learn quickly to read and write so that they might send me letters and books.

"I lived in that house for close on six years. It belonged to a woman who took in children whose parents were in India." Kipling and his little sister did not see their parents again for almost six years.

Kipling has written about these six years in *Something of Myself,* in "Baa Baa, Black Sheep," and in *The Light That Failed.* For him they were years of "calculated torture—religious as well as scientific . . . It was an establishment run with the full vigour of the Evangelical as revealed to the Woman. I had never heard of Hell, so I was introduced to it in all its terrors—I and whatever luckless little slavey might be in the house, whom severe rationing had led to steal food. Once I saw the Woman beat such a girl who picked up the kitchen poker and threatened retaliation. Myself I was regularly beaten. The Woman had an only son of twelve or thirteen as religious as she. I was a real joy to him, for when his mother had finished with me for the day he (we slept in the same room) took me on and roasted the other side . . .

"I was made to read without explanation, under the usual fear of punishment. And on a day that I remember it came to me that 'reading' was not 'the Cat lay on the Mat,' but a means to everything that would make me happy. So I read all that came within my reach. As soon as my pleasure in this was known, deprivation from reading was added to my punishments. I then read by stealth and the more earnestly . . .

"My troubles settled themselves in a few years. My eyes went wrong, and I could not well see to read. For which reason I read the more and in bad lights. My work at the terrible little day-school where I had been sent suffered in consequence, and my monthly reports showed it. The loss of 'reading-time' was the worst of my 'home' punishments for bad school-work. One report was so bad that I threw it away and said that I had never received it . . . I was well beaten and sent to school through the streets of Southsea with the placard 'Liar' between my shoulders . . .

"Some sort of nervous breakdown followed, for I imagined I saw shadows and things that were not there, and they worried me more than the Woman . . . A man came down to see me as to my eyes and reported that I was half-blind. This, too, was supposed to be 'showing-off,' and I was segregated from my sister—another punishment—as a sort of moral leper. Then—I do not remember that I had any warning—the Mother returned from India. She told me afterwards that when she first came up to my room to kiss me good-night, I flung up an arm to guard off the cuff that I had been trained to expect."

After some happy months with his mother, Kipling was sent to the school that *Stalky and Co.* has made real to so many readers. The United Services College at Westward Ho! was, as Kipling writes, "largely a caste-school—some seventy-five per cent of us had been born outside England and hoped to follow their fathers in the Army"; its headmaster was Cormell Price, a cultivated friend of Kipling's family, whom the boy had learned to call "Uncle Crom." Kipling remembered his first term there as "horrible" and his first year and a half as "not pleasant"; his own memories of his last two and a half years there and of the two friends who were the originals of Stalky and M'Turk seem to correspond almost exactly to *Stalky and Co.* (Both Stalky and M'Turk have written their own memoirs, and it is interesting to see how far these agree with and disagree with Kipling's—their general tone is often surprisingly different.) One has the impression that Kipling's memories of literary things—as he gives them in "Regulus," "The Propagation of Knowledge," and his account of the last examination at the school—are more accurate than some of the other memories and inventions that *Stalky and Co.* combines. The Head, for instance, was in reality a far gentler and less conventional man than the awing, omniscient figure of authority of the stories; in *Something of Myself* Kipling tells how he was " 'nursed' with care by Crom and under his orders. Hence, when he saw I was irretrievably committed to the ink-pot, his order that I should edit the School Paper and have the run of his Library Study . . . Many of us loved the Head for what he had done for us, but I owed him more than all of them put together . . . There came a day when he told me that a fortnight after the close of the summer holidays of '82, I would go to India to work on a paper in Lahore, where my parents lived, and would get one hundred silver rupees a month! . . .

"So, at sixteen years and nine months, but looking four or five years older, and adorned with real whiskers which the scandalised Mother abolished within one hour of beholding, I found myself at Bombay where I was born, moving among sights and smells that made me deliver in the vernacular sentences whose meaning I knew not . . . There were yet three or four days' rail to Lahore, where my people lived. After these, my English years fell away, nor ever, I think, came back in full strength." That Kipling should make this last remark after thirty years' life in Sussex seems to me particularly interesting. It is only partially accurate, I think: his first six years in England remained with him in full strength for the rest of his life.

Kipling then lived for some years with the people he loved best: his father and mother and, a little later, his sister. "Not only were we happy but we knew it," he writes; his description of the first days of the new life is full of the delight of a child who is getting to play house exactly like the grown-ups: "I had my own room in the house; my servant, handed over to me by my father's servant, whose son he was, with the solemnity of a marriage-contract; my own horse, cart, and groom; my own office-hours and direct responsibilities; and—oh joy!— my own office-box, just like my Father's . . .

"My Chief took me in hand, and for three years or so I loathed him. He had to break me in, and I knew nothing. What he suffered on my account I cannot tell; but the little that I ever acquired of accuracy, the habit of trying at least to verify references, and some knack of sticking to desk-work, I owed wholly to Stephen Wheeler.

"I never worked less than ten hours and seldom more than fifteen per diem; and as our paper came out in the evening did not see the midday sun except on Sundays. I had fever too, regular and persistent, to which I added for a while chronic dysentery. Yet I discovered that a man can work with a temperature of 104, even though next day he has to ask the office who wrote the article . . . From the modern point of view I suppose the life was not fit for a dog, but my world was filled with boys, but a few years older than I, who lived utterly alone, and died from typhoid mostly at the regulation age of twenty-two . . . Books, plays, pictures, and amusements, outside of what games the cold weather allowed, there were none . . . Death was always our near companion. When there was an outbreak of eleven cases of typhoid in our white community of seventy, and professional nurses had not been invented, the men sat up with the men and the women with the women. We lost four of our invalids and thought we had done well. Otherwise, men and women dropped where they stood. Hence our custom of looking up any one who did not appear at our daily gatherings.

"The dead of all times were about us—in the vast forgotten Muslim cemeteries round the Station, where one's horse's hoof of a morning might break through to the corpse below; skulls and bones tumbled out of our mud garden walls, and were turned up among the flowers by the Rains; and at every point were tombs of the dead. Our chief picnic rendezvous and some of our public offices had been memorials to desired dead women; and Fort Lahore, where Runjit Singh's wives lay, was a mausoleum of ghosts . . .

"My Mother and sister would go up to the Hills for the hot weather, and in due course my Father too . . . Thus I often lived alone in the big house, where I commanded by choice native food, as less revolting than meat-cookery, and so added indigestion to my more intimate possessions.

"In those months—mid-April to mid-October—one took up one's bed and walked about with it from room to room, seeking for less heated air; or slept on the flat roof with the waterman to throw half-skinfuls of water on one's parched carcase. This brought on fever but saved heat-stroke.

"Often the night got into my head . . . and I would wander till dawn in all manner of odd places—liquor-shops, gambling- and opium-dens, which are not a bit mysterious, wayside entertainments such as puppet-shows, native dances; or in and about the narrow gullies under the Mosque of Wazir Khan for the sheer sake of looking . . . One would come home, just as the light broke, in some night-hawk of a hired carriage which stank of hookah-fumes, jasmine-flowers, and sandalwood; and if the driver were moved to talk, he told one a good deal . . .

"My month's leave at Simla, or whatever Hill Station my people went to, was pure joy—every golden hour counted. It began in heat and discomfort, by rail and road. It ended in the cool evening, with a wood fire in one's bedroom, and next morn—thirty more of them ahead!—the early cup of tea, the Mother who brought it in, and the long talks of us all together again . . . Simla was another new world. There the Hierarchy lived, and one saw and heard the machinery of administration stripped bare . . .

"Till I was in my twenty-fourth year, I no more dreamed of dressing myself than I did of shutting an inner door or—I was going to say turning a key in a lock. But we had no locks. I gave myself indeed the trouble of stepping into the garments that were held out to me after my bath, and out of them as I was assisted to do. And—luxury of which I dream still—I was shaved before I was awake!

"One must set these things against the taste of fever in one's mouth, and the buzz of quinine in one's ears; the temper frayed by heat to the breaking-point but for sanity's sake held back from the break; the descending darkness of intolerable dusks; and the less supportable dawns of fierce, stale heat through half of the year . . . Though I was spared the worst horrors, thanks to the pressure of work, a capacity for being able to read, and the pleasure of writing what my head was filled with, I felt each succeeding hot weather more and more, and cowered in my soul as it returned." Later in *Something of Myself* Kipling writes: "I had broken down twice in India from straight overwork, plus fever and dysentery."

Kipling's earliest stories, written when he was only twenty, were *Plain Tales from the Hills*. He was forced to "write short," since these had to fit into a "turnover" of a column and a quarter. Later on Kipling was put in charge of "a weekly edition of the *Pioneer* for Home consumption," with a whole page of "syndicated serial-matter bought by the running foot . . . Why buy Bret Harte, I asked, when I was prepared to supply home-grown fiction on the hoof? . . . Henceforth no mere twelve-hundred Plain Tales . . . but three- or five-thousand-word cartoons once a week." By the time he went back to England, at twenty-three, Kipling had published, in India, *Plain Tales from the Hills, Departmental Ditties,* and "six small paper-backed railway-bookstall volumes embodying most of my tales in the *Weekly.*" With the exception of "William the Conqueror," "The Miracle of Purun Bhagat," and "In the Presence," all the stories in this volume are taken from these books and from the first that followed them—books that, printed in the West, were to make Kipling one of the best-known writers in the world.

In one sentence Kipling divides his early stories into "soldier tales, Indian tales, and tales of the opposite sex." (One might add to these, bureaucratic or governmental stories and stories of death or disease or the supernatural, of extreme situations of every sort.) Kipling makes very few comments about these early stories; but after telling about a tale "of the opposite sex . . . which, because of a doubt, I handed up to the Mother, who abolished it and wrote me: *Never you do that again,*" he continues: "But I did and managed to pull off, not unhandily, a tale called 'A Wayside Comedy,' where I worked hard for a certain 'economy of implication,' and in one phrase of less than a dozen words believed I had succeeded. More than forty years later a Frenchman, browsing about some of my old work, quoted this phrase as the *clou* of the tale and the key to its method. It was a belated 'workshop compliment' that I appreciated."

"A Wayside Comedy" is a merciless and truthful story, one of the best that Kipling ever wrote; one wonders what Kipling's mother had to say about *it.* Both the form and content of this almost geometrical story of love under laboratory conditions are the opposite of what one would expect from a Victorian, English story of a love affair—no wonder some of his first readers were shocked at Kipling's "brutality" and "vulgarity." When Kipling, in his old age, writes about the story entirely in terms of the "economy of implication" of one "phrase of less than a dozen words," and the "workshop compliment" that this got him, isn't he managing to substitute neutral technical considerations for any consideration of the qualities that, perhaps, have come to seem a little shocking to Kipling himself? I cannot identify that phrase—perhaps the reader can; to me the phrase in the story with the most economy of implication is simply the name Ted.

It is interesting to compare "A Wayside Comedy" with "William the Conqueror," a love story that Kipling wrote ten or twelve years later. There is plenty of reality to the famine, the governmental workers who fight it, the two good and attractive people who fall in love—yet how terribly licit their love affair is, how entirely approving and sentimental are the comments of the wise old ones who know what is happening long before the young ones have realized it! The characters are examined—and yet all of them have, so to speak, been given an A before they take the examination. *Plain Tales from the Hills'* comment on Anglo-Indian bureaucracy—"Good work does not matter, because a man is judged by his worst output . . . Bad work does not matter, because other men do worse . . . It is a slack country, where all men work with imperfect instruments"—would seem as out-of-place in "William the Conqueror" as it would seem in a commemorative service. The story is—to pay it that final Victorian compliment—one that any young girl can read without being shocked; whereas "A Wayside Comedy," like many of Kipling's early stories, is supposed to shock not just the girl but the girl's mother with its intimate knowledge of "the other sex." All the once-famous Mrs. Hauksbee stories (I realized with a pang that I could find none to include in this book) are supposed first of all to make the reader exclaim: "How could a *man* know that?" Unless, crouched under a table among corset covers and false hair, the author overheard the whole thing, he must have been on terms of the greatest intimacy with one of the most knowing of women, to have so professional a knowledge of one of earth's ultimate professions. All of these stories and almost all of some even more famous stories, the stories of the Three Musketeers, are hurt by the knowing essayistic remarks they seem almost to exist for, the showing-off of a young man who realizes to his own astonished delight that he can tell you about anything, always, from the inside. (As Kipling says, "all the queer outside world" dropped in at his newspaper office sooner or later; at the Club he met "none except picked men at their definite work— Civilians, Army, Education, Canals, Forestry, Engineering, Irrigation, Railways, Doctors, and Lawyers—samples of each branch and each talking his own shop"; and Kipling had a specialized enough acquaintance with enlisted men to be asked by Lord Roberts, the Commander in Chief in India, "what the men thought about their accommodation, entertainment-rooms and the like.") "The Drums of the Fore and Aft," for instance, begins with a six-page essay on the British soldier under fire, the tone of which is embarrassingly omniscient; and some of Kipling's political and social writing is worse.

Yet the offhand, laconic, matter-of-fact, conversational tone of *Plain Tales from the Hills,* the little asides or pieces of intimate information that remind the insider of what he and the author already know, and impress the outsider with that shared knowledge that constitutes a world—these and the continual understatement, the continual contrast of form and content, the continual "writing short," all help to give the stories their particular force. Only six or eight of the forty *Plain Tales from the Hills* are very good stories, and yet somehow the whole book is better than the best of the stories, and gives the reader a surprisingly vivid and comprehensive feeling of the society that produced it. "Lispeth" is a succinct and conclusive anecdote of the betrayal of a native girl—whom Kipling treats with thorough imaginative sympathy—by English hypocrisy, the Protestant, missionary self-righteousness and self-centeredness that Kipling had so early learned to detest; what the story ironically doesn't say, its entire absence of any palliation or justification of what happens, help to give it its attractive, slightly mannered, concise elegance. Kipling's account of the servant's child who, like a bowerbird, makes his queer little pebble-and-glass-and-feather constructions among the castor-oil bushes of the garden is also notable for what it doesn't say: "The Story of Muhammad Din," a plain, representative anecdote, quite moving and quite unsentimental, seems to me the best of Kipling's early stories about children. (Stories like "Wee Willie Winkie," "His Majesty the King," and "Tods' Amendment"—what you can call, with rough accuracy, Kipling's Little Lord Fauntleroy pieces—are sentimental contrivances that worked with our grandparents and no longer work with us; we have our own.) "A Bank Fraud" is a queerly touching story, ambiguous as life, about the children of darkness being wiser in their generation than the children of light; the "savage self-conceit" of the harshly unworldly accountant, the elaborate, unthanked, unmotivated kindness of the worldly manager, as he sits obediently "reading the Bible and grim 'Methody' tracts" to the dying man, and plans each day's consoling lies—the whole thing is very human and very appealing, down to its last two-faced sentence. "False Dawn," the story of a picnic and a proposal, with complications, makes a reader feel that he has been dipped into Anglo-Indian society for a night, without reservations; by the end of it he is willing to repeat admiringly, with the narrator: "I never knew anything so un-English in my life." It has, perhaps, more sensory immediacy than any of the other *Plain Tales*—or, at least, than any except "In the House of Suddhoo": this presentation of a séance in a native house, and the hodgepodge of attitudes and emotions that goes with it, has at its best an uncanny actuality—Kipling's description of the seal cutter's "unspeakable triple crawl," of the "lip-lip-lapping" of the baby's head in the basin, comes almost too close for comfort. Even the most knowing Anglo-Indians are not much more than accidents at the edge of *this* world. "Jews in Shushan" (it is not actually one of the *Plain Tales* but is so understated, so decidedly "written short," that I always mistakenly remember it as one, along with "At the Pit's Mouth") is a grim, wry little story of the precariousness of life for some other accidents powerless within a large and deadly world; Kipling's picture of the "meek bill-collector at his work, nostrils dilated, lips drawn back over his teeth, and his hands upon a half-maddened sheep" is something else that comes uncomfortably close, and helps to give the story its ambiguous actuality. "At the Pit's Mouth" is a poker-faced story in which all the lines are thrown away. Its organization is as exact as its pictures of the Simla Cemetery, the accident on the Himalayan-Tibet Road, are arresting; the whole story has an unpitying finality about it. It is one of the best and is decidedly the most unpleasant of all Kipling's stories of illicit affairs—it is queer to remember that these were one of his specialties in his early twenties, just as stories actually or ostensibly for children became one of his specialties in his thirties and early forties, and were replaced for the rest of his life by entirely adult stories. "The Man Who Would Be King" is an effective, rather showy adventure story that seems to me romantic in the bad sense of the word; its frame of Indian events is more plausible and attractive than its central action in Kafiristan, which requires a great deal of willing credulity on the reader's part. Many anthologists seem to have said about it, "I guess we'd better put in 'The Man Who Would Be King' for Kipling"; yet, effective as it is, is it really one of his best stories? When I was a boy I used to read, in a magazine called *Adventure,* stories by a thoroughly Kiplingesque writer named Talbot Mundy; it seems to me that "The Man Who Would Be King" is closer to the best of those stories than it is to the best of Kipling's.

"Without Benefit of Clergy," another favorite of anthologists, is different. What begins as an equivocal idyl, glistening in the ornate scrollwork of its exotically romantic wording, customs, costumes, ends as harsh and pitiable actuality. It is not one of those stories of Kipling's that you admire for its perfection of realization: many of the speeches in the vernacular seem, to this reader's ignorant guess, contrived, and the little essays on death and pestilence in India, the introduction of the Member for Lower Tooting—that regular interrupting fool in several of Kipling's early stories—seem badly out of place here. Yet there is something appealing and truthful to the story; it is a real thing you want different, instead of an entertainment you enjoy and dismiss. If only its treatment of native speech were as sweepingly effective as "Dray Wara Yow Dee" 's (a dramatic monologue that is Kipling's prose equivalent of "Soliloquy of the Spanish Cloister") or as quietly and completely plausible as "In the Presence" 's! This last story has the great interest, to a devoted reader of Kipling, of being a late story about India; as you read this new treatment of old material you realize what a delicately skillful writer Kipling has become, and long for him to have written more such stories.

"Namgay Doola" is a lighthearted, lightweight, colorful story of life in an out-of-the-way spot in the Himalayas. It is a little too good to be true, and it presupposes in the reader an attitude toward the Irish that not many readers are likely to have any longer, but if the reader is willing to make a few allowances (more or less as if he were dressing for a ball in honor of Modjeska and Dr. Livingstone) he will enjoy himself. "The Miracle of Purun Bhagat," another story of the Himalayas, needs no such concessions on the reader's part: its pictorial qualities, its style, and its accepting tenderness for the little world it describes, make this tapestry-like legend something one can read along with *Kim*.

"On Greenhow Hill" seems to me quite exceptionally the best of Kipling's stories about the Three Musketeers; what Learoyd says and what Ortheris does, as they approach each other and finally coincide, give the story an extraordinarily effective organization. (When you compare Kipling's knowledge of Learoyd's speech and world with his knowledge of Sussex ways and speech, in a story like "Friendly Brook," he seems only moderately acquainted with the first—yet the story isn't spoiled.) "Black Jack" may very well be the next best of these stories of Mulvaney, Learoyd, and Ortheris. It is a representative piece, full of rude force, that has the partial disadvantage of being told in Mulvaneyese, a creative, more-than-colorful dialect that only Kipling pretending to be Irish has ever quite spoken. These two stories of soldiers, like any of Kipling's early stories about military things, are not nearly so much reports of wartime conditions as is "At the End of the Passage." Much of this account of civil service in India "when she turns herself for six months into a house of torment" is genuinely terrible, in the way that a truthful and detailed picture of an extreme situation always is; it is too bad that, for a few paragraphs, Kipling substitutes for these real terrors the contrived terrors of a supernatural something photographed in a dead man's eyes. Both real and contrived terrors were very dear to the Kipling of those early years; it is only because I am including them in another Anchor book (of Kipling's stories of extreme situations, of ghosts, nightmares, revenge, practical jokes, nervous breakdowns) that I have omitted from this book "The Phantom 'Rickshaw," "The Return of Imray," "The Sending of Dana Da," "The Gate of the Hundred Sorrows," "The Rout of the White Hussars," "A Sahibs' War." Similarly, I have not included in this book such Indian stories as "The Undertakers," "In the Rukh," and "The Maltese Cat," since they are to be part of a forthcoming book called *Other Worlds.**

Kipling might have used for all his stories of the English in India a title like Alfred de Vigny's *Splendors and Miseries of Military Life:* his splendid and miserable civil servants, in their petty and dangerous, homesick and homey little enclave there in the midst of a half-alien, half-familiar world, were living under wartime conditions that the English in England knew nothing of, till they read about them in Kipling's stories. (In the same way, Kipling was the first English writer in many generations to bring home to the English what the life of the ordinary English soldier was like.) Some sentence akin to *What do they know of England who only England know?* is the real motto of this volume: behind most of these stories is Kipling's conviction that he and his Anglo-Indians knew life as the English in England could never know it—knew, that is, the wild, varied, and terrible existence of the planet Earth, and not the tame and restricted existence of a Victorian island. (Of course, the tame and restricted existence of a Victorian island *was* the wild, varied, and terrible existence of the planet Earth, as some of his later stories show—but, in general, it takes a writer greater than Kipling fully to convince us of this.) If the world that Kipling depicts gives these stories some of their individuality, it is his own temperament, his own powers of observation and empathy and invention, that give them their originality—several generations of imitators have left his stories of India unique.

* The projected anthologies mentioned here were never completed.—Ed.

The English in England

To most of us Kipling means India. Kipling's masterpiece, *Kim,* is an Indian story; so are *The Jungle Books;* so are the stories that made Kipling, in his thirties, the best-known writer in the world. It was this Indian Kipling whom Henry James called "the most complete man of genius (as distinct from fine intelligence) that I have ever known." Yet many, even most, of Kipling's best stories are stories of the English in England; the stories of Kipling's old age or late middle age—work that shows the easy and decisive mastery that was the result of a lifetime of imaginative realization—are with a few exceptions stories about England.

Here are fourteen such stories. Ten or eleven of them, perhaps, are among the best stories Kipling ever wrote, and the others have a particular interest of one kind or another. "Baa Baa, Black Sheep" is the one purely autobiographical story of a reticent and private-spirited author (his story of the future, "As Easy as A.B.C.," makes "invasion of privacy" the sin upon which his new society is based); and since "Baa Baa, Black Sheep" is the only early story in this volume, it gives the reader a chance to compare some good and some excellent examples of his later style with an example of the live and effective, but relatively crude, style of the earlier stories. "The Vortex" is one of the funnier examples of a compulsive form, Kipling's practical-joke story; the reader may feel, as I do, that he enjoys Kipling's farce for its charm and landscape, and is indifferent to its point. As for " 'In the Interests of the Brethren,' " it is pure charm—who would have supposed that you could make, of the meeting of an imaginary Masonic lodge, one of the most winning of sketches? I imagine that, except for *The Magic Flute,* it is the most attractive work of art Masonry has produced.

But at this point the reader may feel like remarking: "Autobiography, compulsive practical jokes, Masonry—do the subjects of the stories keep on like this?" Well, yes. But let me sum up the subjects in a sentence, and you can judge for yourself. In these fourteen stories a drugged, lovesick, and consumptive pharmacist, on an icy winter night, writes part of "The Eve of St. Agnes"; an elderly cook tells an elderly countrywoman, her friend, the story of how she took upon herself her lover's cancer; an urban intellectual, after inheriting a place in the country, gradually falls in love with country and county ways; a man visits the house of a blind woman, a house haunted by children; the boys of a Latin class translate an ode of Horace's and apply it to their everyday affairs; two countrymen eat their midday meal beside a flooded brook, and discuss a providential murder the brook has committed; a child from India undergoes five years of bullying and torture in a lower-middle-class English household; the railway station and crossroads of an English village are immobilized by four cartons of bees; a rich and nervous American and his wife are converted to the tranquil country ways of their English forebears; some motorists of varied distinction, fined and insulted in a village road trap, avenge themselves by a geometrical progression of practical jokes that leaves the village the laughingstock of several continents; a shell-shocked artilleryman encounters at the front a little group of admirers of Jane Austen; a middle-aged woman, while burning the effects of a dead R.F.C. pilot, her employer's nephew, finds a wounded German pilot in the underbrush and watches him die there; a man gives up, out of ordinary human feeling, his long-prepared revenge upon a petty and despicable scholar.

Revenge, love, disease and death, the supernatural, extreme situations, practical jokes, country ways, literature: these are some of the things that keep recurring in the stories. Yet the list of subjects seems to me, as I imagine it seems to the reader, a surprisingly varied and unusual one. Kipling is one of the most effectively realistic of writers— his stories are dazzling in their verisimilitude, their extraordinarily broad and detailed knowledge of special ways of speech and life, of a hundred varieties of local color; yet they are never mere slices of life, and are even more notable for their imagination than for their realism. If the reality principle has pruned and clipped them into plausibility, it is the pleasure principle out of which they first rankly and satisfyingly flowered. Kipling is far closer to Gogol than to a normal realist or naturalist: in Kipling the pressure of the imagination has forced facts over into the supernatural, into personally satisfying jokes or revenges, into personally compulsive fantasies or neuroses. Then too, like Gogol, Kipling is one of the great stylists of his language, one of those writers who can make a list more interesting than an ordinary writer's murder. For instance: "Everything his eyes opened upon was his very own to keep for ever. The carved four-post Chippendale bed, obviously worth hundreds; the wavy walnut William and Mary chairs—he had seen worse ones labelled twenty guineas apiece; the oval medallion mirror; the delicate eighteenth-century wire fireguard; the heavy brocaded curtains were his—all his. So, too, a great garden full of birds that faced him when he shaved; a mulberry tree, a sun-dial, and a dull, steel-coloured brook that murmured level with the edge of a lawn a hundred yards away. Peculiarly and privately his own was the smell of sausages and coffee that he sniffed at the head of the wide square landing, all set round with mysterious doors and Bartolozzi prints. He spent two hours after breakfast in exploring his new possessions. His heart leaped up at such things as sewing-machines, a rubber-tyred bath-chair in a tiled passage, a malachite-headed Malacca cane, boxes and boxes of unopened stationery, seal-rings, bunches of keys, and at the bottom of a steel-net reticule a little leather purse with seven pounds ten shillings in gold and eleven shillings in silver."

All the things of the list—beginning and ending with that great thing, money—are alive, and either move us specifically or hold out to us the general possibility of motion. The man who can fill two sentences with those semicolons, and then not use another in the paragraph; who can begin two sentences *So, too, a great garden . . .* and *Peculiarly and privately his own . . .* and give every other sentence a perfectly ordinary beginning; who can invent the passage-work that, from *a rubber tyred bath-chair in a tiled passage,* makes its way, through an elderly invalid's possessions, into the culminating *little leather purse with seven pounds ten shillings in gold and eleven shillings in silver*—the man who can do this, and still not have a word obvious or a rhythm obtrusive, really knows how to write. As Chekhov said, and as everybody remembers, you must never hang a pistol on the wall in the first act unless someone is going to shoot himself with it in the last; here the dull, steel-colored brook murmurs level with the edge of a lawn a hundred yards away only because, twenty pages later, that brook is to flood the whole story.

Yet the story from which I am quoting, " 'My Son's Wife,' " is a live thing with one leg missing. If Kipling had read it and not written it, he could not have helped seeing that the country is created in beautiful detail, favorable and unfavorable, but that the city intellectuals are set up and knocked down with blankly abstract, pharisaical irony; they are just Bandar-log, after all, and the few details Kipling is willing to waste on them are not observed but invented. We more or less gather that Midmore spent his London hours lying on pillows with women, at teatime, but we neither see the women nor feel the pillows. When we finish the story we are as sure that the country Midmore read

Surtees (down to that last haunting sentence: "When at length they rose to go to bed it struck each man as he followed his neighbor upstairs, that the man before him walked very crookedly") as that the idiot wailed, " 'Fraid o' the water! 'Fraid o' the water!" But what did the unconverted Midmore read in London? The Webbs? Wells? Frazer? We respond: "Since you say so," to Midmore's previous condition of servitude, but it is about as real to us as is the earlier career of one of those people in Mark Twain who used to be pirates but have taken to making testimonial speeches for temperance societies, now. Yet, ordinarily, no writer of fiction is better at making literature alive to us as social fact. Literature, in Kipling's stories, is something that makes behavior, is as much an effective part of life as religion or politics. We see this in exaggerated form in "The Janeites": part of the reader's pleasure in the story—as in so many of Kipling's stories— is that it couldn't possibly really have happened so, and yet it is happening before our eyes. But Kipling's treatment of literature and education in "Regulus" seems exactly truthful in both essence and detail—*is* there a better treatment of a class in fiction?

If Kipling had written: "What do they know of England who only England know?" a few years earlier than he did, his readers might have replied: "What does he know of England who has spent most of his life in India and Vermont?" But in 1896, after the public difficulties with his wife's brother that led him to remark: "There are only two places in the world where I want to live—Bombay and Brattleboro. And I can't live at either," Kipling and his American wife went to live in the English countryside, in a house so hauntingly unpleasant to them that Kipling wrote a kind of psychiatric ghost story about it ("The House Surgeon"); they did not find "Bateman's," the Sussex house where they spent the rest of their lives, until 1902. "An Habitation Enforced" is, I think, a fantasy about the way it would have been if the Kiplings had returned to a house and country at once magically their own: the American millionaire and his wife are blank sticks on which a wish is hung. And, too, there is the same family romance behind the story that is behind *Kim* and *The Jungle Books;* it is not until they leave their ostensible ones that the Americans discover their true home and family. ("Baa Baa, Black Sheep" and the chapter on the same subject in *Something of Myself* show us why Kipling, the most devoted of sons, had his lifelong compulsive belief in this fantasy.) "Friendly Brook" and "The Wish House" are two of the stories that demonstrate the microscopic, loving knowledge of Sussex and its inhabitants that Kipling eventually came to have. A farm laborer whom

Kipling knew particularly well said to someone, after Kipling's death, that the old fool did nothing but ask you questions; stories like these are the result of many asked and many unasked questions. The primary pleasure of a story like "Friendly Brook" is the atmosphere ("so choked with fog that one could scarcely see a cow's length across a field") through which it comes to us; grim, plain, warped through work and workaday speech, the happenings have the harshly satisfactory reality that they have in one of Frost's country stories: " 'Dada' he says, an' 'Mumma' he says, with his great rollin' head-piece all hurdled up in that iron collar. *He* won't live long—his backbone's rotten, like . . . No! 'Twadn't no stroke. It stifled the old lady in the throat here. First she couldn't shape her words no shape; then she clucked, like, an' lastly she couldn't more than suck down spoon-meat an' hold her peace. Jim took her to Doctor Harding, an' Harding he bundled her off to Brighton Hospital on a ticket, but they couldn't make no stay to her afflictions there; and she was bundled off to Lunnon, an' they lit a great old lamp inside her, and Jim told me they couldn't make out nothing in no sort there; and, along o' one thing an' another, an' all their spyin's and pryin's, she come back a hem sight worse than when she started. Jim said he'd have no more hospitalizin', so he give her a slate, which she tied to her waist-string, and what she was minded to say she writ on it." The happenings of "The Wish House" are given something of the same atmosphere and the same reality, but the happenings themselves are the strange mixture of love, disease, and the supernatural that had an almost obsessive attraction for Kipling. The love affairs of most stories, compared to those of Kipling's later stories, seem attractive preoccupations of the young; in his the poor and ugly and sick and middle-aged are overwhelmed by something drab, raw, but ultimate.

There are few stories that seem, first of all and last of all, beautiful; " 'They' " is one. It is almost as if the story's extraordinary beauty of picturing, and of the style which pictures, came out of Kipling's desire to have the story a memorial to his own dead daughter. It is a memorial in three tapestries, an early-summer, a late-summer, and an autumn day; the days themselves are hardly more beautiful than the story's movement through the days, the gradual change from loving ignorance into knowledge, the change from the first glimpses of the children, out of the corner of the eye, into the last "little brushing kiss" that "fell in the centre of my palm—as a gift on which the fingers were, once, expected to close: as the all-faithful half-reproachful signal of a waiting child not used to neglect even when grown-ups were busiest—a fragment of the mute code devised very long ago. Then I knew." The treatment of the children is so delicately and hauntingly convincing that it is no wonder "Burnt Norton" should have been influenced by it; yet the tallies with which the blind woman runs her farms, the colored Egg of the soul which the blind woman sees, the blind woman's last piteous, "Oh, you *must* bear or lose. There is no other way"—all this and much more than this are as convincing.

It is interesting to compare the naturally beautiful " 'They' " with the harshly and uncannily colorful " 'Wireless,' " a story that leaves a sort of stained-glass deposit in the memory. It is seen and felt and heard as few stories are: if genius is the ability to perceive (and to make us perceive) likenesses never before seen, in concise hallucinatory form, then " 'Wireless' " is a work of genius. It is certainly a work of astonishing originality, of the most extraordinary professional skill. Here, for instance, is Kipling's description of a drugstore on a cold night: "Across the street blank shutters flung back the gaslight in cold smears; the dried pavement seemed to rough up in goose-flesh under the scouring of the savage wind, and we could hear, long ere he passed, the policeman flapping his arms to keep himself warm. Within, the flavours of cardamoms and chloric-ether disputed those of the pastilles and a score of drugs and perfume and soap scents. Our electric lights, set low down in the windows before the tun-bellied Rosamond jars, flung inward three monstrous daubs of red, blue, and green, that broke into kaleidoscopic lights on the faceted knobs of the drug-drawers, the cut-glass scent flagons, and the bulbs of the sparklet bottles. They flushed the white-tiled floor in gorgeous patches; splashed along the nickel-silver counter-rails, and turned the polished mahogany counter-panels to the likeness of intricate grained marbles—slabs of porphyry and malachite. Mr. Shaynor unlocked a drawer, and ere he began to write, took out a meagre bundle of letters. From my place by the stove, I could see the scalloped edges of the paper with a flaring monogram in the corner and could even smell the reek of chypre. At each page he turned toward the toilet-water lady of the advertisement and devoured her with overluminous eyes. He had drawn the Austrian blanket over his shoulders, and among those warring lights he looked more than ever the incarnation of a drugged moth—a tiger-moth as I thought." One feels after reading this: well, no one ever again will have to describe a drugstore; many of Kipling's descriptive sentences have this feeling of finality.

As he got older, Kipling found it necessary to write more and more elaborately farcical practical-joke stories—stories of revenge,

often; the confirmed reader will immediately think of pieces like
"'Brugglesmith,'" "My Sunday at Home," "The Puzzler," "The Vortex," "The Village That Voted the Earth Was Flat," "The Bonds of
Discipline," "Steam Tactics," "'Their Lawful Occasions,'" "Aunt
Ellen," "The Miracle of St. Jubanus," "Beauty Spots." I myself can read
these stories with pleasure. (But if Kipling had written instructions on
how to make a bed with hospital corners, or how to can gooseberries,
I could read them with pleasure: as one of his characters exclaims, "It
was the tone, man, the tone!") Most of these farces are stories for the
confirmed reader only, since they have been written by the writer for the
writer: in them, often, the writer tells us how he laughs so hard that he
cannot speak or see or stand up, and how that luckiest of all winds, the
dawn wind, comes and whispers to him that the next day everything is
going to be even better. "The Village That Voted the Earth Was Flat"
quite overcomes these humble, compulsive beginnings: a little of it
is a little too good to be true, but what a knowing ingenuity of invention it has, how extraordinarily it is imagined! When the true flat-
earthers strike up their hymn,

> *Hear ther truth our tongues are telling,*
> *Spread ther light from shore to shore,*
> *God hath given man a dwelling*
> *Flat and flat for evermore.*

> *When ther Primal Dark retreated,*
> *when ther deeps were undesigned,*
> *He with rule and level meted*
> *Habitation for mankind!*

you feel like muttering with the envious music-hall impresario: "Curse
Nature, she gets ahead of you every time," till you remember that it is
Kipling himself, here, who is both Nature and Art.

I had always supposed that Kipling wrote "Mary Postgate" a few
months after his son was killed in the First World War, and it had
seemed to me an awful but in some sense normal thing. When you
learn that the story was written several months before his son's death,
you are troubled just as you are when you learn that Mahler's *Kinder-
totenlieder* was written before and not after the death of his child. This
truthfully cruel, human-all-too-human wish-fantasy is as satisfying to
one part of our nature as it is terrible to another. What happens is
implausible but intensely actual: the German pilot isn't really there,

of course, except in our desire, but his psychological reality is absolute, down to the last groan of the head that "moved ceaselessly from side to side . . . as pale as a baby's, and so closely cropped that she could see the disgusting pinky skin beneath"; we are forced to believe in him just as Freud was forced to believe in his first patients' fantasies of seduction. "Dayspring Mishandled," one of the most morally appealing of Kipling's stories, is very human in the opposite sense of the word. When, dying under the expectant scrutiny of his knowing and faithless wife, the knighted and successful Castorley, in puzzled misery, in all the agony of disease and doubt, begs for the reassurance of the man who for twenty years has worked out the ruin he can accomplish with a word, and who now interrupts unsteadily: "I can confirm every word you've said. You've nothing to worry about. It's *your* find—*your* credit—*your* glory and—all the rest of it"—when he gets to this point, Kipling has made his way to something past revenge, past any human division: the sentences are as beautiful in their inclusiveness as the last sentence of the story is beautiful in its precise exclusion: "As, on the appointed words, the coffin crawled sideways through the noiselessly-closing door-flaps, I saw Lady Castorley's eyes turn towards Gleeag."

If you compare one of the best of Kipling's early stories ("Without Benefit of Clergy," say) with some of the best of his late stories, you realize that the late stories are specialized in their moral and human attitudes—in their subject matter, even—in a way in which the early story is not. The early story's subject is a general subject that will repay any amount of general skill or general talent: you can imagine a greater writer's rewriting "Without Benefit of Clergy" and making a much better story out of it. But this is precisely what you cannot imagine with Kipling's later stories: Chekhov and Tolstoy and Turgenev together couldn't improve " 'They' " or " 'Wireless,' " since in each a highly specialized subject has received an exactly appropriate, extraordinarily skilled and talented treatment. These later stories of Kipling's don't compete, really, with "Gusev" and "The Death of Ivan Ilych" and *A Sportsman's Sketches,* but have set up a kingdom of their own, a little off to the side of things, in which they are incomparable: their reader feels, "You can write better stories than Kipling's, but not better Kipling stories." This kingdom of theirs is a strange, disquieting, but quite wonderful place, as if some of the Douanier Rousseau's subjects had been repainted by Degas. If we cannot make the very greatest claims for the stories, it would be absurd not to make great ones: as long as readers enjoy style and skill, originality and imagination—in a word, genius—they will take delight in Kipling's stories.

Good Fences Make Good Poets

BOOK WEEK, NEW YORK HERALD TRIBUNE, AUGUST 30, 1964

Selected Letters of Robert Frost, edited by Lawrance Thompson

FROST'S CLOSE FRIEND, Lawrance Thompson, has selected, introduced, and commented on Frost's letters. What he writes is penetrating, almost severe: the official biography that he is preparing ought to be an extraordinarily interesting book. These letters are, as Thompson says, an invitation to each reader to make his own biography of Frost, since in the letters Frost "unmasks himself, at least partially."

Thompson goes on to say that Frost's readers need, now, a sympathetic explanation of the difference between Frost's public self and his private self; Thompson warns readers of the letters that "those who knew the poet largely from his poetry and his public appearances—and who take pleasure in remembering the evidence of his affirmations, encouragements, cherishings, tenderness, humor, wit, playfulness, and joviality—may not be prepared to see how often his private correspondence reveals periods of gloom, jealousies, obsessive resentments, sulking, displays of temper, nervous rages, and vindictive retaliations."

It is so wonderful to read Frost—was so wonderful to get to see and hear him—that we forget how hard it was to be Frost. He could write: "The conviction closes in upon me that I was cast for gloom as the sparks fly upward . . . I am of deep shadow all compact like onion within onion and the savor of me is oil of tears." Frost's sensitivities were, as Thompson says, excruciating: the world hurt and shocked and delighted the poems out of him. His public self was, in a sense, one more poem, the one on which he worked longest and hardest: these were the terms of his armistice with the world.

To let us know Frost better, his publishers ought to bring us the book of Frost's prose that was planned, but not published, during his lifetime, and a book of the best things that Frost said. Universities, television stations, and broadcasting companies taped Frost's conversations and monologues so often that hundreds or thousands of hours of these recordings survive—a good selection of them would make a fine book.

Frost's letters remind one that his life was as unusual as his poetry. For almost forty years he was poor enough to be able to say: "I wrote about the poor because at the receptive and impressionable age I was poor myself and knew none but the poor." But he said about his poetry, with fierce pride: "My house may be only a one-room shack but it is not the Poor House: it is the Palace of Art." Palace or Poor House, nobody wanted it; when his poetry came to that "trial by market" to which (Frost said) everything must come, the buyers turned it down.

During those years Frost farmed, taught school, and lived off the small income his grandfather had left him. (Nobody seems to have thought much of his farming, but a school superintendent called him the best English teacher in the state.) "I kept farm," Frost wrote, "less as a farmer than as a fugitive from the world that seemed to me to 'disallow' me. It was all instinctive, but I can see now that I went away to save myself and fix myself before I measured my strength against all creation."

Even when, at forty, he had come back into the world and had been improbably successful there, he could feel half safe only because he had been, like a woodchuck, "so instinctively thorough / About my crevice and burrow." The poet who had written, "Something there is that doesn't love a wall," was the man who wrote later, "I'm in favor of a skin and fences and tariff walls. I'm in favor of reserves and withholdings." He wrote to a good friend about his letters to that friend: "I have written to keep the overcurious out of the secret places of my mind both in my verse and in my letters to such as you." And yet, as Frost said, there was a devil in him that defeated his deliberate intentions: anyone who has read his *Collected Poems* and *Selected Letters* has entered some of the secret places of Frost's mind.

Just under the skin of the stocky, rock-faced old success—a great celebrity and a greater poet—the thin, sensitive-faced young failure survived. Consequently Frost felt "an obscure anxiety to please that I imperfectly understand"; he was, he said, "too cowardly to offend anybody intentionally and usually too skillful to do it unintentionally." His good friends and good audiences reassured him, but not enough; he—so to speak—had come so close to starving, fifty years before, that he still couldn't keep from carrying off in his pocket the leftover dinner rolls. He remembered every detail of friendship or enmity: the poem a dead man had rejected in 1910 was still an open wound. He warns a friend of "my Indian vindictiveness. Really I am awful there. I am worse than you know. I can never seem to forgive people that scare me within an inch of my life." The world had scared him within an inch of his life, over and over and over, and he never forgave and never forgot.

Some of Frost's letters, talk, and later poems methodically joke about serious matters; their argument progresses by plays on words, puns, allusions, as though the writer were determinedly staying on the humorous surface of things. Frost himself has a penetrating analysis of this habit of his: "Belief is better than anything else, and it is best when rapt, above paying its respects to anybody's doubt whatsoever. At bottom the world isn't a joke. We only joke about it to avoid an issue with someone, to let someone know that we know he's there with his questions: to disarm him by seeming to have heard and done justice to his side of the standing argument. Humor is the most engaging cowardice. With it myself I have been able to hold some of my enemy in play far out of gunshot."

In public Frost rather enjoyed looking at himself with approving wonder; in private he wrote over and over, as a bad man would not have written, "I am a bad bad man . . . I have been bad and a bad artist," and felt that he himself was somehow responsible for the death and insanity and suicide in his family. He wrote once, "I'm sad about Marj, but I am more busted up than sad. All this sickness and scatteration in the family is our fault and not our misfortune or I wouldn't admit it." During his last years he had left the dark uneasy world of family life—where the greatest can fail and the humblest succeed—for the well-lighted, reassuring world of the friends and audiences his poems had brought him. His deafness made normal back-and-forth conversation difficult for him, so that his private talk more and more resembled those extraordinary monologues that accompanied his public poem-sayings. In the end he talked as naturally as he breathed: for as long as you got to listen you were sharing Frost's life. What came to you in that deep grainy voice—a voice that made other voices sound thin or abstract—was half a natural physiological process and half a work of art; it was as if Frost dreamed aloud and the dream were a poem. Was what he said right or wrong? It seemed irrelevant. In the same way, whether Frost himself was good or bad seemed irrelevant— he was *there,* and you accepted him.

Frost wanted to be convinced not that he was good, but that he was a good poet; and it took all the laughter and applause of audiences and friends, all the love and admiration plain in their eyes, to persuade him of this. He wrote: "I wouldn't give a cent to see the world, the

United States or even New York made better . . . My whole anxiety is for myself as a performer. Am I any good? That's what I'd like to know and all I need to know." But, of course, no artist can ever know this about his own work: so that Frost's most obsessive conviction, all his last years, was the conviction that the best we have to offer "may not be found acceptable in Heaven's sight"—the work can fail like the life.

Frost once had told a friend that he was "non-elatable." Frost's wife retorted, "What a lie . . . You can't talk in public or private without getting elated. You never write but from elation." The last two years of Frost's life were years of elation. One of his strongest feelings was his feeling for American history; now, what with Kennedy's in-auguration, Khrushchev's interview, Frost himself had magically become a part of that history. After all, he had got Pound freed, had helped to join power and poetry in this new age of Kennedy—couldn't his words to Khrushchev help to transform the cold war into an honorable rivalry between the two great powers of the world? The realist Frost had always been romantic about power; his life ended in a dream of power.

Frost had written about old age: "Better to go down dignified / With boughten friendship at your side / Than none at all. Provide, provide!" Frost went down great and elated, with the world his poems had earned him grieving at his side. The death of his wife (all his poems were about her, he said) had been the end of his purely private life, an end so disastrous that he had had to be taught to live without her; the public life of his poems brought Frost the happy ending his private life could not bring him.

What Frost said about all human beings describes Frost: "We people are thrust forward out of the suggestions of form in the rolling clouds of nature . . . the background is hugeness and confusion shading away from where we stand into black and utter chaos; and against the background any small man-made figure of order and concentration." Between the darkness and chaos visible outside, invisible inside, the poet and his poems stand in ordered concentration.

Index

Index